So Far from Allah, So Close to Mexico

So Far from Allah, So Close to Mexico

Middle Eastern Immigrants in Modern Mexico

BY THERESA ALFARO-VELCAMP

University of Texas Press ◆ *Austin*

Cover Photo: Girius Ibrahim Martinos Abraham (naturalized in Torreón as Jorge Martínez Abraham), left, and Estefanaun in the mountains of Lebanon during World War I, circa 1916. Courtesy Archivo Histórico Juan Agustín de Espinoza, S.J., Universidad Iberoamericana, Laguna, Torreón.

Maps are original artwork prepared for the manuscript by Robert H. McLaughlin.

First edition, 2007

Requests for permission to reproduce material from this work should be sent to:
    Permissions
    University of Texas Press
    P.O. Box 7819
    Austin, TX 78713-7819
    www.utexas.edu/utpress/about/bpermission.html

♾ The paper used in this book meets the minimum requirements of ANSI/NISO Z39.48-1992 (R1997) (Permanence of Paper).

Library of Congress Cataloging-in-Publication Data

Alfaro-Velcamp, Theresa, 1967–
So far from Allah, so close to Mexico : Middle Eastern immigrants in modern Mexico / by Theresa Alfaro-Velcamp.—1st ed.
p. cm.
Includes bibliographical references and index.
ISBN 978-0-292-71640-7 ((cl.) : alk. paper)
ISBN 978-0-292-71641-4 ((pbk.) : alk. paper)
1. Arabs—Mexico—History. 2. Immigrants—Mexico—History. 3. Mexico—Emigration and immigration. 4. Arab countries—Emigration and immigration.
I. Title.
F1392.A7A44 2007
972'.0004927—dc22
                                                                2007004251

This book is dedicated to Mustafa (Roman) Itt Alfaro and Magdalena Alfaro-McLaughlin.

Contents

Acknowledgments

This project began more than a decade ago at Georgetown University with John Tutino as my mentor. He guided me through studying, researching, writing, revising, and publishing in Mexican history. I cannot adequately express my gratitude to him for his numerous readings of the text and his invaluable suggestions. It has been a privilege to work with him and many other scholars. Yvonne Haddad, Charles Keely, James Brennan, and Evelyn Hu-DeHart helped me finish a dissertation in history and offered insights to transforming the early research into an accessible book. At Georgetown University, I also would like to thank Dorothy Brown, John Voll, John Esposito, Amira Sonbol, James Collins, and Sonia Jacobson for their continued support. My Georgetown colleagues Michael Socolow, Jennifer Hull Dorsey, Elyse Semerdjian, Kathryn Coughlin, Nadya Sbaiti, and Daniel Bryne have been great friends and critics. The Institute of World Politics in Washington, D.C., and the Georgetown University History Department, Mexico Project, and Center for Latin American Studies provided funding for both research and writing.

Wayne Cornelius and Eric Van Young generously offered me a home at the University of California, San Diego, at the Center for U.S.-Mexican Studies and the Center for Comparative Immigration Studies in 2001–2002. As a joint fellow in both centers, I had the opportunity to work with a terrific group of colleagues. The historians' group of Antonio Ibarra, Kelly Lytle Hernandez, Mark Mairot, Ariel Rodríguez de Kuri, and Daniela Traffano helped me grow more than they realize. At Sonoma State University, Judy Abbott, Steve Bittner, Randy Dodgen, Steve Estes, Mary Halavais, Michelle Jolly, Elizabeth Martínez, Kathleen Noonan, Bill Poe, and Tony White have provided engaging seminars to test many of my ideas. I would also like to thank Sonoma State Provost Eduardo Ochoa and Dean of Social Sciences Elaine Leeder for their continued support of the research and for granting professional leave to write.

At the University of California, Berkeley, Laura Nader, Bill Taylor, Walter Brem, and Misha Klein took a special interest in my project and offered generous support in the final stages of writing. While revising the manuscript, Jeffrey Lesser and Akram Khater graciously read versions of the texts and made insightful suggestions to make it a better book. I would also like to thank the anonymous readers of the manuscript who helped me clarify some points. It has been an excellent experience to work with the editors at the University of Texas.

Early in my explorations of Middle Easterners in Latin America, Gladys Jozami and Ignacio Klich suggested ways to reach the few communities of Arabic-speaking immigrants in Latin America. Their excellent scholarship in the field has been a source of inspiration at every step of this project, and their ongoing support has been invaluable.

In Mexico City, my *tíos y tías* helped me enormously by opening their homes to me and orienting me around D.F. Muchísimas gracias, Tío-abuelo Mustafa (Roman) Itt Alfaro, Ricardo and Lupe Itt, Arturo, Luz María, Arturito, Lorena Hitt Espinosa, Martha Hitt, and Fernando Hitt. In Cuernavaca, the Hitt Orozco family—Tía Hilda, Tío Carlos, Adriana, Karla and Carlos Antonio, and the Hitt Casas family—Pati, Raúl, and Rodrigo. Tía-abuela Nora Hitt Alfaro and the late Tía-abuela Amine Hitt Alfaro also generously opened their homes to me during research trips.

At the Archivo General de la Nación, Patricia Galeana, Jorge Nacif Mina, Arturo Jarrero, and Roberto Beristáin Rocha facilitated my work by offering me access to invaluable documents, and archivists Juventino and Fulencio brightened my days with their gentle humor. My dear friend Rosa María Rojas Montes has often challenged me, leading me to a better understanding of Mexican society.

At El Colegio de México, Francisco Alba introduced me to Moisés González Navarro and María Elena Ota Mishima, now deceased. Professor Ota Mishima facilitated meetings with Doris Musalem Rahal and Zidane Zéraoui, who patiently listened to my ideas about Arab immigration and then provided me with new models for analyzing Mexican immigration history.

The colegiality of Delia Salazar Anaya and Leticia Reina at the Instituto Nacional de Antropología e Historia (INAH) provided encouragement and guidance as I searched for ways to explain my findings. In addition, they extended themselves in helping me locate further sources.

In Mexico City, Martha Díaz de Kuri and Geraldo Gozain Frangie from the Centro Libanés offered me insights about the collaborative projects among the Lebanese in Mexico. Martha has continued to open her personal archives and share with me her sources and insights. Conversations with Father Paul Kerbage of Nuestra Señora de Líbano gave me excellent comparative perspectives on the Lebanese communities in Mexico, Argentina, Brazil, and Australia. Marcela Schott de Tamariz and her husband Carlos Tamariz broadened my understanding of Mexican politics, culture, and history. Mexican Army Brigadier General Eduardo Martínez Aduna not only introduced me to the Tamariz family, but he also wrote letters on my behalf to several Mexican archives.

At the Universidad Iberoamericana in Torreón, Dr. Sergio Antonio Corona Páez, a wonderful colleague, helped me locate archives, introduced me to people in the community, and offered insights into Laguna society. María Isabel Saldaña Villareal also helped with her work in the Family Papers in the Archivo Histórico. The Abusaid family in Torreón was especially welcoming, and I thank Luis Fernando García Abusaid, María Elena Abusaid de Fernández, J. Fernando Abusaid Quinard, and Angelita for their hospitality. I would also like to thank those *laguneros* whom I interviewed for their candid responses to my questions. At the Municipal Archive in Torreón, the late Beatriz González de Montemayor and her staff, especially Martha and José Luis, were very helpful. In Saltillo, Arturo E. Villarreal Reyes of the Saltillo Municipal Archives provided access to several useful documents. Martha Rodríguez García at the Centro de Estudios Sociales y Humanísticos in Saltillo also provided enthusiastic support.

In Beirut, Guita G. Hourani of the Emigration Research Centre at Notre Dame University provided unlimited access to the Centre's holdings, for which I am most grateful. At the Centre de Documentation et de Recherches Arabaes Chrétiennes (CEDRAC), an affiliate of St. Joseph's University, Father Samir Khalil Samir offered me interesting insights on categories of personhood for these early Arabic-speaking immigrants. The Arab Image Foundation was extremely helpful in locating more than thirty-five images of Lebanese immigrants in Mexico. Eliane Fersan has been an excellent research assistant.

Also, Marion Smith, archivist of the former Immigration and Naturalization Service, was invaluable in helping me track Syrian entries along the Texas-Mexico border.

I would like to thank David Stemper, Gloria Almeyda, and Teresa Garza for their wonderful friendship and their continued interest in this project.

This book reflects the ongoing faith and encouragement I received from my parents, Chata Alfaro and John Velcamp. My brother, John Velcamp Jr., was central to the development of this project. Robert H. McLaughlin, my husband, partner, colleague, never ceases to amaze me with his editorial pen, gentle criticisms, and good humor.

So Far from Allah, So Close to Mexico

Introduction

Looking for Antonio Aychur Itt and Finding Hamud Said ʿEid

This book follows my journey to locate Antonio Aychur Itt, my great-grandfather, in Mexico and to trace his birth name, Hamud Said ʿEid, and his birthplace in Lebanon. I never knew my great-grandfather and knew very little of his eldest son, my grandfather Said Itt Alfaro. My grandfather came to the United States as a *bracero* worker in the 1940s, and U.S. immigration officials changed his name to Ruben Alfaro. Stories of these two men have been passed down from generation to generation, capturing my imagination. As I began studying Mexican history, I wondered how and where my great-grandfather's and grandfather's stories fit into Mexican historiography. In the fall of 1998 as part of my dissertation research, I began the task of compiling a database of Middle Eastern immigrants who came to Mexico and registered with the Department of Migration in the 1930s. While in my final stages of examining more than eight thousand immigrant cards, I stumbled upon the *ficha* (card) of Antonio Aychur Itt, my great-grandfather. His picture and description matched my family records. This is the only tangible piece of my family's immigration history that I have ever collected. While doing years of research, however, I realized I had encountered a new dimension of Mexican social history, that there were many ways to be Mexican in the twentieth century.

The title of the book, *So Far from Allah, So Close to Mexico,* derives from Mexican President Porfirio Díaz (1886–1911) saying, "Poor Mexico, so far from God, so close to the United States." Since the book aims to broaden notions of *mexicanidad* and illustrate the diversity of Middle Eastern immigrants, the use of *Allah* (God in Arabic) extends to the beliefs of the Christian, Jewish, Muslim, and Druze immigrants from the Middle East who arrived and eventually settled in Mexico. Some Middle East historians have cautioned that the term *Allah* in North American culture has come to signify those of Islamic faith. This is not my intent in employing the word *Allah;* rather I am using the word to speak generally about God and how Arabic-speaking immigrants acculturated in Mexico. The subtitle, *Middle Eastern Immigrants in Modern Mexico,* accounts for the journey that the Middle Eastern community experienced from arrival in Mexico to becoming Mexican citizens. This journey enabled many of the immigrants to retain aspects of their "foreignness" while joining the Mexican nation. An example of such a Middle Eastern immigrant who naturalizes is Jorge Martínez Abraham (formerly known as Girius Ibrahim Martinos Abraham), who naturalized and founded El Cairo restaurant in Torreón. Martínez Abraham exemplifies how Middle Easterners have both embraced their Arab heritage and become Mexican citizens. Caroline Nagel and Lynn Staeheli, in examining Arab immigrants in the United States, suggest that "it is possible to claim identity as a citizen of a country and to negotiate membership within the bounds of 'belonging,' even without claiming to 'be of' that country."[1]

Book Structure

The chapters that follow examine why Middle Eastern immigrants came to Mexico, where they settled, how many came, where they came from, how Mexicans responded to them, why some areas like the Laguna (the lake district, or Comarca Lagunera, which occupies almost the full width of southern Coahuila and far northeastern Durango states) attracted them, and how they positioned themselves. Each chapter asks how and why Middle Easterners are important to the Mexican nation. Beginning with the first chapter, "Amplifying *Mexicanidad,*" the migration process can be divided into four phases: (1) the first sojourners, often called *turcos* (Ottoman subjects), came between 1880 and 1910; (2) during the Mexican Revolution (1910–1920), some sojourners and newly arrived immigrants became Middle Eastern merchants, providing necessary goods and services; (3) the 1920s and 1930s marked Syro-Lebanese family reunifications; and (4) the 1940s brought some World War II refugees as well as the reconstruction of the Lebanese Mexican community. These four phases are by no means the only migratory periods and settlement processes of Middle Eastern immigrants in Mexico; however, they help explain and demonstrate how different historical events affected the timing of when groups moved to Mexico and how the Middle Eastern community came into being and changed over time.

In Chapter 2, "Locating Middle Easterners in National and Transnational Histories," I examine Mexican immigrant history and how to place

Middle Eastern immigrants in the historical record. The chapter also discusses the relationship between migrations to Mexico and across Mexico's northern border to the United States. Mexico thus became known as a "back door" to the United States and became vulnerable to changes in U.S. immigration policies.

Chapter 3, "*Turco* Sojourners Come to Porfirian Mexico," examines why *turcos* came to Mexico in the late nineteenth and early twentieth centuries. In it I discuss the political instability, increased economic competition, and religious tensions in the Middle East that motivated emigration. In addition, Porfirian development initiatives are examined as attracting immigrants to Mexico. Analysis of immigrant registration cards combined with immigrant histories detail where the immigrants came from in the Middle East and where they settled in Mexico. Their migration experiences were greatly facilitated by Middle Eastern immigrant networks, which provided money and information to family members and friends. During this early phase of migration, Middle Eastern immigrants began positioning themselves in the Mexican nation.

Chapter 4, "Borderland Merchants in Revolutionary Mexico," explores how the early sojourners' networks provided an infrastructure to continue with commercial activities during the chaos of the Revolution. Middle Eastern immigrants provided food and arms to the various revolutionary factions. Their ability to maneuver around the strong anti-foreign rhetoric attests to their skills of self-positioning and their unique role in the Mexican nation. The ability to cross into the United States enabled some Middle Easterners to amass large profits while the rest of the country was fighting. At the same time, the immigrants faced greater risks because of anti-foreign sentiments and revolutionary violence.

After the turbulent decade of the Revolution, Middle Eastern immigration to Mexico nearly quadrupled in the 1920s. The Middle Eastern community grew, and many of its members permanently settled in Mexico. Meanwhile, Mexican citizens became increasingly uncomfortable with the Middle Easterners' presence and marketing endeavors. As Mexicans voiced their opposition to the immigrants, Middle Eastern families became more unified, consolidating their economic enterprises with more kinship ties.

Chapter 5, "Middle Eastern Immigrants and Foreigners in Post-Revolutionary Mexico," analyzes the consolidation of the immigrant community and the slowing of immigration in the 1930s. Tough economic times combined with anti-foreign policies led Mexican citizens to more actively express their dislike of Middle Easterners. This can be attributed to both the larger numbers of immigrants who came in the 1920s and the Mexican citizenry's demand for help from the federal government in times of

Figure I.1. Immigration Card of Antonio Aychur Itt

crisis. Complaints against Middle Easterners varied from allegations of setting up illegitimate companies to falsely declaring bankruptcy, and from establishing monopolies to carrying contagious diseases. Letters from citizens, chambers of commerce, and state governments demonstrate a nation searching for a way to control its immigrant populations in the midst of economic, social and political change.

Chapter 6, "Peddling, Positioning, and Prosperity," explores how Middle Eastern immigrants have peddled their identity by carefully positioning themselves between Mexican society and their own immigrant community. Their identity has been rooted in their economic roles of making profits, especially during conflict. While making their profits, Middle Eastern immigrants (often referred to as "the Lebanese colony") sought to define themselves in relation to events in the Middle East and in Mexico. In response to Mexican nation building, many of the successful immigrants aimed to unite and perpetuate their foreignness. They constructed a Lebanese discourse that largely excluded Arabs, Muslims, and Druzes.

Chapter 7, "Meanings of Multiculturalism," synthesizes the text and offers a new means to examine the manifold ways of being Mexican. This concluding chapter examines how immigrants acquired *mexicanidad* while creating their own Middle Eastern immigrant community, adopting much of the Mexican national discourse, and becoming Mexican citizens. Although retaining their "Lebaneseness," their immigrant positioning suggests that Mexico is indeed multicultural and demonstrates some social acceptance and tolerance for ethnic difference.

In Chapter 7 I also discuss how the construction of the Lebanese community has created a hegemonic voice for anyone of Middle Eastern descent in Mexico today. The constructed history tends to ignore the diversity of immigrant roles in Mexican history and portrays the early immigrants as primarily Christians from Lebanon. The diversity of the immigrants and their contradictory reception in Mexico has largely been overshadowed by the notion that the Lebanese quickly acculturated and economically dominated.

Following the text is an appendix of fourteen tables, largely drawing on Middle Eastern immigrant registration cards compiled by the Mexican government between 1926 and 1951. They illustrate how the Middle Eastern migration changed over time, showing the gender breakdown of the immigrants and marital status, nationality, country and city of birth, religion, place of residence in Mexico, place of entry, and occupation. Throughout the text, I reference the tables in parentheses for readers to further examine the variables under discussion.

The Sources

Historians develop their analyses from the sources available. In this inquiry, official Mexican sources and Middle Eastern immigrant testimonies were examined for their direct information but also in search of inferences from hidden transcripts.[2] Immigrants who did not attain great economic or political success rarely emerged in the historical record, and many seem to have melted into Mexican society. Some were killed in revolutionary conflict or during other moments of chaos. In an effort to develop a more holistic portrait of this community, I used several research methodologies. I drew on 8,240 Middle Eastern immigrant registration cards (1926–1951), Mexican immigration laws published in the *Diario Oficial* (1920s–1940s), citizen complaints about Middle Easterners to Mexican presidents (1920s–1940s), Middle Eastern immigrant community-based sources (newsletters, novels, and letters), U.S. immigration cases involving Syrians crossing into the United States (1904–1945), and my interviews in 1999 with descendants of Middle Eastern immigrants (1999), whom I have given pseudonyms for this book.[3] Middle Easterners are among many immigrant groups who came to Mexico and drew on their foreignness to better their economic and social standing.

The geopolitical changes in the Middle East, Porfirian economic policies, and U.S.-Mexican relations in the nineteenth and early twentieth centuries provide a backdrop against which the analysis here proceeds and interprets 8,240 Middle Eastern immigrant registration cards produced by the National Registry of Foreigners. The Migration Law of 1926 established the National Registry of Foreigners to collect information on immigrants and the Mexican Department of Migration. In trying to get an accurate count of foreigners, these registration cards were processed from 1926 to 1951.

It should be noted that 8,240 is the full sample of immigrant registration cards available. Unfortunately, data were not always provided on certain cards; therefore, the samples from which I draw the following analyses vary. In 1997 Zidane Zéraoui identified 7,533 Arab immigrants in his analysis of the registration cards.[4] In my research at the Archivo General de la Nación (AGN) in Mexico City, I discovered an unmarked box that had additional records of Middle Eastern immigrants. I believe this box explains why my sample has 707 more Middle Eastern immigrants than Zéraoui has documented.

The information obtained for the cards was largely based on immigrant memory, especially for the earliest immigrants. Therefore, the information recorded was probably more of a snapshot of an immigrant's life at the time of registration than at the point of entry into Mexico. For instance, my great-grandfather Antonio Aychur Itt (Hamud Said 'Eid) migrated to Mexico in 1907 but his card was not processed until 1932, thus leaving a twenty-five-year gap over which to recall his migration experience. His card said he had a Mexican wife and six children; however, this information reflects his status in 1932 at age 51, not his situation in 1907.

Despite the limitations inherent to the immigrant registration cards, analyses of the cards enable historians and social scientists in general to better understand Middle Eastern migration to Mexico and how the immigrants positioned themselves in their new host country. In addition to the delay in processing the biographic information of the immigrant, there are other limitations with these immigrant registration cards. For instance, the cards identify only lawful immigrants with money to pay the fee to register with the Mexican government. This sample represents Middle Eastern immigrants who entered legally or had the wherewithal to obtain the papers to register. This was a self-selective group. In 1927 Middle Eastern immigrants were required to pay 10,000 pesos (roughly $1,000 today) to enter the country. Thus the truly destitute Middle Eastern immigrant would not be counted in these statistics.

Another aspect of the National Registry of Foreigners is Mexican officials' lack of understanding of Arab culture and the political situation in the Middle East at the beginning of the twentieth century. Many of the Mexican immigration officials did not understand that the peoples from the Middle East primarily spoke Arabic.[5] Some of the cards stated "Lebanese" and "Syrian" as primary languages, illustrating that some of the Mexican officials did not know that Lebanese and Syrian immigrants predominantly spoke Arabic as their first language. Another possibility is that an immigration official, in taking the immigrants' biographic information, made the assumption that a Lebanese immigrant spoke Lebanese and a Syrian immigrant spoke Syrian. Furthermore, the cards only indicate what languages immigrants spoke and do not explain the language abilities of these immigrants. It also would seem likely that the immigration officials recorded other information incorrectly or haphazardly, especially in the case of the names. Many Arabic names appear Hispanicized on the immigrants' cards, and the order of the names could have been changed. A middle name in Lebanon could have become a first name or last name in Mexico. These subtle variations are endless.[6]

Discrepancies in the data were quite common, particularly in the Mexican census during this period and especially if the enumerators were trying to communicate with people whose first language was not Spanish. Unlawful immigrants (who probably were not captured in the censuses) avoided any government official such as census takers. For the purposes of this discussion, immigrant registration cards are considered a sample of lawful Middle Eastern immigrants. These cards provide valuable information as to places from which they emigrated and where they settled in Mexico. The immigrants also indicated when they entered Mexico, lending insight into how Middle Eastern immigration evolved over time and responded to Mexican and world events (Table 1).

Despite more than a decade of research in Mexico supplemented with studies in the United States and Lebanon, I have not been able to expand the community-based sources.[7] To the best of my knowledge, this book is comprehensive with respect to most of the primary and secondary sources available. It is my hope that future scholars will continue to uncover documents housed in the new centers in Mexico and Lebanon focusing on immigration/emigration. Most of the materials I located were in Spanish, and I have provided my own translations for the reader. While finishing compilation of the immigrant registration database, I consulted with Middle Eastern historian Nadya Sbaiti, a native Lebanese Arabic speaker, to help me examine the immigrant registration cards in order to identify any Arabic names that had been misfiled or miscoded because of the Hispanicizing of names. In my findings I report observed inconsistencies in the data. Hayat Abu-Saleh, a native Arabic speaker from the region, translated letters and other documents from the Lebanese Emigration Research Centre (LERC) in Beirut. Letters from Maronite priests residing in Mexico City in the late nineteenth century describe their difficulties in adjusting to Mexico and request permission to return home. The task of translating these letters was particularly difficult for a modern-day speaker of Arabic. As LERC continues to build its collection, it should be a rich resource for future scholars.

In comparing Lebanese and Mexican sources on immigration, cases of Middle Eastern immigrants, particularly Syrian immigrants, have been well documented in the United States during the twentieth century. The concern of U.S. citizens that Middle Eastern immigrants as well as other undocumented immigrants surreptitiously enter the United States has created a good source of information. For instance, court cases and U.S. Immigration and Naturalization Service (INS) records have led to a better understanding of transnational migration. Mexico was sometimes used as an alternative point of entry for immigrants wishing to enter the United States.

Finding Family

After several years of archival research, I found Hamud Said ʿEid in June 2004. With a travel grant from my university, I went to Lebanon hoping to find a trace of my great-grandfather Antonio Aychur Itt. Some wonderful friends and colleagues there drove me to Sibline, the town shown on my great-grandfather's immigration card. According to his immigrant registration card, he arrived in Mexico in 1907, thus making my quest nearly a century later seem unlikely to succeed. My Lebanese and Syrian friends and I went to the home of the local *mukhtar*, the Muslim administrative leader in the community, explaining that I was looking for information about a family member who had emigrated to Mexico at the turn of the twentieth century. After coffee, long stares, and explanations of my family history, I was told I looked like an ʿEid because of the shape of my face, and I was directed to the ʿEid family in the next village. There, at a distant relative's home, we were treated with caution until an elderly man arrived and said that his prayers had been answered. He had been trying to reach Said ʿEid, my grandfather, in Brooklyn, New York, since the early 1970s. I explained that my grandfather had passed away at that time, and the family was still in Mexico, with the exception of Said's children. The man then said my great-grandfather's name had been Hamud Said ʿEid. The Arabic *ʿEid* became the Hispanicized *Itt*, as many of my Middle Eastern colleagues had suspected; however, he lost the name Hamud and gave the name Said (meaning "happy" in Arabic) to my grandfather. The Aychur name came from his maternal side, and *Antonio* was clearly an attempt at assimilating into Mexican culture. With the pieces of the puzzle coming together, I finally learned how my family's journey began and felt it was time to share this history of Middle Eastern immigrants coming to Mexico.

CHAPTER 1

Amplifying *Mexicanidad*

C onsider Carlos Slim Helú: "Slim is credible as a nationalist because, in all of Latin America, Telmex [Telefónicas de México] is the only major privately owned telco [telecommunications company] that's homegrown. And he has labored to gain the goodwill of people on both ends of Mexico's ideological spectrum." [1] How does a son of Middle Eastern immigrants proclaim himself a nationalist and representative of the Mexican nation? [2] Carlos Slim Helú, the wealthiest man in Latin America, [3] is proudly a Lebanese Mexican. Slim attributes his business acumen to his father, Julián Slim, a Lebanese Christian who escaped the Ottoman Empire's military draft by fleeing to Mexico in 1902. During the Mexican Revolution, the elder Slim bought out his partner in a Mexico City general store and purchased several nearby commercial buildings. Slim Helú said of his father, "Now *that* was courage . . . he taught me that no matter how bad a crisis gets, Mexico isn't going to disappear, and that if I have confidence in the country, any sound investment will eventually pay off." [4] The history of Slim Helú and his family illustrates how a few Middle Easterners and their descendants have positioned themselves in Mexican society and have achieved an elite status as "foreign citizens" in Mexico.

There are, of course, other Middle Easterners who identify with Mexican culture and who appear to have completely acculturated into the Mexican nation. My *tío-abuelo* (great-uncle) Mustafa Itt often said to me, "*Hija, soy mexicano*" (Daughter, I am Mexican). Yet he carries an Arabic surname from his father, who migrated from Sibline in southern Lebanon to Mexico in 1907. How could Carlos Slim Helú feel proudly Lebanese Mexican and my *tío-abuelo* feel solely Mexican without reference to his Middle Eastern ancestry? The difference lies in how Middle Easterners in Mexico have forged immigrant positions, some claiming a constructed Lebanese Mexican identity. This claim has roots in commercial activities from peddling to industrial capitalism and has grown into politics and popular culture. Middle Eastern immigrants position themselves between Mexican society and their Middle Eastern immigrant communities.

The experiences of Middle Eastern immigrants and the construction of the Lebanese Mexican identity raise a broad historical question: How do immigrant groups position themselves to prosper in a nation-state of purported *mestizo* origins? How do nation-states, in turn, create conditions for this positioning and prosperity? This book explores how a few Middle Eastern immigrants and their descendants have drawn on an imagined Phoenician past to create an elite Lebanese Mexican class in modern Mexico. Although Middle Eastern immigrants are a well-known group throughout Latin America, few scholarly works have systematically addressed their presence in the historical record. There are several reasons for this that will be explored in the following chapters. Because Mexican nationalism, *mexicanidad*, a sense of Mexicanness, cannot be explained as monolithic, scholars have had difficulty conceptualizing how to place the members of ethnic minority and immigrant groups outside the *mestizo* (those of mixed Spanish and indigenous descent) construct in Mexican history. To help conceptualize these ideas, revisionist (and post-revisionist) scholarship on race, subalterns, and hegemony has been employed to describe those peoples outside more traditional state formative processes.[5]

Although in later generations it could be suggested that the wealthier children of early immigrants have become active in Mexican state formation with the intention of creating hegemonic power bases, this book focuses largely on the first- and second-generation immigrants who sought to make enough money to return to Lebanon and/or bring other family members to maintain their economic and familial interests. This inquiry examines how the immigrants described themselves and, in turn, forged a place for themselves in Mexican society. As with many immigrant groups, the story is not linear nor clearly demarcated by geography or analytical categories. These immigrants came from a complicated homeland and found a new host country mired in civil strife and nation building.

Unlike various other immigrant groups in the Americas, the homelands of Middle Eastern immigrants changed dramatically in the late nineteenth and early twentieth centuries. The first wave of Middle Eastern immigrants to Mexico, subjects of the Ottoman Empire, left a region known as the provinces of Greater Syria, which encompassed present-day Syria, Lebanon, and Palestine (Figure 1.1).

After World War I and the collapse of the Ottoman Empire, Britain ac-

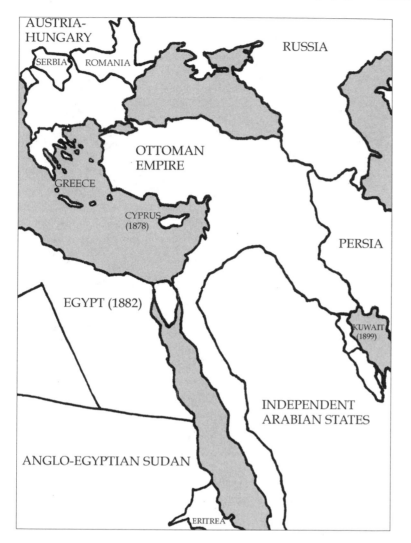

Figure 1.1. The Middle East in 1900

quired control of Iraq, Palestine, and Transjordan, while France took control of the Syrian mandate (Figure 1.2). Under the French, what are now the nation-states of Lebanon and Syria were treated as colonies. In 1920, when the creation of Greater Lebanon was proclaimed, the French objective was to safeguard the Maronite community by making sure it would not be absorbed into a Syrian Muslim state.

In 1926, French officials approved a constitution creating a Lebanese re-

Figure 1.2. The Middle East in 1920

public. However, Lebanon did not declare independence until 1943, while Syrian independence was delayed until 1946 (Figure 1.3).

These geopolitical changes complicate categories of analysis when trying to determine where these immigrants migrated from, how they identified themselves, and how others identified them. I use the term "Middle Eastern immigrants" to refer to peoples from the region that encompasses the contemporary nation-states of Syria, Lebanon, Palestine (the West Bank, Gaza, and British-mandated territory), Israel, Iraq, Iran, Jor-

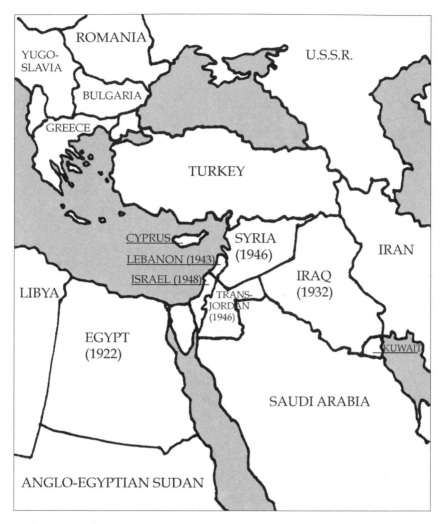

Figure 1.3. The Middle East in 1948

dan, Egypt, and the Arabian Peninsula. Although Armenia and Turkey are not widely regarded as Arab states, peoples from these nation-states are often considered part of the Middle Eastern migration to Mexico.[6] Defining appropriate categories of personhood to describe these immigrants has sparked considerable debate. Moreover, both after the creation of the state of Israel following World War II and more recently following the terrorist attacks of 9/11, the term *Arab* has become politically charged.[7] Scholars such as Zidane Zéraoui and Roberto Marín-Guzmán refer to immigrants from the Middle East as "Arabs," employing the term as an ethnocultural construct.[8] I have chosen to use "Middle Eastern," preferring its geographic connotations in examining the history of peoples who emigrated from the Ottoman Empire at the end of the nineteenth century as well as those who migrated from the region in the twentieth century. Given the departures of early immigrants from the Ottoman Empire, the term *turco* (Turk) is still used occasionally to describe Middle Easterners.[9] "Lebanese" immigrants are thus a subgroup within this larger Middle Eastern migration. Because Lebanon and Syria did not emerge as independent nation-states until the 1940s, earlier immigrants often declared cities and regions as their places of origin and drew on a variety of ethnic and religious identities.

The Mexican case is further complicated by variation among Latin American countries where notable populations of Middle Eastern immigrants have settled. In Argentina and Brazil, the term "Syro-Lebanese," a term coined by the subjects themselves, is used in common parlance; in Mexico and Ecuador, the term "Lebanese" is most often used to encompass all Middle Easterners; in Honduras and Chile, the term "Palestinian" is more common. These variations point to both the problematic nature of these historical categories as well as the particular influx of immigrants and their internal dynamics within each Latin American country. Although "Middle Eastern" can be reductionist (in the same way that "Latin American" can be), it nevertheless offers the most comprehensive nomenclature based on my examination of 8,240 Middle Eastern immigrant registration cards compiled by the Mexican government between 1926 and 1951.[10]

Asher Kaufman's monograph *Reviving Phoenicia: The Search for Identity in Lebanon* carefully traces how, prior to Lebanon's creation in 1920, Lebanese nationalists looked to the Phoenician past to narrate and justify the existence of Lebanon as a viable nation.[11] He argues,

> The idea that the ancient Phoenicians had crossed the Atlantic was a view shared by many Lebanese and supported by dubious scholarly work. It reflected an attempt made by Syro-Lebanese, advocates of the Phoenician identity, to illustrate their contribution to Western civilization since time immemorial. In the American context, it was an attempt to make evident that Syro-Lebanese were actually more American than Americans.[12]

Kaufman suggests that the various Syrian communities in North and Latin America promulgated a Phoenician past as early as 1914;[13] however, in Mexico, Lebanese community newsletters did not begin widespread circulation until the 1930s. Kaufman nevertheless shows that early in the twentieth century, questions of identity circulated among Middle Eastern immigrants in the Americas. As this book will show, while the immigrants observed radical change in their homeland from afar, they also helped to broaden post-revolutionary constructions of the Mexican nation-state and the meanings of *mexicanidad*.

A Question of National Composition

The self-positioning of Middle Easterners in Mexico highlights the contradictions of twentieth-century Mexican nation building and how this immigrant group became both victims and victors of national conflicts. From President Porfirio Díaz (1886–1911) to post-revolutionary President Lázaro Cárdenas (1934–1940), Mexican policy makers aimed to bring Mexico out of underdevelopment by reclaiming "Mexico for Mexicans."[14] This effort, however, has led to an ambivalent treatment of foreigners. Immigrants, mostly Europeans, who were perceived to potentially "better" the nation with skills and capital—and in some cases fair skin[15]—were welcomed by Mexican elites and policy makers. Meanwhile, the Mexican populace often felt exploited by these foreigners. Other immigrants such as the Chinese, Japanese, and Middle Easterners did not meet the criteria of "bettering" Mexico, yet they provided necessary services to the Mexican people. Some even prospered from direct dealings with the poor. These immigrants, often storekeepers or peddlers, improved the lives of *campesinos* (peasants, agrarian workers) and *rancheros* (small-scale independent ranchers) with more commercial options such as purchasing items outside the stores of the *hacendados* (owners of large landed estates), yet many Mexicans still subscribed to anti-foreign attitudes.

The inconsistent treatment of foreigners coincides with a national history that often dismisses the importance of immigrants in Mexico. Why has the history of immigration to Mexico been given scant attention? Mexico has had a long immigrant tradition with enduring foreign influences; however, post-revolutionary discourses in the twentieth century and onward tend to emphasize *mestizo* constructions to the exclusion of others' cultures and ethnicities.[16]

With the dawn of the twentieth century, President Díaz looked in particular to the British and Germans for investments to modernize Mexico and to act as a counterweight to growing U.S. dominance in Latin America.[17] Along with an infusion of cash came British and German immigrants eager to capture their share of the profits. In the process of introducing new economic activities such as mining, money lending, and wholesale trading, the foreigners were also quite visible; thus when Mexicans became frustrated with modernization, they could easily blame foreigners. The early twentieth century also brought an influx of Middle Eastern immigrants who took up peddling, some finding a niche among French immigrant wholesalers. These immigrant groups, collectively and individually, have contributed to the economic development and construction of the Mexican nation-state.

Amplifying *Mexicanidad*

The Spanish are usually seen as an integral part of Mexico, not as immigrants. The Creoles of New Spain, descendants of Spaniards born in Mexico, sought to distance themselves from the Spanish (Bourbon) Crown in the late eighteenth and early nineteenth centuries. In trying to differentiate themselves, they helped create a Mexican nation, separate and different from Spain. Their participation in the construction of the nation-state has launched a two-century debate about *who* is Mexican. The scant discussion in the national discourse about the infusion of other immigrants and their cultures in Mexico attests to the dominance of the Creole legacy.

Historically, the situation of the Spaniards has been the most complex because of their widespread "conquering" influence that has led to the cultural (and some would say biological) construction of the *mestizo* and ultimately, the "cosmic race."[18] The Mexican national discourse tends to assign Mexicans as Spanish or Indian or *mestizo*. This tripartite ethnic scheme began with the Conquest and became the dominant basis of defining who is Mexican. The narrow ethnic construction suited Spanish colonial interests in limiting who enjoyed privileges such as landownership and participation in Spanish government. Although the Mexican national discourse has changed over time, it has tended to employ *mexicanidad* as a means to draw on *indigenismo* and Europeanness in its nationalism.[19] According to José Vasconcelos, post-revolutionary Secretary of Public Education, the cosmic race theory suggests taking the best of Spanish and Indian cultures and creating a new hybrid race:

> The advantage of our tradition is that it has greater facility of sympathy towards strangers. This implies that our civilization, with all defects, may be the chosen one to assimilate and to transform mankind into a new type; that within our civilization, the warp, the multiple and rich plasma of future humanity is thus being prepared.[20]

Vasconcelos contended that it is the contribution of the Spanish that helps the *mestizo* improve himself or herself. Earlier than Vasconcelos' writing, Justo Sierra, Minister of Public Education and Fine Arts from 1905 to 1911, suggested that "foreign elements" indeed helped Mexican social evolution. Sierra wrote between 1900 and 1902: "We need to attract immigrants from Europe so as to obtain a cross with the indigenous race, for only European blood can keep the level of civilization . . . from sinking, which would mean regression, not evolution."[21] Accordingly, the *mestizo* represented a way in which to create a liberal model of homogeneous integration of all ethnic groups. By encouraging individual groups—specifically indigenous peoples—to shed their distinctive characteristics and to become *mestizo*, they could become part of an evolving Mexican nation. Similarly, Yucatecan positivist social critic Andrés Molina Enríquez in 1909 advocated an ethnic scheme of Creoles, Spaniards, and *mestizos*. He believed that the continuation of the *mestizo* as the dominant ethnic group would encompass Mexico's indigenous origins as well as constitute a truly national population.[22] Alan Knight writes, "Mexico could achieve demographic growth without recourse to immigration . . . mestizaje and nationhood were equated."[23] Together Sierra, Molina Enríquez, and later Vasconcelos and others advocated *mestizaje* as the foundation of what it is to be Mexican.[24]

Historian Arthur Schmidt explains that decades after the Mexican Revolution, "*indigenismo* and economic development served as powerful hegemonic symbols for Mexico's national identity, for the image of a homeland that would provide for all Mexicans."[25] With time, however, this national project collapsed. The marginalization of the indigenous peoples and massive Mexican emigration created an "enduring crisis of self definition."[26] D. A. Brading echoes much of Schmidt's assessment and notes of Manuel Gamio, the father of Mexican anthropology and famed excavator of Teotihuacán pyramids, that

> there is little doubt that his *indigenismo* derived from his liberalism and was animated by a modernising nationalism, which promoted the incorporation and assimilation of the Indian communities into the urban, hispanic population. The ultimate and paradoxical aim of official *indigenismo* in Mexico was thus to liberate the country from the dead-weight of its native past, or, to put the case more clearly, finally to destroy the native culture which had emerged during the colonial period.[27]

While some post-revolutionary intellectuals suggested that the lack of ethnic integration and indigenous traditions were at the root of many of Mex-

ico's problems, they also worked to curb the arrival of undesirable immigrants, such as those coming from the Middle East. But as Serge Gruzinski
aptly points out,

> It is hard to know exactly what this "mestizo effect" covers—its dynam-
> ics are not really questioned. Mixing, mingling, blending, crossbreeding,
> combining, superimposing, juxtaposing, interposing, imbricating, fusing,
> and merging are all terms associated with the mestizo process, swamping
> vague description and fuzzy thinking in a profusion of terms.[28]

It is within this "fuzzy thinking" that we find the construction of *mestizaje*, implicit to *mexicanidad*, as a dominant cultural category that fuses the
Spanish and Indian in everything Mexican.

Marilyn Grace Miller successfully challenges the *mestizo* construction:
"Whereas *mestizaje* has been taken as a monolithic discourse and a com-
monplace of *latinoamericanismo*, a tour of its myriad appearances in textual
and other expressive formats divulges a trajectory of tremendous variance,
polarization, juxtaposition, and opposition."[29] The monolithic assumption
derives from the writings of Molina Enríquez, who equated Mexico with *lo
mestizo*; Manuel Gamio reiterated this interpretation in 1916.[30] Miller suggests that intellectuals throughout the Americas have used notions of *mestizaje* and the cosmic race to their ideological ends, causing confusion and
ambiguities as to nationalism, identity, and ethnicity throughout the twentieth century. However, Agustín Basave Benítez succinctly notes that "the
tendency to link mestizaje and mexicanidad responds essentially to a search
for national identity."[31] *Mexicanidad*, in my analysis, has therefore come
to refer to the sense of feeling Mexican by and among Mexican nationals
yet remaining open to a range of individual and collective interpretations
depending on one's own situation and experiences.

The ability of Middle Eastern immigrants to position themselves in
Mexico can be explained in part by the flexibility of the concept of *mexicanidad* and by varying interpretations of what it means to be Mexican.
Henry Schmidt, for example, suggests that allied terms *mexicanidad*, *mexicanismo*, and *lo mexicano* all refer to the Mexican ethos as well as to its
study and therefore become a driving principle for the growth of knowledge related to Mexico.[32] But what is the Mexican ethos? Roger Bartra
argues that "studies on Mexicanness constitute an expression of the dominant political culture. This hegemonic political culture is bound by the set
of imaginary power-networks that define socially accepted forms of sub-
jectivity and that are customarily considered as the fullest expression of

national culture."[33] Accordingly, the Partido Revolucionario Institucional (PRI) has been creating a type of "metadiscourse" that many Mexicans and non-Mexicans use to explain national identity.[34] This discourse is premised on what Bartra terms "*commonalities* of the Mexican character" and founding myths of the Mexican Revolution.[35] It can accommodate and integrate social difference, tolerate difference, and alternately suppress, disregard, and obscure difference such that the terms *mexicanidad, mexicanismo,* and *lo mexicano* promote unified, homogeneous meanings. The mythical accounts of the Mexican Revolution that inform this discourse tend to pertain to Pancho Villa and Emiliano Zapata.[36] Public officials and intellectuals have drawn on carefully selected cultural symbols—such as Zapata and Bénito Juárez—to describe what and who is Mexican. These constructions have ignored the rich cultural mosaic of Mexican society. Instead, they promulgate the tripartite ethnic and racial description—begun during the colonial era—of Mexicans as Spanish, indigenous, or *mestizo.*

Apart from the metadiscourse of *mexicanidad,* however, most Mexicans readily acknowledge the role of the *turco* merchant among other figures such as a Basque supermarket owner in their social landscape. Why, then, does a discrepancy exist between Mexican intellectuals and popular tradition? This discrepancy between the popular recognition of difference and the *mestizo* image reflects yet another difficulty in describing who is Mexican and who ought to be citizens of Mexico. Rodolfo Stavenhagen and Tania Carrasco write, "Mexico is essentially a multicultural country not only for its indigenous and Iberian culture, but also for the contribution of the immigrant cultures."[37]

Ultimately, the *mestizo* construction aimed to temper the influence of foreigners and the visibility of the indigenous, thereby limiting plurality. Despite the intellectuals' and state's attempts to construct a monolithic, homogeneous Mexican, the Mexican populace has come to include diverse immigrants in a pluralistic society in which there are many ways of being Mexican. The ambiguities of what it means to be Mexican beyond the *mestizo* construction have allowed immigrants from the Middle East simultaneously to position their status in the Mexican metadiscourse and to create their own Lebanese discourse.

From Immigrants to Foreign Citizens

The infusion of Middle Eastern immigrants in Mexico increased tensions among classes and affected how Middle Eastern immigrants positioned

themselves and their goods. As Mexican policy makers at the federal and
state levels designed policies to appease displaced middle-class Mexicans in
the 1920s and 1930s, they also tried to accommodate immigrants who supplied a needed part of Mexico's economic infrastructure. While some immigrants were denied admission into Mexico, others were granted it and,
later, citizenship.

The Great Depression that began in 1929, combined with anti-foreign
rhetoric, raised concerns about who should be allowed into Mexico and
who should become Mexican citizens. The international environment—
exemplified to some extent by the United States closing its borders—coincided with these questions among Mexican citizens and policy makers
about which immigrants were "worthy" and which were not. As post-
revolutionary intellectuals pushed the cult of the *mestizo* (that is, mestizophilia), they stressed homogenization as fundamental to the nation's development and health.[38] Portrayals enhancing Mexico's modernization posed
Middle Eastern immigrants, among others, as instead carrying disease and
increasing poverty and criminality. Restrictive policies were made, yet they
were not always enforced. Thus, how Middle Eastern immigrants positioned themselves in Mexican society offers an alternative perspective to
traditional conceptualizations of who is Mexican and who can become
Mexican citizens.

The ability of Middle Eastern and other immigrant groups—Ashkenazi
and Sephardic Jews,[39] Spaniards, French, Germans,[40] Italians, Japanese,
Koreans, and Chinese[41]—to develop commercial enterprises reflects demands in the Mexican economy during the late nineteenth and early twentieth centuries. Immigrants, savvy to market demands, quickly learned how
to supply Mexican consumer demands. Some Middle Eastern immigrants,
as their commercial endeavors led to economic success, began to position
themselves both as Mexicans and as foreigners in Mexican society.

As President Díaz sought to emulate European modernization, he looked
to foreign investment to bring Mexico out of underdevelopment and "back-
wardness."[42] The Mexican Revolution and post-revolutionary regimes in
the 1920s and 1930s aimed to replace the Porfirian model and redefine
the nation as a Mexico for Mexicans. Revolutionary rhetoric often became xenophobic, denouncing those who had pillaged Mexico of its resources. Yet despite the rhetoric, immigrants continued to come and settle
in Mexico. If anti-foreign sentiments were so strong, how could immigrants
continue to migrate and establish themselves in the early twentieth century
in Mexico?

Despite the revolutionary discourse that emphasized the *mestizo,* the

"Mexican foreign tradition" continued. This tradition privileged outsiders who were seen to help Mexico progress. It dates back to the colonial period when the early Spaniards often viewed foreigners as bringing the necessary skills for Mexico to develop. The fear of foreign merchants and their exploitation of native peoples likewise can be dated to the colonial period when foreigners composed much of the merchant class. In 1681 the Laws of the Indies specified that "no foreigner or excluded person be allowed to trade in the Indies, or go to them."[43] In the seventeenth century, poor peasant families from the Basque region often sent their sons to New Spain to make their fortunes. Charles Nunn explains that "since [colonial] immigrants often came to make their fortunes, few had significant assets upon arrival. In Spain, the Casa de Contratación kept a full watch on everyone who sailed from the mother country to the Indies."[44] This pattern of poor families migrating to Mexico with ambitions of wealth has occurred frequently throughout Mexican history.[45]

In the nineteenth century, Mexican intellectuals struggled to create a unique national identity based on European traditions. At the turn of the twentieth century, Spanish peninsular merchants, French and British bankers, and U.S. mining investors provided critical goods and services while maintaining their ethnicity. Unlike less powerful immigrant groups, who tended to acculturate as a tactic of survival, these foreigners with Mexican citizenship often kept their culture and maintained their "foreignness." Many became wealthy through their development projects and established themselves within the Mexican elite.

In looking at North American and European democracies, Bonnie Honig suggests that foreignness can be relational and fungible in that it reflects the values of the society. In particular, Honig examines the role of the capitalist foreigner, who, although "depicted as someone who is interested in material things, . . . quickly turns from someone who has something to offer us into someone who only wants to take things from us."[46] This transition from an inquisitive immigrant to a self-serving materialist resonates with popular Mexican reflections on the role of the Middle Eastern immigrants in the country. Although Honig's analysis is limited to liberal democracies, her usage of *foreignness* and the notion that foreigners enable regimes to import needed skills and talents can be applied to Mexico.

The contradictory reception and treatment of foreigners in Mexico can be described as a "foreign citizen" paradigm. Luz María Martínez Montiel describes this dilemma by arguing that to be foreign in Mexico is a guarantee of wealth, creating a paradox throughout Mexican history. Mexicans feel xenophobic because of foreigners' wealth.[47] Yet foreignness becomes a means of legitimation and path to elite status.[48] Not unlike other countries seeking to develop, Mexico has depended on outside resources. Therefore, those in Mexican society most capable of attracting foreign investment are most able to thrive economically. The "foreign citizen" mediates a contradictory and mutually reinforcing relationship that allows outsiders to maintain multiple identities, including the identity of an "insider" in Mexico. This notion that citizenship can be granted to a foreigner on the promise that he or she brings skills and capital is not uncommon. However, in Mexico and perhaps other Latin American (and other "developing") countries, the ability to declare foreignness across generations helps explain how elites distance themselves from their poor *paisanos* and command a sense of entitlement.

The irony is that to climb the Mexican economic ladder, one needs to have enough Mexicanness to work within the system. Yet once the person has reached economic elite status, he or she often claims his or her foreign roots (as if) to explain success. How have Middle Eastern immigrants participated in this "foreign citizen" trajectory? The first generation often downplayed cultural differences to better acculturate into Mexican society. However, by the second and third generations, with economic ascent, some Middle Eastern immigrants were able to create a new Lebanese Mexican identity,[49] as further addressed in Chapter 6. In contrast, Middle Eastern immigrants who did not make fortunes tended to acculturate into the *mestizo* Mexican culture, similar to my *tío-abuelo*, a middle-class Mexican.

Mexico has a rich immigrant history too often ignored in analyses focused on the Mexican Revolution and *mestizaje*. Moreover, the case of Middle Eastern immigrants demonstrates the diversity of the immigrant flows into Mexico and how Mexicans accommodated social difference in varying degrees. Perhaps most importantly, the evolution of Middle Eastern immigrants creating a Lebanese Mexican community illustrates how the "foreign tradition" has resonated in society to create "foreign citizens." Peter Sahlins in his monograph *Unnaturally French: Foreign Citizens in the Old Regime and After* analyzes how foreigners in seventeenth-century France who naturalized were not treated as citizens, especially in the examination of tax records under the Old Regime.[50] According to Sahlins, "Foreign citizens were, no doubt, a privileged group of immigrants, although not literally in the Old Regime sense, since only a small proportion were nobles."[51] Sahlins suggests that prior to the creation of modern nation-states, notions of citizenship were defined primarily in opposition to the foreigner, and "naturalization as administrative practice, moreover, never fully protected the foreigner from all the civil incapacities, especially the liability to special taxes, that accumulated during the early modern period."[52] Similarly to Sahlins' foreign citizens of seventeenth-century France, Middle Eastern immigrants who naturalized in twentieth-century Mexico often retained elements of their foreignness, manifest in such gestures as opening a restaurant named after an Egyptian city.

Unlike many European immigrants, Middle Easterners often appeared to be Mexican in their dealings with rural communities. Yet, over time their larger investments in industrial projects served national interests and enabled them to then emulate Europeans by seeking to construct a unique Lebanese Mexican community. Despite anti-foreign revolutionary rhetoric, the post-revolutionary Mexican nation continued to draw on foreignness as a means of legitimation, especially in elite circles. Middle Eastern immigrants, by peddling their legitimacy and their wares, fused their immigrant status with Mexican citizenship and in turn expanded the meaning of the Mexican nation in the twentieth century.

Mexican citizens at home and abroad often feel multiple loyalties that extend to the Mexican nation, their regions, and more particularly their towns.[53] Their sense of belonging extends to two (three and four) homelands simultaneously. They identify with their hometown, *patria chica;* their country, *patria;* their adopted country, *segunda patria;* and their adopted hometown, *segunda patria chica.*[54] These loyalties become further complicated by religion and marriage partners. Olga Seba, a second-generation Lebanese, said in an interview, "We carry [have] a double life, when I am in the house, I am Lebanese, and in the street, I am Yucatecan."[55] Like some transnationals,[56] Middle Easterners maintain far-reaching linkages such that immigrants in Mexico have ties to relatives in the United States, Brazil, and Argentina, for example. Their social identities emerge from the globalization of the world economy and the construction of webs of social relations. The links are more difficult to trace and document; however, individual case studies show that some Middle Eastern immigrants and their children feel more Mexican, while others adopt multiple identities.

Immigrants have, for the most part, participated in the Mexican discourse by adopting *mestizo* identities. This illustrates the fungibility of *mexicanidad.* This fungibility denotes the relational and contextual use of identity as theorized by historian Prasenjit Duara.[57] Duara examines national communities as relationships based on inclusions and exclusions and how the competing visions intersect with alternative criteria of identity formation.[58] By building on Duara's framework that nationalism is a continually contested and negotiated space for multiple groups to live, which he applies to Chinese history, I argue that ethnic groups in Mexico vary in their abilities to acculturate, and some choose to maintain their ethnic identities, especially as they ascend the Mexican economic and social ladder.

In contrast, Middle Eastern immigrants who were less economically successful tended to more fully integrate into the metadiscourse of *mexicanidad*. Although post-revolutionary intellectuals aimed to temper the influence of foreigners and the visibility of the indigenous by emphasizing the *mestizo*, Lebanese Mexicans became successful foreign citizens, simultaneously illustrating the diversity of the Mexican nation and the fungibility of *mexicanidad*.

Although many have described Lebanese Mexicans (immigrants and subsequent generations) as having a double identity, one Mexican and the other Lebanese,[59] immigrants' identities tend to be far more dynamic and diverse. At one level, Middle Eastern immigrants became Mexican citizens, yet some constructed a parallel loyalty to Lebanon. In creating their Mexicanness, they built on the Mexican elites' sense of foreignness in Mexico. What becomes particularly interesting is how Middle Easterners, who were traditionally deemed undesirable immigrants, could adopt a sense of foreign superiority. How did the constructed Lebanese community overcome Mexican prejudices to be accepted as elites worthy of foreignness?

The answer, in part, turns on regional differences within Mexico. To be Lebanese in the Yucatán is different from being Lebanese in the Laguna or in Mexico City. Perhaps the most striking difference is between the Lebanese community in Mexico and the Lebanese living in Lebanon. The community's sense of Mexican elitism differentiates them from their Lebanese counterparts living in the Middle East. According to a Lebanese immigrant living in Mexico City in 1999, "You can't compare these Lebanese with the Lebanese in Lebanon . . . most of them [those at the *Centro Libanés*] did not speak Arabic."[60] This disjunction between those from Lebanon and the descendants of Middle Eastern immigrants exemplifies both how the construction of Lebaneseness has been unique in Mexico and how immigrant homeland memory may depart from homeland reality.[61] As the second and third generations retold and perhaps reinvented family stories, the lines between the real and imaginary became blurred and distorted, creating a distinct Lebanese Mexican community.

CHAPTER 2

Locating Middle Easterners in National and Transnational Histories

Jorge Amado, in his popular novel *Gabriela, Clove and Cinnamon*, describes a Middle Eastern character, Mr. Nacib, as follows: "His many friends called him Arab or Turk, and they did so as an expression of intimacy, of affection. He did not much mind Arab, but he hated to be called Turk. . . . 'Call me anything you want except Turk. I'm a Brazilian.'"[1] Although Amado's character reflects the Middle Eastern experience in Brazil, this fictional anecdote resonates throughout Latin America, showing how some Middle Eastern immigrants felt about the term *turco*. As Ignacio Klich and Jeffrey Lesser point out, *turco* is an imposed rather than a self-constructed identification.[2] The term refers to an area of the former Ottoman Empire. Despite its historical and geographical orientation, however, the term carries negative connotations in Mexico. In this chapter I begin an interrogation of the term *turco* and its alternatives as they exist in the historical record, and I explore the role of Middle Eastern immigrants in twentieth-century Mexico.

I begin by examining Mexican immigrant history and ways to account for Middle Eastern immigrants in the historical record. By exploring various sources, I hope that readers begin asking questions to further studies in the area of immigration to Mexico. In tracing Mexican immigrant history, the foreign merchant tradition emerges by which some of the Middle Eastern immigrants positioned themselves in Mexican society to later become foreign citizens.

Mexican Immigrant History

Charles Gibson has suggested that the modern migratory past began six centuries before the arrival of the Spanish in 1519 during "a time of new immigration, by Tolteca, Chichimeca, Otomi, and 'Aztec' peoples."[3] The Aztecs, or "Mexicas," were believed to be migrants from northern Mexico who built Tenochtitlán at a site in what is now Mexico City. Once the Spanish arrived, they cleverly negotiated with rivals (Tlaxcallans and Chalcans) to help overthrow the Aztecs.[4] With the assistance of these rivals, the Spanish eventually took formal power in 1521 and ruled until 1821.

As colonizers for three centuries, emigrants from Spain continued to come to Mexico to develop the "New World." These *peninsulares,* as the Spaniards were called because they were from the Iberian Peninsula, often worked as wholesale merchants, providing goods and services to the Spanish communities in Mexico. The role of merchants in colonial Mexico thus became assigned to foreigners.[5] Harold Sims explains that "*peninsulares* had always enjoyed social and economic advantages in Mexico, of course, by virtue of their undisputed *limpieza de sangre* (purity of blood) . . . The importance of Spaniards in Mexican society—a condition inherited from the colonial period—was reflected in their continued prominence in commercial enterprises. . . . Commerce was a predominant occupation of Mexico's Spaniards."[6] Although many of the important *comerciantes* were *peninsulares,* not all *peninsulares* were *comerciantes.*[7] The Spanish Crown tried to regulate who could come to the Americas. In principle, only Spanish subjects of "pure" blood—those not from Moorish or Jewish descent—were permitted to emigrate. Estimates suggest that between 1504 and 1650, approximately 450,000 Spaniards migrated to the Americas, the majority opting for New Spain (Mexico).[8] Emigration was voluntary and regulated by the Spanish House of Trade and the Council of the Indies that oversaw the reports and licenses of the migrants.

As the Spanish colonies grew in the sixteenth and seventeenth centuries, however, immigration became more difficult to regulate. A recent translation of a travel memoir of a Chaldean priest named Elias al-Mûsili suggests that Middle Eastern interest in the Americas and Mexico in particular can be dated to the seventeenth century as well.[9] European politics at the time are generally viewed to have determined the makeup of the foreign community in Mexico. It is estimated that Portuguese, Dutch, Germans, Italians, and English comprised 2,000 of the non-Spanish European community during the colonial period; scholars also speculate that Mexico received more than 200,000 Africans during this time.[10] Like these Africans, many Asians came to Mexico as slaves. In the seventeenth century, about 600 Asians entered Mexico each year. According to D. A. Brading's study of Guanajuato, Mexico, in the late eighteenth century, non-Spanish European males composed only 3 percent of the workforce in 1792.[11] Labor depended heavily on these other groups.

During this colonial occupation, the Spaniards imported many African slaves to sugar-producing communities such as Veracruz and Morelos. These slaves were forced into migration, and their presence in Mexican society has further challenged who belongs to the Mexican nation.[12] Nancy P. Appelbaum, Anne S. Macpherson, and Karin Alejandra Rosemblatt suggest that Afro-Mexicanness employs a racialized discourse whereby regions with black populations are not fully considered part of the nation.[13] Given the widespread dispersal (Veracruz, Morelos, and Oaxaca) of Africans throughout Mexico, it seems quite probable that Afro-Mexicans have also positioned themselves among *mestizos* from the colonial period through the present day.[14]

After the war for Mexican independence from 1810 to 1821, Mexico struggled to define the role of Spanish immigrants in Mexico. In 1824 Mexican officials asked Spaniards to leave the country and ordered the expulsion of Spaniards by 1828.[15] Harold Sims argues that

> in light of the Iberians' dominance of commerce, I would suggest that although the expulsions were the result of a broadly based, nationalistic anti-Spanish movement, a substantial source of criollo pro-expulsionist sentiment was mercantile rivalry between Mexicans and Spaniards during a period of severe economic decline.[16]

When Mexican liberals later accused conservatives of being anti-immigration and unprogressive, some elites sought to reestablish ties to the Spanish Crown in 1836. As Mexicans fought over how to build the new nation, Texas declared its independence from Mexico in 1836, and the United States took advantage of its position and went to war with Mexico in 1846. As an outcome, in 1848 Mexico lost more than half of its territory. Despite the war, American entrepreneurs continued migrating to Mexico to make their fortunes. An estimated 5,412 foreigners resided in Mexico in 1852, and by 1910 more than 20,000 Americans lived in Mexico.[17]

Also during the nineteenth century, French immigrants came to Mexico, often replacing the *peninsulares* as merchants and sometimes becoming wealthy.[18] While the British and French founded Mexico's first modern banks, French immigrants from Barcelonnette, along with Germans and

Spaniards, owned many of the warehouse stores that formed the hubs of an extensive wholesale network.[19] These foreigners enjoyed diplomatic protection and maintained their status as "outsiders" as Benito Juárez pushed for increased immigration to infuse the Mexican populace with Protestant values.[20]

However, Napoleon III decided to extend his empire and in 1863 sent Archduke Maximilian Von Habsburg to take control over Mexico. By 1867 Maximilian was executed and the Mexicans expelled the French, further fostering anti-foreign sentiments among many Mexicans. Meanwhile, the U.S. Civil War had come to a close, and some newly freed black slaves who sought a new life migrated to northern Mexico.[21] Yet the arrival of these immigrants did not fit with notions of "bettering" the nation, and within a few decades a large portion of Afro-Americans returned home.

With the hope of transforming Mexico's "backward" indigenous past and mounting debts, President Porfirio Díaz promoted immigration to alleviate Mexico's ills. In 1883 the government passed the Colonization and Naturalization Laws of the Republic to encourage settlement in sparsely populated areas and to bring development to Mexico. Immigrants from Italy were among the first colonists. Díaz' openness to immigration extended to Japan and China. In November 1888 the Treaty of Friendship, Commerce, and Navigation between Mexico and Japan facilitated the immigration of Japanese. Between 1891 and 1908, roughly thirty-four Japanese emigration companies sent thousands of Japanese emigrants abroad.[22] In 1893 Mexico and China signed a Treaty of Amity and Commerce containing a "most favored nation" clause welcoming Chinese immigrants. After the United States terminated Chinese immigration by the Chinese Exclusion Act of 1882,[23] Mexico became an attractive alternative for Chinese immigrants.[24] However, by 1896 the colonization program was abandoned for being too costly and inefficient and taking too long to implement.[25]

It is within this context that Middle Eastern migration to Mexico can be explored, locating immigrants in national and transnational histories.

Exploring National History

The trajectory of Middle Eastern immigrants becoming itinerant traders selling small trinkets and goods throughout the Americas is well known. A paucity of sources, however, has left the Middle Eastern communities in the Americas to construct their histories as told to them by their relatives.[26] Although literary works like the aforementioned *Gabriela, Clove and Cin-*

namon make references to the role of the *turco*,[27] a comprehensive history of Middle Eastern immigration to the Americas has yet to be written. Scholars have only begun to develop comparative studies on how Middle Eastern immigrants position themselves in various Latin American countries. With the exception of the edited volumes by Ignacio Klich and Jeffrey Lesser and by Albert Hourani and Nadim Shehadi,[28] most studies on Middle Eastern immigrants tend to focus on specific countries.

Moreover, while some scholars have described the Middle Eastern immigrant experience in the Americas, few address the historical significance of Middle Eastern immigrants in Mexican history and Latin American history in general.[29] This study examines how the conflicts of revolutionary Mexico provided Middle Eastern immigrants the opportunity to prosper and create their own unique community in the post-revolutionary nation. Middle Eastern immigrants successfully positioned themselves in Mexican society by exploiting conflictual moments and building on the Mexican tradition of foreign entrepreneurship.

During the late nineteenth century, immigrants from the Middle East came to Mexico intending to make their fortunes quickly and to return to their home countries or pass through to the United States. As the immigrants entered Mexico at the turn of the twentieth century, admissions into the United States became more difficult, Mexico became embroiled in its Revolution, and the Ottoman Empire participated in World War I. Together these events indefinitely delayed the immigrants' return to their homelands. Consequently, many immigrants permanently settled in Mexico and subsequently brought over other family members.

Historical events in the Middle East as well as Mexico and other parts of the Americas helped to determine where immigrants landed. Their settlement patterns reflect economic motivations, politics, and complex social networks. Between 1895 and 1940, approximately 36,000 Middle Eastern immigrants migrated to Mexico.[30] According to the Centro Libanés Website (www.centrolibanes.org), approximately 380,000 of Mexico's 100 million people have Lebanese ancestry.[31] The Centro Libanés is a social club throughout Mexico for those of Lebanese descent, with nine clubhouses: in Mexico City, Guadalajara, Veracruz, Chihuahua, Mérida, Puebla, Monterrey, Tampico, and San Luís Potosí. Although this immigrant group is not numerically large, it commands substantial economic and political power in Mexico, as will be discussed in Chapter 6.

Most Middle Eastern immigrants arrived in Mexico not knowing Spanish. Many were illiterate, had few skills, and were not particularly interested in farming. Their circumstances encouraged them to start peddling.

Although not all Middle Eastern immigrants began as peddlers, many did; historical records tend to describe many Middle Eastern immigrants beginning with this occupation. As the Mexican nation developed, it had limited networks for the distribution of household goods and with small villages separated by long distances, presenting opportune circumstances for the peddler to play a critical role.[32]

Much of the status of Middle Easterners derived from their roles in the Mexican economy. Early immigrants often brought their initial goods from other countries and then borrowed capital from their immigrant countrymen. According to Lebanese Mexican oral tradition, the first Middle Eastern immigrant to Mexico was Butros Raful, a Lebanese missionary who arrived in the nineteenth century and was later followed by his family. In interviews with members of the Lebanese community, anthropologist Luz María Martínez Montiel notes that "they arrived bearing relics they had brought from the Holy Land. Their oriental attire was looked upon admiringly. People here [in Mexico] kissed their hands and garments, and on learning that they came from the East, would ask them for news of the family of Jesus Christ."[33] The Raful family exchanged rosaries and crucifixes they had brought for pens, threads, knives, and cloth, and they used earnings from the sales of relics with glass, hardware, cutlery, perfume, and toys. Once they had developed a clientele, Middle Eastern immigrants would accumulate stock to satisfy their customers' demands and consolidate the immigrant businesses. The immigrants' greatest help came from friends and relatives who had already settled in Mexico.[34] Some of these early immigrants capitalized on their peddling activities and expanded into other commercial ventures such as real estate and industrial production. Whether real or perceived, Middle Eastern entrepreneurship seemed to overcome the difficulties of the Mexican economy and thrive.

The *turco* sojourners, these initial immigrants who quickly escaped the collapse of the Ottoman Empire with short-term goals of working and returning home, realized the need to legitimate themselves as trustworthy suppliers. They needed to market themselves and their goods for their personal safety as well as for societal acceptance. In this process, Mexican elites often found Middle Eastern immigrants a valuable resource in appeasing their workers and *campesinos* with goods.[35] Middle Eastern immigrants offered workers and *campesinos* new economic freedoms in their purchasing decisions through the ability to pay in installments, called *abonos*. Middle Eastern peddlers thus competed with a rising Mexican middle class, which became increasingly frustrated by Middle Eastern economic strategies. Letters written by Mexican merchants to the various presidential administrations in the 1920s and 1930s complaining of unscrupulous Middle Eastern merchants manifest these frustrations, as will be examined further in Chapter 4. These letters helped to initiate anti-immigrant legislation and raise issues of who could be members of the Mexican nation. They also locate Middle Eastern immigrants in the historical record.

Mexico Becomes the Back Door to the United States

As Latin American countries struggled to handle their foreign populations, the United States became increasingly concerned about controlling diseases associated with immigrants. From 1879 to 1883 the U.S. National Board of Health was established to support state and local health efforts, but the feeble agency never imposed national quarantine standards to suppress diseases. Some immigrant smuggling rings began to see Mexico as "America's 'back door,' "[36] a place from which immigrants could slip through a porous border. In March 1891 a U.S. federal immigration law known as the Disease Act required that steamship companies medically examine emigrants to certify their health prior to their departure.[37] Alan Kraut notes that with the passage of the Disease Act of March 3, 1891, "the federal government acted decisively to exclude diseases borne on the bodies of immigrants."[38] This law meant that immigrants would undergo health inspections before departures and upon arrival in the United States. More specifically, steamship companies were required to certify the health of their passengers prior to departure and were liable for the cost of housing and feeding passengers that were detained by American authorities. To maintain their customer base, steamship companies began to actively use Veracruz as an alternate port of entry. Upon entering Mexico, Middle Eastern immigrants could travel to Ciudad Juárez and then enter the United States at El Paso, Texas, or other border towns.

The U.S. Disease Act of 1891 revolutionized migratory patterns from the Middle East to the Americas. The health standard barred previously legal entries into the United States, prompting corruption and new entrepreneurial migration patterns. Savvy immigrants, steamship agents, and doctors quickly learned ways to evade immigration laws intended to exclude diseased immigrants such as those with the contagious bacterial eye disease commonly known as trachoma.

Trachoma afflicted many immigrants coming to the Americas because of its prevalence in areas of overcrowding and poor hygiene and because it is passed to others by hands, on clothing, or by flies that are attracted to faces and runny noses.[39] Cramped steamships and entrepots were prime locations for the disease to spread. And as trachoma became a concern among U.S. immigration officials in the late nineteenth century, more stringent regulations became instituted to stop the flow of diseased immigrants. Nayan Shah also has suggested that the U.S. Public Health Service more frequently diagnosed Middle Eastern and Asian immigrants with trachoma than the European immigrants because of racial bias.[40]

In 1905 the Annual Report of the U.S. Commissioner-General of Immigration to the Secretary of Commerce and Labor noted:

> In Marseilles [France], the "treatment" of trachoma has assumed quite remarkable dimensions. Here most of the emigrants from the Orient, from Syria, Armenia, etc., come on their way to the United States. Most of the Orientals report to one Anton Fares, who refers them to a boarding house. After the usual preliminaries, such as inquiries as to the amount of money in their possession, their destination, etc., the emigrants are referred to Doctor Reynaut for examination. Those who are found free from contagious disease are given tickets and at once sent to Havre. As is well known, these races are especially prone to trachoma and in a large proportion of instances the doctor does discover its presence. These are given by M. Fares the choice of two alternatives: Either to go via St. Nazaire to Mexico, where Fares claims to have agents to conduct them across the frontier to the United States, which is quite expensive and tedious process, and of late very uncertain, or submit to a course of treatment by Dr. G. Reynaut, 20 Boulevard d'Athénee, Marseilles, who claims to have been very successful.[41]

Reynaut charged one franc per treatment, and the average duration of treatment was about two weeks. However, not all of Reynaut's patients did in fact have trachoma. Rather they were people with money who were diagnosed with "curable" trachoma. After a period of treatment and boarding, these individuals were certified as "cured" and easily passed into the United States. Syrian immigrants convinced of Reynaut's abilities and Fare's connections became excellent advertisers among the Middle Eastern community.

As Middle Easterners anxiously waited to cross the Atlantic and U.S. immigration policies became more stringent, Mexico emerged as a host of undocumented immigrants seeking to enter the United States. The concerns about trachoma and diseased immigrants illegally entering the United States led to an undercover investigation, which was conducted in late 1906 *goes under cover.*

by U.S. Inspector A. Seraphic. On October 16, 1906, A. Seraphic was given "confidential instructions" in Washington, D.C., by the Bureau of Immigration to "proceed to the Republic of Mexico and investigate the Syrian Immigration to the United States through the Republic of Mexico in all its phases as well as the conditions at the Border stations."[42] His report reveals a complex, well-coordinated smuggling ring that began in France and brought immigrants to Mexico who would otherwise be denied admission into the United States. These immigrants would then cross the U.S.-Mexican border at towns such as El Paso and Brownsville. The report documents the ease of crossing the U.S.-Mexican border for Mexicans and for Middle Eastern immigrants. As the Seraphic report reveals, immigrants were coached to "become Mexican" in order to more easily enter the United States. Posing as Mexicans, Syrians and in some cases Greeks who were able to "dress Mexican" and pretend to be drunk could bypass poorly paid inspection officials. One informant told a disguised Seraphic, "let him walk across briskly and say he is Mexican."[43] In examining the comparable case of the Chinese immigrants seeking to cross the border, Grace Delgado notes that "two Chinese women adorned themselves in the customary dark veils garnished by Mexican women of the time."[44] Responding to such practices, Commissioner-General F. P. Sargent complained that the inspectors at the El Paso bridge "apparently pay but little attention to persons having the appearance of being Mexicans, which has led to that form of disguise being adopted by aliens of other nationalities who are desirous of finding an easy means of ingress to this country [the United States]."[45] Sargent then contacted the San Antonio office and stated:

> It would appear that the dress and appearance of a Mexican is about
> all that is needed for any European alien, regardless of his condition, to
> secure admission through that port . . . It is further shown that there is
> a small boat plying regularly between Eagle Pass and the Mexican shore,
> carrying passengers who are passed with no further examination than
> that of an inspector stationed on the bridge, who contents himself with
> looking at the passengers going back and forth on the boat.[46]

According to INS records, several smuggling operations existed to facilitate a growing market demand to bring relatives to the United States. The smugglers operated throughout Mexico in Tampico, Veracruz, Mexico City, Monterrey, Nuevo Laredo, Matamoros, Ciudad Juárez, and Torreón. In Veracruz, Syrian immigrant Nicolás Homsey, for example, ran a dry goods store and restaurant with some "filthy" rooms for arriving compatriots. When there were not enough beds to accommodate the immigrants, they would sleep in empty lots or near the docks in front of the U.S. Consulate. Homsey would charge the Syrian immigrants $1.00 to $1.50 per day for board and lodging and $2.00 each for his services in buying them tickets and acting as an interpreter for them. Seraphic describes Homsey as

> a grafter of the first degree and a combination exists between him and Geo. Roume and Mitri Assi of Marseilles, who are the principal steerers of Syrian Immigration to the United States through Mexico. The combination extends to Mexico City with the Hotel keepers and to Monterey [*sic*] and Torreon with dry goods merchants.[47]

According to the report, French and German steamers had brought about two hundred Syrians to Mexico, of whom 40 percent left for the Yucatán via steamships and eighty were found in Homsey's house.

Although Nicolás Homsey and other merchants in Mexico City, Monterrey, and Torreón appeared to be helping Syrian immigrants get to the United States, Seraphic contends that in fact they were putting up every possible obstacle to induce these immigrants to stay in Mexico. With more Syrian peddlers in Mexico employed by store-owning countrymen, there was greater market coverage and therefore an increased opportunity for profit. For example, many of the immigrants leaving from Europe to Veracruz intended to make it to the United States; they were told in France that railway tickets from Veracruz to New York were only sixteen dollars, and these immigrants got the idea that they could cure their cases of trachoma in Mexico before entering the United States. Once in Veracruz, however, and if they had money, Homsey suggested that they proceed to Yucatán where, after six more months, they could proceed to New York by steamer. Apparently, U.S. inspectors were not as strict on steamships arriving from Mexico as they were with steamships coming from Europe.

Those Syrian immigrants who arrived without money in Mexico began peddling in Veracruz or were sent to Mexico City by friends or relatives. Selim Almshiti was the "chief immigrant robber in Mexico City, after Nicolas Homsey has divested them of as much cash as he can through himself and some of his agents who work for him."[48] Seraphic notes that "deported immigrants cannot get back at them for false guarantees and representations."[49] These immigrants had no recourse. The human smuggling ring operating in Mexico to serve and exploit Syrian immigrants acted with impunity.

One extreme case involved Aziz Barondi, who was known to collect full fares to El Paso from immigrants in Mexico City and purchase transportation for them only to Torreón. Barondi and his colleagues also would exchange money for the immigrants at much less than the prevailing rates.

For immigrants going to Mexico City from coastal ports, Syrian handlers greeted them at the train station and escorted them to five places —Josi Ali y Selim Abdalla, Correo Mayor No. 1; Ayar Assad, Meleros No. 1; Rashid Galahon, Correo Mayor No. 7; Youseff Simaan, Avenida Oriente No. 1; Manuel Daraskoui and Selim Amshiti Yousef, Rejas de Valvanera No. 5. Immigrants often slept on the floor and were packed like sardines. One or two rooms were converted into a restaurant in which immigrants could sleep and eat. Although these filthy places further spread trachoma and other contagious diseases, they also served as places to coach immigrants as to what to say during inspection at the U.S.-Mexican border. Meanwhile, as immigrants waited for remittances from relatives in the States, they would begin peddling goods for their countrymen who owned stores in Mexico. There were reportedly 900 Syrians living in Mexico City in 1906 whose chief occupation was peddling. Seraphic reported:

> The Syrians endeavor to, and succeed very readily in becoming Mexicanized. They dress in Mexican attire while peddling through Mexico and they show great aptitude in learning Spanish. Their mode of life in Syria is not dissimilar to that of the low Mexican and as both the Arabic and Spanish abound in insincere expressions of politeness, bordering on servility, they assimilate with Mexicans easier than all other races.[50]

Although the Middle Easterners had a propensity for integration into Mexican society, many still wished to immigrate to the United States to join family members and friends. If immigrants were able to save enough from peddling or receive sufficient remittances from friends or relatives in Mexico City, they would travel to one of the border cities and try to enter the United States. Many immigrants traveled to other Latin American destinations and then similarly tried to enter the United States. Immigrant Fares Nasser of St. Louis, Missouri, told immigration officials in August 1906 that he traveled from Marseilles to Buenos Aires because his brother lived in Buenos Aires. Nasser then left Buenos Aires for Veracruz and then Mexico City. From Mexico City, he traveled to El Paso and crossed the border with nine other immigrants with the assistance of Alexander Hakeem, whom he paid two dollars.[51]

The Mexican Herald published an article in July 1906 with the headline "Thousands of Turks: Immigrants of this Class Arriving at Veracruz."

The article began, "Three special cars were attached to the regular Mexican train from Veracruz yesterday morning on account of a large number of Turkish immigrants brought to that port by the German steamer which arrived there Thursday."[52] A Spanish steamer also brought a large influx of immigrants. It was estimated that more than 450 immigrants from both steamers arrived in Veracruz. Some of the immigrants stayed in the vicinity to secure work, and others would "eventually work their way to the border and cross into the United States."[53] In December 1906 the *San Antonio Express* commented that "while Mexico wants immigrants, nevertheless, she does not want any more than does the United States the objectionable classes."[54]

In Ciudad Juárez, an active smuggling ring included a medical inspector, Dr. Coffin; a translator, Salim Mattar; and customs officials. When word leaked that A. Seraphic was not in fact an undocumented Syrian immigrant trying to cross the U.S.-Mexican border with a pregnant cousin but rather an undercover investigator from the Immigration Service, accusations began to fly. Unfortunately, only Seraphic's account survives in the historical record. As with drug trafficking rings, the total number and scope of human smuggling rings are difficult to document.

In Ciudad Juárez, Seraphic noted that Kalil Koury of El Paso was the main contact for Syrian immigrants seeking to cross the U.S. border. Koury had adobe houses with about ten rooms in total, and the immigrants huddled together on muddy floors without any bedding or cover "in a condition that Mexican peons do not care to reside in."[55] After charging each immigrant various fees for boarding, transportation pick-up and drop-off, Koury would then take the immigrants to Dr. Coffin's treating day. Dr. Coffin, wrote Seraphic, was the man who "monopolizes the treatment of Syrian trachomatous eyes." For twenty dollars, Dr. Coffin would guarantee the cure of trachoma and would employ the following procedure:

A Syrian to open the eye of each patient and two drops of a solution of nitrate silver in the eye constituted all the patients received. Every three days one of each treatment or ten a month, but usually eight. This with the payment of $20 cash is a positive guarantee to cure every case in a month.[56]

However, as of January 1907 Dr. Coffin was to raise his fee to twenty-five dollars per cure. On treatment day, Koury would pull out a book reminding the doctor of which immigrants were cured or not, and then the doctor would write out a certificate saying: "This is to certify that I have treated bearer for one month, and he is now cured (Sgd.) C.W. Coffin." Coffin would agree to certify four immigrants in one day.[57] However, Koury would sometimes lie about the date of the certificate, forcing the immigrants to stay for additional nights at his boarding home and to incur more debt.

Meanwhile at the El Paso inspection station, Seraphic suggests, Dr. Sinks, the medical inspector, was connected to Dr. Coffin and was in fact taking kickbacks for admitting "cured" immigrants. According to the report, Dr. Coffin and Dr. Sinks formerly had their offices together, and their families were very close. "Dr. Sinks pointed out Dr. Coffin to Kalil Koury to treat the Syrians. He has a monopoly of it, netting from $600 to $1,000 per month. All that are treated by Dr. Coffin, Dr. Sinks passes."[58] In a seeming grudge against Dr. Sinks, Seraphic goes as far as approaching the former Mrs. Sinks for additional information. However, Seraphic was not able to obtain sufficient evidence to warrant Dr. Sinks' dismissal; rather, Seraphic advised that Sinks be transferred.[59]

While making accusations against the medical inspectors in El Paso in 1906, Seraphic also investigated an interpreter, Salim Mattar, for charging immigrants additional fees for translation. Mattar was employed by the federal government to translate for inspection officials. When Seraphic approached the Santa Fe, G.H. and S.A., and Rock Island railroad ticket agents about Mattar, they all stated that they never paid any commission to the interpreter. Rather, Seraphic suggested, Mattar and Koury were partners who defrauded immigrants. Mattar had helped Koury get started in his business in Ciudad Juárez. In El Paso, Mattar had a Turkish bazaar that paid him well. In the end, Seraphic's main complaint against Mattar was that he was not proficient in English.[60]

The U.S. Department of Commerce and Labor also took note of Kalil Koury. In 1907 the department reported that Abraham Assad, a Turk of Syrian race, entered the United States in violation of the Act of Congress approved March 3, 1903. After being rejected at El Paso as suffering from trachoma, Abraham Assad was smuggled into the United States by Kalil Koury.[61] Koury, known for his famous immigrant boardinghouse in Ciudad Juárez, was reported to have smuggled at least 500 Syrians into the United States in 1906. Salim Mattar, who worked at El Paso inspections, apparently aided Assad in obtaining a doctor to help him overcome his trachoma.[62] This account, combined with the Seraphic report, offers a glimpse into human smuggling of Middle Eastern immigrants into the United States.

Interestingly, despite the numerous allegations of S. M. Mattar accepting kickbacks, he was reemployed by the Immigration Service in late 1906 with compensation of two dollars per diem. In December 1906 and again in February 1907, the Immigration Inspector in El Paso wrote to headquarters:

> Through the cooperation of boarding house keepers and others of his [Mattar's] nationality whom he has befriended, and some of whom are doubtless under obligations to him, I am kept fully informed as to the illegal entry of Syrians. Within a few hours after Syrians cross without inspection, I am enabled to locate them. While some successful efforts have been made to smuggle Syrians in the past, the Syrian immigration now is under almost complete control, through the means indicated. Under the circumstances, would not Mr. Mattar be a valuable man to retain, and would not his separation from the service, when he is now willing to remain, place this office at a serious disadvantage in dealing with the class of aliens under consideration?[63]

The inspector continued: "It is a significant fact that the Syrian immigration through this port has fallen off to almost nothing since Dr. Sinks was displaced, and I see no reason why Interpreter S.M. Matter should not be again permanently appointed at $300. per annum."[64] In 1915 a New Orleans special agent of the Justice Department located Mattar's Immigration Service badge. Apparently Mattar failed to surrender his badge when he stopped working for the government.[65]

Ultimately, the Seraphic report recommended better salaries for the interpreters and more oversight to help eliminate corruption. However, Seraphic concluded, "my very careful study of the Mexican Border problem and alien immigration has convinced me that the wisest and most effective solution will be to close the Mexican border to aliens."[66] Clearly, Seraphic's recommendations were not implemented. Rather, the permeable border continued to allow Middle Eastern immigrants to enter the United States, although many of these immigrants either failed to cross the border or chose not to continue their migration to the United States. In these cases, Middle Eastern immigrants rooted themselves throughout Mexico.

At the same time, Japanese and Chinese immigrants were entering the United States illegally through fraudulent papers. In March 1907 the El Paso Immigration Office wrote headquarters in Washington, D.C.:

> Since the influx of Japanese, the Chinese have evidently taken advantage of our hampered condition to overrun us. Since July 1st [1907] last 237 Chinamen holding certificates of residence and other papers, all from points of the country, have appeared at this office and have asked to have

their papers stamped so that they could proceed to their various destinations, claiming that they were unable to find work here, for which they came in search. These Chinese have all entered from Mexico . . . In other words, Chinese in El Paso holding good papers occupy the same status that they would in Cincinnati or any other place, irrespective of the fact that there is no record of their arrival from the interior to this place, and that they make ridiculous and contradictory statements accounting for their presence here.[67]

It appears that the El Paso immigration center was overwhelmed in its responsibilities and looked to Washington for support. It was estimated that in 1906 and 1907 more than 10,000 Japanese had been brought to Mexico. But according to INS records, "Now, at the present moment [1907] you cannot find a thousand in all the Republic of Mexico,"[68] suggesting that many of these Japanese immigrants had migrated to the United States. Grace Delgado, in examining the Chinese in Sonora, found that "by 1900, Mexican businessmen in Sonora believed they were unable to compete equally with Chinese merchants and grocers . . . During the *porfiriato*, the Chinese received government upstarts and incentives that, under the law, the Mexican merchant was not entitled [to receive]."[69] Delgado suggests that this tension between Mexicans and Chinese merchants had "foreboding consequences," referring to the 1911 revolutionary violence directed at foreigners. Anti-Chinese sentiments may have thus caused some Chinese immigrants to cross the U.S.-Mexican border as well.

Mexican-U.S. Policy Exchanges

While some Middle Eastern immigrants tried to enter the United States illegally, the U.S. government recognized the fluid boundaries between the United States and Mexico. U.S. bureaucrats began to seek help from Mexico, France, and other countries to curb the clandestine entry of diseased immigrants. According to U.S. State Department records, as early as 1903 the U.S. government sought to have Mexican railroad companies stop the movement of diseased Europeans from entering into the United States from Mexican ports.[70]

The intergovernment correspondence between the U.S. Ambassador to Mexico and the Minister of Foreign Affairs (SRE) in Mexico City, Ignacio Mariscal, dramatizes this concern about undocumented Syrian immigrants. In 1906 U.S. Ambassador David E. Thompson asked Minister Mariscal to help control the borders against the "undesirable" Syrians coming to Veracruz, Mexico. They corresponded for nearly a year on this subject. The United States' first letter states that

> there is an increase in the immigration to Veracruz, Mexico, of Syrians who are destined to the United States, but who on account of their inability to secure direct passage to our ports by reason of the loathsome or contagious diseases with which they are afflicted.[71]

Mariscal reported that 1,500 Syrians lived in Mexico City, the majority of them illegally. The U.S. government argued that these Syrians were waiting for a favorable opportunity to "evade the requirement of our emigration laws" by surreptitious entry across the Texas border.[72] This exchange between Thompson and Mariscal also indicated that an unknown number of Syrians lived along the border and that U.S. immigration officials were seeking to keep out this "undesirable class of persons."[73] The U.S. State Department was clearly trying to pressure Mexico to alter its immigration policies and enforcement practices. The U.S. concern with health issues can be underscored by the publication of Upton Sinclair's *The Jungle* in 1906 as well as two measures endorsed by U.S. President Theodore Roosevelt, the Pure Food and Drug Act and the Meat Inspection Act, both passed in 1906.

After two additional letters from the United States,[74] Minister Mariscal responded to U.S. pressure and wrote the Governor of Veracruz, the Minister of the Interior, and the Sub-Secretary of Communications of the Ministry of Foreign Affairs expressing the U.S. Embassy's concern with trachoma and the incoming Syrian immigrants. Mariscal indicated to the Ministry of Economic Development (Secretaría de Fomento) that it was important to differentiate between the need for immigrants and the health issue,[75] illustrating that Mexicans had their own internal debates on how exactly to handle their new immigrant population. By August 1906 the various governmental officials had written Mariscal describing the measures they were taking to control the Syrian immigrants.[76] During the remaining months of 1906, Mariscal and the Mexican government tried to implement a more comprehensive immigration policy.

This correspondence between the United States and Mexico underscores both the U.S. fear of Middle Eastern immigrants bringing trachoma to the Americas and the international scope of the Middle Eastern migration. The letters also exemplify the pattern of U.S.-Mexican relations throughout the nineteenth and twentieth centuries, with the U.S. government seeking to influence Mexican policy makers. Many other Latin American countries had taken their cues from the United States and had begun implementing restrictionist immigration policies. Mexican policy makers struggled to adhere to Mexican national interests. U.S. immigrant agent Marcus Braun noted:

> The Mexican Government fears . . . the accumulation of diseased persons within the borders of that country, but such condition prevails at the present time, as hundreds of aliens who have been excluded at boundary ports upon account of their afflictions, are harbored at points in Mexico and are proving a menace to the population.[77]

Despite the "undesirability" of Middle Eastern immigrants, Mexican officials also saw these immigrants as providing necessary services that Díaz deemed important.

To further complicate the Mexican position, Thompson inquired about the Mexican Superior Board of Health and its sanitary regulations with respect to trachoma. He cited Article 26 of the Mexican Sanitary Code, which "sets for the measures taken at the ports of the Republic to prevent the importation of epidemic and infectious diseases."[78] Thompson ended the letter saying that without the sanitary code, sick immigrants would have a detrimental effect on legitimate Mexican laborers who might seek work in the United States. Again, this thinly disguised threat to stop Mexican immigrants from entering the United States because of disease demonstrates how the U.S. government attempted to compel Mexico into taking harsher measures to prevent Syrian immigration across the Mexico-U.S. border. To reinforce his point, Thompson enclosed an eleven-page monograph on trachoma prepared by the Surgeon-General of the Public Health and Marine Hospital Service of the United States. The monograph stated that "trachoma is a disease of the conjunctiva . . . [in which the sufferer becomes] restricted in his activities and may eventually become a public charge . . . During a prolonged period, he remains a constant danger to the community at large by his ability to disseminate the disease."[79]

The Law of September 22, 1908, which established the Mexican Immigrant Inspection Service, could be seen in part as a response to Thompson's letter-writing campaign in 1906. This service began functioning in 1909 to maintain statistical data concerning migration. Prior to 1910 these statistics covered only immigration to Mexico, but after 1910 data on both immigration and emigration were to be maintained.[80] Although the U.S. State Department reported in 1929 that some statistics were available, little evidence has been shown to demonstrate that this law was implemented systematically prior to the Mexican Revolution. It is probable that this law aimed to prohibit foreign workers from arriving in Mexico because of the 1908 economic crisis and the threat to the subsistence of Mexican workers.[81]

In December 1908 Francisco J. Ituarte, a member of the Congress of Deputies, wrote Deputy Francisco Alfaro asking the Mexican Congress to reexamine Articles 8 and 10 of the 1886 immigration law. Ituarte argued that the law was too drastic and would scare potential investors, giving them the wrong impression of Mexico.[82] This fear of losing potential investors has been a periodic concern throughout Mexican history and was particularly acute for Porfirio Díaz, who linked much of the nation and its future to foreign capital investment.

As U.S. and Mexican governments debated the best way to slow Middle Eastern migration, news of economic opportunities in the Americas circulated in the Middle East. For instance, *Al-Mircad*, M. Fares' newspaper, had wide circulation in Syria and was considered "in character a good advertising sheet for emigration to America."[83] When Immigrant Inspector Maurice Fishberg asked French authorities why they permitted him to operate in France, they responded that "there were certain powers at work; the steamship companies need him here."[84] Fares was known to ship forty to fifty immigrants weekly on the Compagnie Génerale Transatlantique, and the steamship companies in general approved of his activities to help the immigrants. It should be noted that steamship companies were fined one hundred dollars for each case of trachoma that passed, and it was the duty of the authorized physicians of the companies to treat and "cure" such cases of trachoma.[85]

As the United States, via the State Department, sought to share responsibility for this immigrant population and its "loathsome disease," Mexico began to follow U.S. immigration policy as a barometer on how Mexican officials ought to handle its immigrant populations.

When Immigrant Inspector Marcus Braun visited Mexico City in 1907, he reportedly met with President Porfirio Díaz, who agreed to develop an immigration agreement similar to the one Mexico shared with Canada. According to Braun, Díaz mentioned that "anyone not good enough for the United States ought not be good enough for Mexico."[86] Among the more than twenty-one ports of entry along the U.S.-Mexican border, Laredo, El Paso, and Eagle Pass saw the largest number of alien crossings.

The number of aliens who were known to apply for admission at Mexican border ports was roughly 10,000 a year. A State Department report in 1908 found that the Japanese were the largest group of U.S. border crossers, followed by Syrians and Spaniards. Of the immigrants most likely to be ex-

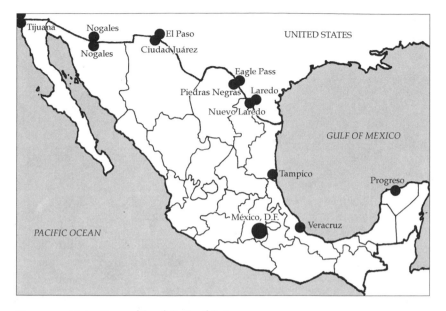

Figure 2.1. Major Sea and Land Ports of Entry

cluded, Syrians comprised the largest number, followed by Japanese. The report noted that "it is not an unusual instance for an alien to be arrested in the United States after surreptitious entry and deported to Mexico three and four times within as many months."[87] In February 1908 the U.S. Department of Commerce and Labor sought to have an agreement consisting of eight articles with the Government of Mexico and several Mexican transportation companies regarding immigration. However, it does not appear that such an agreement came to fruition despite Inspector Marcus Braun's earliest attempts, in 1903.

As the Mexican regime faced increasing economic difficulties around 1908, the Porfirian policy of welcoming immigrants began to be reexamined. New technological innovations and the European abilities to extract critical resources from colonies led to increasing trade imbalances and a reconfiguration of world powers. These events created an explosion in world migration.[88]

Concluding Comments

The role of the *turco* merchant illustrates how Middle Eastern immigrants have been part of the Latin American social fabric for the last century.

Not only have Middle Easterners entered the Latin American landscape, but they have traversed national boundaries, thereby intersecting and linking national histories throughout the Americas. Mexican-U.S. policy exchanges on immigration grew out of a concern about immigrants using Mexico as a back door to the United States. More specifically, U.S. immigration policies such as the 1891 Disease Act transformed transatlantic migration patterns, giving rise to smuggling rings. To further complicate this history, Mexican policy makers during the presidency of Porfirio Díaz were seeking to both attract foreign investors and to placate the United States. The dynamics of Porfirian policy makers will be further examined in the next chapter.

By locating Middle Eastern immigrants in Mexican national history and more broadly in Mexican-U.S. relations, the difficulty of placing these immigrants in historical categories becomes transparent. The Middle Eastern experience in Mexico can be best explored through an examination of a myriad of sources with attention to nationalist agendas and dramatic changes in geopolitics. Through this historical context, Middle Easterners are seen to participate in Mexican society and later to join the Mexican nation as foreign citizens. The following chapter focuses on Middle Eastern historical events and how they intersect with Mexican history and the demographic profile of the early Middle Eastern immigrants.

CHAPTER 3

Turco Sojourners Come to Porfirian Mexico

In 1907 U.S. Immigration Inspector T. F. Schmucker asked Syrian alien Soulaiman Mahmoud if he knew he had done something illegal when crossing the U.S. border. Mahmoud responded, "I don't know the difference between Mexico and the United States."[1] Mahmoud was promptly arrested and deported. A few months later, in August 1907, *The Mexican Herald* printed an editorial on such situations:

> Mexico has long been the stamping [*sic*] ground of Syrians and other
> foreigners, who come to this country because they have been denied or
> know that they will be denied admission to the ports of the United States
> because they are victims of the disease . . . With respect to Mexico, the
> steamship companies will hereafter have to be more than usually careful in
> selecting the class of their passengers, for if they bring trachoma sufferers
> to this country they will be at the expense of giving them a free ride back
> to their homes.[2]

This editorial captures a widespread consciousness shared among people, governments, and businesses that international relations affected migration patterns of the late nineteenth and early twentieth centuries. This chapter explores the conditions for Middle Eastern immigrants leaving the Ottoman Empire, their migration experience, the context for their arrival in Mexico, and a demographic profile of these immigrants. Since many early immigrants departed as subjects of the Ottoman Empire, prior to World War I, they were often called *turcos*, or Turks. At the time of the immigrants' departure, many were sojourners, those with the intent of working for a short time and then returning home. Their emergence in Mexico as foreign citizens would take place in the decades that followed.

Mexican policies under President Porfirio Díaz and events in the Middle East coincided to make Mexico a destination point for 2,277 Middle Eastern immigrants who later reported having entered Mexico between 1878 and 1909. These 2,277 immigrants registered with Mexican officials from 1926 through 1951. In trying to build a "modern" nation, President Díaz allowed foreign immigration into Mexico, yet this policy led the United States to pressure Mexico to better monitor its borders and control "Syrian" migrants, as discussed in Chapter 2. Meanwhile, in the Middle East, the Ottoman Empire faced increasing debts to European nations and escalating religious tensions in the Levant (*al-mashriq* in Arabic), which generally refers to present-day Lebanon, Syria, Israel, Jordan, and Palestinian territories. The result was an exodus from the Levant and elsewhere in the Middle East to the Americas. Mexico in particular was a destination point because of established immigration networks and the ability to circumvent U.S. officials along the Eastern Seaboard by traveling first through Mexico. After a long journey to Mexico, many Middle Eastern immigrants turned to countrymen like Domingo Kuri for help in locating their family and friends in Mexico. Kuri's network of Middle Eastern immigrants gave new arrivals instant credit and the ability to penetrate remote areas of the Mexican interior. In this early stage of migration, Middle Eastern immigrants often became peddlers and small-scale merchants, providing key goods and services. As an emerging immigrant population, Middle Easterners often tried to maintain their culture while simultaneously striving to integrate themselves in the Mexican economy.

When Middle Easterners decided to migrate at the end of the nineteenth century, they faced a world divided between rising industrial powers and colonial occupations. The capacity to mass-produce goods through factories supplied inexpensive products and stimulated a demand for cheap raw materials. Western countries relied on regions abroad to supply the raw materials needed to produce finished goods that could be sold for large profits.

By supplying the Western powers, nations in Latin America and in the Ottoman Empire became dependent on exports to generate revenue and foreign credit.[3] In Mexico, liberal army commander Porfirio Díaz, who seized power in 1876 and ruled Mexico directly and indirectly for the next thirty-four years, dedicated his regime to economic expansion. His policies aimed to create the necessary conditions and incentives for capitalist enterprises and to eventually make Mexico modern.[4] Edward Beatty argues that "for Mexico's elites, industry meant modernity . . . Industry also promised to promote national sovereignty by reducing Mexico's dependence on foreign imports."[5] The Díaz regime's attempts at modernization had mixed long- and short-term results. Consequently, foreign investment and Díaz' heavy-handed approach in political and social matters enabled some aspects of the Mexican economy to prosper while the poorer segments of society became more marginalized.

The policy makers of the Díaz regime, often called *científicos,* were influenced by Herbert Spencer and Auguste Comte, who emphasized that government policy should be carried out according to "scientific" laws.[6] José Y. Limantour, Díaz' treasury minister and a son of French immigrants, said in 1901 that "the weak, the unprepared, those who lack the tools in order to emerge victorious against evolution, must perish and leave the struggle to the more powerful."[7] This pseudo-scientific language was used to justify Díaz' consolidation of power over regional bosses and to stimulate the Mexican economy by giving preferences to foreigners both as investors and settlers.[8]

European and American capitalists responded to Porfirian policies and invested heavily in many enterprises, from retail establishments to large-scale mineral exploitation. Rodney Anderson has noted that "industrial production doubled from 1877 to the turn of the century, as great factories and mills were built and as mines, utilizing the latest techniques of extraction and smelting, supplied the raw materials for the industries of Europe and the United States."[9] The United States became Mexico's leading trade partner as mineral exports expanded beyond gold and silver to include copper and zinc. Mexico's own modest industrialization centered on textiles, cement, iron, and light consumer goods. In Orizaba, Veracruz, Mexican textile mills were considered among the largest and most modern in the world at the time. In addition, the mechanization of sugar plantations and processing of Morelos developed parallel to those of Hawaii and Puerto Rico.[10]

Foreign investors saw a great potential for profit in financing railroad routes that facilitated the transportation of products to ports or to the northern border of Mexico. Railroads enabled the quick distribution of goods to other parts of Mexico as well as the transportation of manual laborers to industrializing areas. In turn, this stimulated small markets for a wide variety of easily transportable articles. These circumstances favored itinerant trade beyond the railroad terminals, and Middle Eastern immigrants quickly took up this form of commerce.[11] While the immigrants began peddling in Mexico, they also attempted to maintain ties to their homelands, hoping to return or to bring other family members to the Americas.

The Middle East of the Late Nineteenth Century

The Ottoman Empire's extensive landholdings and coastlines (Figure 1.1) enabled the export of Egyptian cotton, Lebanese silk, wool and hides of the Maghrib, Tunisian phosphates, oranges from Palestine, wine from Algeria, and olive oil from Tunisia for trade with European countries. The Ottoman Empire imported textiles, metal goods, tea, coffee, and sugar. The Ottomans granted the French trading concessions, and silk was a linking factor between Mount Lebanon and France.[12] The French used their economic influence to try to spread Catholicism. Overall, the Ottoman Empire had an unfavorable balance of trade because the Europeans had extended large loans to governments of the Middle East, thereby increasing European financial control in the region.[13] This exchange of goods, although not particularly beneficial to the peoples of the Middle East, did help some indigenous merchant groups. For instance, Syrian and Lebanese Christians, Syrian and Iraqi Jews, and Egyptian Copts all traded with their European counterparts, primarily with British, French, and some German merchants. Some of these Christian and Jewish merchants became landlords in the late nineteenth century because they had accumulated sufficient resources to purchase land within the Ottoman Empire.[14]

Beirut became a major center for the export of silk and the import and distribution of European goods. Thus people from nearby Mount Lebanon, referring to the mountain range that extends across Lebanon and was semi-autonomous during the Ottoman Empire, became aware of what was happening abroad.[15] The integration of Beirut and Lebanon more generally into the world economy was accelerated by the expansion of the silk industry in the nineteenth century. The cultivation of silk led to the diffusion of small-scale ownership in which almost every male inhabitant in Mount Lebanon was a small proprietor of land.[16] In 1846 silk accounted for 57 percent of the value of gross agricultural output of Mount Lebanon, but in 1917 silk reeling only generated roughly 7 percent of the Lebanese national income.[17] The opening of the Suez Canal in 1869 sparked the change, enabling trade between Europe and the Far East to bypass the Levant and thus facilitating the shipment of Japanese silk to European markets at competitive prices.[18] The people of the Levant were unable to compete in this new environment, and silk production in the region declined drastically. To exacerbate the problem, in the 1890s, phylloxera invaded Syrian vineyards.[19] Thus, many people became displaced by the devastation of the vineyards and competition from the Japanese silk industry in the early twentieth century. Many of those affected chose to migrate.

Oral testimonies further reveal religious tensions, mandatory conscription, food shortages, and brutal authorities as contributing factors for leaving the Middle East. However, every emigrant's motivation was different, and no one push factor can be singled out as "the" reason for migration; rather migration is, as Douglas Massey explains, "cumulative" and based on social networks. Massey suggests that migration develops a life of its own and that the interconnections among individual, household, and community-level factors lead to the cumulative causation of migration. These processes are reinforced by dynamic microeconomic relationships among regional labor markets. In short, migration is a social and economic process that involves relationships to homelands and host countries.[20]

As noted, religious tensions also shaped emigration, particularly from Mount Lebanon. The population has traditionally been divided between Muslims and Druzes on one hand and Christians on the other. In 1860 a complex set of civil wars began pitting Maronite Christians and Druze in violent conflict with one another. According to Robert Brenton Betts, in 1860 the Druze killed 12,000 Maronites in Mount Lebanon, and 10,000 Christians were killed in Damascus.[21] A sectarian outburst erupted in Mount Lebanon and spread to uprisings between Sunni Muslims and predominantly Greek Orthodox Christians in Damascus.[22] With the Ottoman Empire weakening in the nineteenth century, local rulers began asserting greater power and authority, especially over local Christians. The increased prestige of Christian Europe—France, in particular—and economic encroachment on Ottoman sovereignty fostered resentment against the Christians in Greater Syria and created colonial intrigue.[23]

The massacres of 1860 led to international intervention in which France, Great Britain, Austria, Prussia, and Russia helped the Ottomans restore stability to Mount Lebanon, and Lebanese Christians were granted a degree of autonomy. This increased autonomy, combined with the Christian community's push for greater equality, threatened the sense of security among Muslims. Michael Suleiman compares the Muslim population to the "poor white trash" of the American South during of the Civil War and the civil rights movement. He notes that the Muslim population in the Syrian province, although poor and oppressed, still enjoyed a social status that was greater than that of non-Muslims, particularly the Christians.[24] The threat of losing this high status made many Muslims susceptible to suggestions from local Ottoman rulers that their Christian neighbors were the cause of Muslim troubles.[25] This perception became substantiated with the 1864 statute that created a political entity in the Ottoman Empire called the *mutasarrifiyya,* which usually had the subdivisions of the provinces (*vilayets*),[26] administered by a non-Lebanese Christian Ottoman governor (*mutassarrif*). This governor, appointed by the sultan, led a central administrative council in which Muslim and Christian sects were proportionally represented.[27] The conflicts among the Christians, the Druze, and Muslims in the 1860s prompted the 1864 statute and its division of religious sects.

Continual European involvement in the Ottoman Empire not only prevented the Ottoman government from directly controlling the areas that comprise Lebanon today but also precluded reconciliation of religious differences, giving some the impetus for emigration in the late nineteenth century.[28] Antonio José Budib, for instance, the first registered Middle Eastern immigrant from Beirut, arrived in Mexico in 1878 and declared himself a Christian. Religious differences also spilled over to military service. General conscription into the Ottoman armed forces was first introduced in 1855. At the time, Christians and Jews paid a tax to be exempt from service.[29] However, the concession was abolished with the takeover by the Young Turks, a group of army officers who rebelled in 1908 and ruled until 1918 with the aim of reforming the Ottoman Empire through constitutionalism. Mandatory conscription was reintroduced in 1909.[30] Conscription was very unpopular with most religious groups because the people were not accustomed to military service. Many fled their homes and emigrated to avoid the draft. Zain Chamut, a Shiʿite Muslim from Braachit, Lebanon, decided to migrate to Mexico only after his brother, Hassan, was forced to fight in the Ottoman army in the Balkans. Hassan became a prisoner of war and suffered a severe stomach injury. He escaped and returned to Braachit, but he was a different man. Zain, fearful of repeating his brother's misfortune, left his homeland in 1907.[31]

Ottoman treatment of Christians, Druzes, and local Muslims in the Levant has long been debated as a stimulus for emigration; historians have reached little consensus on this issue. According to historian Engin Deniz Akarli, Muslim migration from the Ottoman Empire was seen as an embarrassment to the regime, and "the Ottoman government viewed the increase of emigration of the Muslim population in the areas neighboring Mount Lebanon with grave concern."[32] Historian Kemal Karpat points out that "the available Ottoman documents indicate that, in fact, the number of Muslim immigrants was substantial."[33] He suggests that the Muslims' departure from the Ottoman Empire was necessarily clandestine, since they were forbidden to emigrate even before general restrictions were imposed.[34] This level of secrecy probably skewed many of the early immigration records of Ottoman subjects arriving in American cities because they may have feared admitting their religion and risking deportation.

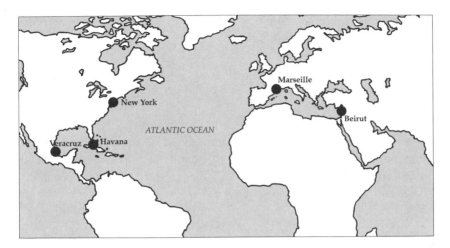

Figure 3.1. Major Ports of Early Transatlantic Migration

The degree of Ottoman control over the subjects of the empire is clearly open to speculation. However, the point that Muslim emigrants have been underreported helps illuminate a question about the tendency of historical records to report Middle Eastern immigrants in Mexico as mostly Christian.

In addition to political, economic, and religious circumstances, many emigrants from the Middle East left for more personal reasons. For example, Juan Chayet Abusaid left Sejoud,[35] Lebanon, to evade local authorities. According to the Abusaid family story, Juan was herding sheep and got into an argument with a good friend. He threw a rock at the friend, and his friend was knocked out. (It was unclear whether he killed his friend or just knocked him unconscious.) Without knowing the friend's actual fate, Abusaid got so scared that he ran to the first ship and left, not even saying goodbye to his father. Afterward, he felt guilty for his hasty departure and sent word to his father that he was "OK" through a cousin in Tabasco, Mexico. He also sent money. According to his youngest daughter, Juan Chayet Abusaid's reason for leaving was *miedo*—fear.[36] Although his story does not mention relatives as the reason he went to Mexico, it is highly probable that his cousin in Tabasco helped him migrate to Mexico.

Family members and friends often played a critical role in how the immigrants migrated from the Middle East to the Americas. Figure 3.1 shows several key transatlantic ports of migration; immigrants typically departed Beirut, stopped in Marseilles, and then arrived in the North American port cities of New York, Havana, and/or Veracruz.

Financial resources, information on migration routes, and contacts in Mexico formed vital networks for Middle Eastern immigrants. Many immigrants borrowed money from friends or relatives and received money through remittances. Remittances from the Americas to Greater Syria were estimated at $8 million in 1914 and $19 million in 1924; and $20 million was sent back to Lebanon in 1952, which compared to exports of $22 million, or 4 percent of the national income in that year.[37] Although the recipients used much of the money to buy land and build houses in their home villages, they also used money to send other family members to the Americas to work in family-owned businesses. When remittances were not available, some mortgaged property to purchase tickets to emigrate.

At the beginning of the twentieth century, the cost was approximately 230 to 250 francs for a one-way fare to South America and 190 francs to New York City.[38] Immigrant testimonies also indicate that it cost $36.40 in gold to take a steamer from Marseilles to Veracruz and another $37.50 to take a train from Veracruz to El Paso, Texas.[39] Emigrants with financial resources were able to purchase tickets leaving from the Lebanese ports of Beirut and Tripoli. In an 1896 Beirut travel agency advertisement, no price was mentioned; rather, the agency listed the ships' amenities such as a doctor and cheaper agents. It states that "tickets to America, Brazil, and other destinations to which the passengers wish to go once they get to Marseilles can be purchased from the same agency. This is 25 percent cheaper than [the price offered by other agencies in Marseilles]."[40]

Shipping lines employed brokers who sent out agents to recruit immigrants. Given Ottoman regulations on travel, military police were stationed on roads leading to the port cities and in the ports themselves. Despite the restrictions, ticket agents often bribed Turkish police and smuggled people out. According to Samir Khalaf, steamship agents "did play a definite role in 'smuggling' immigrants at a time when exit from Ottoman ports was strictly forbidden."[41] At night, agents rowed the emigrants out to international ships anchored off the Mediterranean coast of Syria.[42] In the late 1880s the passenger ships stopped at western European ports such as Marseilles, Athens, Genoa, Trieste, Cherbourg, and Le Havre.[43] In these port cities, agents approached the immigrants, selling tickets to North and South America. Due to commercial trade earlier in the nineteenth century, many of these cities had countrymen to assist the immigrants in their journey. In Marseilles, Middle Eastern immigrants often stayed in the boarding house of Butres Shadiak.[44] Novelist Elmaz Abinader describes the Middle Eastern network in Marseilles in her story of protagonist Mayme's migration to the United States:

Mayme hopes she remembers Marseilles well enough to find the Lebanese doctor who gave them their medicines when she and Shebl [her husband] went to Brazil. Many new things have been built since Mayme's last stop in this city, but the port district and the neighborhood where the Lebanese and Syrians keep their shops are little changed.[45]

Although Mayme's recollection is presented as fiction, her experience reflects the breadth of the migrants' international network in the late nineteenth century. With time, the network alerted countrymen to fraudulent agents and increasingly restrictive immigration policies. Despite the warnings, many emigrants were misrouted to unknown destinations because of ignorance and agents' indifference. Ticket agents received a commission on each ticket sold and often made significant profits on their sales. This in turn made would-be immigrants more susceptible to fraud. A Presbyterian mission report of 1907 summarizes the situation:

The emigrant business has become a very profitable one; the method used in Germany in the seventies (1870s) is used here. A native, usually that has been to America, visits a village, holds meetings, tells of the wonderful way to make money, where to go, what to do, in fact everything necessary for an emigrant to know. It is a poor day when he does not obtain a number of deposits for steamer tickets. This man is one in a long chain whose links are located all the way from Syria to North and South American seaports. From time to time, this chain of workers will send and receive warnings to avoid or to go to this or that place. Word will come to avoid New York if diseased; then go to Mexico, and then go north, etc. At the present writing the flow is towards Argentina. We could tell of the harvest of gold that has been reaped by the officials, steamship agents, boatmen, etc., at the ports. It is a system that results in much human suffering, troubles, jealousies, and sometimes crime.[46]

As the report notes, some immigrants were tricked by ticket agents and steamship lines into believing that they were going to the United States when they were in fact taken to Latin American ports.[47]

Most Middle Eastern immigrants probably preferred the United States as their final destination, and the influence of an extensive American Protestant missionary movement in Lebanon must have been a factor for some of these immigrants. Yet, many Middle Easterners faced rejection at U.S. immigration ports of entry such as Ellis Island because of illiteracy and/or trachoma and other health problems. In cases of deportation, such as that of Zahya Baroudy and her two children, the return cost from New York to Marseilles was $34 per adult for steerage on the Fabre Steamship Company in June 1907. Children under one year were carried free, while the rate for those from one to twelve years was half fare.[48] With the risk of this penalty, migrating to Latin America, and more specifically to Mexico, became a much more desirable alternative.

Learning from immigrants like Baroudy, many came to Latin America because they felt that they could more easily enter the United States by an indirect route from Latin America. Others were probably ill aware of their migratory destinations. Given the difficult circumstances in the Middle East, "some of the early migrants did not care where exactly they were going and were prepared to take the first ship heading in the right direction."[49]

There were also cases of immigrants running out of money and being forced to peddle while in route to their final destinations. Once they arrived in western European ports, some needed to raise additional funds to make it to the Americas. Zain Chamut first went to Marseilles,[50] then Paris, spending approximately eight months working in the two French cities to earn enough money for a passage to Mexico.[51] He left from Le Havre, France, and arrived in Veracruz, Mexico, in 1908. At that time, the typical voyage lasted between forty-two days to six months by boat.[52] The cost of a third-class fare from New York to Veracruz was $54 in 1934 (compared to $34 in 1907) and from Havana, Cuba, to Veracruz cost $30.[53] Once Zain Chamut arrived in Veracruz, Domingo Kuri helped him find his way to his father's cousin Alfredo Chamut. This cousin had migrated in 1906–1907 to a small town near Saltillo, Coahuila. Zain Chamut's story of incremental migration and eventual contact with his cousin through a network of Middle Eastern immigrants is a common one.

The contact, Domingo Kuri (1885–1971), played a pivotal role in connecting members of the Middle Eastern community throughout Mexico. Kuri, formerly known as Abd el Ajd, of Kártaba (Cordoba), Lebanon, arrived in Mexico in 1903. He migrated at the age of eighteen after studying two years in a seminary where he learned French and Latin. His language training enabled him to quickly master Spanish and to become a conduit for newly arrived Arabic-speaking immigrants. He purchased a house, Chalet Josefita, in Veracruz with the purpose of helping fellow immigrants. Chalet Josefita had twenty-eight bedrooms and a dining room that seated twenty-four and served food twice daily. Kuri would ask immigrants their places of origin, last names, family relatives, and any known address of other *paisanos*. He kept all of this information in an elaborate archive over the decades.[54] From an interview with his son, Ahmed,[55] and other family members, the current existence of the archive is uncertain. With few Ottoman diplomatic representatives in Mexico, Domingo Kuri became an "honorary consul" (*consul honorario*) whereby port authorities and consulates in Veracruz would come to his store, El Arca de Noé, to advise him of incoming ships.[56] Badía Yabur, in an interview with Teresa Cuevas Seba and Miguel Mañana Plasencio, described her migration experience to Mérida, saying that "in Veracruz, a *paisano* named Domingo Curi [*sic*] bought us a ticket to come here."[57] By all accounts, from Torreón to Mexico City, Domingo Kuri made an enormous impact on the dispersal of the early Middle Eastern immigrants throughout Mexico.

The Porfiriato and Its "Open Door" Policy

As the Ottoman subjects faced difficulties in migrating, social and economic policy in Mexico during the Porfirian years (1876–1911) was led by the *científicos,* who, inspired by social Darwinism, believed that Indians and thus *mestizos* were inferior to Europeans and North Americans.[58] The *científicos* advocated an "open door" immigration policy. A preference for Anglo-Saxons was part of a long Latin American tradition of trying to "whiten" indigenous populations. And Middle Easterners were not automatically or universally viewed as whites.[59] In addition, contrary to Porfirian policy designs, many non-European (i.e., non-white) immigrants came to Mexico. These immigrants would not "better" Mexico, according to the *científicos,* and would certainly challenge the desired composition of the nation. According to Ignacio Klich and Jeffrey Lesser, "What placed Arabs in such a contradictory and perplexing role is that they were never officially designated as 'non-white' since they were not from the Far East or Africa, and instead bore some resemblance to other Mediterraneans."[60] Consequently, Mexicans were often uncertain about how to treat this immigrant group, especially in the context of broader political and cultural debates. Moisés González Navarro notes that although elites favored immigrants during the Porfiriato, many of the common people felt contempt toward foreigners. Others, such as positivist Andrés Molina Enríquez, saw immigrants as receiving undeserved special favors. Moisés Navarro suggests that the "official xenofilia produced various nationalistic reactions."[61]

While some foreigners and elite Mexicans thrived economically under Díaz, the middle classes and poor became increasingly disenfranchised by political authoritarianism and low wage rates. Many Mexicans lived in

How did indiginals pay to the middle easterners?

poverty and did not have easy access to consumer goods outside of company stores. Thus, when Middle Eastern immigrants arrived at the end of the nineteenth century, opportunities to sell goods and services were facilitated by the credit system of paying in installments, *abonos*, to these sectors that had been marginalized by Porfirian policies.[62]

Some of the early immigrants went as far as to learn indigenous languages to communicate with customers. Moisés González Navarro notes that by learning indigenous languages often before Spanish, Middle Eastern immigrants were able to tap into new markets.[63] Of the 8,036 Middle Eastern immigrant registration cards that report on language, 50 indicated that they spoke Maya. In interviews with Middle Easterners in the Yucatán, María Beatriz de Lourdes Cáceres Menéndez and María Patricia Fortuny Loret de Mola found that Middle Eastern family members often learned Maya before learning Spanish.[64]

Other Middle Eastern immigrants went to Oaxaca and interacted with and sold goods to the indigenous populations there. Historian and political scientist Jeffrey Rubin notes that the Lebanese community, exemplified by Manuel Musalem Santiago (Tarú) of Lebanese descent, played important roles in the maintenance of Zapotec identity in Oaxaca.[65]

Anthropologist Leticia Reina observes this role at another level, one of social practice. Through her research, she describes a festival that takes place in Huamelula, Tehuantepec, in Oaxaca. Every year on June 27, twelve people dress up as *turcos,* soldiers of Muhammad, and show their gratitude to Muhammad.[66] Beyond the expression of a Middle Eastern presence in Mexico, some may interpret the festival as a representation of the centuries-long historical tensions between Moors and Christians that date back to the eighth century.

More generally, anthropologist Anya Peterson Royce, in exploring Zapotec women in Oaxaca, found Lebanese Christians to occupy positions as middlemen while intermarrying with Mexican nationals, especially in the second generation. Although Lebanese intermarried, "many Lebanese actively maintain their Lebanese identity in spite of their successful accommodation to the Mexican nation."[67] Royce notes that the first Lebanese families to the Isthmus of Tehuantepec came at the end of the nineteenth century and were drawn by a railroad being built across the isthmus between the Gulf of Mexico and the Pacific Ocean. Attracted to the opportunity to invest along the railroad route, one of the first Lebanese immigrants opened a hardware and general dry goods store in Juchitán. Unlike the daily markets in the area, these Lebanese businesses became some of the first commercial establishments requiring initial investments of capital. During ethnographic fieldwork beginning in the late 1960s, Royce has found that Lebanese and Zapotec women continue to compete amiably in the markets.[68]

By the early twentieth century, the Lebanese controlled hammock making and the weaving of artifacts out of palm fiber; in both they still function as middlemen between Juchitán and the outside market. According to Royce, "The Zapotec feel that they are treated fairly and are willing to let the Lebanese continue in their role."[69]

By speaking indigenous languages as well as Spanish and establishing themselves among the indigenous peoples, Middle Eastern immigrants facilitated their credibility and the extension of commercial credit in the countryside.[70] Comparative migration scholars will note that the Lebanese community in West Africa replicated this pattern, in which the immigrants would "grant credit to the Africans with less risk than the European." The Lebanese often had earlier indications of shifts in consumer demands or crop prospects because they came from the outside and maintained communications through their networks; thus they could manage the repayment relationships more skillfully.[71] Middle East historian R. Bayly Winder contends that Lebanese merchants generally had low business and personal costs, increasing their competitiveness relative to their European counterparts. It appears that many Middle Eastern immigrants in Mexico emulated this low-cost business approach.

Many early Middle Eastern immigrants carried goods on their backs or on pack animals, going from village to village selling products to these disenfranchised communities. They sold "the merchandise of ribbons, sashes, lace, and adornments, [along] with linen, thread and yarn in order to be sold to the poor and the *rancheros* by walking the streets. These initial experiences yielded [them] the capital growth of uncommon value."[72] Once in Mexico, immigrants often sold the goods they brought with them from abroad and then borrowed capital for additional peddling from their fellow Middle Easterners. Julián Arista Nasr, for example, recalled the story of his grandfather selling his shoes to a Mexican when he landed in Veracruz because he had no money. With the money from the sale he bought another pair of shoes and began peddling.[73] In several court cases involving the arrest of undocumented immigrants, Middle Eastern immigrants claimed to have peddled in Mexico to earn enough money to enter the United States. Immigrant Zelim Zakarya testified in February 1905 that as his family left Laredo due to being infected with trachoma, "they proceeded into the interior of Mexico making their living by peddling until in March they arrived at Matamoros, Mexico."[74] After using a prescribed medicine to treat trachoma and earning a bit of money, Zakarya and his family reapplied for admission to the United States.

Peddling of course required sources of initial capital. Newly arrived immigrants turned to a network of Middle Easterners in Mexico. Yamil Darwich Adí describes how he spent his first year in Mexico with his uncle in Veracruz learning Spanish and the merchant occupation. After this first year he went to Mazatlán, Sinaloa, to find his cousin, who helped him start peddling.[75] Family-based networks thus created and consolidated an ethnic enclave of itinerant salespeople.[76] Hassan Zain Chamut reported that many Middle Eastern immigrants arrived knowing established *paisanos* who would give them merchandise to sell in small pueblos.[77] Early itinerant peddlers often carried their own goods and recorded who owed them money and the payment schedules in small notebooks.

These early peddlers laid the commercial infrastructure for immigrants who followed. Like their Mexican counterparts, early Middle Eastern immigrants in southeastern Texas would migrate "to a town where another Syrian immigrant was already established and could speak the English language. With that security the new migrants could get a start in their new country."[78] In interviews with Syrian immigrants in the 1980s, Sarah John found that the immigrants would provide housing and merchandise for the newer arrivals, and sometimes business relationships developed along these ethnic lines despite religious differences.[79]

Middle Easterners similarly flourished in the Laguna, an arid region in the northern states of Coahuila and Durango (Figure 3.2), because of factors such as northern Mexico's religious tolerance (manifest in the enduring religions of the Tarahumara and Rarámuri Indians) and proximity to the United States. Middle Eastern immigrants could also work closely with their *paisanos* in the United States and have greater access to the borderlands.

As noted, the porous U.S.-Mexican border enabled the crossing of both goods and of people, establishing a Middle Eastern borderland trade culture. Several U.S. government immigration reports cited crossings by Syrians into the United States from Mexico.

> No doubt, by 1905 a significant number of Syrians were crossing into El Paso from Mexico, as a Syrian named Salim M. Mattar was hired that year as an interpreter for the Immigration Service in El Paso . . . Presumably, there would have been no need for an Arabic-speaking translator unless the number of immigrants from Syria at the entry port warranted such attention.[80]

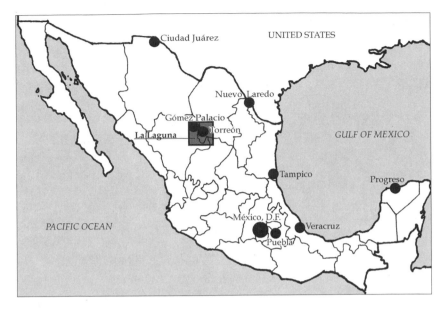

Figure 3.2. The Laguna Region and Other Areas of Middle Eastern Immigrant Settlement

Unlike the Chinese, Middle Easterners did not encounter the intense hatred among Mexicans that led to wide-scale deportations. In the state of Sonora, the Chinese became the "most visible foreigners" because as "immigrant entrepreneurs they settled wherever they established businesses."[81] Why these immigrant groups were treated so differently has been explained as a type of racial hierarchy prevalent in Mexican society.[82] My research, however, has not found a conclusive racialization of Middle Eastern immigrants nor a specific racialized discourse among Middle Easterners nor among specific Mexicans. Rather, my research has shown variation in the Mexicans' treatment of immigrants based on many factors of immigrant positioning including their religious, economic and social integration into Mexico. That said, since the Middle Eastern population was smaller in the Laguna and perhaps perceived as less physically or visibly different than other immigrant groups, it could be argued that these Middle Eastern immigrants were able to more easily assimilate into the existing culture.

Furthermore, it does not appear that initially Middle Easterners directly competed with the Chinese in rural dry goods stores in the Laguna. Rather, it seems that Middle Easterners were able to barter with sharecroppers. By 1900 many *hacendados* rented out portions of their land for sharecropping in the Laguna, and sharecropping was used as a means to reward and retain good workers. Although the *hacendados* had very specific policies on what the sharecroppers could do with their harvests, the sharecroppers preferred to barter rather than comply with the policies.[83] The sharecroppers' ability to barter "under the table" gave them more economic independence and the opportunity to get more for their food items. Middle Easterners were well positioned to participate in this economy, walking from village to village to sell their goods.[84]

The story of Francisco Marcos of Monterrey, Mexico, further illustrates the importance of networks and business relationships to immigrant positioning. In October 1910 Francisco Marcos, a man of Middle Eastern descent, arrived at Ellis Island on the steamer Kaiser Wilhelm II. He was returning to the Americas from the Middle East, and upon his arrival, immigration officials discovered that his wife, Regina, and brother, Salomon, had trachoma. Unprepared, Francisco contacted the Mexican consul general, who verified that Francisco indeed had been a Mexican citizen for ten years and was "established in a large merchandise business" in Monterrey.[85] The Mexican Consulate asked the U.S. government to allow Francisco and his family to travel to Mexico.[86] A few days later, Regina, Salomon, and Francisco Marcos were permitted to travel, providing that they took precautions to prevent the spread of trachoma. This case shows that some of the early Middle Eastern immigrants had developed the economic means to facilitate the immigration of other Middle Easterners.

In this economic and political environment, the Porfirian regime passed one of the first laws to naturalize foreigners residing in Mexico. In May 1886 Mexico's Immigration and Naturalization Law (Ley de Extranjería y Naturalización de 1886) stated that foreigners who resided two years in Mexico could petition to become citizens, and those immigrants who came to work for the Mexican government were to be treated as Mexican citizens.[87] The 1886 law also conferred Mexican citizenship on those who owned property. If immigrant property owners wished to maintain their foreign nationalities instead, they would need to declare this decision before the proper authorities.[88]

Conversely, the law deprived Mexican women of Mexican citizenship if they married foreigners. Therefore, a Mexican woman who married a Middle Eastern immigrant was considered to share her husband's nationality, Lebanese or Syrian.[89] These Mexican women remained "foreign" even after becoming widows.[90] Thirty-nine women (roughly 0.005 percent of the 8,036 registered Middle Eastern immigrants between 1878 and 1951) claimed Lebanese, Arab, or Syrian nationality *por matrimonio* (by marriage), illustrating how the Mexican law could formally change a woman's citizenship and nationality. How representative these thirty-nine cases are of this law is difficult to say; however, they illustrate the effect of marrying a foreigner. This law was enforced until 1934.[91] It should be noted also that women who bore the children of foreigners had to register those children as "foreigners."[92] The 1886 law thus exemplified patriarchal attitudes about the composition of the Mexican nation, the vulnerability of Mexican women, and the "need" for the nation to be "protected" from foreigners. The particular notion that the state ought to carefully monitor foreigners to safeguard Mexican women had been a long-standing concern in Mexican history.[93]

During this same time, other Latin American countries were struggling with how to respond to new Middle Eastern immigrant populations. Unlike Mexico, Uruguay, Haiti, and Guatemala tended to restrict immigration. In June 1890 the Uruguayan government banned "the immigration of Asians and Africans" and proclaimed the need to protect Uruguayans from the influence of "inferior races."[94] Haiti was not far behind Uruguay and in 1903 "debarred all Arabic-speakers from involvement in petty trade and set a ten-year waiting period for those wishing to naturalize."[95] Following Uruguay and Haiti, Guatemala passed an immigration law in 1909 that rejected Asians. Although these laws limited the immigrants, Latin American governments paradoxically acknowledged the presence and importance of Middle Eastern immigrants in Latin America through these acts of legislation.

The ability of Middle Easterners, Chinese, and other immigrants to prosper in their commercial activities suited Mexican modernization projects yet contradicted the *científicos'* aim to whiten and "better" Mexico. The large capitalist investments of the Americans, British, and French during the Porfiriato seemed to follow the Mexican trajectory of progress, but the prosperity of unknown "other" foreigners undermined the confidence of the middle and lower classes in modernization. The ambivalent sentiments about immigrants demonstrate the inherent dualities—both the successes and failures—of the Porfirian regime.[96]

Profile of *Turco* Sojourners

The immigrant registration cards and census figures indicate that between 2,277 and 5,756 Middle Eastern immigrants came to Mexico between 1878 and 1910. According to my calculations for 1878 to 1950, the second-highest immigration occurred during much of the Porfiriato, between 1878 and

1909, when 28 percent of the Middle Eastern immigrants who migrated to Mexico arrived.

The *turco* sojourners tended to be married men. Of the early Middle Eastern immigrants, 61 percent were men and 39 percent were women. Among these early immigrants, 54 percent were married, 37 percent were single, and 8 percent were widowed. The widows and widowers probably migrated because they had less to hold them in their homelands, thus making migration a more attractive option. Or perhaps these widows and widowers were the only family providers, and therefore the need to make money quickly encouraged them to migrate. The large percentage of married men shows that men were coming to earn enough money to send home through remittances and help their families. During this early immigration period, many sojourners came to Mexico to avoid the economic, social, and political dislocations occurring in the Middle East.

Although 71 percent of immigrants who arrived during the Porfiriato declared themselves Lebanese (Table 2), it should be noted that the immigrants declared their nationalities to Mexican officials in the 1930s. Therefore, their sense of a strong nationality could be seen as a reflection of events in the Middle East and Mexico in the 1930s rather than a claim of status based on events between 1878 and 1909. Despite this bias, the early immigrants did identify with some of the other various Middle Eastern countries. For instance, 12 percent called themselves *sirio-libanés,* and 8 percent called themselves Syrians. An additional 7 percent were called Arabs, perhaps reflecting that some earlier immigrants were not aware of where they were born; many could only recall the names of their villages. In interviews with Lebanese Yucatecans, Teresa Cuevas Seba found this also; despite the ages of the informants, they could remember the names of their hometowns and villages.[97]

Given the many changes in geopolitics at the beginning of the twentieth century, it is quite possible that many immigrants were not able to keep abreast of historical events in their hometowns and villages to be aware of where post–World War I and World War II boundaries were redrawn (Figures 1.1, 1.2, and 1.3). Other Middle Eastern immigrants considered themselves Egyptians or Iraqis; some indicated Palestinian or Arab nationalities; and two individuals called themselves Turks. Despite these national identities, all of these immigrants were still considered subjects of the Ottoman Empire and therefore categorized as *turcos* during this period.

The nature of these early immigrants' political and ethnic identities becomes even more complex when examining where they were born: 53 percent of the early sojourners listed Lebanon as their place of birth, 8 percent listed Syria, and 0.5 percent of immigrants indicated *Arabia* as their place of birth.[98] *Arabia* could have been a category among Mexican immigration officials who could not understand the immigrants and simply wrote that they were from *Arabia*. Or perhaps *Arabia* could have signified modern-day Saudi Arabia. In *Destino México,* for example, Arabia Saudita (Saudi Arabia) is listed as a nationality in 1921.[99] Mónica Almeida contends that the category *Arabia* "referred not to citizens of Saudi Arabia but rather to Arabs in general."[100]

Several immigrants of Middle Eastern descent were born elsewhere in the Americas, illustrating a trend of earlier immigrants going to several American countries and then trying to reunite their families. Perhaps more importantly, the variation in national identities and places of birth illustrates the long and complex history of those who partook in emigration from the Middle East. For instance, someone born of Lebanese parents in Costa Rica, the United States, or Mexico was still considered "Arab" and obligated to register with Mexican authorities as a foreigner. The significance of identifying foreigners in Mexican society served as a double-edged sword. By separating "foreigners" from citizens in law and registering the former, the Mexican government helped Middle Easterners to form a community, drawing boundaries around these communities whose members would later assert themselves as "foreign citizens." They were ethnically and culturally different from Mexicans, yet they could maintain their foreignness and still hope to join the Mexican nation as citizens.

More than 50 percent of the emigrants came alone or, over a decade, with a few members of their communities to Mexico. In Lebanon nearly 13 percent came from Beirut, yet 60 percent came from villages and towns with fewer than seventeen emigrants, suggesting that these early emigrants were the first sojourners from their communities (Table 3). The same situation occurred in Syria, where 52 percent came from cities and towns with fewer than five emigrants, while 23 percent of the early immigrants came from Damascus (Table 4). Other towns listed as points of origin such as Nabatiyeh and Saida reflect that Muslims as well as the Christians in Mount Lebanon emigrated, as did Jews from Aleppo.

Another distinctive attribute of the immigrant registration cards is that 759 Middle Eastern immigrants between 1878 and 1909 indicated that Mexico was their place of birth. Lacking an explanation of the apparent contradiction of immigrant status and Mexican birthplace, I identified these cards as a subset of the sample to better analyze immigrant data. The 759 cards are puzzling for another reason. Approximately 756 out of these 759 Middle Eastern immigrants were registered with an entrance date of

September 26, 1902. The significance of this date is unknown. The date may show a collaborative effort on the part of the immigrants to use an official date to document when they entered Mexico. Or perhaps someone simply had a stamp with this particular date during immigrant registration in the 1930s. It may also have been used to incorporate the children of early Middle Eastern immigrants. Such children were still considered foreigners, and their parents were obligated to fill out the foreigner registration cards. Their identity as foreigners is especially interesting because a Middle Easterner born in Mexico could never "enter" Mexico since he or she was born there (Table 5).

The 759 cards also raise the possibility of fraudulent documents. The ability to obtain such documents to gain legal residency in Mexico was clearly facilitated by the Middle Eastern immigrant network. According to Teresa Cuevas Seba and Miguel Mañana Plasencio, since many immigrants arrived without passports, they paid to get papers saying they were born in the Yucatán.[101] Other interviews conducted by Cuevas Seba in the Yucatán revealed that many paid a *mordida* (bribe) to obtain legal cards. She indicates that many of the Lebanese in the Yucatán were still fearful of speaking of this aspect of their migration in the late 1980s, with many claiming, "I am not from there, I was born here."[102] Cuevas Seba and Mañana Plasencio conclude that much of this fear was rooted in being an *extranjero*, a foreigner, in Yucatecan society.

An overwhelming 86 percent of the *turco* sojourners declared themselves Catholic. As with the issue of nationality, these early immigrants declared their religion in the 1930s and may have tried to "fit in" with Mexican society. Although Maronites, members of an Eastern Catholic Church dating back to the fifth century, are often considered Catholics, only five immigrants between 1878 and 1909 specifically declared themselves Maronites. Apart from these five, it is likely that many of the Maronite immigrants simply called themselves Catholics. Only seventy-one (3 percent) of the immigrants identified themselves as Orthodox Christians. Of the early Middle Eastern immigrants, 2.2 percent said they were Muslim, 0.7 percent said they were Druze, and 3.7 percent declared themselves Jewish. Only 0.9 percent said they were Free Thinkers, and 1.6 percent gave *ninguna* (none) as their religion. This category of "none" may have enabled immigrants to avoid offending Mexican officials by being something other than Catholic or Christian, and at the same time it freed the immigration officials of knowingly breaking international laws. Karpat has noted that during this time, it was illegal for Muslims to leave the Ottoman Empire.[103] It is probable that some who declared themselves Free Thinkers or having no religion were Muslims or Druzes (Table 6).

The religious linkages often influenced where the immigrants settled in Mexico. A salient example is the Maronite community in Mexico City, an immigrant community large enough to attract several priests from the Middle East as well as some 2,000 parishioners by the late nineteenth century. Letters from three Maronite priests to their superiors back in Lebanon reflect religious and personal differences within the Mexico City Maronite community of the time. From 1892 to 1897, the priests wrote of their difficulties in adjusting to life in Mexico, and they requested permission to return home to Lebanon. During those years, the priests—Yosef Zghieb, Daoud Ass'ad, and Elias Karam—complained of the life in the "New World" and of trying to maintain French and Arabic language instruction in the immigrant community.[104] In particular, Daoud Ass'ad wrote, "Whereas this land is not open for Eastern Priests, the locals think there is no existence for the Catholic ceremony other than the Latin one, so they asked us to worship in Latin."[105] Daoud Ass'ad then complained that Priest Bolus Al-Hasrouni had been living without an "official order" for seven years and that Al-Hasrouni was "stupid, silly, arrogant, running after money and bringing shame on us because of his impoliteness."[106] Yet in 1892, of the 2,000 members of the Maronite community in Mexico City, 92 asked that Priest Bolus Al-Hasrouni be granted license "to conduct his religious task."[107] (Many of the 92 members listed their places of origin as the same locations indicated on the 1930s immigrant registration cards.) Apparently by 1896, Bolus Al-Hasrouni had created further problems for his fellow priests, for example "by spreading rumors among the people of the homeland [in Mexico City] that I [Daoud Ass'ad] am a Druze man with no consent to serve them."[108] These intrigues of the Maronite community provide insights into both the varied experiences of Middle Easterners in late-nineteenth-century Mexico and how the largest Christian sect in Lebanon acculturated in Mexico.

The Maronite priests appeared to have responsibility for outlying areas and not just Mexico City. For instance, Father Daouad Ass'ad traveled to Jalapa, Veracruz ("Khalppa, Vrkrosh"), in September 1894 to investigate the murder of Antonious Sam'an Bolus from Zahleh, Lebanon. According to a court brief that Ass'ad obtained, Antonious Sam'an Bolus died when the gun he carried dropped and fired: "In attempt to pick it up, a bullet released and injured him. He died three hours later."[109] Father Ass'ad then reported that the local government sealed a small wooden box with some goods belonging to Bolus. In July 1894, seven months after the death, a man named Bakhous claimed that he was the brother of Bolus, took the box with the goods, and disappeared. Father Ass'ad, seemingly concerned about the family of Bolus, had money sent to the deceased man's father. He wrote:

> The money was transferred to the Ottoman Bank in Beirut. I would also like to inform you that his excellence Al-Vekeut De Petitevel, Ambassador of France in this capital, had expressed every interest to complete your order of what we have recommended to Minister of Interior of Mexico, and the government of Vrkrosh [Veracruz] state . . . Although, there is great confidence in us from the government here, but a letter from you in French and not in Arabic will foster their trust in us.[110]

Ass'ad finished the letter mentioning that an article was published in the local papers about their sect. Despite the publicity, the priest cautioned the Maronites in the homeland that the "numbers of community's members and their poverty don't allow establishing a private chapel to practice our ceremonies."[111] Most importantly, this 1894 letter reveals how precarious life and death were for an immigrant in Mexico, the reliance on French authorities residing in Mexico, and the fact that these early immigrants did not have sufficient resources to even build a church.

While the early Maronites sought to create a place for themselves in Mexico, Muslims also looked to establish a community. As mentioned, Zain Chamut was a Shi'ite Muslim, and he ended up settling in Torreón, Coahuila. For many of the early Muslim sojourners, Torreón became a gathering place for Islamic worship and has continued as such to the present. The state of Coahuila was the fifth-largest recipient state of Middle Eastern immigrants, followed by Durango. Together these states received 220 immigrants, compared to 230 immigrants who settled in Puebla (Table 7). Part of the two adjoining northern states forms the Laguna. Torreón in Coahuila state attracted many of these immigrants. Of the total 8,240 Middle Eastern immigrants, only 343 identified themselves as Muslim; however, 15 percent (51 of 343) came during the Porfiriato. The early Muslims who came to the Laguna were from the southern Lebanese towns of Nabatiyeh, Braachit, and Sidon, while others came from Tripoli, Damascus, and Aramta.

The ability of newly arriving immigrants to find kinsmen was greatly enhanced by the knowledge and advice of Domingo Kuri in Veracruz. For instance, immigrants from Bikfaya tended to settle in Tehuácan, Puebla.

Those immigrants from Zgharta, Lebanon, resided in Toluca, Mexico. Those from Antaurín went to Pachuca, Hidalgo, and families from Beit Mellat went to Nueva Rosita, Coahuila. The Palestinian immigrants tended to go to Monterrey, Nuevo Leon, and Saltillo, Coahuila. Those from Tannourine, Lebanon, went to Durango, Durango. The families from Deir el Qamar, Lebanon, settled in Tehuantepec in Oaxaca.[112]

Most of the Middle Eastern immigrants (58 percent) first arrived in Veracruz, while 4.4 percent arrived in Progreso, and 1.6 percent came to Tampico. Regardless of which port they entered, though, they would often take a train to the capital or go to a town that Kuri recommended. Their dispersal throughout all regions in Mexico is impressive. According to Luz María Martínez Montiel, the first wave of immigrants tended to disperse in an irregular pattern and later settle in urban centers.[113] Her observation reinforces the important role of Domingo Kuri in advising the immigrants. The first known sojourner, in 1878, settled in Ciudad del Carmen in Campeche. In 1882 Mexico City became the next place of settlement, followed by Jalapa in Veracruz; Tlaxcala in Tlaxcala; Mérida in Yucatán; Oaxaca in Oaxaca; Mulege in Baja California; Puebla in Puebla; Morelia in Michoacán; Salinas Victoria in Nuevo León; and Tepic in Nayarit state in 1892. By 1894 Parral in Chihuahua was settled and Saltillo in Coahuila in 1896. Sonora, San Luis Potosí, Zacatecas, Colima, Aguascalientes, Guanajuato, and Querétaro were also locations of the first *turco* sojourners.

Concerned about Middle Eastern migration routes, undercover agent Seraphic noted:

> Yucatan, Mexico, is the port at which the greater bulk of European aliens coming to the U.S. ports, embark for New York, after landing at Vera Cruz and being utilized in peddling operations for about six months. This fact points to the necessity of a rigid examination of aliens coming to New York from Yucatan and the Commissioner at Ellis Island should be so instructed.[114]

U.S. immigration authorities closely monitored immigration patterns into Mexico. One report indicated that "transportation companies in Europe are making an effort to get as many emigrant passengers as possible for the United States via Mexico."[115] The report noted that, "Mexico does not want to lose any of its labor, even though it may be temporary, because they need every pair of working hands they can get; Mexico does not want to restrict immigration into its country."[116]

The Porfirian call for "working hands" helped to shape where migrants entered Mexico but did not quite correspond to the immigrants' propensity to work in commerce. For instance, 47 percent of the early immigrants participated in some form of commercial activities, with 40 percent declaring themselves merchants and less than 2 percent calling themselves peddlers. Given that the immigrant registration cards were processed in the 1930s, it is likely that with time, Middle Eastern immigrants preferred calling themselves merchants rather than peddlers (Table 8).

The second most common occupation listed during this early stage of migration was *ama de casa* (homemaker), at 32 percent. Although the term implies women, sixteen men declared themselves homemakers, challenging traditional roles assigned to men and women at the turn of the twentieth century. Clearly, these house-spouses played integral roles in their families' commercial ventures. The broad use of the term "homemaker" could also include an array of activities in which the spouses participated, such as tailoring, baking, and managing stores and employees.

Just as some men worked in the domestic sphere, 10 percent of Middle Eastern immigrant women were identified as merchants, and fewer than 1 percent of the women were peddlers. Although the number of women merchants and peddlers appears small, it reflects their smaller numbers and their active involvement in commerce from the onset. With respect to other women's occupations, 1 percent were employees, although none was specified as an employee in a sector such as accounting, jewelry, office administration, industry, and drapery. Early immigrants listed other occupations for themselves, such as baker, miner, travel agent, tailor, mechanic, and teacher. Only 1.8 percent of the *turco* sojourners said they had no occupation. Although 4 percent of the sample said they were students, 90 of these 92 were born in Mexico, which could suggest that a student status sounded prestigious among Mexican-born children and could have been a sign of middle-class status.

During this period, Porfirian policy makers aimed to attract agricultural laborers. Despite their intent, only 2.6 percent of the early immigrants called themselves farmers. This failed Porfirian policy can be partially explained by the Middle Eastern immigrant network that enabled the early immigrants to receive instant credit from their *paisanos* and embark on their commercial endeavors. The immigrants' network combined with a tenacity to succeed led to further opportunities during the Mexican Revolution.

Concluding Comments

At the end of the nineteenth century, subjects of the Ottoman Empire suffered from severe economic, political, and social dislocations, while in Mexico, President Porfirio Díaz and his *científicos* welcomed foreigners as part of a nationalist modernization program. These changes, combined with U.S. immigration policies, motivated many Middle Easterners to migrate to Mexico. Some among them intended to cross the U.S.-Mexican border. By using their kinship ties, Middle Eastern immigrants developed migratory networks that enabled them to make their way to the Americas, where *paisanos* would assist them in their settlement and/or further migration. During the Porfiriato, 2,277 documented Middle Eastern immigrants came to Mexico, and many began peddling.

The network of Middle Eastern immigrants provided Mexicans, especially the poor and marginalized in rural areas, with necessary goods and services that the Mexican nation could not otherwise offer them. The immigrants' ability to obtain credit within the Middle Eastern network and peddle in remote areas of Mexico created unique opportunities during the Mexican Revolution that ended the Porfiriato and continued for another decade. In this early stage of migration, however, Middle Eastern immigrants positioned themselves as providing critical commercial functions, which in turn played on the Mexican tradition of privileging outsiders who were seen to further Mexican progress. Immigrants who accumulated substantial wealth in Mexico often kept their culture and "foreignness" while also establishing themselves among the Mexican elite. Although they did not entirely fit the científicos' criteria for "bettering" Mexico, Middle Easterners during the Porfiriato often appeared to be Mexican in their dealings with rural communities and were seen to be joining the Mexican nation. Middle Eastern immigrants therefore arrived as *turcos* and came to be known as *árabes* who would eventually situate themselves as foreign citizens.

(what are the borderlands?)

CHAPTER 4

Borderland Merchants in Revolutionary Mexico

They're tormenting animals, and they're holding their mouths to stifle cries that might disturb Don Acacio while he's slipping between the heavy thighs of his Cristina, the girl with the twisted nose. By the devil, she's ugly! But her ass must have some enchantment, for he takes her everywhere with him and buys her boxes of scented soap whenever the Turk comes.

B. TRAVEN, "SCENES FROM A LUMBER CAMP"

Particular immigrant figure.

This Turk who came to the mahogany camps of Chiapas where the German socialist writer B. Traven encountered an informant named Matías who spoke of Don Acacio and Cristina is known only as "the Turk."[1] He has no name but is rather known by a term that marks him as a particular type of immigrant figure. Although the anecdote illustrates indigenous exploitation, it also gives insights on how to extrapolate a Middle Eastern (*turco*) peddler presence in the historical record, especially during and after the Mexican Revolution, 1910 to 1930. In this chapter I examine how the early sojourners' network developed into a commercial infrastructure during the chaos of the Revolution.[2]

The revolutionary conflicts created a demand for food and arms that Middle Eastern immigrants often supplied to various revolutionary factions, particularly in the borderlands. For this discussion, "borderlands" refers to a geographical place that often includes the communities along the U.S.-Mexican border (Mexican territories until 1848). It also refers to the regions of intersection between Mexican and North American cultures. In the borderlands, the immigrants maneuvered around the violence and strong anti-foreign sentiments by showing their commercial value to Mexican citizens. The ability to cross into the United States enabled some Middle Easterners to amass large profits while Mexicans found their country in turmoil.[3]

After the violent decade of the Revolution, Middle Eastern immigration to Mexico nearly quadrupled in the 1920s. As the country struggled to rebuild from the revolutionary destruction, the growing Middle Eastern community fulfilled commercial needs. Yet many Mexican citizens disapproved of the presence and marketing endeavors of Middle Eastern immigrants and merchants. An increasing xenophobic attitude during the Revolution and into the 1920s culminated in the official restriction of immigrants of certain nationalities in 1927. This restriction affected Arab workers and became a turning point for Middle Easterners and their decision to become naturalized Mexicans and foreign citizens.

Overview of the Mexican Revolution

Mexican Rev. = Mexican Civil War

Debates endure over the Mexican Revolution, also called the Mexican Civil War. For instance, how long did the Mexican Revolution last? Did the Revolution end when Álvaro Obregón became president in 1920? Or did only the worst of the violence end then? Here I discuss the violent decade of the Mexican Revolution—1910 to 1920—and events leading up to it. However, revolutionary changes continued throughout the 1920s and 1930s.[4]

Porfirian development projects dramatically slowed with the 1906–1908 economic downturn. Dependent on foreign export markets, Mexico suffered the consequences of the collapse of the silver market, which led to unsettling price fluctuations, inflation, a growing national debt, and budgetary shortfalls. In addition, a worldwide financial panic in 1907 forced banks to call in loans and tighten credit in Mexico. The value of the peso in relation to the dollar declined. Copper prices fell to low levels, and by the fall of 1907 many miners in the states of Oaxaca, Hidalgo, Durango, Sonora, and Chihuahua were unemployed. These economic events fueled the tensions already brewing in Porfirian Mexico.

By 1910, the working classes became increasingly frustrated with the weak Mexican economy and Porfirian economic policies. At the same time, Emiliano Zapata led a group of peasant villagers in a dispute over sugar estate lands in the state of Morelos, and he quickly became known as the defender of villagers' rights against the *hacendados*. Meanwhile, Francisco Madero, a member of one of the wealthiest families in northern Mexico, began the Anti-Reelection Campaign against Porfirio Díaz. In short, Madero claimed the presidency by the end of 1911 and tried to neutralize Zapata. Díaz fled to France. However, Madero not only failed to defeat Zapata, but his failure helped encourage General Victoriano Huerta, who ousted and killed Madero in 1913 and took control of the government.

While agrarian insurgents in Morelos kept fighting for land rights, Venustiano Carranza, a wealthy estate owner from Coahuila, contested Huerta's usurpation with his Plan de Guadalupe in March 1913. The plan denounced Huerta and recognized Carranza as head of the Constitution-alist Army, representing those who felt that Huerta had violated the 1857 Constitution. U.S. President Woodrow Wilson decided to oppose Huerta and sent U.S. Marines to occupy Veracruz in 1914. Because Huerta could not withstand the U.S. arms embargo and fighting from both the north and the south, he fled into exile in July 1914. After his resignation, military leaders held a convention in Aguascalientes in which Carranza and Zapata dissented, along with Francisco "Pancho" Villa.

Villa in northern Mexico formed an alliance with Zapata in the south, joining the Conventionalists, who represented the more marginal elements of Mexican society. In 1914 and 1915 the Constitutionalists, led by Car-ranza, and the Conventionalists fought for power. From 1913 to 1915, "no state effectively ruled Mexico: there was no national monopoly of coer-cion, of justice, and of the rules of property."[5] For two and a half years, regional factions fought to control the Mexican state. By 1917, Carranza gained control of the government and supported a new constitution that allowed minimal land distribution. With the assistance of a few remaining Zapatistas, former Carranza military commander Álvaro Obregón ousted Carranza in 1920 and soon claimed the presidency.[6] In return for support-ing Zapata, villagers in parts of Morelos state received expropriated land.[7] Hence, throughout the 1920s many *rancheros* feared that they would be the next victims of agrarian reform, which had an antecedent in the 1917 Constitution.

The 1917 Mexican Constitution sought to compensate for favoritism of early regimes toward foreigners. In particular, Article III on foreigners notes that "the Federal Executive shall have the exclusive power to compel any foreigner whose remaining he may deem inexpedient to abandon the national territory immediately and without the necessity of previous legal action. Foreigners may not in any way participate in the political affairs of the country." The Mexican Constitution clearly states that Mexican nation-ality is acquired by birth (*jus sanguinis*, someone born of Mexican parents) or naturalization. Regardless of the nationality of the parents, someone born in Mexico has the right to Mexican citizenship (*jus solis*, birthplace determining one's nationality).[8] Despite the attempt in other articles of the Constitution to address previous foreign abuses of the Mexican nation, questions of how to handle foreign investment and foreign populations continued to garner considerable post-revolutionary political debate.[9]

President Álvaro Obregón (1920–1924) faced a Mexico devastated by ten years of conflict. He was a revolutionary general and part of the Sonora Triangle along with Adolfo de la Huerta and Plutarco Elías Calles, the three of whom pushed for Obregón instead of Carranza for president in 1920.[10] In trying to accommodate the military, regional strongmen, labor, and agrarian leaders, Obregón attempted to address land reform, improve education, and gain recognition from the United States. During these endeavors, Obregón appeared to have a good working relationship with the Middle Eastern community, as will be shown later in this chapter.

In 1924 Plutarco Elías Calles became president and was hesitant to proceed with radical reform, seeking rather to unite all the revolutionary factions under one national revolutionary party.[11] Calles aimed to create a nation of institutions and laws that included professionalizing the military and reducing military budgets. He also invoked the anti-Church provisions of the 1917 Constitution, causing some, especially in west-central Mexico, to rise up against anti-clericalism. This uprising, known as the Cristero Revolt, lasted from 1926 until 1929 and signaled to elites in Mexico City that rural Mexicans could not be easily pacified. Although Calles had some setbacks, he flourished as a political strongman, influencing three subsequent presidential administrations. During the presidency of Emilio Portes Gil, the 1930s Depression hit Mexico, further weakening the economy and many of the elites' power structures. Calles was called Jefe Máximo; his reign of power, known as the Maximato, began to diminish with the presidency of Lázaro Cárdenas (1934–1940). Cárdenas used the stable institutions created by Calles to consolidate a power base and sent Calles into exile in 1936.[12]

Middle Easterners in the Mexican Revolution

Despite the chaos of the Mexican Revolution, large zones of the country were completely untouched by fighting. John Womack offers the compelling argument that "whatever the disorder and violence, the Mexican economy functioned from 1910 to 1920. It was predominantly, although not solidly, capitalist, its regions very unevenly developed . . . production of oil and henequen boomed throughout the decade."[13] While some sectors of the Mexican populace fought and died during the Revolution, other sectors continued with their modes of production and consumption, illustrating the complexity of the Mexican Revolution from 1910 to 1920. Therein lay economic opportunities for Middle Eastern immigrants who traveled Mexico with aspirations to make money.

Womack suggests twelve theses regarding the role of the Revolution in the Mexican economy. Two theses highlight the ability of Middle Eastern

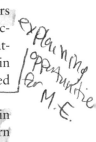

M.E thrive

immigrants to thrive with their networks in Mexico and the United States. Womack explains that after 1913, the destruction and deterioration of the railroads became more serious, especially with their use by the military and political factions. This "encouraged black markets and extortion."[14] The use of a black market and smuggling were probably areas in which the Middle Eastern immigrants could more easily participate as foreigners because of their ethnic network extending from Mexico to the United States.

M.E easily got into black market

The cases of Cecilia Attal, Saleem Talamas, Issa Talamas, and Toyokichi Saito illustrate how immigrants who tried to escape revolutionary violence often began peddling to the soldiers and rebels both to raise funds and to resettle in the United States. For instance, Cecilia Attal, a 30-year-old widow from Soor, Syria, was denied entry into the U.S. at Laredo, Texas, in October 1913, and found peddling in northern Mexico profitable. When Albert Warren, chairman of the U.S. board inquiring into her case, asked Attal how long she had been in Mexico, she responded, "It has been four months since I left Syria, I remained about one month on the road, landed at Vera Cruz [*sic*] and went direct from there to Mexico City where I remained twenty days, and from Mexico City I came by way of Tampico to Monterey [*sic*] and remained there—I don't know how long—and came to New Laredo and have been there for eighteen days."[15] When the chairman asked her why she had spent eighteen days in New Laredo, Attal responded, "We were told by the people that it was very strict here [in Laredo, Texas] and that they were not allowing anybody to go through, that's why I remained there, we said to ourselves, 'We are not any better than the others.'"[16] According to Attal's testimony, the hotel keeper in Marseilles, France, Elias Haddad, also from Soor, Syria, told her that Mexico was nearer to El Paso than New York and bought her a ticket to Veracruz. Cecilia therefore decided to migrate to Mexico first.

A few days after the meeting of the first Board of Special Inquiry, in 1913, Cecilia's sister, Heleney Attal, testified in El Paso that she had three stores in partnership with Simon Michael. As Heleney claimed to need her sister's help in the stores and to have the resources to support her, the inspectors became increasingly curious about her relationship with Simon Michael, suggesting the existence of an improper sexual relationship. Heleney denied this accusation, saying that the interpreter, Salim Matter, had a grudge against Simon Michael. According to Heleney, "The interpreter's intention at the time was to ruin Simon Michael, and the interpreter told me to say so, and so, and so, and the Lord knows what he said to the Board."[17]

Whether the interpreter was fraudulent in his translations is never fully determined in the records, but the possibility does suggest that immigrants were often at the mercy of translators. At the time, if an immigrant wished to retract a statement from an earlier testimony, blaming a translator might offer a convenient way to pursue resolving questions of immigration status more favorably.

Following Heleney's testimony, the documents show Simon Michael further substantiating the sisters' claims. In November 1913, another meeting of a Board of Special Inquiry in Laredo, Texas, determined that Cecilia Attal was likely to become a public charge.[18] In December 1913 her attorney successfully requested that she be allowed to travel from Nuevo Laredo through the United States to Juárez, Mexico, passing through El Paso. U.S. Department of Labor Supervising Inspector Berkshire stated:

> Ordinarily this office would recommend that the privilege be denied and
> insist upon the alien proceeding through Mexico to Juarez, but as it is
> a well known fact that she could not, at this time, reach Juarez through
> Mexico, owing to revolutionary disturbances in that country, it is felt that
> the request should be granted.[19]

A second inquiry board chairman, T. E. Edwards, asked Cecilia Attal in November 1914, "Then you came to Mexico with the intention of coming to the United States?" and she responded, "Yes, sir."[20] Cecilia Attal planned to join her sister, Heleney, in El Paso, Texas. Heleney had a dry goods store and needed help. Although the first document from 1913 on Cecilia Attal indicates that she could not read or write, nor could she speak English or Spanish, it does not state who provided the Arabic translation.

Four months later, Cecilia Attal appealed her debarment on the grounds of becoming a public charge. Her attorney suggested that she be admitted into the United States under a bond. In November 1914 a court brief noted that although Cecilia did not speak Spanish, she was able to earn $60 by peddling in Chihuahua, Mexico, from April through November 1914. "The testimony shows that in a short time she increased her savings from $40.00 to $100.00 by peddling in a foreign country, whose language she did not understand."[21] The brief explained that Cecilia Attal clearly had the entrepreneurial spirit needed to work in the United States. In October 1915 Simon Michael, by then her brother-in-law, held a bond on Cecilia's behalf showing that she was a clerk in a store in El Paso and received $4.00 a week in wages, including board and lodging. It was claimed that she had saved another $200 since entering the United States. She augmented her salary by washing clothes for Syrian families and making and selling Syrian laces.[22]

The situation of Saleem Talamas likewise remains unresolved in the rec-

[handwritten margin note top: denied entrance to U.S. for failing to pay a head tax.]

[handwritten margin note left: He wanted to leave mexico b/c no more business]

ords. In December 1913 Saleem Talamas and his thirteen-year-old son, Issa Talamas, of Bethlehem, Syria (now Palestine/Israel), were denied entry into the United States for failing to pay a head tax. When the Board of Special Inquiry asked why they were leaving Mexico, Saleem responded, "on account of the trouble—there is no more business in Mexico—that is why I am coming to the United States."[23] The elder Talamas was then asked how much he made per day while in Nuevo Laredo, and he answered, "At the time the soldiers were there I made $6 or $7 a day peddling fruit, when there were no soldiers I could only make $2 or $3 a day, but my boy makes $1 or $2 a day shining shoes."[24] During the inquiry he was asked how he was supporting his wife and daughter in Monterrey, Mexico, while away, and he answered that he was sending them money. However, Talamas noted that the Revolution compromised his ability to maintain contact: "I sent them $30 by telegraph before the wires were cut."[25]

Dirham Kazay also anxiously awaited entry into the United States in 1913. Despite a bond posted by his brother and a letter from attorney Walter S. Reynolds saying that "the boy is anxious to get out of Mexico owing to the troubled condition there,"[26] Dirgam Ghazi was deported from Laredo, Texas, on November 12, 1913.[27]

Middle Easterners were not alone in their efforts to cross into the United States from Mexico. For instance, Japanese alien Toyokichi Saito, also known as Saito Tomy, tried to enter the United States from Mexico in September 1913 but was denied entry because he had no passport. Immediately following his exclusion, Saito offered a bribe to one of the board members. He was therefore charged with offering a bribe to a government official and sentenced to a thirty-day imprisonment in the county jail. After Saito's release, he returned to his mercantile business in Juárez, Mexico. However, in November 1913 Saito tried again to enter the United States because he wanted to enter El Paso "for the purpose of buying goods." He continued, "I want to buy such things as I can not obtain in Mexico at the present time, I have opened up a store in Juarez, and I am going to get my stock."[28] Saito produced documents showing that he rented a store at Degallado and Morelos Streets in Juárez. Saito made the concluding statement: "I wish only to enter the city of El Paso to go no other place, and my sole reason for wishing to do so is that it is impossible to buy everything that is necessary to run a store in Juarez at the present time, I can not buy the things necessary there at the present time."[29] Despite his plea, his application was rejected.

Shinkichi Kitagawa was denied entry to the United States in 1912 as well. Having worked in Colima, Mexico, on the railroad, he later settled in Chi-

[handwritten margin note bottom left: Own ran small store, Chihuahua, had a servant in Juárez, cook]

huahua, Mexico, where he ran a small store and then served as a house servant. In 1910 he moved to Juárez and worked as a cook and house servant for two years. After leaving his last employer, he decided to attend school in El Paso; however, he did not have sufficient funds to pay for his education.[30] After this inquiry, no further mention of Kitagawa appears in the INS records. These cases illustrate that immigrants, Japanese and Middle Easterners alike, were interested in commercial enterprises during the Revolution; however, circumstances beyond their control often dictated their successes and failures. *Dictated success & failure!*

Thanks to the Middle Eastern network, immigrants were able to buy and distribute goods, which was both extremely risky and highly profitable. Some Middle Easterners even played significant roles in supplying basic necessities to revolutionary troops.[31] The merchants traveled throughout the country, coming into contact with all of the sectors participating in the armed conflict.[32] Middle Easterners' apparent deftness in their maneuvering with many revolutionary factions not only served them well financially, but it also gave them a certain amount of leverage in the communities within which they operated. As in all moments of conflict, food and bartering skills became valuable commodities, and Middle Eastern immigrants appeared to have obtained both, as well as the ability to make a profit. The money that was available tended to come from *hacendados,* wealthy merchants, or officials who had participated in unseemly activities such as looting, bribery, or extortion.[33]

Returning to Womack's analysis of the Mexican economy during the Revolution, he also notes the collapse of the banking system by 1914 and the dispersal of the financial authority in 1915 and 1916. The Constitutionalists, who controlled the largest commercial centers, arranged for credit to finance their military campaigns. The lack of a banking structure pushed Mexicans to look for alternatives, and Middle Eastern immigrants were able to provide credit to Mexicans and give them the opportunity to purchase necessary items in installments, *abonos.*[34] This type of financial activity enabled Middle Easterners to further develop their capital resources, expand their networks, and increase Mexican dependency on them. The revolutionary violence thus created economic opportunities for Middle Easterners to become critical providers and sources of credit to the Mexican nation.

However, not all Middle Easterners participated in commerce; some joined warring factions in the Mexican Revolution and obtained military ranks. Said Assam Rabay, for example, said he knew two Middle Easterners who fought in the Revolution. Escandar Lauchi, who changed his name to Carlos Ochoa, became one of Plutarco Elías Calles' generals. The other, Julián Wehbe, fought in the south.[35] How many Middle Easterners were killed due to revolutionary violence is speculative. Moisés González Navarro indicates that 7.25 percent of foreigners born in "Arabia" in 1910 were killed.[36] Assuming the numbers are based on the 1910 Mexican census, it would suggest that more than 112 Middle Easterners died in the Revolution.[37] Sources to date, however, have not revealed whether Middle Easterners overwhelmingly sided with one revolutionary faction over another or displayed regional differences or whether and to what extent Middle Eastern participation was welcomed. Rather, available sources have tended to focus on Middle Eastern economic activities as well as migratory behavior.

Their commercial activities led some to join the fighting. Middle Eastern immigrants José, Jorge, Elías, and Juan Abraham Guaida opened a clothing store and cantina in Amecameca, Mexico. General Emiliano Zapata sometimes visited the cantina and ate Middle Eastern food in their houses. In 1914 José Abraham Guaida closed his store to fight with the *zapatistas*. After Zapata's death, José reopened his business.[38] According to former Zapatista soldier Félix Fayad, Zapata indicated that many Lebanese soldiers had joined his political movement and that he had great confidence in them, as evidenced by naming Fayad first sergeant.[39]

In northern Mexico and in the Laguna region particularly, Middle Eastern immigration decreased considerably during the chaos of the Revolution, although commercial activities continued. Immigrant registration cards show that from 1910 through 1919, five Middle Eastern immigrants went to Gómez Palacio, Durango, and ten went to Torreón, Coahuila. The smaller number of immigrants could perhaps explain their concern as targets and an unwillingness to participate in revolutionary violence. The population of Torreón was 30,000 by 1910.[40]

On May 15, 1911, a group of 4,000 unruly, lower-class Madero supporters (*maderistas*), men and women, descended upon Torreón's business district and looted and destroyed commercial establishments. Besides pillaging, the rampaging mob indiscriminately killed 303 foreigners, the majority of whom were Chinese.[41] Drawing on Pierre van den Berghe's typology of race relations, Alan Knight has explained the pogrom as "competitive racism," or racism based in a socioeconomic rationale.[42] Mexicans' resentment of Chinese immigrants' success created a xenophobia rooted in economic and physical difference. The massacre symbolizes that Mexicans felt deeply betrayed by Díaz' concessions to foreigners and held strong prejudices against foreigners, especially the Chinese.

Friedrich Katz, in describing Pancho Villa's darkest phase from 1917 to 1920, corroborates that Villa allowed pillaging on a large scale in Chihuahua and against foreigners in particular. In looting a government shoe factory, a mob of mostly women quickly grew and spread the rampage to other parts of Chihuahua. "Next to the Chinamen, the mob directed its savage instincts to the business places of the Syrians, or the Arabs, as they are called in this country and who are particularly hated by the natives."[43] A mob of women looting the stores of foreigners reinforces a long tradition of women rebelling against those controlling food supplies in Mexico.[44] When food supplies are limited, women often take to the streets, and in this case they pillaged Middle Eastern and Chinese stores. These acts further illustrate the xenophobia rooted in the tradition of having foreign merchants in Mexico.

Even more specifically, Hassan Zain Chamut describes how the revolutionaries stole from his father, Zain Chamut, and left the elder Chamut with nothing; and at one point, they were going to kill him just because he was "nothing more than a foreigner."[45] Zain Chamut, Alfredo Chamut, and other Middle Easterners were about to be executed when José Chamut pleaded with Pancho Villa to spare their lives.[46] This family story and other testimonies reveal how Middle Eastern immigrants were victims of anti-foreign sentiments at the same time that they were enterprising merchants who sometimes benefited from the Revolution. These contradictory roles of simultaneously suffering and benefiting from this violent decade have painted a somewhat one-sided picture of Middle Eastern immigrants. The stories and written documents tend to reflect those Middle Eastern immigrants who survived and became successful from the revolutionary events rather than to describe the poor Middle Eastern immigrants and/or those killed during this period. It is the contradiction of needing foreign-owned stores yet resenting their presence that led to the ambivalent treatment of Middle Easterners during and after the Revolution.

The history of Antonio Aychur Itt (Hamud Said ʿEid) of Sibline, Lebanon, who emigrated to Nazas, Durango, in 1907, appears to follow the well-known Middle Eastern merchant migration pattern. However, outside of his immigrant registration card, no official documentation of his migration exists. According to a community member, he was Muslim and owned a large house with a store in front in Paso Nacional, approximately one mile from Nazas.[47] Given that Aychur Itt was the only known Middle Eastern merchant in the area during the Revolution,[48] it is likely that he traded with the rebel leader Cheche Campos and Campos' four hundred men who were based out of Nazas in 1913. Campos and his men were fighting the federal cavalry, which included four hundred state troops and two hundred federal

Figure 4.1. Antonio Aychur Itt (*far right*) in Paso Nacional, circa 1926

cavalry based in Torreón.[49] The circumstances surrounding this commercial relationship are unknown, but to support four hundred rebels would have required substantial merchandise and the means to obtain it.

Not only did Middle Eastern merchants have to be extremely careful in their maneuverings among revolutionary factions, but they also had to be discreet in financial dealings in order to temper anti-foreign sentiments. If they survived the Revolution, they probably developed certain diplomatic skills and in turn gained some leverage in the communities where they operated.[50]

Juan Abusaid, a renowned Middle Eastern merchant in northern Mexico, made substantial profits during the Mexican Revolution and gained community respect.[51] According to family members, Abusaid traded for Pancho Villa and helped his troops. Abusaid had a store in Jiménez, Chihuahua, and sometimes crossed into the United States by mule to get food and arms.[52] In March 1924 Abusaid obtained a visa from the U.S. Consulate to go into El Paso for a "few days for the purpose of buying some goods."[53] With Lebanon under the French Mandate, he had a French passport and was considered a French citizen. The visa shows that some Middle Easterners could enter the United States with fewer obstructions than their Mexican merchant counterparts, which in turn gave them a competitive advantage as "transnational merchants."[54] Villa protected Abusaid and called him *el árabe*.[55] Many in the Torreón community corroborated this story and added that Abusaid stole a sum of money from Villa and hid it in an attic and a water well.⁵⁶ After the Revolution, Abusaid began lending money to *paisanos* and other *laguneros*. He also developed a lucrative cotton business in San Pedro de las Colonias, Coahuila, where he then began other financial ventures.

Antonio Ayub, a contemporary of Juan Abusaid, established a small store on Bolívar Street in Chihuahua. After nearly losing the store to *villista* troops, Ayub pleaded with Pancho Villa and explained the sacrifices he had endured in order to open his store. Villa then let Ayub have his store, and they subsequently built a friendship and a commercial arrangement that lasted many years. Like Abusaid, Ayub helped provide supplies to Villa and his troops in the states of Durango and Chihuahua.⁵⁷ These Middle Eastern men probably went to El Paso or other U.S. towns along the border to trade with their *paisanos*.⁵⁸

Not all Middle Eastern immigrants fared well during the Mexican Revolution, including some in the Laguna. According to Nicolás Abusamra Hadad's family history, on December 6, 1916—his wedding day—the *federales* sent a train to evacuate and protect foreigners against the incoming *villistas*. The *villistas* then looted foreign businesses,⁵⁹ including Abusamra's store. However, Abusamra "decided to stay at his wife's side and hide together in the house of Leopoldo Olvera and his wife Juanita Martínez for 30 days full of anguish."⁶⁰ The *villistas* took Señora Afife and Señor Antonio Díaz, a loyal employee of the family, as prisoners. The *villistas* "threatened to kill them unless they informed of Don Nicolas' whereabouts." According to the story, Leopoldo Olvera and his wife, Juanita Martínez, did not follow the *villistas'* orders.⁶¹ Their fate was unclear in the records.

After the *villistas'* expulsion from the town, Nicolás Abusamra Hadad was so discouraged by his great economic loss that he considered migrating to St. Louis, Missouri, but his family and friends convinced him to stay in Mexico. In 1917 he changed the name of his store from Las Nuevas Fábricas de México (New Factories of Mexico) to La Internacional.⁶² The new dry goods and toy store was located on Juárez Avenue between Cepeda and Rodríguez Streets. The business grew for the next twenty years, during which time Abusamra began manufacturing clothes and mattresses.⁶³

The chaos of the Revolution not only robbed Abusamra of some of his fortune, but it also took the lives of his brothers. Major Ricardo Trigo killed Elías Abusamra Hadad in November 13, 1919, and two years later, Trigo killed Jorge Elías Abusamra Hadad. The family records do not explain why this major killed the two brothers or what revolutionary faction, if any, Trigo supported. Rather, the family history notes only that Nicolás Abusamra Hadad and his mother considered returning to Lebanon, but they could not return due to the French occupation of and turmoil in their homeland.

Jalife family correspondence collected over several decades beginning during the Mexican Revolution describes the family history of Ahmed Mustafá Khalife (Carlos Jalife) from Ghaziye in southern Lebanon. According to early records, Carlos Jalife and Salomón Bujdud,[64] both Muslim Lebanese, had a business together in Torreón. Although the documents do not explicitly address their religious link as Muslims, Torreón was shown to attract Muslim Middle Eastern immigrants. On stationery reading "The City of Damascus, J. Bujdud and Jalife, merchants and agents" (*La Ciudad de Damasco, J. Bujdud y Jalife, comerciantes y comisionistas*), Carlos Jalife wrote to his girlfriend (who later became his wife), Esther Cervantes, on July 13, 1913, that since May 14 he and his partner had not been able to take a train because Carranza supporters (*carrancistas*) had taken the plaza under control on May 20. He was writing from Tancanhuitz, San Luis Potosí, and noted that he had not received any of her letters from Zacatecas or Aranzazu "for reasons that she would understand" (*debido a las causas de Ud. ya comprenderá*).[65] In other words, the chaos of the Revolution was foiling their ability to communicate.

Despite revolutionary disruptions, Bujdud and Jalife opened a store in Torreón in November 1917 called Al Paso del Aguila, which sold clothing, groceries, and novelty items. On November 27, 1917, in the newspaper *La Opinión*, a full-page story featured the new store. "[Since] the merchandise was imported from the United States and Japan and then entered into Mexico from the border town of Eagle Pass, the owners decided to name the store 'To Eagle Pass or literally to the Pass of the Eagle.'"[66] Bujdud and Jalife maintained a lucrative business despite the revolutionary forces who often looted the store.

Although the revolutionaries sometimes pillaged store goods, Bujdud and Jalife's importing business became attractive to Mexico City stores such as El Palacio de Hierro and El Puerto de Liverpool that wanted additional merchandise. The increased business encouraged the owners to expand into selling shoes. At the same time, Bujdud and Jalife maintained the *abono* system. Their store was located on the corner of Avenida Juárez and Blanco Street in downtown Torreón.[67] The documents, however, do not offer much more information on how long the store was in business and how it fared into the 1920s. It is known, however, that Jalife later opened his own store called El Nuevo Fenicio (The New Phoenician) on Acuña Street in front of the Juárez market.

A few years after Jalife opened El Nuevo Fenicio, his extended family in Lebanon wrote asking for money. One of his brothers, Adib Khalife, attended the American University in Beirut and studied medicine, and throughout the 1920s and into the 1930s, Adib continued to ask for money to pay for his education and school supplies. In a letter dated September 4, 1919, from Beirut, the brother acknowledged receiving 1,000 francs and noted that British pounds were being sold in Beirut.[68]

As the violent decade of the Revolution started winding down, and probably due to the success of the store, Carlos Jalife subscribed to a Lebanese cultural and political journal called *Al-Bayan*. The editor, Suleiman Baddour, based in New York,[69] responded to a March 1919 letter from Jalife containing $45 and asking for nine subscriptions for family members and friends. In April 1919 Baddour wrote Jalife asking for the list of names and addresses in order to fulfill Jalife's request. This subscription marked the beginning of a more politically conscious and wealthy Carlos Jalife.

Also in April 1919 the Arab Union Committee wrote Jalife acknowledging their brothers [of Torreón] in the fight for their Lebanese *patria*. The president of the committee, Abdallah Omar Saleh, wrote from Boston, Massachusetts, saying that Jalife should not lose patriotism for his native country.[70] This politicization of Jalife and the rise of an international Arab alliance coincided with an increase in the wealth of Middle Eastern immigrants.

The Borderlands During the Revolution

Mexico's proximity to the United States facilitated trade within an expansive Middle Eastern network. Sarah John notes that "by the early twentieth century, Syrians in El Paso had made their way to Texas from the east coast, and others had begun to use the Mexican border as an alternative entry port."[71] These immigrants were known to peddle before and after they opened small stores. The ability of many to speak three languages—Arabic, Spanish, and English—and to trade with their *paisanos* on both sides of the border probably gave them a great advantage over their Mexican counterparts in terms of market accessibility. For instance, some Middle Easterners peddled merchandise on both sides of the border, whether they lived in El Paso or Ciudad Juárez.[72] In a U.S. Department of Labor hearing, it was suggested that Simon Nicola, alias Brom Yamo, "entered from Mexico, without inspection, presumably at El Paso, Texas, on or about March 1st,

1917."[73] Chinese and Japanese immigrants also entered surreptitiously and were sometimes caught.[74]

Other trading towns along the U.S.-Mexican border, such as Nogales, Arizona, had communities of Middle Easterners demonstrating the strength of their network and commercial interests in the borderlands. Some sources have claimed that President Plutarco Elías Calles was actually the son of Elías, a camel tender who came "out west" before the U.S. Civil War.[75] The surname Elías was his father's name, and in 1910 Calles opened a store called Elías, Smithers y Cía., which sold fertilizer, seeds, and flour in Guaymas, Sonora.[76] During this time, Calles went by the name Plutarco Elías, as evidenced in an announcement in *El Correo de Sonora*, Guaymas, on February 22, 1911.[77] With the store in Guaymas and rising political tensions throughout Mexico, Calles sent his wife, Natalia, and their children to Nogales with the help of a friend.[78] The location was chosen both for safety and for business. How much business Calles did in Nogales is difficult to ascertain; however, sending his family to Arizona during the Revolution indicates that Calles probably had sufficient business dealings in the borderlands area to feel comfortable relocating his family there, especially as the United States vacillated over which revolutionary faction to support.[79]

As the Mexican Revolution polarized and destroyed much of the Mexican nation from 1910 to 1919, U.S. immigration officials struggled with issues of state and federal jurisdiction over immigration and immigrants. With the creation of the Border Patrol and the regulation of immigration under the auspices of the Department of Commerce and Labor, Mexicans were to be inspected before entering the United States. In August 1921 an international agreement lifted all passport requirements for Americans and Mexicans living within a forty-mile zone on both sides of the border.[80] Because the Border Patrol was not in place until 1924, immigrants from the Middle East as well as China and Greece could cross the relatively open U.S.-Mexican border unimpeded, evading stringent immigration regulations.

However, Alexandra Minna Stern has revealed that reports of epidemics "ravaging Mexico" prompted the U.S. Public Health Service and Bureau of Immigration to draft new policies requiring the examination of immigrants coming from Mexico as early as 1916.[81] With immigrants entering on foot, inspection became incorporated into the process of entry, including forced nudity and totalizing disinfections.[82] In May 1917 the U.S. Secretary of State wrote the Secretary of Labor regarding the Immigration Act of 1917 and his concern with

a large number of European aliens seeking to enter this country by clandestine methods . . . the Department has sent appropriate instructions to
the American consulate at Veracruz as well as the American Consuls at
Tampico and Progreso, Mexico, directing them to endeavor to procure the
information desired by your Department and to forward the information
to the appropriate immigration officials.[83]

By 1918 U.S. Immigration officials began questioning the 1882 head tax
on immigrants, which was increased in 1907 from 50 cents to $4.00.[84] They
feared that with respect to Mexicans, the head tax may have caused more
illegal entries into the United States because the immigrants could not afford the $4.00 to enter. In a letter to Congressman John N. Garner, the Act-
ing Secretary of the Department of Commerce and Labor responded to a
concern voiced by Mrs. Ella Pomery of Dallas, Texas, who apparently complained that trachoma had spread in Texas because Mexicans were entering
illegally. The Department of Commerce therefore advocated removing the
head tax from Mexican immigrants.[85]

In 1921 the U.S. federal government took full responsibility for the health
inspection of international travelers. And from 1917 to 1923 in the United
States, Mexican labor became regulated through the issuance of provisos
(labor certificates), though not in a particularly systematic way. Therefore,
the Seraphic Report discussed earlier coincided with the relative lack of in-
stitutional control from both sides of the border and a U.S. concern to rein
in the situation. A 1921 report from the American Consulate in Veracruz
was titled "Aliens Landing in Mexico for the United States."[86] U.S. concerns about European immigrants illegally entering from Mexico can be
traced throughout the nineteenth and twentieth centuries and are clearly
documented throughout INS records.

According to INS records, in 1911 there were several cases of Syrian boys
trying to cross into the United States from Mexico.[87] The Supervising Inspector in El Paso wrote to headquarters: "There is a considerable number
of Syrians applying for admission on this border, particularly at Laredo,
Texas, at the present time, among whom are quite a number of boys under
sixteen years of age, and it appears that there must be some unusual reason for diverting this immigration by way of the Mexican border."[88] When
fifteen-year-old Sarey Hanna El Baba was asked why he went to Mexico,
he replied: "I don't know, the runners [at Liverpool, England] routed me
that way."[89]

In 1912, concern over Middle Eastern crossings into the United States
increased. Various cases suggest that immigrants would spend a few days

to several weeks in Mexico waiting for money to arrive from family members and/or friends in the United States before trekking from the Mexican interior to the Laredo or El Paso port of entry. Once these immigrants, predominantly males like Sarey Hanna El Baba, made it to their respective ports of entry, they were mostly rejected as potentially becoming a "public charge." Stories of cousins and brothers sending the immigrants money in Marseilles and Veracruz are repeated throughout the immigrants' testimonies. In particular, U.S. immigration officials were concerned about the route between Laredo, Texas, and Sioux City, Iowa. When Khalil Shaaban was asked why he came by way of Mexico, he responded: "I had to wait 19 days in Marseilles for a New York steamer so I came this way on the advice of some person who said it cost the same, but I found it cost more to come this way."[90]

In reading the immigrant testimonies and records from boards of inquiry, it becomes clear that board members did not agree on the value (or disservice) of peddling. Some board members applauded the immigrants' abilities to peddle in Mexico, while others saw the immigrants' peddling as a sign of problems to come in the United States. Such disagreement among U.S. officials clearly sent confusing messages to non-English-speaking immigrants. Khalil Shaaban's attorney wrote on his behalf in 1912:

> The fact that an alien might possibly become a peddler in case he is admitted also appears to operate against him, by the members of the board. Why should this exclude a person from being admitted to the United States? It is an honorable avocation, and in fact the foundation of much of the wealth and prosperity of the people of this country.[91]

Mohammed Ramadan from Batroun, Syria (now Lebanon), stated to his Board of Special Inquiry that he came to the United States "to better myself."[92]

As the Mexican Revolution continued, many immigrants remained in Mexico. Youssef Daher had been in Mexico for four months in 1913, most of that time in Mexico City. He indicated to U.S. immigration authorities that "he intended to come to this country, but was delayed on account of the railroads not being in operation [in Mexico]."[93] According to Daher's testimony, he spent three and a half months in Mexico City because no trains were running.[94]

While earlier immigrants who had settled in Mexico contended with the cross-fire of the Mexican Revolution, other Middle Eastern immigrants continued to arrive, fleeing violence in their home countries. In the case of

Murad el Kady from Beirut, his sister, Mateel Joseph (Youssef), testified to U.S. immigration officials that her brother would be "forced into the Turkish army and get killed . . . they are Chirstians [sic] and don't want to fight for the Turks; then I was afraid they would get killed so I asked my husband to help them get to America. They will work and pay him back the money."[95] According to Immigrant Inspector A. D. Faulkner, the members of this Syrian family "are much above the average Syrians in appearance and are intelligent and refined." Murad was one of the few permitted to enter the United States in 1913. Perhaps his admission and the ascription of intelligence to him can be attributed in part to the family's economic position and Christian background.

In August 1913 Khaleel Moustafa from Bateen, Syria, claimed that his brother was helping him migrate to the United States. While trying to reach the United States, he said, "I was peddling goods in Monterey [sic]."[96] Moustafa said he had arrived in Mexico with $10 or $12, and in eight months of peddling had earned $60 in gold. To verify his story, the Chicago Inspector-in-Charge interviewed his brother, Mohamed Mustafa, and his English-speaking friend, Kall Solomon. Solomon declared himself a "supply headquarters for peddlers" in Chicago and said that there were forty to sixty peddlers. The Chicago report ends with this observation:

> It would seem that the aliens could not be legally barred from entering the
> United States even if promised employment as peddlers (which is denied),
> as it is the nature of merchandising. From a superficial examination of
> these merchants supplying these peddlers of whom there are a great many
> in Chicago, it seems that there is a big profit in the importation of laces
> from the Orient, ranging from 200 to 400 percent gross. That at the same
> time a lot of laces and other things more or less imitation manufactured in
> the United States are handled in which there is also a big profit.[97]

In October 1913, the Bureau of Immigration suspected that Khaleel Moustafa did not have a brother in Chicago, although he was likely to have been part of a peddling operation. The commissioner-general asked that Moustafa be deported, and he concluded: "It is difficult in Syrian cases to determine what the facts really are, so easy do some aliens of that nationality find it to stray away from the truth."[98]

U.S. immigration officials continued to distrust Syrian immigrants seeking to enter the United States from Mexico. In October 1913, Syrian housewife Zaineb Ameen from Tibneen, Syria, sought to migrate to Michigan City, Indiana, to rejoin her husband. She had been deported at New York because of trachoma and then illegally entered the United States from the Canadian border to Detroit, Michigan, to join her husband, Mahmoud Ajami. However, during 1912 she had an affair with Said Abdallah. In Laredo, Texas, she tried to enter with an alleged male cousin "with whom she had cohabited." The document continues: "The record shows that while this woman was unlawfully within the United States and pretending to be the wife of her alleged husband she was carrying on an intrigue with the alleged cousin, who, it is shown, even went so far as to present a fraudulent marriage certificate during the course of the investigation had looking to her expulsion."[99] The record also indicates that Ameen's husband, Mahmoud Ajami, cancelled transportation orders sent to her because of his own debts. The supervising inspector concluded that the twenty-five-year-old Syrian woman was "falling into a disreputable life" and should be denied entry into the United States.[100] Such cases of Middle Eastern immigrants using Mexico as a back door to the United States complicate the historical trajectory.

As Middle Easterners developed their commercial enterprises, the Mexican nation continued to struggle with revolutionary chaos and international pressures. At the urging of the Brazilian Foreign Ministry (whether pressured from Middle Easterners in Brazil is unclear), the U.S. State Department wrote the Mexican government in May 1915 to inquire about the violent deaths of three Syrians during the *carrancista* intervention against Huerta in Mexico City in February 1914.[101] The U.S. State Department and the Brazilian Ministry's concern over these deaths could have been a pretext for the United States and Brazil to get involved in Mexican political events for larger purposes. When Ismael Palafox of the SRE wrote the Inspector General of Mexico City, the inspector responded that there was no record of such deaths.[102]

Although Mexican policy was inconsistent in its dealings with Middle Easterners, the immigrants continued to trade in the borderlands during the Revolution, which overlapped with World War I. One Middle Eastern merchant, Antonio Letayf, working with the Kuri cousins, asked the U.S. government to allow the passage of goods from Glasgow, Scotland, into Mexico. In March 1918 the company, Kuri Primos Sucesores, received permission to allow the goods to go forward because "the firm . . . does not appear upon the British Statutory list."[103] Middle Eastern economic interests in Mexico seemed to prevail despite world events and the Mexican Revolution, demonstrating the business acumen and successful economic positioning of Middle Easterners within the international arena.

Yet, as the Middle Eastern immigrants cleverly "worked" the system, they simultaneously became more visible as having money in a time of great economic hardship. In December 1919 the Diplomatic Department of the SRE viewed the Syrian colony as part of the French Protectorate and therefore sought to extract from the colony a loan of 50,000 pesos; however, the details and purpose of such a loan were not clear in the documents. The Syrian colony in the state of Tabasco was asked to pay 50,000 pesos. Although Mexican government officials wrote the French Consulate, it appears that neither the French nor the Middle Easterners responded to the request. It is possible that the Syrian colony paid the obligatory loan to temper the still-brewing anti-foreign sentiment in the final years of the Mexican Revolution, but this transaction remains undocumented. Alternately, the Middle Eastern community may have simply ignored Mexican authorities.

Although international forces tried to intervene on Middle Eastern immigrants' behalf, such as the Brazilian government's inquiry, they do not appear to have had much impact. Meanwhile, Mexican policy makers, who were desperate for resources, looked to the Middle Eastern colony in Tabasco for assistance. These incidents of Brazilian diplomatic intervention and perceived French monetary backing show the growing influence and resentment of Middle Easterners in the Mexican nation during conflict.

World War I and the Middle East

As Middle Easterners in Mexico struggled with revolutionary conflict, their families and friends faced the devastation of World War I. When the Ottoman Empire sided with Germany during World War I, the Allied fleets blockaded the Syrian coasts and prohibited the entry of all imported food supplies. Meanwhile, the Ottoman military confiscated wheat and other grains in order to assure adequate food supplies for the army.[104] Local production was not enough to feed the population, and famine spread all over Syria, especially in the densely populated area of Mount Lebanon.[105] Approximately one-eighth of the population died from starvation and starvation-related diseases during the war as a result of famine.[106] In *Children of the Roojme*, novelist Elmaz Abinader describes how the protagonist, Mayme, goes to Tripoli to sell one of her bracelets to obtain flour, oil, salt, lentils, and rice to feed her daughters.[107] Mayme reflects, "It was World War I, the Turks occupied Lebanon, and those who weren't dying of starvation were ill from the Spanish flu. Everyone counted these events in his history."[108]

After the Ottomans surrendered to the Allies in 1918, much of their territory was occupied by Allied military forces. In 1920 Mustafa Kemal organized a nationalist Turkish movement designed to radically secularize the Turkish nation. This exclusion of Muslim law combined with Christian Allied occupation left many Muslims feeling dislocated. The Ottoman Empire had provided its subjects a sense of security and belonging to a large universal order with Islamic institutions. The Ottoman Empire offered hope that a distinctly Islamic state could survive in a world of expansionist European powers.[109]

After World War I the French occupied all of Syria and in 1920 used their new mandate to create Greater Lebanon. Pleas from many Lebanese Maronite Christians led the French to split Syria and Lebanon into four new divisions, which extended the area of Lebanon. At this same time, members of the Maronite community in Mexico City wrote in support of Lebanese independence. Hashaen Alazar and Rashid Khalifa, leaders of the Lebanese Renaissance, for example, wrote from Mérida in 1919:

> Dear Beatitude Ayub Al-ʿAlami of Mar Elias:
> The Lebanese in the new world were thrilled to hear that your great self didn't spare an effort to claim their rights, which are the independence of their Lebanon and giving back its original borders for the sake of its sons blood shed in the war and for what had been scarified on the stand of freedom . . . On behalf of the homeland, we depend on your Beatitude after your appointment for Lebanon to represent the sons of Lebanon at the Peace Council and to claim their holy rights. The members of the Lebanese Renaissance (Al-Nahda Al-Libnaniah) give you the consent to represent them during this term.[110]

According to Maronite priests living in Mexico in the early 1920s, the Middle Eastern Maronite community ranged from 800 to 2,000 members — perhaps suggesting a decline in membership since 1892 — who aimed to teach their children Arabic and French.[111] In another gesture of support for a Lebanese nation, the Tanauring Charitable Association in Mexico made a contribution of 2,000 francs (100 French lira) to their needy *paisanos* in Lebanon.[112] Such transnational exchanges further empowered the Maronites' position in the Lebanese homeland.

The French Mandate embraced Christians in lands outside the old *mutassarrifya*, but it also included thousands of unwilling Muslims who would have much preferred to be part of Syria.[113] At the time, a slight Christian majority of 5 percent over Muslims indicated that Lebanon was no longer a Christian province but rather a diverse religious society.

The Sunnis, the dominant Muslim sect at the time, replaced the Druzes as the Maronites' political partners. The Sunnis refused to recognize Lebanon as an independent state and deplored French government. Before 1920 the Christians had argued for the need to enlarge Lebanese borders to make up for the exodus of so many Lebanese emigrants. Although the French tried to restrict permits to leave, emigration continued.[114]

The French involvement in Lebanon continued to favor Christian elements, leading to a representative council in 1922 that was subsequently replaced in 1925 by General Maurice Sarrail. The general, known for his unwise tactics, fomented quarrels between the Maronites and Druzes and appointed an unpopular Frenchman as governor of Lebanon. Meanwhile, the French pushed Christians to develop a Lebanese constitution stipulating that there would be representatives of both Christian and Muslim peoples in government. The Lebanese Republic was proclaimed on May 23, 1926, with Charles Dabbas, an Orthodox Christian, as president. Muslim leaders lobbied for separation from Lebanon and union with the Syrian Confederation, but the Maronites refused to give up any Greater Lebanon land. These profound changes in Syria and Lebanon left many people displaced socially, economically, and politically, and migration became an attractive option despite French restrictions.

During and after World War I, peoples of Syria and Lebanon received news of the opportunities abroad. One Middle Eastern immigrant remembered, "We heard that the streets of America were paved with gold."[115] Letters, telegrams, occasional returnees, and money sent back to the community (remittances) formed the basis of a social network in which Middle Eastern emigrants felt confident in their ability to "make it" in America. Whether emigrants generally understood the difference between the United States, Mexico, and Brazil is unknown; however, many probably believed that they could go to the "Americas" and quickly become rich and return home. Akram Khater notes, "Those who were boarding the ships at Beirut vaguely knew to go to 'Amirka,' south or north."[116] Middle Eastern immigrants in the United States who departed before 1905 and those who followed until World War I said that they had come to make money and then return within two or three years to live better in their villages.[117] Khater suggests that historians have not fully explored the role of return migration and states that "these scholars appear to have barely noticed that over one third of the people left and many came back."[118] In my research, however, I did not find many cases of immigrants returning to Lebanon permanently; rather, once immigrants had "made it" in Mexico, they would sometimes visit their homeland.

After fifteen years in Mexico, Zain Chamut saved enough money to go back to Braachit and find a bride. He married his first cousin and brought her back with him to Torreón in 1924. At that time, immigrant plans to bring relatives to America became complicated by strict U.S. immigration policies. One interviewee indicated that her Muslim parents, from Bourg El Barajni, Lebanon, intended to migrate to the United States, but her mother was denied admission because of a case of trachoma. After forty-four days of quarantine in 1923, her parents came to Mexico and settled in Tampico.[119]

Many of these first-generation Middle Easterners also probably realized that they were not returning to Lebanon and were therefore seeking a way to maintain their culture. Letters to Carlos Jalife from his family in Lebanon plead for him to return home. His brother Muhammad Khalife wrote Carlos in 1926 not to forget about his homeland.[120] In 1928 Ibrahim Khalife, another brother of Carlos Jalife, wrote that "it is time to come home" (*es tiempo de regresar*).[121] Other letters continue to ask Carlos to return, and in 1934 his mother, Khadiya, wrote the strongest letter, imploring her son to come back. She pleaded for Carlos to return to Lebanon even if he did not have money.

> For this reason, if you want to help your sad mother, hurry back, by all means because I will not rest until you come back, and be assured that the construction and destruction of our houses depends on your quick arrival, and if [it] is the lack of money [then] I implore you to come here, I will give it to you as soon as you need it, we will send it to you. We cannot forgive you still that you delay as a stranger, do not look for pretexts to write again, I repeat that you come back because the situation is between life and death economically and morally.[122]

From the letters it appears that Carlos Jalife, who died in 1940, never returned to his homeland. His son Salvador Jalife, however, visited Ghaziyeh in 1955 and met the family.[123] Stories of other second-generation Middle Eastern immigrants returning to Lebanon to visit are quite common throughout the Laguna.[124] Despite many immigrants' intention to return home, developments in the Middle East, Mexico, the United States, and elsewhere further divided their home communities and indefinitely delayed their return, leading many more to migrate.

Middle Eastern Immigrant Profile During the Revolution

The Revolution and World War I affected the number of Middle Eastern immigrants who came to Mexico and increased the importance of the Middle Eastern immigrant network. Middle Eastern immigration decreased between 1910 and 1919, when 919 (11 percent of the total available sample of 8,036) came to Mexico.[125] The majority (64 percent) of these immigrants who arrived between 1910 and 1919 said they were married when they later registered in the 1930s (Table 9). Among the immigrants who arrived in that period, 62 percent were male, and 38 percent were female (Table 10). During this immigration phase, as compared to the Porfirian period, more married men migrated. This increase could illustrate how the Middle Eastern network provided a sense of opportunity and gave some Middle Eastern men the impetus to leave their families in the Middle East. The informal network offered migrants the ability to immediately begin commercial activities in Mexico.

Among immigrants from the Middle East, regional identities remained important. The majority (64 percent) said they were born in Lebanon, and 53 percent said they were Lebanese; 26 percent declared Syria as their place of birth, and 19 percent called themselves Syrians; and 11 percent called themselves *sirio-libanés*. This discrepancy between place of birth and nationality illustrates that the early immigrants did not necessarily see themselves as Lebanese or Syrian only, but rather as belonging to the Middle East, both generally and specifically through various forms of identity. For example, some immigrants still called themselves *árabes* to reflect both a regional and cultural identity. Compared with the Porfiriato, a higher percentage of immigrants were born in other American countries during this period—2 percent compared to less than 1 percent (Table 5).

As in the earlier immigration period, most of those who migrated to Mexico between 1910 and 1919 came with only a few members of their communities. For instance, 63 percent of those born in Lebanon came from towns or villages with fewer than ten emigrants. The largest exodus, 13 percent of all Lebanese immigrants, came from Beirut (Table 3). Damascus sent 23 percent of all Syrian emigrants to Mexico, and 52 percent of Middle Eastern immigrants from Syria came from cities and towns with fewer than five emigrants (Table 4). Again, this shows that only a few individuals, not entire villages, were migrating to Mexico.

The immigrants' regional identities were also clearly linked to their religious affiliations. When they registered in the 1930s, 68 percent of the

Middle Eastern immigrants of this period declared themselves Catholic, and 19 percent called themselves Jewish; compared to the Porfirian period, Jewish immigration increased nearly sixfold, from 3.3 percent, and Catholic migration decreased considerably, from 86 percent (Table 6). It is not clear why Jewish immigration began to increase between 1910 and 1919. Of the Middle Eastern immigrants who arrived in this period, 5.4 percent called themselves Orthodox, and 3 percent identified themselves as Muslim. As noted earlier, Muslims or Druzes probably were not comfortable admitting to a non-Christian religion (Table 6).

Another critical aspect to the Middle Eastern immigrant profile during the Revolution was their use of the network to avoid places of conflict. The points of entry started to diversify during this period of immigration. More than 80 percent of Middle Eastern immigrants entered in Veracruz, and 8.4 percent entered in Progreso, Yucatán, or Tampico, Tamaulipas. During the Revolution, immigrants also began entering Mexico at Ciudad Juárez, Chihuahua, and Nuevo Laredo, Tamaulipas (Table 11). Although the immigrants entered in various locations, nearly 38 percent settled in Mexico City, and 13 percent settled in Veracruz (Table 7). As noted earlier, these places of settlement could reflect the immigrants' lives in the 1930s at the time of registration, not their actual residences during the Revolution. Overall, the new places of entry demonstrate the breadth of the Middle Eastern immigrant network in this second immigrant wave and their commercial activities throughout Mexico.

The Mexican Revolution, in sum, enabled a few Middle Eastern immigrants to diversify their enterprises and become more prosperous. It afforded Middle Easterners the opportunity to sell goods and services while the rest of the country was involved in revolutionary violence. Due to the scarcity of goods, prices fluctuated, enabling the Middle Eastern merchants to use some discretion in setting prices. These merchants often had a fixed establishment, while other family members peddled goods in remote areas. Middle Eastern immigrants found these conditions favorable for increasing their wealth.[126] The Chinese massacre, combined with a fighting Mexican population, increased the demand for goods and services that Middle Easterners could provide. As the Revolution unfolded, Middle Eastern immigrants who survived the violent decade became more united as an immigrant group. They began to use their resources to help their fellow Middle Eastern countrymen in Mexico and in their homelands.

Middle Eastern Immigrants in the 1920s

The border trading that began during the Porfiriato had long-lasting reper-
cussions and continued into the 1920s and 1930s.[127] In 1927 the U.S. Consulate complained that despite immigration restrictions, Middle Easterners
needed their visas so they could keep buying goods in El Paso to sell later
in Juárez, thereby helping U.S. business interests.

> There are in Ciudad Juarez, a number of aliens, principally Syrians and
> Russians, who upon their arrival here several years ago applied for quota
> numbers to enable them to enter the United States for residence. Not being
> able to secure quota numbers they have established themselves in business
> in Ciudad Juarez and do most of their buying in El Paso, Texas, just across
> the border. As restrictions in reference to the issuance of passport visas
> were much less severe at the time, upon their requests they were granted
> temporary passport visas to enable them to go to El Paso occasionally to
> buy merchandise. Several of these merchants within a short time apply
> at this Consulate for renewal of this privilege. In view of late instruction
> further restricting the issuance of temporary passport visas would this
> office be justified in issuing new visas to these applicants? If these visas are
> refused it may mean considerable loss of American trade.[128]

This letter signifies not only the legacy of Middle Eastern immigrants living
along the border and trading in both countries, but it also foreshadows the
ongoing dilemma of how to handle immigrants from many countries who
hope to enter the United States from Mexico and provide good business
opportunities.

After the Revolution, Middle Eastern migration to Mexico quadrupled.[129] In 1921 the American Consulate in Veracruz became especially concerned with European immigrants trying to evade U.S. immigration laws
and entering the country via Mexico. An INS report dated March 1921
stated:

> The feature of this immigration movement through the port of Veracruz
> is that a very large portion of the incoming passengers from European
> countries consist of persons who are unable or who did not obtain visas in
> the country of origin. A great majority of these upon arrival here do not
> present themselves at this Consulate nor at any other but through some
> arrangement, which has not yet been traced, go to the frontier and attempt
> to pass illegally at points some distance from the regular ports of entry.[130]

As train services resumed across the U.S.-Mexican border, aliens who arrived at the U.S. side were to first be inspected and, if necessary, vaccinated by the Public Health Service. Since many of these arrivals to the United States were "second-class" passengers on the trains, they were also bathed and deloused and had their clothing and baggage fumigated by the U.S. Public Health Service. Acting Assistant Surgeon General Irving McNeil explained the process in a 1923 report: "After the clothing has been removed and passed into the disinfecting room, the nude person is next inspected by a male or female attendant, as the case requires, for vermin infestation, for eruptions of any sort, enlarged glands or any abnormality to which the doctor's attention should be called."[131] Then, the eyes of all aliens other than the Mexicans were examined closely in order to detect eye diseases. Unless the medical examiner's suspicions were aroused, Mexican immigrants' eyes were rarely examined.[132] In 1921 the U.S. Immigration Service recommended that certain stations outside of El Paso more closely inspect trains in which contraband aliens may have traveled to the interior of the country.[133] European aliens were being apprehended at various ports of entry along the U.S.-Mexican border for illegal entry into the United States.

During this time, reports from El Paso, Texas, expressed concern that immigrant smuggling rings were operating from Veracruz to the U.S. border.[134] One report notes that many apprehended aliens had been the "Hebrew" race, which could be Eastern European Jews or those migrating from the Middle East.[135] According to the U.S. Department of Labor in 1923, "large numbers of people coming into the United States from Mexico . . . [suggest] that the immigration laws are not as strictly enforced along the Mexican border as they are at our ports of entry on the oceans."[136] The report also notes that the literacy test for admission was often overlooked with regard to immigrants arriving from Mexico. In the period following the Revolution, it appears that Middle Eastern and other immigrants seeking to enter the United States faced more rigorous health inspections and literacy tests than their Mexican counterparts.

The U.S. government continued its vigilance against undocumented immigrants by maintaining passenger lists of steamships arriving in Veracruz. The French lines usually carried Syrian, Polish, Italian, Greek, and Turkish immigrants. In 1922 the INS Acting Commissioner General noted that "as conditions in Mexico at the present time apparently are not such as to attract immigration of this class, there seems to be a fair likelihood that a considerable percentage of these aliens will eventually endeavor to gain entry to the United States, in all probability without complying with the formality of applying to the immigration authorities."[137] A consular report from Berlin indicated that the scheme to enter the United States through Mexico reached German immigrants as well in 1921.[138]

The U.S. Consulate in Veracruz also expressed concern about smugglers and in particular a man named Carlos Munves, a Mexico City importer who met all the Holland-Lloyd Steamship Line boats in Veracruz and helped immigrants disembark, change their money, and travel to Mexico City. It seems that once in Mexico City, arrangements were made for immigrants to enter the United States.[139] By comparison, according to the American Consulate in Antwerp, Belgium, although the Holland America Line operated ships directly to Havana and Veracruz, it was not an important line competing for the transportation of passengers in the Gulf of Mexico. Rather, Compagnie Generale Transatlantique, which operated the steamers *La Fayette, Espagne,* and *Flandres,* tended to dominate the business, taking passengers from St. Nazaire, France, to Havana and Veracruz. The Pacific Steam Navigation Company also competed with Compagnie Generale Transatlantique. The company periodically issued bulletins describing the favorable conditions in Mexico, such as the "plentiful supply of work for emigrants." The consulate in Antwerp reported, "Their agent [of Compagnie Generale Transatlantique] informs me that this propaganda had already had the desired effect and that emigration to Mexico is increasing steadily."[140] Clearly, international steamship companies played a critical role in the dissemination of information among potential emigrants, whose visions of the Americas motivated migration.

As a result of steamship information and U.S. border enforcement, the profile of Middle Eastern immigrants who came to Mexico changed from mostly married immigrants (64 percent) from 1910 through 1919 to more single immigrants (40 percent) in the 1920s (Table 9). Also between 1920 and 1929, more Jewish Middle Easterners (26 percent) migrated (Table 6), and 26 percent of the immigrants declared themselves Syrians (Table 2). The larger number of Middle Easterners who arrived in Mexico in the 1920s was thus a more diverse immigrant population.

The occupations of Middle Eastern immigrants changed slightly in the 1920s with an increase in immigrants defining themselves as employees. This gradual shift from merchant (or more likely peddler) to employee reflects the changes in the patterns of commerce. By the 1920s, Middle Eastern families would have some family members working in the stores as employees while other members were often engaged in peddling. Immigration began to concern family reunification and enterprise. It should be noted that the broad use of the terms *comerciante* and *ama de casa* gave immigrants a great deal of latitude in categorizing their occupations (Table 8).

Middle Eastern immigration dramatically increased after World War I and the initial decade of the Mexican Revolution. Of the total sample of Middle Eastern immigrants, 3,657 of them (46 percent) arrived in Mexico between 1920 and 1929. Many immigrants were escaping the dislocations that followed World War I and seeking a better life in Mexico. The majority (64 percent) were male, and 36 percent were female (Table 10). Unlike the previous immigration phase, only 54 percent of all of the immigrants were married, compared to 64 percent in the preceding decade, and 40 percent were single (Table 9). This higher proportion of unmarried immigrants probably reflects a younger group at the time of registration. This increased number of unattached immigrants shows that the Middle Eastern community had grown sufficiently to give incoming immigrants the prospect that they could find a partner in Mexico and come to depend on the extended immigrant network. This period of immigration in the 1920s marks a significant change in the immigrant profile and how the community developed.

Reports of birthplace and nationality are similar to those in earlier immigration phases. The majority (55 percent) of the Middle Eastern immigrants who entered Mexico between 1920 and 1929 said they were born in Lebanon, and only 43 percent said they were Lebanese; 33 percent said they were born in Syria, and 26 percent said they were Syrian (Tables 2 and 5). The discrepancy between place of birth and nationality can be partially explained by the 11 percent with a hyphenated identity of *sirio-libanés*. Whether the immigrants called themselves *sirio-libanés* or the Mexican officials put this label on them cannot be discerned from their registration cards. Again, this shows the variation noted earlier in region, ethnicity, and nationality as terms of identification. Some post-revolutionary and post–World War I immigrants felt a pan-Arab nationalism, especially Muslim and Druze Middle Easterners who sometimes had strong anti-French sentiments. During this migratory phase, immigration attracted people with diverse religious backgrounds from many parts of the Middle East (Table 6).

The 1920s marked a period of a more rural Lebanese migration and a more urban Syrian migration to Mexico than in earlier decades. The Lebanese cities of Beirut and Tripoli together sent nearly 19 percent of the immigrants born in Lebanon. In Syria, Damascus and Aleppo accounted for nearly 60 percent of the Middle Eastern immigrants born in Syria. This trend shows that immigrants born in Lebanon tended to come from towns that fewer people left; 59 percent came from cities or towns with fewer than twenty emigrants (Table 3). Conversely, immigrants born in Syria tended to come from large cities; 32 percent of the Syrian immigrants came from cities and towns with fewer than nine emigrants (Table 4). Many of the immigrants born in Aleppo, Syria, were Jewish.

As emigration varied among cities and towns, so did the religious background of the immigrants. The large Catholic migration of 68 percent that had occurred between 1910 and 1919 decreased to 53 percent between 1920 and 1929 (Table 6). This change could be partially explained by the immigrant registration in the 1930s for which early immigrants had had more time to convert (either by choice or assimilation), but it could also reflect that Jewish immigrants from the Middle East (26 percent) played a more significant role in the immigration flow of this period. Another potential reason for the decline in immigrants identifying with Catholicism was that the French Mandate restricted Christian emigration. Although there may have been trepidation on the part of the immigrants to admit to being Christian, 6.5 percent called themselves Orthodox.

The French colonial administration that favored Catholics and discouraged Christian emigration also may have caused Orthodox Christian immigrants to deny their religion to Mexican immigration officials, resulting in underrepresentation of Orthodox immigrants in the historical record. Of the Middle Eastern immigrants, 6 percent were Muslim and 2.4 percent were Druze. Clearly, the increased number of immigrants coincides with greater religious diversity among the Middle Eastern immigrants who came to Mexico between 1920 and 1929.

As during earlier immigration periods, the majority of the immigrants came through Veracruz, using Domingo Kuri's extensive knowledge of the Middle Eastern network throughout Mexico to locate friends and family. Again, 85 percent used Veracruz as a port of entry as compared to 83 percent during the Revolution (Table 11). Mariscal, Chiapas, became a more common place of entry, as 0.4 percent of the immigrants apparently migrated from Guatemala or other Central American countries.

The post-revolutionary immigration differed from earlier periods, with immigrants obtaining their paperwork through Mexican consulates abroad; 0.49 percent obtained their travel visas from the Mexican Consulate in Beirut, and 0.77 percent obtained their visas in France. These Middle Eastern immigrants were probably of middle- to upper-class backgrounds and had the economic resources and literacy to begin their paperwork in the Mexican consulates overseas and registered with the Mexican National Registry of Foreigners.

Although the Middle Eastern immigrant settlement was regionally wide-spread, immigrants often settled in concentrated areas, with 49 percent reporting their place of residence as Mexico City (Table 7). However, the place of settlement could reflect the immigrants' status at the time of registration rather than the place of residence from the time of arrival in the 1920s forward. Nearly 8 percent of the Middle Eastern immigrants indicated that the state of Veracruz was their place of settlement, especially the cities of Orizaba and Jalapa; 4 percent declared Puebla as their residence, and many resided in Tehuácan. In the north, Coahuila attracted 4.45 percent of the immigrants, with many residing in Torreón. In Chihuahua, 3.5 percent settled in the state and many in the city of Chihuahua. Of the immigrants, 2 percent indicated that Durango was their state of residence, in particular the cities of Gómez Palacio and Durango. As noted earlier, Muslims tended to settle in the north, while many of the Jews resided in Mexico City, and often newly arrived immigrants began peddling in Veracruz. Despite the urban concentration, Middle Eastern immigrants' regional dispersal provided many rural Mexicans with needed goods but at the same time triggered the anti-foreign sentiments often associated with immigrants in Mexican history.

Anti-Arab Sentiment in Post-Revolutionary Mexico

Throughout the 1920s Mexicans distrusted foreigners, especially Middle Eastern immigrants. Anti-Arab sentiments, which began during the Porfiriato, escalated with the immigrants' increasing visibility in Mexican society. The Mexican public's distrust probably began with the Middle Easterners' *abono* system of credit and disagreements about payments. However, reports of criminal activities further manifest this distrust and by 1927 evolved into the restriction of Middle Eastern immigration. Both individuals and organizations throughout Mexico wrote to the federal government about their troubling experiences with Middle Eastern immigrants.

Following ten years of violence and chaos, President Álvaro Obregón's administration needed funds and began imposing a fee structure on incoming immigrants. On October 10, 1922, the U.S. Consulate in Veracruz reported that "all immigrants [to Mexico] must have on their person the sum of 50.00 pesos ($25) or the equivalent in other money, besides passage money to cover expenses to their destination in Mexico. Chinese and Negroes are compelled, however, to have the sum of 500.00 pesos ($250.00)."[141] The provisions of this regulation aimed to deter not only the indigent and undesirable, but also the "visually other"—the Chinese and "Negroes"—from entering Mexico. More importantly, the differing fee structure illustrates how anti-immigrant sentiment started and how policy became an instrument of racial and ethnic prejudice.

Despite President Obregón's supposedly good relations with Middle Eastern immigrants, the Consular Affairs of the SRE received and recorded reports of crimes committed by Middle Easterners.[142] For example, in January 1922 José Helú was accused of injurious crimes, though no details were provided.[143] Although Helú was accused according to one government file,[144] Obregón responded nine months later to Helú and Naoum Mokarzell's telegram, saying he wished all Syrian-Lebanese immigrants would make Mexico their second *patria*.[145] Mokarzell was president of La Liga Progresista Libanesa de Norte America. The friendly exchange with an accused man seems to indicate a prior working relationship whereby Helú had perhaps helped Obregón in some commercial matter during the Revolution.

Meanwhile, the Mexican citizenry began expressing misgivings about the Middle Eastern immigrant population. The headline of a 1923 article in *El Universal* read: *Una muchacha de la clase humilde dio muerte a un árabe que quiso ultrajarla* (A young girl of humble origins killed an Arab who tried to rape her).[146] According to the article, María Rosario Ortega of humble origins in Guadalajara, Jalisco, was waiting for her partner's return when the *árabe* returned to her house; he had come earlier requesting payment for some clothes she had purchased, but she had not had sufficient money to pay him. The Middle Eastern merchant had asked to use her bathroom, and after using the toilet, he had tried to rape María Rosario. She had grabbed a shaving blade and stabbed him. Salomé Bernabé, the Middle Eastern merchant, died. Yet at the end of the article, the author notes that Bernabé was Ukranian: *que era ukraniano de nacionalidad*. The linking of Middle Easterners and Ukranians illustrates the general confusion about foreigners and the belief that all immigrants selling clothes were *árabes*.[147] Both the press's construction and the populace's concern that foreigners were not to be trusted with Mexican women had continued from the time of the Porfiriato. This distrust of foreigners and especially Middle Easterners as peddlers and members of the community later became institutionalized in restrictive policies toward Middle Eastern immigration.

During the Plutarco Elías Calles presidency (1924–1928),[148] immigration restrictions against the Middle Eastern community become the most stringent. Obregón, who chose Calles to become president, had alienated Adolfo de la Huerta of the Sonora Triangle, who felt that he was entitled to the presidency. As a result, some landlords, clergy, and military officers rebelled against Obregón and Calles in 1923 and 1924. During this three-month revolt, 7,000 people died. Later, many Mexicans who wanted Middle Easterners deported would claim that the latter had supported de la Huerta and were *delahuertistas*. This use of Mexican politics to influence immigration policy is a subtle but effective tool employed by the Mexican citizenry.[149]

On March 13, 1926, a Mexican immigration law passed that expanded the list of medical reasons for which immigrants could be refused entry.[150] In compliance with this new law, the French Consulate in June 1926 contacted the Mexican Office of Migration to warn that a steamship en route to Mexico had thirteen passengers with trachoma.[151] The Consular Section of Protection asked that the thirteen Syrian-Lebanese not be permitted to disembark in Veracruz. Although the law was based on health reasons, it was clearly linked to concerns that the Middle Eastern immigrants would deplete Mexican resources. Therefore, official documents had to be presented upon entering or leaving Mexico, along with the possession of 10,000 pesos to satisfy basic living expenses while in Mexico.[152]

In response to Mexican protests that foreign merchants' unfair competitive practices undermined Mexican economic interests,[153] Armenians, Syrians, and other Arabs were prohibited from entering Mexico in 1927. According to Mexico's *Diario Oficial* on July 15, 1927, an order to the Mexican Migration Department stated the following:

> Whereas the immigration of persons of Syrian, Lebanese, Palestinian, Arabic and Turkish origin has reached a limit that makes itself felt in the national economy in an unfavorable manner on account of the conglomeration in urban centers;
>
> Whereas, while the number of foreigners of the said nationalities, shown by the incomplete census that by order of this Ministry is being taken in the republic would not be sufficient to establish restrictive measures against the said immigrants, the activities of same do justify a limitation, even if it be temporary;
>
> Whereas these activities do not constitute a useful economic factor in the development of the public wealth, nor can be considered as a productive contingent, as the industrial characteristics of the immigrants under consideration are those of trading in the smallest way and money-lending; the former exercised in the form of street peddling with practically no capital or a precarious credit; a system that far from promoting industrial

progress has occasioned a notable unstableness in the large trade and had deprived our own countrymen of the small trade;

Whereas a selection based on the professions of those immigrants would not give satisfactory results as a majority of them have noted on their passports and identification cards that they are farm laborers and none of them on arriving in the republic engage in field work, the Secretariat of the Interior, in use of the faculty granted it by Article 65 of the Migration Law, orders:

FIRST—Commencing the last four-monthly period of the present year and during the years of 1928 and 1929 the admission of laboring immigrants of Syrian, Lebanese, Armenian, Palestinian, Arabic and Turkish origin is suspended; considering as laborers those persons who on their arrival in the country do not possess a capital of ten thousand pesos as a minimum.

SECOND—Excepted from the foregoing restrictions are:
   a) husbands and wives of those who have immigrated legally.
   b) The ascendants and descendants of persons who have legally immigrated, provided that the latter have an honest means of earning a living and are in a good financial positions.

THIRD—During the period referred to in the first part of this order Mexican Consuls will refrain from visaing passports and issuing identification cards to the persons affected by same.[154]

This law clearly reveals anti-Arab sentiments in post-revolutionary Mexico; the most indicative aspect of the law is the second point. Not only were the immigrants supposed to be legal, but they were also to have an "honest means of earning a living." Obviously, the peddling and commercial activities of foreigners were not deemed sufficiently honest and were even perceived as destructive to Mexican citizens. The third paragraph states that Middle Eastern trading was not helping the Mexican nation progress; rather, it deprived Mexican citizens of small trade. Ultimately, the law implied that while Mexican peddlers and merchants were acceptable, Middle Easterners in the commercial sectors caused economic and social instability. Daniela Gleizer suggests that these post-revolutionary regimes tried to create Mexican immigration policy on selective criteria based on those who could easily assimilate into Mexican society, criteria that became more clearly manifest in subsequent laws.[155]

Although the U.S. State Department applauded the Mexican restriction as a means to curb Middle Eastern immigration into the United States, the American Consul General in Mexico City was skeptical that Middle

Eastern immigrants would stop coming to Mexico in hope of eventually entering the United States.[156] This decree attempted to appease the U.S. government as well as to quiet disgruntled Mexicans; however, as later diplomatic letters indicate, it does not appear that there was much enforcement of the law.

Despite the Mexican government's legal restrictions prohibiting Middle Eastern immigrants into Mexico, complaints about Middle Easterners and their practices continued. In 1926 José Abraham Serpel, a Persian merchant, wrote to the Secretary of the Interior complaining that "Turkish" merchants were falsely passing as priests in order to use orphans to work for them. Serpel identified Daniel Benjamín and Isaac Jorge of the Hotel Cairo in Mexico City as the guilty parties and asked that they be deported.[157] Why would a Persian want to deport fellow Middle Eastern merchants? Perhaps Serpel wanted to eliminate his competition, and it is quite possible that home-country hostilities still existed among Persian and other Middle Eastern immigrants. Also, the complaint could point to tensions within the Middle Eastern community in Mexico.

State governments as well as federal officials expressed frustrations with Middle Eastern immigrants and their accumulation of wealth. In 1928 the Governor of Hidalgo wrote to the French Consulate complaining that a Middle Eastern immigrant, Alejandro Athié, had not acted appropriately as a foreigner.[158] Athié had not paid taxes on his *haciendas*, La Florida and San Miguel Ocoza, in the municipalities of Cardonal and Ixmiquilpan, respectively.[159] According to the governor, the foreigner had also treated the renters poorly. More importantly, the governor claimed that Athié had helped Gaudencio Garduño, his employee, during the Revolution, that he had provided food, arms, money, and spies to overthrow the Obregón government during the de la Huerta uprising.[160] The letter continues that the *haciendas* in dispute were properties taken during the Revolution and given to Athié. This situation demonstrates how post-revolutionary politics continued as Mexico struggled to recover from the destruction of the Revolution.[161] Athié's particular case did not get resolved until 1932 when he finally agreed to make payment for back taxes. However, he continued to challenge the Hidalgo government every step of the way.

In 1927, Cecine Farres, a Middle Easterner, was accused of falsifying documents to say that he was a doctor. As a charlatan, he sold drugs from his house on Mesones Street in Mexico City.[162] The accuser appears to be Mexican citizen Antonio Pérez, who asked the Ministry of Security to investigate the *extranjero pernicioso* (harmful foreigner) and consider deportation. It was not evident how the case was resolved.

Another accused criminal was Josefina José Mabarark, also known as the *vampiresa árabe* (Middle Eastern *femme fatale*). She was charged with having an affair with Dr. Joaquín Aguilar and ruining his family. Aguilar's son, Juan Aguilar González, began writing in December 1927 to have her deported.[163] He claimed that she was married to a Middle Easterner in Puebla who had left her because of her prostitution and that Josefina José had a police record in Puebla as well. To further damage her case, the younger Aguilar said she had an abortion in 1925 and had supported the *delahuertistas* in 1923.[164] According to the story, she was a lover of a colonel who later claimed she was a rebel and a spy.[165] In 1928 the Governor of Veracruz wrote the State Attorney General of Justice (Procurador General de Justicia) to say that Josefina José deserved to be deported. At the same time, her lover Dr. Joaquin Aguilar went on record saying that she should not be deported on the basis of having an affair with him.[166] She also visited the French Consulate for assistance, but it was unclear what the Consulate provided. Sometime during the case, a newspaper ad ran trying to solicit more information about Josefina José and her activities. By October 1930, it appears that she was to be deported.[167]

This illustrates how Middle Eastern women were constructed as dangerous to Mexican men and Mexican families. In the particular case of Josefina José, it is difficult to evaluate the situation based on the limited information available; however, it is clear that an adulterous relationship was grounds for expulsion. The various letters from her neighbors and lover's family members paint an ugly picture of a *vampiresa*. Yet in telling her story, the Jalapa community gives power to this woman and her ability to manipulate men. The case of Josefina José Mabarark exemplifies the cumbersome and lengthy nature of implementing the immigration laws as well as methods used by Mexican citizens to employ national politics against immigrants (such as calling them *delahuertistas*) to get foreigners deported. Pablo Yankelevich, in analyzing the expulsion of foreigners pursuant to Article 33 of the Mexican Constitution, found that not only were Middle Easterners accused of smuggling contraband but that the presidential administrations of Pascual Ortiz Rubio (1930–1932) and Abelardo L. Rodríguez (1932–1934) were especially aggressive against immigrant commercial activities, as will be seen in the next chapter.[168]

After Calles' presidency, Obregón won reelection but was murdered in July 1928. Calles quickly arranged that a congressional selection have General Emilio Portes Gil, a Tamaulipas governor, named as president (1928–1930). Calles then organized the official party, the Partido Nacional Revolucionario (PNR), to ensure the selection of General Pascual Ortiz Rubio as the presidential candidate in the 1929 election that would complete the Obregón term. Through the PNR, progenitor of the present-day Partido Revolucionario Institucional (PRI), Calles consolidated power in "the revolutionary family," from which he emerged as Jefe Máximo.[169] Portes Gil, as part of this "family" of leaders, continued many of Calles' immigration policies.[170]

In 1928, sixteen residents of Estación Creel in Chihuahua wrote to the governor of the state asking for the expulsion of three Middle Eastern merchants, David Daher, Antonio Daher, and Jorge Kirk. These citizens had collected fifteen complaints against these Middle Eastern men stating that the foreigners had violated the law of worship and were clandestinely selling intoxicating drinks.[171] Whether these Middle Eastern immigrants were deported is not documented; however, they were incarcerated in June 1928. This complaint represents one of the first cases in the late 1920s and early 1930s in which groups of citizens, and in particular Mexican merchants, wrote to the federal government asking for Middle Easterners to be deported. Requests for the deportations of Middle Eastern immigrants escalated in the 1930s and coincided with the peak of the Depression.

In response to such a complaint in October 1928, the municipal president of the cities of Motozintla and Mariscal, a municipality in a district of Chiapas, wrote in defense of Middle Eastern immigrant Felipe Dejuky, who had been accused of illegally taking lands from Inés Verdugo in 1911.[172] Amador Coutiño, the municipal president, noted that there had been antagonism for some time between the gentlemen but that Dejuky had been able to provide proof of a land purchase from Ricardo Arturo Lobato. The letter states that Dejuky had donated 75 meters of land for the construction of a new plaza and municipal building.[173] This letter raises questions about why this Middle Eastern immigrant would have made these donations to the municipal government and what the result of these donations had been. For example, had the evidence of his land purchase materialized as a result of the donations? It also seems quite possible that Felipe Dejuky had used the revolutionary conflicts to obtain his land. This case could also point to the fact that some of the Middle Eastern immigrants were learning to "work the system" by bribing government officials in order to prove that their land expropriations were legitimate.

As Middle Easterners became more clever in their dealings, the Mexican government temporarily suspended the entrance of all workers in 1929.[174] This was probably a result of the inability to enforce the 1927 Mexican immigration law. On August 30, 1930, the Migration Law of 1930 ruled that those immigrants from cultures similar to the Mexican culture and with a propensity for easy assimilation could be granted entry as determined by the Secretariat of the Interior (Article 5).[175] Taking its cue from the United States, Mexico's immigration policy became more restrictionist. These laws clearly determined whether Middle Eastern immigrants could enter the country and, once in Mexico, how they would earn their living.

In October 1929 the Mexican Consulate in Beirut prepared a report examining Syro-Lebanese immigration to Mexico and the impact of the 1927 law. This report concluded that the law had not been particularly effective for several reasons. To begin with, the problems of spelling and pronunciation between Spanish and Arabic often led to duplicate passports and confusion in reporting immigrants.[176] The report also noted that the 1927 law was "ambiguous" regarding bringing spouses back to Mexico and left room for interpretation.[177] If the immigrant was legal, then technically he or she could bring back his or her spouse to Mexico. Mexican officials were also concerned about illegal immigration. The third aspect of the report expressed concern about how the immigrants were obtaining their 10,000 pesos to enter Mexico. Consulate Officer Gaspar O. Almanza noted that certain individuals were taking advantage of the gullibility of the Lebanese by offering to obtain illegal documents for them for 300 pesos. Coincidentally, the person named for running this business was Alejandro Attié,[178] who was most likely the same Alejandro Athié of Hidalgo who was not paying his taxes. Finally, there were doubts about whether the Secretary of the Interior in Mexico or the Consulate Office in Beirut was ultimately responsible for deciding whether an immigrant was to emigrate. This detailed report underscores the Mexican problem of handling both the immigrant population residing in Mexico and those intending to migrate from Lebanon.

The evidence from the 1920s demonstrates that the Middle Eastern community continued to gain momentum and visibility in Mexican society. As many Mexican citizens became frustrated with the Middle Easterners' presence both for legitimate deals as well as perceived evils, Middle Eastern immigrants successfully employed the French Consulate to mediate their situations. As part of the French protectorate,[179] the immigrants would write the French Consulate asking for its intervention on their behalf. How active the French Consulate was in protecting the Middle Easterners is unclear; however, I would suggest that the symbolic French role tempered the Mexican government's responses. As a result, the Middle Eastern immigrants had some credible standing against the Mexican complaints.

Many Mexican citizens nevertheless felt that foreigners were not helping native-born Mexicans or the country and should be deported. Although

Obregón made a gesture toward the Middle Eastern community, the Calles machine still aimed to prohibit immigration. The 1927 decree, which followed the U.S. quota laws from 1921 to 1924,[180] appeased the U.S. government interest in Mexico's own border controls. Yet, the active Mexican Embassy in Beirut in the 1920s showed Middle Eastern influence in Mexican political circles as well as profound concern over continuing Middle Eastern immigration. It appears that Mexican policy makers were caught between responding to their constituents and appreciating the cheaper goods and services provided by the Middle Eastern merchants. Thus, although Middle Easterners were not particularly well liked, some such as Alejandro Athié/Attié and José Helú successfully positioned themselves in Mexican development and competed internationally.

In the Laguna, the largest influx of Middle Eastern immigrants to the region occurred during the post-revolutionary period. More than 50 percent of the Middle Eastern immigrants who came to the region arrived and settled there between 1920 and 1929, with thirty-four immigrants going to Gómez Palacio and seventy to Torreón.[181] The increase in the Middle Eastern population, combined with French and British occupation of Greater Syria, mobilized many of the first-generation Middle Eastern immigrants into celebrating their fraternal unity. As the Mexican nation struggled to rebuild itself, the early immigrants along with the newer immigrants began creating a sense of Arab consciousness.

Concluding Comments

The early sojourners' network established an infrastructure for Middle Easterners to provide the necessary food and arms to the various revolutionary factions. While fighting occurred in many parts of Mexico, some Middle Eastern immigrants perished, some amassed large profits, and others just managed to survive. Their ability to overcome the chaos of the Revolution helped them position their foreign merchant status during the 1920s as had earlier generations of immigrants in the Mexican nation. As the Ottoman Empire collapsed, the French occupied Syria and Lebanon, and the British controlled Palestine, Middle Eastern immigrant identities changed. Ottoman subjects (*turcos*) were transformed into the colonial subjects of the French and British, and yet a sense of Arab identity grew. Many Middle Eastern immigrants in Mexico emerged as *los árabes*.

As the Middle Eastern community grew in the 1920s, Mexican citizens became increasingly uncomfortable with the presence and marketing endeavors of these immigrants and voiced opposition. The result was that foreigners and immigrants, once the symbols of Porfirian progress, became the scapegoats of the Mexican Revolution and post-revolutionary nation building. However, the Mexican tradition of having foreign merchants combined with a porous U.S.-Mexican border enabled the Middle Easterners to continue with their commercial activities. With increased migration, the reunification of Middle Eastern families signaled their long-term settlement in Mexico, even while some migrated to the United States. The commitment of those who stayed in Mexico would provide the basis for a permanent Lebanese Mexican community and the construction of foreign citizens.

CHAPTER 5

Middle Eastern Immigrants and Foreigners in Post-Revolutionary Mexico

D uring the 1930s, Mexican citizens manifested ambivalent attitudes about immigrants and specifically Middle Easterners. As in earlier immigration periods, Middle Eastern immigrants and their children responded by positioning themselves as foreign citizens in Mexican society. As I have shown in earlier chapters, the historical record presents only a somewhat linear trajectory of Middle Eastern immigrants arriving as *turco* peddlers, becoming Middle Eastern merchants, and evolving into Syro-Lebanese store owners.[1] Although many in the community followed this path, not all did. Individual narratives and general patterns combine and overlap. Anomalies, however, are difficult to document. In this chapter therefore I explore how some Middle Eastern immigrants responded to events in the Middle East by constructing liminal identities, such as declaring themselves Syro-Lebanese or reporting disjunctive birthplaces and nationalities. "Syro-Lebanese" can be a translation of *sirio-libanés,* which is used in Argentina and Brazil and in most of the Mexican immigration records. The term entered common parlance between the 1920s and 1940s as Lebanon and Syria established political identities. Following World War II and the creation of Israel, these identities become layered with complexity, as we will see in this chapter.

Although the 1930s were marked by ongoing anti-foreign sentiments, Middle Eastern immigrants and their descendants registered with Mexican authorities and began the process of naturalization. Mexican policy makers struggled to control the influx and activities of foreigners and to appease the Mexican populace's concern with Middle Eastern business practices. In 1932 Mexican policy makers decided to manage the immigrant population through immigrant registration. Foreigners were obligated to appear before authorities of the Mexican Migration Department and to show per-

sonal identification papers. The registration policy forced Middle Easterners to declare themselves foreigners irrespective of their length of residence
in Mexico. Policy makers thus perpetuated the "foreign citizen" paradigm
whereby an immigrant could maintain multiple identities while becoming
part of the Mexican nation. Furthermore, events surrounding the registration in the 1930s laid the groundwork for the formation of the Lebanese community in the 1940s. Letters complaining about Middle Easterners
offer insights into the dynamics between Mexican citizens and the post-
revolutionary presidencies.

The presidencies of Pascual Ortíz Rubio and Abelardo Rodríguez continued President Plutarco Elías Calles' policy of restricting Middle Eastern
immigration. During the same period, the number of letters of complaint
from Mexican citizens about Middle Easterners substantially increased,
especially during Lázaro Cárdenas' presidency. Cárdenas' populist style
combined with his perceived ability to stand up to foreigners, such as the
American and British oil interests in 1938,[2] created an expectation that he
could handle foreigners.

Pressures from the United States

As post-revolutionary governments took shape in Mexico in the 1920s and
1930s, the U.S. government began repatriating Mexicans. "According to
figures attributed to the U.S. Labor Department and cited by *El Universal*, on August 22, 1932, 2,000,000 Mexicans had returned home during
the past fifteen months."[3] The newly repatriated Mexicans raised issues
of how to deal with Mexico's own immigrant populations, especially in
light of how Mexicans were being treated by their North American neigh-
bor. As the post-revolutionary regimes struggled with foreign policy questions, these regimes also sought ways to handle immigration as a domestic
issue.

The world Depression in the 1930s and more stringent immigration laws
in the Americas led to a decrease in Middle Eastern immigration to Mexico,
yet the U.S. government remained concerned about smuggling operations
in Mexico. On January 29, 1934, the Conference of American and Mexican Immigration Officers met in El Paso, Texas, to discuss various pro-
posals. Prior to the meeting, D. W. MacCormack, U.S. commissioner of
immigration, cabled Washington, D.C.: "We have much to gain in establishing friendly relations with Mexican immigration officials and in obtaining their cooperation direct or through their government in preventing alien

smuggling."[4] The Chamber of Commerce also wrote and suggested that "Europeans, Asiatics or other aliens residing in Mexico desiring to visit the United States should not be made subject to passport restrictions and should be entitled to the crossing card privilege on the same basis as Mexicans should be entitled to it and for the same reasons."[5] Apparently, many European businessmen residing in Mexico had found it impossible to visit American border cities on legitimate buying trips because of an inability to produce current passports. The United States was particularly concerned about corruption among Mexican Customs guards. A U.S. consular report from Ciudad Juárez in June 1934 notes:

> Our border patrol is probably attributable to the tightening down on Mexican Custom Guards by the present Mexican Collector of Customs at Ciudad Juárez. It was rumored, and probably had some foundation, that at the time of the informal meeting [January 1934] when the situation was so bad, that Mexican Customs Guards were frequently aiding smugglers in protecting their crossing the river by firing on American patrols from places of concealment on the Mexican side.[6]

Following the conference in 1934, the *El Paso Herald Post* reported that "nearly 100 smugglers since 1929, will be discussed directly with the Mexican government."[7] The smuggling of aliens and goods remained a pervasive problem along the U.S.-Mexican border. In September 1940 both *El Universal* and *Excelsior* printed articles describing how certain individuals falsified admissions documents of the Mexican Foreign Service and produced telegrams dated in Mexico and bearing falsified facsimile signatures of the functionaries of the genuine secretary. According to the newspaper reports, the "trick" was discovered in time and foiled, thus keeping those "undesirable" immigrants from entering Mexico.[8] As the U.S. government also pressured Mexico to keep unwanted immigrants from entering Mexico (and eventually the United States), Mexican officials sought to balance Mexican national interests against U.S. demands.

Mexico in the 1930s: Controlling Immigration

During the Ortíz Rubio administration (1930–1932), the SRE continued to report on the limitations of the 1927 law that prohibited Middle Easterners from immigrating to Mexico. In a 1930 consular report from Beirut, Gaspar O. Almanza noted irregularities in granting permission to emigrate.

He identified two Lebanese men, Alejandro Attié (discussed in Chapter 4) and Antonio Letayf, who helped immigrants obtain the necessary documents for 300 pesos per person. According to Lebanese community documents, Antonio Letayf was one of the most important men in the immigrant community and a man of much respect, a *don*.[9] Yet according to Mexican diplomatic records, he was a criminal generating fraudulent documents. He was also reported as working for the Kuri cousins, who had declared bankruptcy under dubious circumstances.

The report from Beirut argued against allowing these individuals to immigrate into Mexico as arranged by Attié and Letayf. It claimed that the children were educated to worship money, be secretive, lie, and cheat. It charged that the Syrian-Lebanese people in general were inculcated in selfishness and carried in their blood the need for immediate personal benefit.[10]

The report described a scenario in which a young Lebanese migrated to Mexico, changed his last name, naturalized as a Mexican, and made a good salary but lived without luxuries. After saving his money, he returned to Lebanon and purchased expensive property. This immigrant then returned to Mexico to begin the process all over again. The report claimed that another tactic of accumulating wealth was for a Middle Easterner to defraud Mexicans by purchasing goods on credit and then leaving the country without having paid for those goods. Almanza suggested that the capital requirement of 10,000 pesos was not enough to compensate for the damage caused by such immigrants.[11]

Almanza closed the report by saying that the Lebanese could not be held responsible for these defects; rather their shortcomings were due to their background and perceived lack of education. Although they were admittedly physically attractive people, Almanza said that mixing with Arab blood would spoil the *mestizo*.[12] This stereotype that Middle Easterners were contaminating the national population was shared by many Mexicans and other Latin Americans. Nancy Leys Stepan notes that Syrians and Lebanese were seen as "weighed down by psychic and physical defects."[13]

Registering Middle Eastern Immigrants in 1930s Laguna

The economic success of Middle Easterners in the 1920s fueled anti-Arab sentiments during the Depression of the 1930s. As the federal government sought to consolidate its power, the Secretary of the Interior began writing to the Torreón municipal president to push for order in the region. In particular, the federal government aimed to get control of the foreign population living in Mexico. From 1930 through 1939, only 3.4 percent of the Middle Eastern immigrants migrated to the Laguna.

For the federal government, via the Secretary of the Interior, registering immigrants was one way to better monitor the immigrant population.[14] In March 1932 the Secretary of the Interior ordered municipal governments to document the specific occupations of its foreigners.[15] The Torreón Municipal Presidency had Middle Eastern immigrants fill out a specific alien questionnaire to ascertain their employment and to identify how many employees worked for immigrants.[16]

In 1934 the Inspector General of the Police in Torreón wrote to the municipal president about the various immigrants.[17] In response to tough economic times, post-revolutionary reforms, and anti-Arab attitudes, federal and municipal governments corresponded in the early 1930s to correct, verify, and clarify information on Middle Eastern immigrants.[18]

In 1934 J. Ignacio Uribe and F. Sifuentes from San Pedro, Coahuila, contacted President Lázaro Cárdenas to have Juan Abusaid expelled for financing small businesses in a harmful way.[19] Although Abusaid was never deported, he apparently made a donation of some of his "less used" lands in order to avoid expropriation during the Cárdenas administration.[20] It could also be inferred that Abusaid's gesture was a successful attempt to temper some of the anti-Arab objections to him and his business practices. He became a naturalized Mexican citizen in 1938.

In 1936 Luis Rodríguez of the Factory Workers Clothing Union wrote to the Governor of Coahuila complaining of Yadala Marcos. Marcos owned El Venado (The Deer) clothing factory and was accused of savagely hitting workers who demanded their rights.[21] The union asked to have her deported in compliance with Article 33 of the 1917 Constitution. José Ayub also faced similar charges when the Federation of Municipal Workers of Matamoros, Coahuila, asked to have him deported for using false forms and taking advantage of their good faith. They wrote: "This gracious city [complains that] enemy José Ayup [sic] tries to surprise you by [using] false reports, taking advantage of the good faith [of] those signators referred, we appeal to your correct, esteemed criteria so justice justifies honorable behavior observed [by] slanderous elements."[22]

This anti-Arab attitude escalated in 1937 with the threat of the Ku Klux Klan (KKK) coming to Coahuila. A letter from the Syrian, Lebanese, and Polish colonies indicated that thirty Syrian, Lebanese, and Polish families were threatened with grave harm in Nueva Rosita.[23] Interestingly, although the KKK threatened to come into Coahuila in 1937, Shawn Lay found that the KKK had been in decline in the El Paso area since 1923.[24] Yet the

Klan was known to be keenly interested in issues of law, order, and social morality. Through Mexican official R. Medina Guzmán, President Cárdenas responded to Alejandro Chaib, José Name, and Owszei Sladownik, secretaries of the Syrian, Lebanese, and Polish colonies, that he would guarantee their safety by directing the governor of Coahuila to protect them.[25]

This order to the state government exemplifies how the federal government handled many difficult problems. It would order the governor or municipal president in a given state to remedy a controversial issue at the same time that the president would promise to help one or both sides. This incident not only shows the state-federal government tensions, but it also illustrates that the proximity to the United States brought American racialized ideas on the need to limit certain immigrant populations. The question remains how the KKK knew about a small community of Syrian, Lebanese, and Polish families in Nueva Rosita. Did disgruntled Mexican workers and merchants contact the KKK? Did successful Middle Eastern immigrants antagonize white Americans in their border dealings? Or could it have been an imagined threat?

In July 1937 the *Diario Oficial* announced the need to protect Mexican merchants and the request of the federal government for the cooperation of the municipal governments.[26] A few days later, the National Chamber of Commerce and Industry of Torreón (Cámara Nacional de Comercio e Industria de Torreón) wrote the various municipal and federal government agencies complaining that immigrants were violating the law and were making Mexican middle and lower classes poorer.[27] By August 1937 the Torreón Municipal Presidency instituted its own registry to comply with the request of the Secretary of the Interior. This additional registry also served to confirm that all immigrants had F14 immigrant cards issued by the National Registry of Foreigners.[28]

According to Torreón municipal government records, a total of 567 aliens—200 Chinese, 150 Spaniards, 84 Middle Easterners, 43 Americans, 37 Germans, 8 Greeks, and others—were registered in 1938.[29] Nearly 87 percent of the Middle Eastern immigrants in Torreón were merchants in 1938, and of those 74 merchants, 26 had Mexican employees. Jacobo Zarzar recorded having 25 Mexican employees. The predominance of Middle Eastern immigrants as merchants differs from the immigrant registration from 1930 through 1939, a decade when 45 percent of all the Middle Easterners identified themselves as being in commerce (Table 8). The Laguna Middle Easterners were notably more inclined toward the trading profession as compared to their *paisanos* dispersed throughout Mexico.

The concern with foreign merchants continued with letters to President

Cárdenas. The Veracruz Union of Small Peddlers complained that some foreigners were unscrupulous and the country needed to exterminate the "plague of the Jews," who were making them poor and dishonorable.[30] This "plague of Jews" probably referred to all Middle Eastern merchants, including Middle Eastern Jews and non-Jews alike. The Veracruz Union wrote: "We hope that you continue your patriotic and purging work until exterminating that plague of Jews that discredits us, makes us poor, and dishonors us."[31] The letter also noted that the practice of selling in *abonos* hurt the poor and harmed the Mexican economy. Manuel Sánchez Cuen of the Secretaría de la Economía Nacional wrote in 1938 that Middle Easterners controlled the clothing market and employed Mexicans as servants.[32] The Nationalist Committee of Nueva Rosita complained that Middle Easterners charged five or six times the value of an article and that they sucked the small economy (*chupan las pocas economías*).[33] These letters claimed that Middle Easterners were violating Article 123, which provided for equal pay for equal work regardless of nationality. The concerns resulted in a policy that required all foreigners to go through the federal government in order to naturalize.

By 1939 those wishing to naturalize had to go directly to the SRE in Mexico City to register.[34] This policy to take alien registration and naturalization from the municipalities and states and to put these functions in the hands of the federal government coincides with Cárdenas' overall drive to concentrate more power in the central government. It is also similar to U.S. immigration policy that increasingly put immigration under federal jurisdiction in the late nineteenth and early twentieth centuries.[35] A few months later, the SRE wrote again, asking about the availability of cotton in order to supply a French request.[36] Despite intentions to temper regional independence, the Laguna remained a powerful economic force in Mexico, challenging the federal government's desire to centralize its power.

Written exchanges in the 1930s reflect tensions between the municipal and federal governments and how officials struggled to handle the immigrant populations. The Secretary of the Interior would write the Torreón municipal president for additional information on Middle Eastern immigrants, and the Torreón municipal president would consistently reply that Middle Easterners were upstanding and valuable community members. The municipal government sided with Middle Eastern immigrants, who provided the necessary goods and services to spur development in the Laguna. Meanwhile, the federal government attempted to respond to middle-class concerns by establishing specific procedures and regulations for the immigrants to naturalize, thereby hoping to deter further migration and naturalization. Ultimately, it appears that Middle Easterners and the various Torreón municipal presidencies were able to outmaneuver the various presidential administrations.[37] Not only did Middle Eastern immigrants stay in the Laguna, but they naturalized and continued as foreign citizens in their economic and political activities to support both of their *patrias*.

Immigrants, Complaints, and Restriction

The dynamics present in the Laguna correspond to the widespread patterns of complaint and restriction concerning Middle Eastern immigrants in Mexico during the 1930s. For their part, pro-Middle Eastern interest groups began pressuring the Mexican government to act on their behalf. The Congress of Syro-Arab Associations for Independence (Congreso de las Asociaciones Siro-Árabes Pro Independencia) based in Buenos Aires, Argentina, even petitioned the SRE in February 1931 to advocate independence for the Arab peoples in the Middle East. The letter detailed foreign aggression against Middle Easterners and asked that Mexico advocate foreign withdrawal from the Levant.[38] No response was found in the records; however, these records do show that the Middle Eastern community supported a free Lebanon in 1943 and 1944, illustrating their political connections as well as their sense of community consciousness.

At the other end of the political spectrum with a domestic focus, the Mexico City National Chamber of Commerce (Cámara Nacional de Comercio de la Ciudad de México) wrote the Secretary of the Interior complaining of Middle Eastern merchants falsely declaring bankruptcy.[39] The complaint corroborated Gapsar O. Almanza's 1930 report from Beirut that Middle Eastern immigrants were taking advantage of Mexicans' trust and goodwill. This particular letter from the Chamber of Commerce identified Antonio Cid of Progreso, Yucatán, and Halim B. Nassar of Irapuato, Guanajuato.[40] The president of the Junta de Administración Civil de Irapuato defended Halim Nassar, saying he was honest and hardworking.[41] The municipal president said that Cid also was a man of good behavior and not known to have any vices.[42] Although resolutions to these cases were not recorded, they mark the beginning of a decade of citizens claiming injustices committed against them by Middle Eastern immigrants.

In this context, in 1932 the Mexican government established a National Registry of Foreigners over fifteen years of age. All were obligated to appear before the proper authorities and show their personal identification papers.[43] Growing anti-foreign sentiment, combined with the Depression, gave Middle Eastern immigrants the incentive to register with the Mexican Migration Department, where they could become "legal" and begin the process of naturalization. In complying with the new law, the municipal president of Mazatlán, Sinaloa, issued a notice to aliens in January 1932. The notice stated that "only Chinese, Russians, Syrians, Czechoslovaks, Hungarian, Bulgarian, and Turks . . . have been given a period of 15 days in which to present their immigration documents to the Municipal Authorities."[44] Non-compliance would be considered an act of disobedience, although the law did not mention any specific punishment. However, the strong language helped push adherence to the law. Of the Middle Eastern immigrants who registered, 72 percent did so between 1930 and 1933, and 89 percent registered between 1930 and 1939.

Despite the laws of 1927 and 1932, Mexicans continued to complain about Middle Easterners in letters to government officials. In San Luis Potosí, an organization called the National Block of Defense Pro Patria (Bloque Nacionalista de Defensa Pro Patria) was established to control Mexican commerce and industry by Mexicans and to prevent the "degeneration of the race" by Asians, particularly the Chinese. The organization's first tenet was: "To ask for the expedition of a law that will restrain the immigration of Turkish, Syrian-Lebanese, Czechoslovakians, Poles, and Jews, or of any nationalities of the many that are invading the markets with serious injury to the National commerce."[45] This organization was one of several groups that aimed to publicly impede Middle Easterners and their economic activities.

During Aberlardo Rodríguez's administration (1932–1934), the Committee for Race (Comité Pro-Raza) began a letter-writing campaign asking the president to put a quota on the number of "exotic" races permitted into Mexico.[46] The Committee for Race circulated a detailed constitution in October 1933 stating that the invasion of little-desired immigrants such as the Chinese, Turks, Arabs, and Lithuanians ought to be curbed because of their payment schemes and mafia connections.[47] In November 1933, five hundred people in Santiago Ixcuintla, Nayarit, demonstrated to protest against foreign merchants, in particular against the Chinese.[48] During this same month, telegrams to the president from the Committee for Race in Guasave, Sinaloa, Chihuahua, Chihuahua, and Mexico City described demonstrations of up to eight hundred people protesting the influx of undesirable immigrants.[49]

In February 1934 Rodríguez extended the ban on immigrants who had fewer than 10,000 pesos, except for those with approved technical skills; those skills were to be determined by the Secretary of the Economy. Investors with the minimal capital of 20,000 pesos and interested only in agricultural and industrial businesses were allowed, but nobody interested in commerce (*de ningún modo comerciales*) was to be permitted.[50] In response to economic dislocations and discontented citizen groups, the president strove to curb Middle Eastern immigration.

Despite Rodríguez' efforts, the Turkish government complained to the Mexican government about its acceptance of Turkish citizens who had not obtained permission to migrate. Although the Mexican government had signed a Friendship Treaty with Turkey in 1927 to continue trading between both countries,[51] by 1934 the Turks believed the Mexicans were violating the spirit of the agreement. In November 1927 the Turkish Embassy issued its first complaint that Mexico was already in violation of the treaty. Subsequently, the Turkish government suspended visas to Mexican citizens.[52] The Turkish government argued that since 1900, many people had migrated to Mexico with Turkish passports or declared themselves Turkish and were able to acquire Mexican citizenship, particularly Jews from Istanbul, Andrinople (Edirne), Kirklar-Eli, Izmir, Los Dardenelos (Chanak-kale) and Silivri. Since many of the emigrants first went to the Mexican Consul in New York, the Turkish government requested that the Mexicans not extend passports to those Jews who were registered as Turkish citizens.[53]

In response to the Turks' complaint and U.S. pressures, the regulations to enter Mexico appeared to tighten. A 1934 shipping document explaining Mexican immigration regulations, particularly the rights to a tourist card, stated:

> [S]pecial permission had been granted by Mexican Immigration Authorities to this [unnamed shipping] Company to issue a Tourist Card to first cabin passengers, 15 years or older, purchasing roundtrip tickets, who are entering Mexico solely for sightseeing purposes (except to Ministers of the Gospel and foreigners of origin Syrian, Lebanon, Armenian, Palestine, Arabian, and Turkish, whose entrance into Mexico is prohibited.)[54]

These restrictions in obtaining a Mexican tourist card were an attempt to appease the Turkish government's concern about the unauthorized migration of Turkish Jews, who could easily enter Mexico via New York. However, it is more likely that the restrictions aimed to curb Middle Eastern immigrants altogether.

In the face of rising xenophobia and international pressures, Middle Easterners in Mexico began lobbying the Mexican government. Julián Slim, President of the Lebanese Chamber of Commerce, wrote to the president requesting clemency and justice in reference to the expulsion of Lebanese Luis Ferrer.[55] Five days after sending this note, José Magro Soto responded, saying that the Secretary of the Interior was reviewing the situation.[56] The quick response suggests that the Lebanese Chamber of Commerce and Julián Slim commanded sufficient economic power to get the attention of Mexican political elites.

This emerging political power of the Middle Eastern community extended beyond Mexico. A Brazilian journalist wrote asking the president's opinion of the progressive Syrian colony and its cooperation with the progress and civilization of Mexico.[57] The tone of this letter indicates that Middle Easterners in Brazil were becoming increasingly prominent.[58] Although the letter does not appear to have received a response, it demonstrates that Middle Easterners were becoming more united and determined to position themselves as a community not only in Brazil but also throughout the Americas. As a result, President Lázaro Cárdenas sought to strike a political balance between Mexican citizens and Middle Eastern immigrants.

The popular administration of Lázaro Cárdenas (1934–1940) constructed an image of fulfilling many of the revolutionary promises, such as land distribution and nationalization of the oil industry.[59] However, scholars debate the degree to which he challenged foreign investors and immigrant populations. In breaking from the Jefe Máximo, President Plutarco Elías Calles, Cárdenas went to the people. As a populist, he appeared to successfully address citizens' concerns and orchestrate power within a single political party.[60] As Cárdenas sought to consolidate political power, right-wing newspapers such as *El Hombre Libre* urged the Labor Department to visit "the different stores headed by Syrian-Lebanese and the rest of that Jewish plague who invaded our dear fatherland, to practice disloyal competition in commerce, industry and even in the most humble activity, that of *tamale sales.*"[61] Another right-wing newspaper, *Omega,* noted that "one cannot find a place [on the streets of Mexico City] where one does not trip over a Chinese, an Arab, a Jew, or another foreigner, swarming the plazas and markets, and even engaging in such traditionally national pastimes as the sale of lemonade, candies and other items."[62] Such right-wing elements not only vilified foreigners but also set the context in which Cárdenas began his tenure.

In October 1935 the SRE prepared a study examining foreigners' acquisition of property in Mexico. The study reiterated Article 27 of the 1917 Constitution, which stated that only Mexicans born in Mexico or naturalized Mexicans had the right to acquire property.[63] The study also underscored that publicly traded Mexican companies had the ability to acquire unlimited urban properties, suggesting that the Mexican government struggled to curtail foreign acquisitions in Mexico.[64] At the same time, the Mexican government needed foreign investment in order to maintain its reform programs. This attempt to balance national interests of generating revenue for the state against sacrificing Mexican sovereignty plagued the Cárdenas administration.

Meanwhile, cases against Middle Eastern immigrants continued. In December 1935 the National Chamber of Commerce and Industry noted that Jewish and Arab immigrants were falsely declaring bankruptcies and were showing a lack of ethics in their businesses in León, Guanajuato.[65] In April and July 1936 the Union of Mexican Merchants and Industrialists of Aguascalientes asked President Cárdenas to look at the "immoral" commercial practices of Middle Eastern immigrants that included changing their names to avoid the law.[66] The Aguascalientes union wrote Cárdenas again in July insisting that he combat Middle Easterners and push the public to conduct business through Mexican establishments.[67]

In response, the Population Law of 1936 (Ley General de Población 1936) aimed to resolve fundamental demographic problems by establishing and maintaining more comprehensive records on the immigration and repatriation of foreigners.[68] This law prohibited the entrance of alcoholics, drug addicts, prostitutes, anarchists, and salaried foreign workers. It also banned the exercise of commercial activities by foreigners except when such activity was necessary.[69] Although the law did not explicitly mention Middle Easterners, it clearly attempted to restrict Middle Eastern merchants and regain "Mexico for Mexicans."[70]

With this post-revolutionary emphasis on Mexico for Mexicans, letters from Veracruz, Mexico City, Chihuahua, and Chiapas called for increased restrictions on Middle Eastern immigrants. In September 1937 the Union of Mexican Merchants and Industrialists of Veracruz asked for a law to stop foreigners (Chinese, Japanese, Poles, Jews, and the rest) from peddling because they were charging 300 percent more for the value of the goods by using payment in installments, *abonos*.[71] The letter claimed that the *abono* system was hurting the small-scale Mexican merchants who were trying to compete. The group advocated a complete halt to the migration of these immigrants.[72]

President Cárdenas also received a letter accusing the Middle Easterner Cherif Kassem of exploiting Mexican workers in Mexico City. Kassem was said to have entered Mexico on a tourist visa and then to have remained in order to open a store. He was charged with having various young ladies working for fifteen or more hours a day and for less than minimum wage.[73]

He was also supposedly the landlord of a house in which the renters suffered from poor living conditions and were forced to pay a doorman 55 pesos daily.[74] The letter recommended deporting Cherif Kassem, illustrating how Mexicans were expressing their discontent with Middle Eastern immigrants. The unidentified writer further claimed that Kassem was exploiting Mexican women. Once again, these themes reinforce the notion that foreigners were not to be trusted with Mexican women, and therefore action needed to be taken against them.

In Chihuahua, the Workers Union Chamber of the City of Juárez (Cámara Sindical Obrera de Ciudad Juárez) wrote Cárdenas in November 1937 asking for a prohibition against Jews, Arabs, and Japanese who dedicated themselves to selling fruit and other articles.[75] The presence of these foreigners, the group argued, created unfair competition for Mexican merchants. In addition to the competition, the fruits, vegetables, and meat sold by foreigners carried "contagious diseases" that could infect Mexicans.[76] This notion of foreigners carrying diseases that "threaten the health of the nation" by infecting Mexican food demonstrates the extent to which Mexicans resented foreigners.[77] In June 1938 the National Alliance of Chihuahuans sent a letter to the president complaining that the numerous foreigners, especially those in commerce, were monopolists.[78] Many citizens in Chihuahua found the immigrants to be unacceptable. Although it is difficult to document precise numbers, U.S. INS records further suggest that many undocumented immigrants from the Middle East resided in Chihuahua, often waiting to cross the border into the United States.

On the southern border in the state of Chiapas, the same concern was voiced with regard to foreign merchants. In a letter to the president in November 1939, citizens asked that the government put a stop to undesirable immigrants and their commercial activities, which were displacing Mexican merchants.[79] Despite these various requests, it does not appear that these complaints resulted in any further legislative changes.

Governments elsewhere in Latin America likewise adopted restrictions on Middle Eastern immigrants. Guatemala,[80] El Salvador,[81] and Nicaragua[82] began implementing legislation aimed against Arab, Turkish, Syrian, Lebanese, and Palestinian immigrants, in some cases prohibiting them from engaging in commercial activities. The Honduran government went so far as to say that Arab immigrants should only be allowed to do agricultural work.[83] The Colombian government instituted even more rigorous requirements for Middle Easterners in 1937.[84] In the most severe restriction, Bolivia issued ordinances forbidding consuls to consider visa applications from Semite candidates in April and May 1940.

These restrictions illustrate the extensive prejudices that Middle Eastern immigrants faced in coming to the Americas. Brazil, Argentina, and the United States were the largest recipients of Middle Eastern immigrants, and each set its own rigid barriers. Inspired by U.S. immigration policies, the 1937 Brazilian Constitution introduced a quota of 2 percent per nationality for those who had entered the country between 1884 and 1933.[85] According to Jeffrey Lesser, in June 1937 Brazilian President Getúlio Vargas authorized Secret Circular 1,127, which "prohibited the concession of visas to persons of 'Semitic origin.' "[86] Lesser suggests that the term "Semites" conflated Jews and Arabs, with the policy aim of reducing both Jewish and Arab emigration to Brazil.

Cárdenas, similar to Vargas in his populist style, did not take such extreme measures in immigration policy. Rather, he stressed Mexican nationalism, a sense of social justice, and a very centralized state apparatus that built upon the strength of a single political party, the PRM (Partido Revolucionario Mexicano).[87] This newly constructed Mexico became more nationalistic and anti-foreign, which helps explain the many letters to the Mexican government complaining of Middle Eastern immigrants. Like its Latin American neighbors, Mexico sought to enact laws to restrict immigration. However, as in all immigration debates, laws needed to be enforced to act as deterrents. The letters therefore signified not only the xenophobic attitudes at that time toward Middle Eastern immigrants but also the Mexican government's ambivalence about enforcing the existing laws.

Cárdenas also grappled with the question of how to deal with the Spanish Civil War and the rise of General Francisco Franco. Fearing the spread of fascism, he supported the Spanish Republic and refugees of the Civil War. In January 1939 the Mexican government officially welcomed Spanish refugees and formed a special commission to help accommodate them.[88] Between 1939 and 1942, some 12,000 Spanish Republicans resettled in Mexico, and by 1943, almost 30 percent of them had acquired Mexican citizenship.[89] His treatment of the Spanish refugees reflects how Cárdenas worked within the international theater. Cárdenas continued to give Spanish Republicans and leftists special treatment as foreigners in accordance with precedent, which suggests that political refugees such as the defeated Spanish left had acquired a certain legitimacy that others lacked and were welcomed by ruling Mexican "revolutionaries." Unlike Middle Easterners, the Spanish were seen as a race more similar to the Mexicans and therefore desirable.[90]

As Cárdenas and Mexican policy makers struggled to define the Mexican nation for Mexicans, Syria and Lebanon sought independence from the French Mandate. After decades of Mexican residency and xenophobic backlashes, many immigrants decided to naturalize. Although they became Mexican citizens, some still clung to their regional and ethnic roots in Lebanon and Syria, thus becoming foreign citizens. The Middle Eastern immigrants' ability to become Mexican while retaining their foreign identity enabled some members—in particular the wealthy, Christian elite from Lebanon—to in turn create a unique Lebanese Mexican identity.

Syria and Lebanon on the Eve of WWII

As Mexicans wrestled with issues surrounding foreigners in their midst, the French Mandate faced resistance movements throughout Syria in the 1920s. In 1925 Homs and Damascus were in full revolt against the French, so in October 1925 the French bombed Damascus for forty-eight hours. Despite the bombing, the revolt lasted until 1927, two years. Roughly 6,000 Syrians died, and a new Syrian political organization, the National Bloc, emerged. The National Bloc consisted of many nationalists from the Ottoman period who called for independence and territorial integrity for Greater Syria. Although they demanded French withdrawal, the leaders of the National Bloc wanted to retain their dominant local positions. Therefore, they presented themselves as intermediaries to the French, much like they did during the Ottoman Empire.

In 1930 France imposed its own constitution on Syria, rejecting the Syrian Constituent Assembly's constitution in 1929. The 1930 constitution upheld France's role as the mandate authority and prevented Syria from adopting any measures that might infringe on French Mandate privileges. Although Syrian presidents and prime ministers held office and Syrian legislatures met in annual sessions, French power to veto legislation left the Syrians with little ability to self-govern. In 1936 a treaty was drafted by the National Bloc, which prepared itself to assume power of a semi-independent country. However, in 1938 the National Bloc's coalition unraveled. The French refused to ratify the Franco-Syrian treaty, and Syria remained under French control. In 1939 the high commissioner suspended the Syrian constitution, dissolved the parliament, and reestablished the autonomy of the Alawite and Druze states.

Lebanon, with its pro-French Maronite community, was more receptive to the mandate than Syria. As they did in Syria, the French retained much control over Lebanon's domestic and international affairs. The French high commissioner also had the right to dissolve parliament and suspend the constitution, both of which he did in 1932 and again in 1939. Despite the restrictions, Lebanon was provided with a constitutional framework that allowed for electoral politics and some measure of self-government.

During the 1930s the conflicting aspirations of the Christian and Muslim communities framed Lebanese politics, and national leaders needed to persuade the communities to work together. Maronite politician Emile Eddé was premier and served as president of Lebanon from 1936 to 1941. He believed that the purpose of Lebanon was to preserve the Maronite dominance and to link Lebanon's interests with those of France. Despite Eddé's distrust of Muslims, he appointed Khayr al-Din al-Ahdab, a Sunni Muslim, as his prime minister. This appointment established the principle that the president of the republic would be a Maronite, and the prime minister a Sunni Muslim. The appointment of al-Ahdab also prompted Muslim leaders to realize that it was more beneficial to work within the system than to remain outside it.

In 1936 French and Lebanese representatives agreed on a treaty similar to the one that France and Syria had agreed upon but that the French chamber refused to ratify. As a result, Lebanon failed to achieve independence. At the onset of World War II, the high commissioner once again suspended the Lebanese constitution and dissolved the parliament. While Lebanon achieved independence in 1943, Syria had to await the end of World War II.

Profile of Middle Eastern Immigrants to Mexico in the 1930s

With the French Mandate in the Levant during the 1930s and increased immigration restrictions in the United States and Mexico, Middle Eastern emigration decreased. Between 1930 and 1939, only 585 Middle Eastern immigrants and resident foreign nationals registered in Mexico, compared to 3,657 in the previous decade. This significant reduction can be attributed to the world Depression and the fact that less money was circulating among the Middle Eastern community. Of the 585 immigrants, 62 percent were men and 38 percent were women. As in the 1920s migration, the immigrants tended to be married, although in a smaller proportion (49 percent) than during the 1920s; roughly 8 percent were widowed; and 43 percent were single, an increase over the previous decade (Table 9). Single and widowed migrants tended to join family members in Mexico and to work in family enterprises, demonstrating family reunification to be an important pattern of migration.

Most of the Middle Eastern immigrants (57 percent) called themselves

Lebanese in the 1930s, an increase from 43 percent in the 1920s (Table 2). However, 63 percent of the immigrants said they were born in Lebanon (Table 5). This discrepancy between place of birth and nationality could be explained by the strong Maronite presence in Lebanon in the 1920s and 1930s. It seems probable that some Muslims born in Lebanon were more inclined to call themselves Arabs than Lebanese. As noted earlier, immigrant registration cards began to be compiled in 1926, which coincides with the declaration of the Lebanese Republic. The reported identities on immigrant cards probably reflect the "Lebanization" of Middle Eastern immigrants in the 1920s and 1930s.

Among the Middle Eastern immigrants in the 1930s, nearly 22 percent called themselves Syrian (Table 2), with 24 percent saying they were born in Syria (Table 5). This slight discrepancy could be explained by the French Mandate altering Syrian borders in the 1930s. A smaller proportion than before, 8 percent, called themselves *sirio-libanés*, which also could underscore the ongoing disjunctions between nationalities and places of birth.

Approximately 8 percent of the immigrants called themselves Arab, which may have signified attachment to the Middle East through a pan-Arab identity. It is also possible, however, that some Mexican officials continued to label anyone from the Middle East as Arab, as opposed to specifying a declared nationality. Besides the Arab, Syrian, Lebanese, and Syro-Lebanese nationalities, 1.5 percent were Iraqis, 1.2 percent were Egyptians, and 0.17 percent were Jordanians, that is, Transjordanians (Table 2). These variations in identity show the diversity of the Middle Eastern immigration to Mexico. A greater proportion than before, 3 percent, were born in Mexico, and 1.4 percent were born in other American countries (Table 5), again showing that an Arab identity did not always equate to being born in the Middle East. Rather, Middle Eastern communities had proliferated throughout Latin America and the United States and maintained ethnic identities.

Emigration from Lebanese cities became more diffuse in the 1930s. Of the immigrants born in Lebanon, 66 percent came from communities from which fewer than five emigrants left for Mexico in the decade. In the 1920s, 59 percent came from Lebanese cities and towns with fewer than twenty emigrants (Table 3). Most of the immigrants born in Syria migrated from Aleppo (38 percent) and Damascus (20 percent), and 36 percent came from communities with fewer than two emigrants (Table 4). Although emigrants from Syria tended to embark from larger cities compared to emigrants from Lebanon, a significant number from both Syria and Lebanon also migrated from towns with fewer emigrants than during the previous decade.

Of the 585 immigrants, only 45 percent called themselves Catholics, possibly reflecting a lack of time to convert between their entry into Mexico and their registration. Since the immigrants were arriving and registering during this decade, they had less time to choose between maintaining or changing their religions than earlier immigrants to Mexico had been afforded. Jewish immigration declined to 19 percent in the 1930s, down from 26 percent in the 1920s (Table 6). While 13.5 percent of Middle Eastern immigrants called themselves Orthodox Christians in the 1930s, only 6.5 percent did so in the 1920s. Although the French Mandate was probably more stringent on Maronites migrating, 7 percent nonetheless declared themselves Maronites. Of the Middle Eastern immigrants, 5.3 percent were Druzes and 4.1 percent were Muslims. Those in the "none" and "other" categories could have included Jews, Muslims, or Druzes who felt intimidated or for other reasons chose not to disclose their faith (Table 6).

To a greater extent than in earlier migration phases, modes of transportation changed, as immigrants arriving by boat then moved overland by trains, cars, and/or buses. This in turn affected how immigrants came to Mexico and where they arrived and settled. Only 65 percent of Middle Eastern immigrants in the 1930s used Veracruz as a port of entry, as compared to 85 percent in the 1920s (Table 11). The state of Tamaulipas continued to be the second main destination, although the primary port of entry switched from Tampico to Nuevo Laredo in the 1930s. This change could reflect more immigrants using the land ports of entry along the U.S. border rather than the port city of Tampico. Of the Middle Eastern immigrants, 6 percent obtained their visas in the Mexican Consulate in Beirut, and 4 percent apparently arrived directly in Mexico City by plane.

After their arrival, roughly 50 percent of Middle Eastern immigrants in the 1930s settled in Mexico City. As in earlier periods, many also resided in the states of Veracruz, Yucatán, Puebla, Chihuahua, Nuevo León, Coahuila, and Durango (Table 7). What makes this migration phase different is that many immigrants claimed to be tourists and therefore did not indicate a place of residence. After the 1927 law to stop Middle Eastern immigration, many Middle Easterners entered Mexico on tourist visas. However, data on immigrant departures has not been adequately documented to verify how many immigrants had these visas and how many overstayed their tourist visas to settle in Mexico.

In the 1930s, 45 percent of Middle Eastern immigrants described themselves as being in commerce, and 35 percent stated that they were homemakers (Table 8). The occupations listed do not reflect substantial increases in property merchants or employees, suggesting that immigrants did not wish to draw much attention to themselves or to their possible commercial activities. The increase in the number of students to almost 9 percent from less than 1 percent may also reflect a younger group of Middle Easterners migrating to be reunited with their families and educated in Mexico, as well as children born in Mexico. Family reunification enabled the immigrants to merge their resources so that often one family member could still peddle goods in the rural areas while another family member could open a family store in a more urban area. This phase of family reunification not only gave the family unit more workers, but it also consolidated wealth and resources within the nuclear and extended family.[91]

The 1940s Immigration and World War II

During World War II and Manuel Ávila Camacho's administration (1940–1946), immigration continued although Mexican anti-foreign sentiment was modified.[92] The Middle Eastern community, through various Lebanese clubs, began insisting that the Levant region be free of foreign aggression. Middle Easterners lobbied President Ávila Camacho in 1943 to demand French withdrawal from Syria and Lebanon.[93] Letters from presidents of Syrian-Lebanese clubs from nearly every Mexican state flooded the president's office, and the Middle Eastern community repeated the letter-writing campaign in 1944.[94] These letters show a united immigrant group mobilized to participate in Mexican society. After arriving as poor peddlers, within two decades some were able to make enough money to emerge as powerful Mexican actors in the 1940s.

President Miguel Alemán (1946–1952) saw immigration as a form of international collaboration and a mechanism of national development. He offered hospitality to those foreign populations displaced by the war, in particular Jewish refugees. However, as with the earlier legal proscriptions, those admitted had to be able to "ethnically fuse with national groups."[95] This clause in the law gave Mexican policy makers latitude to interpret which ethnic groups would be most useful to the Mexican economy and nation. According to Article 7 of the 1947 law (Ley General de Población), the Mexican government "will facilitate the collective immigration of foreigners . . . who are easy to assimilate into our environment, with benefits to the race."[96] According to Rosa María Meyer and Delia Salazar, the 1947 law aimed to attract immigration of foreign investors, especially those interested in agricultural industry.[97] Economic and ethnic classifications remained firmly codified in Mexican law.

Meanwhile, other Latin American countries continued to impose similar restrictions on foreign populations. For instance, Panama's Constitution of 1941 banned the immigration of peoples of "the black race whose mother tongue is not Spanish, the yellow race and races original from India, Asia Minor and North Africa."[98] However, despite the discriminatory language of other Latin American countries' laws, the events of World War II tempered some of the extreme anti-immigrant sentiments in Mexico. As Mexico profited from war enterprises and economic conditions improved, xenophobic attitudes decreased. In particular, the war helped both the Mexican economy and many Middle Easterners' economic endeavors.

World War II Refugees

The World War II and immediate post-war periods (1940–1951, the year the immigrant registration records ended) brought slightly more registered Middle Eastern immigrants to Mexico than had the 1930s. This can be explained by dissipating anti-Arab sentiments and a more powerful Middle Eastern lobby within Mexico. Those seeking to leave the Levant needed to obtain their passports from the French Surete General, whereby the presidents of Syria and Lebanon were authorized to issue passports as of March 15, 1942.[99] Between 1940 and 1951, 598 Middle Eastern immigrants migrated to Mexico, among them 59 percent men and 41 percent women. This period is perhaps the most gender-balanced, possibly indicating that many of the war refugees were fleeing in family units. The majority (55 percent) of the immigrant population were married, 31 percent were single, and 12 percent were widowed (Table 9). The consistently high marriage rate among the immigrants corresponds to family migration.

The immigrants of this period comprised one of the most religiously diverse migrations to Mexico. Of the Middle Eastern immigrants, 45 percent called themselves Catholic, and nearly 5 percent were Maronites. This period saw the highest Arab Jewish migration to Mexico, 30 percent, followed by nearly 7 percent who were Orthodox Christian. Another 3.9 percent were Muslims, and 2.3 percent were Druzes (Table 6). World War II clearly caused extensive dislocations for many Middle Easterners and added more complexity to the configuration of Middle Eastern immigrants in Mexico.

Compared to earlier immigration periods, the difference between nationality and place of birth decreased. Of the Middle Eastern immigrants, 56 percent called themselves Lebanese, and 59 percent reported being born in Lebanon; 33 percent said they were Syrian, corresponding closely to the 32 percent who were born in Syria. The proportion of immigrants calling themselves *sirio-libanés* plummeted from 8 percent in the 1930s to a mere 0.84 percent in the 1940s, reflecting Syrian and Lebanese independence movements. Muslims and Druzes might have been more inclined to call themselves Arab rather than Lebanese; 4 percent of the immigrants were registered as Arabs, while 0.5 percent were born in Arabia (Table 2). Migration in this period also included many immigrants from various regions in the Middle East, such as Jordan and Morocco, and other areas of the world.

A trend similar to that in the 1930s immigration is that the majority (63 percent) of Middle Eastern immigrants born in Lebanon came from communities with fewer than five emigrants (Table 3). In Lebanon, more cities and towns, such as Douma, Bhamdoun, Ghazir, and Tannourine, began to emerge as places of departure. These newer locations indicate an extensive network between Lebanon and Mexico. Middle Eastern immigrants born in Syria tended to leave from three cities, Aleppo, Damascus, and Homs, which together accounted for 76 percent of the Syrian-born immigrants (Table 4).

Where Middle Eastern immigrants entered Mexico reflects the geopolitical changes of the 1940s as well as the boom in air travel. Nearly 10 percent obtained their visas in the Consulate in Beirut, and almost 7 percent processed their paperwork in Jerusalem (Table 11). Others went to consulates in other countries, such as Havana, to obtain visas to enter Mexico. Nearly half (47 percent) of all Middle Eastern immigrants from 1940 to 1951 entered at Mexico City, indicating that some arrived by air (Table 11). Of the immigrants, 8 percent entered through Nuevo Laredo, Tamaulipas, showing an increase in U.S. border crossings. Less than 3 percent indicated that Veracruz was their place of entry.[100] The decrease in seaports as entrances into Mexico demonstrates the changes in transportation as well as the use of various consulates that could have functioned as ports of entry to Mexico. Changes in port cities also reflect global migration during and soon after World War II.

During that period, settlement information is lacking for more than 75 percent of the Middle Eastern immigrants, though most appear to have settled in Mexico City (Table 7). The immigrant registration cards indicate that of the 1.8 percent who reported settling in Veracruz state, most settled in Orizaba; another 1 percent settled in Nuevo León, specifically in Monterrey. During all immigration periods, Middle Eastern immigrants largely settled in places with *paisanos* from their villages or cities in the Middle

East. This type of regional concentration suggests that the period of immigration and occupation did not necessarily determine the immigrants' settlement process. Rather, the strong ties of family and networks appear to have played the strongest role in the immigrants' residence once they were in Mexico.[101]

In similar proportions to earlier immigration periods, 44 percent of the immigrants classified themselves as merchants. Nearly 38 percent of Middle Eastern immigrants, mostly women, declared themselves homemakers. As noted earlier, it is highly probable that these homemakers helped in the family's commercial activities. Of the immigrants, 4.5 percent were students, suggesting that although the first generation often continued with the family's occupations, the second and third generations began to pursue other professions (Table 8). The ability to develop other professional careers was clearly linked to the family's economic standing.

By the end of the 1940s, some Middle Eastern immigrants had become wealthy entrepreneurs. From approximately 1925 through the 1940s, Middle Easterners made substantial investments in the textile industry. While many factories were closing and declaring bankruptcy in 1928–1929, Middle Eastern immigrants acquired bankrupt companies.[102] In 1932 there were twelve Middle Eastern immigrants in the textile industry in Puebla, and by 1940 there were twenty.[103] Middle Eastern immigrants in Puebla, like their counterparts in the Laguna, had begun as peddlers selling in the marginal zones and then slowly accumulated enough capital between peddling and their small stores to become industrialists.

For the first time, 2.3 percent of the immigrants identified themselves as industrialists. Although some Middle Easterners in the 1930s and 1940s had accumulated sufficient capital to become store owners, only a very few had become industrialists, as the majority continued in some commercial enterprise.[104] The rise of Middle Eastern industrialists nevertheless corresponds to the constructed Lebanese Mexican history whereby Middle Eastern immigrants began as peddlers, later became merchants and store owners, and eventually emerged as an elite minority of industrialists.

The World War II refugees and post-war immigrants had different experiences in obtaining visas, in transportation, and in settling in Mexico. The early Middle Eastern immigrants struggled to position themselves in Mexican society as legitimate suppliers and eventual Mexican citizens, while immigrants in the 1940s participated differently in Mexican society, often joining as foreign citizens almost upon arrival in Mexico and encountering a more welcoming Mexico with established ethnic networks to help them in their settlement process.

Concluding Comments

As in earlier periods, Mexican policy makers struggled to both control foreigners and appease the Mexican populace about Middle Eastern business practices. The registration policy made Middle Easterners declare themselves foreigners while at the same time enabling them to acquire citizenship. Inadvertently, policy makers perpetuated the "foreign citizen" paradigm whereby outsiders maintained multiple identities while joining the Mexican nation. With registration, Mexicans treated Middle Easterners in confusing and often contradictory ways. In the 1930s, Mexican citizens wrote the federal government asking for economic help by demanding the expulsion of Middle Eastern immigrants. Letters from citizens, Chambers of Commerce, and state governments demonstrate a nation searching for a way to control its immigrant populations. The new post-revolutionary regime tried to contain the Middle Eastern problem through restricted immigration policies; however, subsequent letters of complaint indicate that the enforcement of immigration laws remained variable.

Although many Middle Eastern immigrants secured legal status and citizenship in the late 1930s and early 1940s, some of the immigrants still faced socioeconomic marginalization and discrimination. Mexican citizens often excluded Middle Easterners from the mainstream,[105] helping establish Middle Easterners as permanent ethnic minorities.[106] Some of the wealthy Middle Easterners then used the "foreign" label and minority status to differentiate themselves from Mexicans. This became the basis of constructing "Lebaneseness" and distinguishing themselves among the various Middle Eastern communities. The impetus to claim Lebaneseness probably stemmed from the overpowering French Mandate that favored Christians over Muslims and Druzes. While non-Christian Arabs in Lebanon felt increasingly disenfranchised, Middle Easterners in Mexico faced a citizenry that perceived them as parasitic.

Despite some Mexicans' sentiments, Mexican policy makers seemed to recognize the value of Middle Eastern economic enterprises and their role in the Mexican economy. Although the letters do not specifically state the importance of Middle Eastern commercial activities, the registration of the Middle Eastern community implicitly signaled acceptance of their presence in the Mexican nation and conceded expansion to the revolutionary *mestizo* construction. The historical conditions explored in this chapter further shaped how Lebanese Mexicans would construct their community in Mexican society.

CHAPTER 6

Peddling, Positioning, and Prosperity

Carlos Slim Helú recalled his father telling him: Respect your commercial activities . . . Commerce ought to introduce a useful system, its activities and its purpose rest in the small profit in sales. It ought to furnish the consumer with fine and cheap articles, and one ought to deal directly with the consumer, giving him payment options and adjusting your actions to the strictest morality and honor.

MARTHA DÍAZ DE KURI AND LOURDES MACLUF, *DE LÍBANO A MÉXICO*

Slim Helú has followed his father's advice by developing innovative products and providing services to his customers. Slim Helú has come to symbolize the idealized Lebanese Mexican citizen—wealthy yet still connected to his Lebanese ancestry. The story of Slim Helú and his economic prowess are part of a constructed Lebanese Mexican history of Middle Eastern immigrants. Many Middle Easterners came to Mexico aspiring to make money and return home.[1] The presence of Middle Eastern itinerant traders in Mexico is well known; yet few researchers have questioned why Mexican *campesinos* traded with these foreigners. How did Middle Eastern immigrants, with their growing knowledge of Spanish and Mexican customs, attract Mexicans to purchase Middle Eastern products?

Questions also remain concerning how Middle Eastern communities evolved. How did communities construct their identity? In this chapter, I explore how Middle Eastern immigrants have continuously positioned themselves between Mexican society and their own Middle Eastern communities, creating a foreign citizenry. While making their profits, Middle Eastern immigrants (later constructed as the Lebanese colony) sought to position themselves in relation to events in the Middle East and in Mexico. In response to Mexican nation building, the immigrants aimed to unite themselves and establish their foreign elitism by employing a Lebanese discourse that largely excluded Arabs, Muslims, and Druzes. Today, the Lebanese community speaks with a hegemonic voice for all those of Middle Eastern descent in Mexico. The newly constructed history tends to portray the early immigrants as primarily Christians from Lebanon with Phoenician roots. The diversity of the immigrants and their contradictory treatment and reception in Mexico have largely been overshadowed by the notion that the Lebanese quickly assimilated and economically dominated.[2] Here I examine how leading Middle Eastern immigrants reconstructed themselves as Lebanese Mexicans by their positioning during conflictual times and their construction of "Lebaneseness."

Profit and Dealing in Conflict

As discussed earlier, the *campesinos* in Mexican society needed the Middle Eastern merchants' goods. Consequently, Mexicans may have looked past the foreignness of merchants and viewed them as merely suppliers in a developing market economy. The credit system of *abonos* also probably gave the *campesinos* and *rancheros* new economic freedoms from the system of *patrones* and company stores. Middle Easterners were able to cut across class and ethnic lines, and this ability afforded them a unique position in selling clothing and other goods to the poor and middle classes.

At the same time that they sold their products, they were positioning themselves as important providers within Mexican society. Mexican reactions to Middle Easterners vary by region and class. In Torreón some Mexicans actually seemed to accept and help Middle Eastern immigrants. Leopoldo Olvera and his wife, Juanita Martínez, hid Nicolás Abusamra Hadad in their house from xenophobic rebels during the Mexican Revolution.[3] Conversely, in the Yucatán, many Middle Easterners faced discrimination, which led the Middle Eastern community to insulate itself and to, in turn, discriminate against *yucatecos*.[4] It is difficult to ascertain, however, whether these two states reflect broad patterns among other regions in Mexico or anomalies, and further immigrant studies will help explain these regional differences.

As tensions increased between Middle Eastern communities and middle-class Mexicans throughout Mexico, Middle Easterners often looked to an "imagined" past in order to authenticate themselves in their new homeland. Unlike the Spanish and Barcelonette French immigrants, Middle Eastern peddlers traded with *campesinos* for small goods, thereby developing a bond in the countryside. These relationships were clearly strategic and mutually reinforcing as tactics of survival: they fomented autonomy for workers and laborers and acceptance in a foreign land for Middle Eastern peddlers.

Middle Eastern immigrants have often faced xenophobia because being foreign in Mexico has often been equated with prosperity, and Mexicans have resented foreigners' wealth.[5] Indeed, foreigners have tended to dominate in commerce throughout Mexican history. Paradoxically, the tradition of foreign merchants and wealthy immigrants has helped Middle Eastern entrepreneurs and propagated foreign elitism—and with it, the notion that being foreign in Mexico gives one the ability to profit as he or she pleases.[6] These Middle Eastern immigrants are foreign citizens.

The historical trajectory of Middle Eastern merchants trading with Mexicans facilitated a measure of tolerance for Middle Easterners in Mexican society. Mexicans may not have liked these immigrants, but the immigrants nonetheless developed the ability to market themselves as legitimate agents. Middle Easterners learned that they had to please Mexicans in order to ensure their own acceptance and safety in Mexican society. Obviously, each Middle Eastern entrepreneur had his or her own economic strategy and clientele. In the quest to make profits, Middle Eastern immigrants needed to establish themselves as trustworthy suppliers. This positioning of both goods and societal acceptance between Middle Easterners and Mexicans has been ongoing and often problematic.

Middle Eastern immigrants saw profit as the essence of the success that would provide them the ability to return home. Moreover, the ability to trade and profit was heavily dependent on networks of family and friends. "Network migration" describes the complex relationships between the immigrants and members in the receiving community.[7] However, these networks were sometimes unfair and exploitive.[8] For example, Yamil Darwich Adí felt that his uncle exploited him by charging him 200 pesos for living in his home during his first year in Mexico.[9] Although the Middle Eastern network provided Yamil Darwich Adí and other immigrants their initial capital from their fellow countrymen, cases of exploitation or perceived exploitation may have been quite common.

Dib Morrillo recounts in his memoirs that he had deposited 800 pesos with Pedro Slim, but when he returned six months later to get his money back, his money had devalued and merchandise had increased in price. Slim did lend Morrillo the cash to purchase the merchandise, but it took Morrillo three years to pay him back.[10] Morrillo indicates that it was the circulation of Pancho Villa's currency that led to the devaluation during the Mexican Revolution. This anecdote highlights not only the informal network among the Middle Eastern immigrants in lending money and merchandise to one another, but it also illustrates that Middle Easterners did not necessarily afford one another any special opportunities. Although these were ethnic networks, their business transactions appear focused on individual pursuits of profit.

In his novel *En el verano, la tierra*, Carlos Martínez Assad also describes how Pedro Slim purchased merchandise from some friends in Puebla. In adopting the voice of a Lebanese grandfather, Martínez Assad cleverly tells the story of a Lebanese immigrant by exploring the fictional grandson José's feelings toward Lebanon. José's grandfather believed that Pancho Villa's troops respected the Lebanese *aboneros*,[11] because they helped provide the soldiers with clothes once in awhile.[12]

Admittedly, the Middle Eastern system of allowing customers to pay in installments, *abonos,* gave them a competitive advantage over other merchants and increased their profits. This innovative system gave a poor family the opportunity to buy two or three dresses even though the family did not have the money up front to pay for the dresses. The Middle Eastern merchant would then sell the dress for double the price, asking for some initial deposit such as a peso, and the consumers only had to give their name and pay a weekly peso or 50 centavos.[13] This credit system has endured into the digital age in which Carlos Slim Helú and his son Carlos Slim Domit now allow customers to purchase desktop computers for a $100 down payment and 24 monthly installments of $50.[14] What distinguishes the *abono* system is its application to all markets as well as its continued success with both consumers and merchants. The *abono* system combined with the network's infrastructure of providing the immigrants necessary capital proved to be quite profitable.

Mexican conflicts facilitated the Middle Eastern pursuit of profit. During the various conflicts of the Porfiriato, Mexican Revolution, and postrevolutionary nation building, Middle Eastern immigrants found a way to venture into varied commercial enterprises. By taking enormous risks, they were able to exercise great freedom in pursuing their economic strategies. As demonstrated in earlier chapters, it was this latitude in the commercial sector that particularly frustrated middle-class Mexicans. What ultimately resulted from these moments of conflict was a contradictory role for Middle Easterners. They were both victims and victors in the conflicts because they became targets of xenophobia and simultaneously profited from the tensions. It is within this conflicted role that they constructed their Lebanese community.

The Mexican Revolution afforded Middle Easterners the opportunity to sell goods and services while many parts of the country were involved in violence. Recall that due to the scarcity of goods, prices fluctuated and enabled the Middle Eastern merchants to mark up prices. In the 1920s, by having a fixed commercial establishment and one or more family members who peddled in remote areas, the Middle Eastern immigrants created a great economic advantage that would increase their wealth.[15] In the Yucatán, the devaluation of Mexican money along with a lack of trusted currency reduced property prices. With their savings, Middle Easterners were able to monopolize the circulation of money and to invest heavily in real estate that would later yield large profits.[16]

In addition to trading along the border, money lending was common for Middle Eastern immigrants in such places as Torreón in the north. Immigrants such as Antonio Achem also had a history of money lending.[17] While the post-revolutionary government struggled to define the parameters of the Mexican nation, Middle Eastern immigrants began an informal lending practice that helped Mexicans to subsist. The peddlers' *abono* system employed during the Porfiriato and Revolution enabled the peddlers to offer credit to their fixed customers in the 1920s, thereby providing an alternative to formal banking institutions.[18] Juan Abusaid's successful enterprises had led to a family fortune by the end of the 1940s.[19]

The Depression of the 1930s caused some Lebanese families to move from the Yucatán to Mexico City. Those merchants who stayed in Mérida developed extensive networks and increased their wealth.[20] In Torreón, Juan Abusaid and Antonio Achem had accumulated sufficient resources to begin money lending in the post-revolutionary period. Abdelour Aboumrad opened a small store to exchange money, and by 1937 the business had grown to the point of establishing the Banco Aboumrad. Miguel Abed also opened a bank in Puebla.[21] Thus, while the post-revolutionary government struggled to rebuild the Mexican nation-state, Middle Eastern immigrants began providing both formal and informal segments of the banking structure that was needed for the Mexican economy to survive and develop.

Middle Eastern immigrants in Puebla, similarly to their northern and southern counterparts, began as itinerant traders selling in the marginal zones and slowly accumulated enough capital between peddling and their small stores to become industrialists. Early immigrants Antonio Jacobo y Abdo and Antonio Cassab opened a factory to produce tights in Puebla in 1907. Then, Abraham Cheban Bechelani founded the Sociedad Musalen y Cheban to also produce socks and tights in 1909.[22] These early industrialists laid the groundwork for fellow *paisanos* in the mid-1920s. From approximately 1925 through the 1940s, Middle Eastern investment in the textile industry was substantial, and when many factories began to go bankrupt in 1928–1929, Middle Eastern immigrants acquired them.[23] This period also corresponds to the world economic crisis and increased demands for Mexican products during World War II. Thus, while many Mexicans suffered from the 1930s economic downturn, some Middle Easterners flourished.

This prosperity gains partial explanation among Lebanese Mexicans through the notion that Lebanese culture is unique in cultivating profit and that it is their Phoenician past that has helped them succeed financially. One interviewee stated that "the Lebanese make money precisely because we had the background preparation. . . . We come from the Phoenicians, we are merchants by origin."[24] The emphasis on a 6,000-year history of trading and their Phoenician roots is echoed throughout Lebanese literature, as will be discussed later in this chapter.[25] The assertion that Phoenician ancestry gave Middle Eastern immigrants their enterprising talents to make a profit in Mexican society provides the basis for analyzing their community in terms of Benedict Anderson's theory of the imagined community: "Communities are to be distinguished, not by their falsity/genuineness, but by the style in which they are imagined."[26] Middle Eastern immigrants have drawn on their own cultural constructions and on Mexican historical events to find their niche in Mexican society. These mutual constructions of Middle Eastern culture and Mexican nation building are founded on continuous conflict and negotiation.[27]

Economic and Social Positioning: Climbing the Ladder

Much of the foreign status of Middle Eastern immigrants derived from their roles in the Mexican economy. Early immigrants often brought their initial goods from other countries and then borrowed capital from their fellow countrymen. Family-based connections created and consolidated the ethnic network. Jeffrey Lesser notes that "the use of ethnicity to construct wholesale-retail linkages provided new economies of scale."[28] The economic, ethnic, and family links created a network of itinerant salespeople. However, this network was informal and difficult to trace outside of oral testimony.[29] This Middle Eastern network enabled many of the immigrants to participate in the Mexican economy by providing initial capital to one another and to Mexicans, allowing the immigrants to start peddling.

This pattern recalls Walter Zenner's definition of a middle-man minority, of which "a substantial and disproportionate number of its members are engaged in small commercial enterprises or are employed in such enterprises by other members of their groups." Middle Eastern immigrants in Mexico fit his construction. "Some . . . see the culture of the ethnic group in its fostering of ethnic cohesion and familism as an independent variable . . . while others emphasize the role which trade and ethnic cohesion play in the survival of the individuals and the group in a particular context. . . . Whichever stress is given, the 'middleman minority' concept links ethnicity to the political economy."[30] However, middleman minorities also have tended to refer to those who mitigate between colonial regimes and a subject population. In the case of Middle Easterners in Mexico, these immigrants lacked a colonial relationship and its dynamics of power with respect to Mexican society. This in turn helped foster a commercial identity whereby Middle Eastern immigrants largely described themselves as participating in the commercial sector.

During the 1930s immigrant registration, more than 45 percent of the Middle Eastern immigrants registered themselves as *comerciantes,* merchants.[31] The second-highest reported immigrant profession was homemaker, *ama de casa,* with nearly 34 percent of all immigrants declaring this as their profession.[32] Yet, many of these homemakers assisted their spouses in the families' commercial activities.[33] This participation both justified the settlement of Middle Eastern immigrants in Mexico and led to their construction of a meaningful and relevant history.

The majority of the peddlers carried their own merchandise and kept track of their accounts in small notebooks (*libretitas*). They would keep records of those who owed money and the payment schedules. According to Patricia Jacobs Barquet, "They filled a void between the peripheral towns and the commercial interior."[34] Middle Eastern immigrants could peddle goods in the marginalized small towns along the Nazas River in the state of Durango from a commercial base in the city of Torreón in Coahuila state.[35] The Middle Eastern immigrants often established commercial networks in major cities, and then countrymen would peddle the goods. As some peddlers improved their economic positions, they began to strive for better social standing, in which they emphasized their foreign roots to explain and justify their successes.

The importance of Lebanese identity and community preservation is perhaps best exemplified in a 1948 census taken in Mexico that coincided with the new independence of Lebanon and Syria, each nation trying to imbue a separate identity and citizenship in its people. Journalists Julián Nasr and Salim Abud spent two years compiling a 621-page census, *Directorio Libanés: Censo general de las colonias—libanesa—palestina—siria: Residentes en la República.*[36] This Lebanese directory served many functions, among them giving a renewed sense of ethnic pride in Mexico. More importantly, the Lebanese directory listed 70 percent of the Middle Eastern families living in Mexico by dividing the community into the Lebanese, Palestinian, and Syrian colonies. The census in particular celebrates the Lebanese community's success and constructs the ethnic differences among the Middle Eastern immigrants in Mexico.

Tables 12 and 13 demonstrate how analyses of the community census varied. Louis J. Maloof examined the marital status of all people (whom he calls Arabic-speakers) reported in the census (Table 12). The nearly 90 percent endogamous marriage rate is probably a skewed number, given that many of the informants did not list their spouses, and women and Jews were not counted. Also, this was only a 70 percent sample of the actual community in 1948, and it probably reflected the middle- and upper-middle-class Middle Easterners. It is likely that the poorer Middle Easterners had been absorbed into the Mexican society and did not participate in the census. Páez Oropeza focused only on endogamy and exogamy of the Lebanese among all the Middle Eastern immigrants (Table 13). Her estimation that nearly 73 percent of the Lebanese married within the Lebanese community faces the same limitations as Maloof's calculations. Despite the limitations of the data, however, the roughly 73 to 90 percent of the Middle Easterners who claimed to be intermarrying in their community indicates a high rate of endogamy.[37] According to immigrant registration cards between 1940 and 1951, 59 percent of the Middle Eastern immigrants were male and 41 percent female. More than 55 percent who entered during this period were married, 31 percent were single, and nearly 12 percent were widowed—including almost half of the women as widows. However, the immigrant registration cards do not consistently indicate whether the marriages were between Middle Easterners or with Mexicans.

Conversely, from 10 to 27 percent of the Middle Easterners were marrying outside of the community. It is highly probable that many of these exogamous marriages were contracted with Mexicans, although a few Middle Easterners may have married other foreigners. The marriages with Mexicans could have been arranged for economic reasons as well as for emotional attachments. Although there are still more endogamous marriages, there may have been a gradual shift in Middle Eastern immigrant community attitudes regarding endogamy. These attitudes probably varied as immigrants assimilated into Mexican society.[38] It is also likely that poorer Middle Easterners had higher exogamous marriage rates because they could not have afforded return trips to the Middle East to find spouses or pay for potential spouses' voyages across the Atlantic; this in turn would have necessitated finding spouses within Mexican society.

Overall, there is a clear tendency for prosperous Middle Easterners to intermarry and maintain a community in Mexico. In an interview with Professor Juan Estafan in 1957, Louis Maloof described that "to them, marrying an outsider was like 'the hand of death crashing down upon the glorious inheritance' they had received from 'the cradle of civilization.'"[39] Maloof explained that Middle Eastern women wanted to preserve their own "flesh and blood" through endogamous marriages. In some cases, "the Lebanese parents did not permit their children to marry with Yucatecans, saying they did not want to change their race and mix [blood]."[40] This fear for the composition of the community from intermarriages led some Middle Eastern families to arrange marriages between first cousins. Although these marriages are not common in Mexico today, earlier immigrants wanted to "at least keep family patrimony within the line of descendancy."[41] Akram Fouad Khater notes that "the overwhelming predominance of cousin marriage—common to most Mediterranean societies—arose from the economic conditions in Mount Lebanon."[42] Cousin marriages kept land and capital within the family units and established social linkages within the community.

Maloof also traced the ethnic differences of the Middle Eastern immigrants and their years of migration to Mexico. Maloof, writing in 1959, found that at the end of 1948 more Arabic-speaking Middle Eastern immigrants identified themselves as "Lebanese" than other Middle Eastern nationalities (Table 14). Of the 5,509 Middle Eastern immigrants living in Mexico in 1948, 4,472 (81 percent) claimed a Lebanese identity; in contrast, during the Mexican immigrant registration in the 1930s, only 55 percent of Middle Eastern immigrants described themselves as having a Lebanese identity. However, Maloof notes that no Jews were counted in the census,[43] and only the males of the family were counted: "only the patriarch and his sons were named in the genealogy."[44] The discrepancy between the community census and the Mexican immigrant records can be explained not only by the dates when the Middle Eastern immigrants were questioned but also by the exclusion of Jews and women from the tally. The Mexican immigrant registration cards had been produced in the early 1930s, when the Middle Eastern community was still struggling to find its voice in Mexican society. However, by 1946, when the two-year census was begun, the Lebanese community had become more strongly committed to bringing together its members, consolidating a Lebanese identity.

Within Middle Eastern families, women have helped create wealth in their dual role of helping the family business (as peddlers, bookkeepers, and store employees) and carrying the cultural traditions necessary for the creation and maintenance of Lebaneseness.[45] Evelyn Shakir has suggested that in the United States, Middle Eastern women peddlers were often more proficient than their husbands because they could more easily enter the American household. The situation of women peddlers in Mexico has yet to be fully explored in this regard and is worthy of further research. It is clear, however, that although women typically were not paid directly in their families' businesses, their labor contributed to the consolidation of family wealth.[46] The consolidation of wealth by Middle Eastern families can also be described as part of the ethnic identity of the community. Middle Eastern families have tended to be patriarchal and to form a symbiotic unit in which each family member performs a function to help maximize savings and capital; and within this economic unit, family members also aimed to maintain their ethnicity and their immigrant positioning in Mexican society.

Creating a Lebanese Community

The presence of Middle Eastern immigrants has often been understood to have evolved from *turco* peddlers to Middle Eastern merchants to Syro-Lebanese store owners and to Lebanese industrialists. In fact, the community has formed in a far less linear way, with peddling, store owning, and industrial production overlapping in various periods and regions. The community has employed *diasporic* elements,[47] thereby perpetuating a myth of uniqueness.[48] This myth was largely founded on the Phoenician past and fostered by the creation of organizations, newspapers, churches, and films. The creation of community was linked to the amount of time individual immigrants and the larger group had spent in Mexico.[49] With time, the immigrants sought to bring *paisanos* together to uphold the values of the *patria*, the motherland. While the immigrants contributed to the Mexican economic and industrial infrastructure and their own personal fortunes, the first and second generations started to develop a collective consciousness.[50] This collective consciousness can first be documented in 1922 with the founding of the Liga Libanesa by José Helú.[51]

The construction of identity can be linked as well to the Lebanese efforts to declare an independent state. On May 23, 1926, the Lebanese Republic was proclaimed, and Charles Dabbas, an Orthodox Christian, was chosen president. At this time the Lebanese constitution was drafted. With Lebanese state formation, the Cámara de Comercio Sirio-Libanesa advocated bringing more *paisanos* to Mexico to help solidify a collective identity of Lebaneseness in Mexico. In 1943 the Unión Libanesa de la Laguna became the Comité Central Libanés Pro-Aliados y Pro Francia Libre, openly demonstrating its World War II dedication to the Allies and a liberated France.[52] The Academy of Arabic Language was founded by Professor Juan Aaún in 1945 in the classrooms of the Unión Libanesa in Mexico City.[53]

Immigrants sharing an affiliation with Syria were similarly organized and interested in the politics of their homeland. On November 29, 1920, the Syrian Union Committee of Torreón (Comité Unión Sirio de Torreón) wrote U.S. President Woodrow Wilson to ask for French and British withdrawal from Syria and Palestine. The letter (with misspellings retained here) stated: "There fore we are sorry for Angl-French behavior in Syria & Palestine wich will kepp our Country in disturbances for ever, and wich is also perfectly contrary to the hig ideals for wichAmerican People struggled in Europe—Only withdrawal of invasors from Syria & Palestine would restore normal conditions."[54] This letter shows a more politically active and unified Middle Eastern immigrant community with the determination to preserve their homeland *patria*.

By late 1927 the Syrian Union Committee became the Lebanese Union of the Laguna (Unión Libanesa de La Laguna). This group was established on December 17, 1927, with Nicolás Abusamra as president, Simon M. López as secretary, Pedro Jaik as treasurer, and Antonio Farhat as first voice.[55] Its principal objective was to unify the general opinion of the Lebanese who had settled in Mexico, principally those in the Laguna. The founders also sought all possible means to help fellow Lebanese and to influence a morally and intellectually Lebanese culture,[56] thereby establishing themselves as foreign citizens.

In the United States, Lebanese immigrants began to feel an increased sense of ethnic consciousness in the 1920s. This rising consciousness ignited controversy within the Syrian American community because many insisted on being known simply as Lebanese, an identity to which Syrians on the whole would not accede. In 1946 and 1943, when Syria and Lebanon respectively achieved full independence, this matter appeared to be resolved in the United States.[57] Yet, in Mexico the Lebanese became a dominant voice compared to the other Middle Eastern groups.[58] The Lebanese were more affluent and more politically connected.

The Lebanese further developed their sense of community through the use of newspapers and newsletters that galvanized the community around a Lebanese identity.[59] In 1905 Father Chaya started *Ask Shark* to help educate the Middle Eastern community about its history. *Ask Shark* was followed in 1909 by *Al-Gurbal*,[60] begun by Youseff Mousalem and later taken over by Salim Abud.[61] Publication of *Al-Jawater* (The Ideas) began in 1909; in 1927 its publication in both Arabic and Spanish began.[62]

In 1937 Alfonso Negib Aued began publishing *Emir*, which addressed the Lebanese elite in the 1920s and 1930s in Mexican society. *Emir* highlighted social events and provided general community information. *Líbano*, which began publication in August 1937, encouraged a more politically involved community. Under *Líbano* Director General Nasre M. Ganem, columnist Nemesio García Naranjo wrote about the prejudices that the Lebanese community faced and the importance of destroying stereotypes. The message was that the Lebanese community needed to proclaim its origin with pride and always maintain its cultural traditions.[63]

Emir and *Líbano* both had sections on women's issues in order to recognize their female readers. The editors appeared to promote idealized Middle Eastern women who were concerned with their appearance as well as their families. As noted earlier, Middle Eastern women in the family environment helped create wealth through the family business and carried the cultural traditions, making Middle Eastern immigrant women important to the creation, maintenance, and reproduction of Lebaneseness.

In *Líbano*, the Femininas section suggested in one issue that women needed to develop a personality to be "attractive." This article maintained that true beauty is natural beauty.[64] In *Emir*, a section called Página Feminina discussed beauty and health. Although the article format varied, the women's column offered advice on dieting, sunbathing, dressing attractively, improving one's smile, and achieving self-awareness.[65] Anne Rubenstein discusses how the New Woman of the 1920s was an "idealization of lean, androgynous, youthful women."[66] Magazines in North America, South America, and Europe offered advice for women to attain this international image.[67] This image of the New Woman was portrayed in many of the advertisements in Lebanese Mexican magazines in 1937. However, in looking at photographs of the Middle Eastern women during this time, few appear to fit this idealized female image.

Emir also included a section on women's social clubs, such as La Asociación de Damas de San José, noting how the "honorable" families of the community intermingled with Mexican society.[68] Both newspapers recognized the importance of a gender discourse to reach Middle Eastern women and address women's roles within the patriarchal community. At this time, similarly to Mexican discourses on women's behavior,[69] the Lebanese community itself encouraged its women to be physically attractive and morally upstanding. Interestingly, articles in *Líbano* and the other periodicals demonstrate that women in the immigrant community have been critical to the construction of Lebaneseness. In the 1940s immigrant women responded by establishing the Club Feminil Libanés in Mérida.[70] In 1943 *Emir* prominently displayed the Unión de Damas Libaneses for their philanthropic work and "zeal to respond to the destitute in Mexican society."[71] These immigrant women's groups show the importance of Lebaneseness and how the community was adding value to Mexican society.

The film industry addressed some of the tensions between the rising Middle Eastern elites and Mexican society. During the 1940s Gregorio Wallerstein produced two films about Middle Eastern peddlers, *El baisano Jalil* and *El barchante Neguib*. Filmex financed both, and actor Joaquín Pardavé directed the films and played the protagonists.[72] *Baisano* in the earlier film's title is a dialectic version of *paisano*. Many Middle Eastern immigrants have been known to mispronounce the letters "p" and "b" because the Arabic language does not have distinct, comparable phonemes for these sounds. In *El baisano Jalil*, Pardavé uses an Arabic accent and confuses words such as *majacano* to mean *mexicano*. Through the father character of Jalil Farad, the film *El baisano Jalil* tells the story of a courtship between his son, born to a Middle Eastern immigrant family, and the daughter of an aristocratic Mexican family that has fallen on hard times. The romantic and comedic narrative tacks between these young adults and the confused interventions of their families. Although the film is imbued with melodramatic flair, *El baisano Jalil* also reflects the anxiety about foreigners and foreign citizens in Mexico.

In one memorable scene, the daughter of this Mexican aristocratic family rejects Selim Farad, Jalil's son. Overcome by emotion, Jalil cries: "Have I not worked as if I was Mexican? Have I not made more for this country than that entire family? Don't I love Mexico as if it were my own mother? The son of my soul is not Mexican?" Although the Farad family lives in a large, spacious home, Jalil, his wife, Suad (played by Sara García), and son Selim (played by Emilio Tuero) still face painful discrimination in their new home country. This narrative of Farad becoming an owner of a large fabric shop in Mexico City illustrates the common perception among Mexicans that Middle Eastern immigrants, through economic prowess, quickly came to dominate the Mexican economy. However, the ability of the Middle Eastern immigrants to climb the economic ladder has not always corresponded to acceptance in Mexican society.

Middle Eastern immigrants have been able to maintain their foreignness while joining the Mexican nation. As *El baisano Jalil* depicts the family's situation, to be foreign in Mexico is seen as a guarantee of wealth, and yet Mexicans are often hostile because of foreigners' wealth. As the character Farad experiences flashbacks to his peddling days, he both fears losing his new status as a store owner and celebrates his new home in Mexico. In one scene, Jalil and Suad visit the home of Guillermo de la Rada, patriarch of the Mexican aristocratic family that has lost most of its wealth and fiercely clings to its social status. Needing money to maintain the family's social position, Guillermo invites the Farads to the family hacienda in the hope of encouraging a relationship between Selim (Jalil's son) and his daughter (Marta). Meanwhile, Marta's aunt and uncle scheme to have her marry Billy, a member of their own social class. Encouraged by Guillermo's invitation, Jalil desperately wants to impress this aristocratic family for his son. However, throughout the visit, Jalil and Suad break societal rules. For example, they wear over-the-top clothing: Jalil appears in a tuxedo with coattails, while the other men are in open shirts and blazers, and Suad wears dangling earrings and heavy eye makeup. Selim, embarrassed by his parents, suggests that his father has perhaps overdressed, to which Jalil replies, "It is because they have no money." Jalil's comment suggests that immigrants, whatever their origin, are not above their own prejudices and can make disdainful references to their host country's inhabitants.

During this comical yet uncomfortable visit to the hacienda, the audience sees Jalil and Suad in *charro* outfits (which typically include a sombrero, a silver-trimmed bolero jacket, and tight trousers) trying to ride horses and entertaining their hosts by singing and dancing to an Arabic-sounding song. Selim, meanwhile, realizes that his hosts are laughing at his parents and says, "My parents, as all simple and good people, have wanted to win you over. The music of our land that you have just finished listening to is not an odd thing." Then, with the camera sweeping on Selim's face and the sound of a full orchestra, Selim begins to play the piano while singing Rimski Kórsakov's *Scherezada* in Spanish, capturing the hearts of the young women guests and, in particular, Marta.[73] Billy realizes Selim's romantic gesture and makes a snide comment about "the young Sheik" (*el joven sheik*). Meanwhile, Jalil and Suad are proud of their son and the sacrifices they have made for him.

As the romantic tension rises between Selim and Marta, he fumbles in expressing himself, and she assumes he is uninterested in her. She returns to Billy. Selim becomes withdrawn, and Jalil decides that he must act on his son's behalf. Unbeknownst to Selim, Jalil goes to Guillermo's home to ask for Marta's hand for Selim. Marta's mother, aunt, and uncle respond that she cannot marry a poor "*abonero*," "a foreigner," "a son of an Arab!" Jalil, feeling rejected, begins to experience flashbacks to his peddling days.

When Jalil returns to his spacious home full of mosaics and arches, he finds Suad and Selim eating dinner. Jalil begins to sob and tells them about what happened. At first, angry at his father for acting on his behalf and without permission, Selim denies any interest in Marta ("a frivolous woman") and is confused by his father's emotions. Suad responds, "Your pain is that of your father's and my pain . . . we are alone in the world and have each other to help one another." The scene touches on a common theme of Mexican cinema in the 1940s, that families must be strong and united, and the Farads fit this Mexican ideal.[74]

Suad decides that after Selim's lack of self-awareness and Jalil's meddling, it is time for her to save her family's happiness. She tells Jalil, "My heart of a mother tells me that something has happened to Selim and my heart never makes a mistake." In the scene that follows, Suad and Marta chat in a restaurant. Suad asks Marta to help her stop Selim from traveling to Europe. Initially, Marta says she cannot do anything but soon admits to her feelings for Selim. Sara García, often described as "the mother of Mexico"[75] and the "perfect incarnation of the Latin mother,"[76] transcends cultural boundaries and becomes "the mother of all mothers," determined, in her character of Suad, to keep her family happy and together. Despite being a foreign, Middle Eastern character, Suad embodies the mother spirit associated with the ideal Mexican family.

Although members of the Middle Eastern (and more specifically the Lebanese) community did not produce *El baisano Jalil*,[77] the film signals that Middle Easterners composed a notable part of the Mexican cultural fabric in the 1940s. The popularity of the actors Sara García and Joaquín Pardavé, both individually and as an ensemble, demonstrates that Mexican filmmakers and Filmex believed that the film's themes would resonate with Mexican audiences. To this day, when I mention the topic of *árabes* or *turcos* in Mexico, many Mexicans ask me if I know about this film because they have seen it. In my analysis, director Pardavé and producer Wallerstein, through *El baisano Jalil*, suggest that immigrants have been central to Mexico's development and that the immigrants aimed to integrate themselves into Mexico yet retain some of their ethnicity.

Ultimately, Pardavé and Wallerstein's film shows that despite Middle Eastern economic power in Mexico, the immigrants and their children faced painful discrimination. To overcome prejudice, Middle Eastern families would rely on tight family bonds to cope with daily struggles. As the Farad family pulled together as an idealized Mexican family, they also drew strength from their Arab culture, showing how foreign citizens survive in Mexican society. For instance, none of the Mexicans in *El baisano Jalil* act with the same compassion for their fellow citizens as Jalil, and many of the de la Rada family are not interested in working, as Selim is. Thus, the immigrant values of work appear to coincide with the values of the idealized Mexican family to underscore the economic and personal—if not societal—success of the Farads.

A Lebanese Mexican Elite Class

Carmen Mercedes Páez Oropeza suggests that ethnicity has sometimes been manipulated to serve class interests.[78] She argues that the Lebanese "clubs and casinos constructed more a show of class than of an ethnic group."[79] Interestingly, stratification among Lebanese on economic grounds also existed in twentieth-century West Africa.[80] The Lebanese Mexican colony often dismissed poorer Middle Easterners in order to create and celebrate a history of wealthy Lebanese profiting in Mexico. While the Mexican government gave Middle Easterners the opportunity to naturalize as Mexican citizens in the 1930s, as a community they reestablished explicit ethnic ties to advance their foreign citizenship in Mexico.

In particular, the community stressed the notion of Lebaneseness, which became the basis of the Centro Libanés, founded in 1959.[81] The planning of the Centro, however, had actually begun in 1941.[82] During the development process, the Syrian community hoped to join efforts with the Lebanese by making significant monetary contributions. In exchange, they asked to have the club named *sirio-libanés*. However, the Lebanese community members who were involved did not want to attach "Syro" to the Centro's name because they wanted to establish a Lebanese-only club; they subsequently rejected any Syrian donations.[83] The Lebanese's ability to refuse such funds was in part due to their own wealth and not necessarily a reflection of widespread tensions between Lebanese and Syrians in Mexico. Rather, as Martha Díaz de Kuri notes in contrast, "there is a good number of integrated families in which the mother is Syrian and the father is Lebanese or vice versa."[84]

During World War II and afterward, the Mexican textile industry boomed, generating large profits, especially in Puebla. Mexican and Middle Eastern industrialists began producing all types of cotton and wool to supply the national and international demand. This, combined with their money lending, enabled many of the Lebanese Mexicans to make their fortunes and make contributions to the Centro Libanés during this period.[85]

Ironically, the self-positioning of the Lebanese was both facilitated and hindered by the Centro Libanés. The Centro, with its luxurious branches throughout Mexico, draws on the constructed Lebanese history to create the Lebanese Mexican. The Lebanese viewed themselves as economic role models for Mexicans as the country struggled to develop. Carmen Mercedes Páez Oropeza has noted that in 120 interviews with Lebanese immigrants and their descendants, only two Lebanese admitted that they lacked economic resources. The Lebanese community described those two impoverished members within their community as having less wealth and of being less competitive, less intelligent, and lazy.[86] Páez Oropeza found that her informants projected an image of themselves as being more responsible, hard-working, and capable of maintaining stable homes than Mexicans.[87] The Centro, therefore, has tended to function as an elite social club that advocates Lebanese cultural superiority.

The Unión Nacional de Jóvenes Mexicanos de Ascendencia Libanesa (JOMALI) is a youth organization affiliated with the Centro Libanés and holds annual conventions for Lebanese descendants throughout Mexico. In 1998 its conference was held in Pachuca, Hidalgo, and in 1999 in Cancun, Quintana Roo. JOMALI, founded in 1983, serves to elevate awareness of the Lebanese culture and introduce youth to *paisanos*.[88] Although it was never explicitly stated in the founding literature, JOMALI functions as a means to introduce future spouses at the same time it reproduces what it means to be Lebanese Mexican.

Today, JOMALI and the Centro Libanés are the most active organizations in Mexico that promote the Lebanese Mexican. Yet these organizations are not especially visible to the Mexican public. They tend to exclude those who have fully assimilated into Mexican society. Where are those Middle Eastern descendants outside the construct who did not attain wealth? What has happened to middle-class Middle Eastern immigrants? And what has happened to those who could never advance beyond peddling? The answer is that poor and middle-class immigrants generally did not maintain their Middle Eastern identities because survival depended on their assimilation into Mexican society.[89] Therefore, many second- and third-generation Mexicans of Middle Eastern descent now feel little or no connection to Middle Eastern cultures.

Scholar David Nicholls, in studying Middle Easterners in the Caribbean, notes, "One prominent Lebanese businessman put it like this: 'There is a terrifying division within the community on a class basis'. A young Syrian woman complained about the fate of the less wealthy: 'Certain families living in the Belmont area [of Trinidad] have gained little recognition and acceptance from the [Levantine] community at large'."[90] Middle Eastern Mexicans of lesser means are not discussed in the Lebanese community, yet they are worthy of further research.

The Lebanese Mexicans who affiliate with the Centro and JOMALI tend to accentuate their Christianity, downplaying any Muslim and Druze constituencies. This has helped them to demonstrate their "Mexicanness" among Mexicans. There are two Maronite churches in Mexico City, La Iglesia de Nuestra Señora de Balvanera, located downtown, and Nuestra Señora de Líbano, located in Coyoacán. In addition to the Maronites, the Lebanese community includes some Melkites (Byzantine-rite Catholics) and Orthodox Christians, some of whom attend Iglesia San Jorge in Colonia Roma in Mexico City.[91] Although there is a mosque in Polanco where Muslim diplomats and some recently converted Mexican Muslims pray, the Centro Libanés deemphasizes its Muslim *paisanos* who migrated to Mexico.[92] According to my analysis of 8,240 Middle Eastern immigrants who came to Mexico between 1878 and 1951, 343 were Muslim. Of the Muslim immigrants, 56 percent arrived between 1922 and 1927.[93] Roberto Marín-Guzmán and Zidane Zéraoui found 345 out of 7,533 (4.6 percent) to be Muslim and 157 to be Druzes (2.1 percent).[94] More recently, the constituency of the Muslim community has changed with the influx of Muslim immigrants from other areas of the Muslim world.[95] Yet, Muslim Lebanese are generally not members of the Centro Libanés, nor are they mentioned in the larger Mexican discourse.

The Lebanese Mexican organizations, newspapers, and churches all perpetuate the myth of uniqueness rooted in Christianity that has been part of the Lebanese Mexican self-positioning. The myth is a complement to the claim of a deep Phoenician past. Although this claim to uniqueness was a response to the discrimination directed against them, the Lebanese community has since developed a sense of foreign elitism. The sense of distinction coincides with the increased economic and social standing of the Lebanese community. Their elevated class standing enabled them to create their own identity, a Lebanese Mexican identity.[96] This Lebanese Mexican construction reflects these immigrants' economic power and their ability to maintain their position and to protect community interests.

Community scholars such as William Nimeh and Alfonso Negib Aued have written books addressing both the historical and political aspects of Lebanon, subtly stressing Lebanese superiority. Negib Aued, as editor of *Emir*, published *Historia del Líbano* in 1945 through *Emir*'s publishing house.[97] Nimeh's work also was titled *Historia del Líbano* and published in 1945; in its prologue, José Vasconcelos suggests that the Lebanese community was contributing to building Mexico's future and the cosmic race.[98] Negib Aued argued for Lebanese sovereignty in the Middle East, addressing an educated Lebanese Mexican audience seeking to clarify political stances. Nimeh's work was overall more academic, describing Lebanese history for an audience of interested Mexican and community readers. The books may have served different audiences and purposes, yet both were attempts to inform public opinion about Lebanon and the Mexican Lebanese community. It is unlikely that the books had wide circulation or ever reached those outside of the Lebanese community because they served mainly as affirmations of the significance of Lebaneseness in Mexico.

Through film, newspapers, associations, and centers, wealthy Middle Easterners successfully created a Lebanese Mexican colony drawing on a constructed Phoenician past. As these Middle Eastern immigrants and their descendants positioned themselves economically, they looked for ways to situate themselves socially. Those who had sufficient resources began reinterpreting their past and justifying their place in Mexican society. This in turn led to political positioning and increased prosperity.

Political Positioning and Economic Dominance

A brief survey of the 1940s and 1950s until the late twentieth century reveals how some Middle Eastern immigrants adapted to Mexican society and in some cases rose in economic and political prominence. Although my archival research ends with 1951, the last year the cards were kept, ethnographic studies and other community-based works offer insights into how Lebanese Mexicans have navigated their role in Mexican society into the present.

Since the early twentieth century, descendants of Middle Eastern immigrants have participated in Mexico's public sector. In 1910 the Middle Eastern community in Mexico, still subjects of the Ottoman Empire, donated to President Porfirio Díaz an Ottoman clock to commemorate Mexico's centennial. The clock can be found today at the corner of Bolívar and Venustiano Carranza Streets in Mexico City, across from the Miguel E. Abed Building.[99] Ironically at the time of this gesture, Middle Eastern immigrants experienced xenophobia at the outset of the Mexican Revolution. Many nevertheless fought with the revolutionary factions during the Mexican Revolution, while others continued to pursue commerce.

Later in the twentieth century, the children and grandchildren of these Middle Eastern immigrants became more visible in public service positions. This may be explained by the community's focus on economic success as well as the dominant role of the PRI in Mexican politics since the 1930s. By having much of the political power concentrated in the PRI and its leaders, newcomers to the field of politics could not easily enter. That said, a few descendants of Middle Eastern immigrants attained ambassadorships, others won gubernatorial elections, and a couple became cabinet members. Rodulfo Figueroa Aramoni, whose family was from Aramún and Chuayfett, Lebanon, was an ambassador to Colombia from 1987 to 1989.[100] Ricardo

Figure 6.1. Ottoman Clock, Mexico City

Villanueva Hallal, whose family was from Lebanon, has been ambassador to Saudi Arabia and Finland.[101]

In state gubernatorial races, some descendants of Middle Eastern immigrants have won elected seats. According to a preliminary examination, seven past and present governors (of thirty-one states, excluding Mexico City) are of Middle Eastern ancestry.[102] And of these seven governors, six claimed a Lebanese background. Most of these Middle Eastern politicians began serving as governors in the late 1990s or later. Their governorships illustrate that second and third generations are entering the public sphere after their immigrant parents and grandparents have become financially established. It is also interesting to note that these sons of Middle Eastern immigrants have succeeded politically in southeastern Mexico. Although the majority of legal immigrants settled in Mexico City, Veracruz, and Puebla, the prevalence of governors of Middle Eastern descent in southeastern Mexico suggests that larger numbers of undocumented immigrants may have settled in the states of Campeche, Quintana Roo, Morelos, and Oaxaca. And these Middle Easterners seem to have entered the political elite.[103]

Descendants of Middle Eastern immigrants have become cabinet members as well as governors. Fernando Rafful Miguel became Secretary of Fisheries in the 1990s,[104] and Emilio Chuayffet Chemor of Chuayffett and Chemor, Lebanon, was Secretary of the Interior from 1995 to 1998, after serving as governor of the state of Mexico from 1993 to 1995.[105] According to Zidane Zéraoui and Roberto Marín-Guzmán, five senators and four congresspeople have had Arabic names; nearly eighty Middle Easterners have entered the ranks of state government; and an additional thirty-one descendants of Middle Eastern forebears have held political positions in the various federal ministries and the Supreme Court of Justice, among others.[106] The descendants of Middle Eastern immigrants have thus begun entering the ranks of public service as well as holding critical roles in the Mexican economy.[107]

The Lebanese community's century-long evolution in Mexico formed a basis for its members' entry into Mexican political ranks in the 1980s and 1990s—and for the critical role that one Lebanese Mexican would play economically in the twenty-first century. *Forbes* reported Carlos Slim Helú as the third-wealthiest man in the world in 2006 and worth $30 billion.[108] Although the story of Slim Helú and his economic prowess are well known (and perhaps exaggerated),[109] few have questioned how much power he wields in Mexico and how he has influenced Lebanese Mexican history.

According to Philip Peters, a senior fellow at the Lexington Institute, a Virginia-based think tank that monitors regulatory agencies in Latin America, "Mexican officials often point out that [Slim Helú's] Telmex accounts for more than a fourth of the [Mexican] stock market. A ruling against the company would put the Bolsa [the Mexican stock market] at risk."[110] Although this characterization of his economic power may be somewhat inflated, Slim Helú undoubtedly influences much of the Mexican economy with his control of the telecommunications industry. "The running joke about Slim is that he began investing outside Mexico because there was nothing left to acquire inside the border." [111]

How Slim Helú has been able to consolidate his wealth so quickly can be attributed in part to his use of family resources. From the early immigrants to Carlos Slim Helú's family-run enterprises, Middle Eastern families often operate as a unified organization in weathering social, political and economic changes. [112] As a result, the ability to accumulate and concentrate wealth within the family unit has enabled some Middle Eastern families to be self-employed. It has been suggested that Slim Helú's wealth was greatly increased during the PRI-led Carlos Salinas de Gortari presidential administration when Telmex stock was sold to Slim Helú at deflated market value. Accordingly, Carlos Salinas' brother Raúl was particularly well compensated for this transaction. [113] The exact details of this business deal are rather speculative and need further exploration.

Slim Helú has carefully drawn on his Mexicanness while simultaneously funding the creation of Lebanese centers throughout Mexico. The history of Slim Helú and his family parallels the smaller-scale histories of a few Middle Easterners in Mexico who have achieved economic prominence while successfully positioning their social and cultural acceptance and ultimately their citizenship in the Mexican nation. His cousin Alfredo Harp Helú also resides on the list of the world's wealthiest, with $1.8 billion associated with his interest in Banamex. [114]

Finally, the history of Middle Eastern immigrant positioning implicates dynamics of gender and the contributions of women. Slim Helú's late wife, Soumaya Domit Gemayel, was the niece of Amin Gemayel, ex-president of Lebanon and helped solidify the Lebanese cultural ties of the family. Intermarrying within the community also has been important for both socioeconomic and political reasons.

Constructing a Lebanese Identity

The economic, social, and political positioning of Middle Eastern immigrants in Mexico corresponds to their construction of a Lebanese identity by which to relate to one another and to Mexicans. In Lebanon, identity has tended to be associated with villages and religious affiliations. Shi'ites, Sunnis, and Druzes from Lebanon have often called themselves "Arabs," while those of Maronite or Orthodox backgrounds have called themselves "Lebanese" or "Phoenicians." [115] Maronite communities both in Mexico and Lebanon have largely constructed what it means to be "Lebanese" in

Mexico. Maronites have often asserted that their Phoenician ancestry gave them their enterprising talents to make a profit in Mexican society.

Historically, demographic changes caused great disparities between Lebanese Christians and Muslims during the nineteenth century in Mount Lebanon,[116] and these differences became more pronounced in the 1920s when the Maronites, helped by France, established Greater Lebanon within the French Mandate of Syria. Many of the Middle Eastern immigrants looked to this 1920s period as part of an idealized past that they sought to replicate in Mexico. However, as Meir Zamir comments, the Maronites' dominant position was eroded during the Lebanese civil war:

> The Maronites, who considered themselves to be the founders of the Lebanese state, assumed the role of guardians of its independence, sovereignty, and Christian character. They demanded and secured for themselves a preeminent position in its political and administrative systems and in the armed forces, initially with French assistance during the Mandate, and later after independence, when they exploited the National Pact of 1943 to retain and even enhance their privileged status. They not only controlled the presidency but also secured the position of commander-in-chief of the army and head of the judicial system. Indeed, their share in the administration was much greater than their proportion in the general population, and they took advantage of their dominance and access to state institutions to increase their power and wealth.[117]

The construction of a Lebanese identity in Mexico has drawn on the strong links between the Maronites and the French. As with the Mexican tradition of looking to European—in particular to French—origins and traditions for cultural legitimation, these twentieth-century "Lebanese" Mexicans have promoted themselves as the saviors to Mexican underdevelopment. The Maronites' close affinity with the French probably caused some of the Middle Eastern immigrants to position themselves as members of this "desirable" culture. As Zamir continues, "The Maronites determined Lebanon's national identity, which distinguished it from Syria and the rest of the Arab world."[118] This notion of promoting a Christian Lebanese identity was extended to communities located throughout the world, and the World Maronite Union was established in the late 1970s. The First World Congress of the Maronite Union met in Mexico City in February 1979.[119] Although many Maronites met to celebrate their transnational identity, their dominance in Lebanon began to unravel in 1975 with the Lebanese civil war. Many Muslim Lebanese blamed the Maronite leadership for

Lebanon's ills, and the war lasted nearly twenty years, ending in 1991. In October 1989 the Ta'if Agreement forced Maronites to make many political concessions, stipulating among its provisions that Christians and Muslims be equally represented in the Lebanese Parliament. Zamir notes: "Whatever the future holds for the Maronites, Christian Lebanon under the Maronite hegemony, which had existed until 1975, is a thing of the past." [120]

Meanwhile, Lebanese Mexicans have distanced themselves from Middle Eastern immigrants of Muslim and Druze background and implicitly asserted that Lebaneseness, in positive connotations, is equivalent to being Maronite. Many members in the Lebanese Mexican community note their Phoenician roots and strong work ethic to explain why they have succeeded. Other Mexicans discreetly imply that immoral business practices have enabled these foreign peddlers to take advantage of Mexican goodwill and make large profits. Apart from these explanations, the breadth of Mexicanness—who can belong to the Mexican nation—enables this immigrant group to position themselves in Mexican society and attain influence. How this immigrant group had acquired power by the latter part of the twentieth century can also be explained by the tradition of having foreign merchants working in Mexico as well as by Mexican historical events such as the Mexican Revolution.

Concluding Comments

The immigrants' principal drive to make profits led them also to promote their acceptance into Mexican society. The desire to improve their well-being required them to market themselves as legitimate forces in Mexican society. As consumers, Mexicans tended to buy from trusted sources with reliable products, so the newly arrived immigrants immediately began a process to establish themselves as a trusted part of the Mexican economic infrastructure. The Mexican tradition of immigrant merchants allowed Middle Easterners to become entrepreneurs. These immigrants began as peddlers selling to *campesinos* and indigenous populations. Therefore, unlike previous foreign merchants, early Middle Eastern immigrants targeted the poorer, traditionally marginalized consumer classes. With the profits they would earn, the immigrants originally planned to return home as wealthy men and women.

Instead, the immigrants settled in Mexico and constructed their community by promulgating an idealized version of Lebaneseness that emphasized the Christian and European linkages. As they watched events in the

Middle East unfold in the twentieth century, some resolved to maintain their culture. The immigrants' identities tended to be complex, constantly changing and evolving. The fungibility—the relational and contextual use of identity—of *mexicanidad* has enabled the community to draw on a sense of foreign elitism, yet it has also differentiated them from their Lebanese counterparts living in the Middle East.

A further complication has been the regional differences in Mexico, for to be Lebanese in the Yucatán has been very different than being Lebanese in the Laguna or in Mexico City. According to a Lebanese immigrant living in Mexico City in 1999, "Most of them [those at the Centro Libanés] . . . were racist against Muslims." He felt that the Centro was full of Maronite Lebanese "who measure people by their wealth, who [are] very arrogant against Mexicans. They felt superior to Mexicans." He continued, "You can't compare these Lebanese with the Lebanese in Lebanon." The Lebanese community in Mexico was perceived as trying to "exclude themselves" and to claim Arab characteristics when convenient. Within the Mexican context, they were accused of being "opportunists."[121] This disjunction between recent Lebanese immigrants and the descendants of earlier Middle Eastern immigrants exemplifies how the construction of Lebaneseness has been created by a Mexican myth of uniqueness wherein the second and third generations blended the real and the imaginary, thereby fashioning a hybrid Lebanese Mexican community.

The accuracy of the immigrant history becomes less significant when we examine how Lebaneseness extends into the Americas. The Middle Easterners' sense of belonging extended to two, three, or four homelands simultaneously. Currently, a larger "American Arab" identity or "Lebanese American" identity seems to pervade the Middle Eastern immigrant community in Mexico, in which a sense of "transnationalism" ties immigrants and their descendents to relatives in Mexico, Brazil, and Argentina. For example, in the case of the Abusaid family, one of Juan's sisters migrated to Bogotá, Colombia, and her family started a textile factory. Juan's other sister settled in Tucumán, Argentina. Both sisters came to Torreón, Mexico, and visited Juan. But ultimately, it is the economic ties and their pursuit of profit that has helped define Middle Eastern immigrants. In Mexico, "Arab immigration is a marvelous example of the economic life in Mexico."[122] Mexico's economic opportunities have clearly enabled Middle Eastern immigrants to position themselves between Mexican society and their own constructed Lebanese community, to become foreign citizens.

CHAPTER 7

Conclusion

Meanings of Multiculturalism

D
uring the reign of President Porfirio Díaz, it was said: "Mexico, mother of foreigners and stepmother of Mexicans."[1] By interpreting this metaphor with regard to Middle Eastern immigrants, they can be seen as both the children and stepchildren of the Mexican nation. Assuming that their father is a foreign country and their mother is Mexico, the children born to Middle Eastern immigrants remain foreign, their citizenship deriving from their father in early-twentieth-century Mexican law.[2] Middle Eastern immigrants can also be described as stepchildren of the foreign father, whereby the father had an additional, prior, or perhaps even an adulterous relationship with a foreigner. This interpretation becomes particularly salient after 1934 (the post-revolutionary period) when children would obtain Mexican citizenship by *juis soli,* meaning the place of birth determines citizenship. These offspring could thus be deemed stepchildren of Mexico.

In describing the foreign citizens in France of the seventeenth and early eighteenth centuries under Louis XIV, Peter Sahlins notes, "The mixed metaphor of the fatherland as mother was, in fact, the complement of the widespread tropes in legal and political thought that identified the king as 'father' and considered naturalized foreigners as 'adopted children.'"[3] Applied to Mexico, the notion that foreigners can be adopted children of the nation and therefore explicitly and legitimately part of the Mexican family amplifies the meaning of *mexicanidad.* Middle Eastern immigrants, as both children and stepchildren of Mexico, provided necessary skills and labor to help the "family" develop and prosper. In subsequent generations, by building on Mexico's foreign tradition, elite Middle Eastern immigrants have both integrated into the Mexican nation and created their own communities, while other Middle Easterners have acculturated to join the *mestizo* nation.

Middle Easterners are part of the Mexican cultural landscape and belong to the Mexican nation. Since the Porfiriato, post-revolutionary regimes have adopted contradictory attitudes toward immigrants. Municipal governments, on the one hand, have often benefited from the Middle Eastern merchants' activities and *abono* system of payment; on the other hand, national policy makers have often adopted an anti-immigrant discourse and advocated a Mexico for Mexicans based on the *mestizo* construct. Mexican citizens often resented Middle Eastern entrepreneurial successes and wrote letters of complaint about the immigrants' business practices.

The post-revolutionary construction of the *mestizo* was in large part based on the ideas of intellectuals such as Justo Sierra, Andrés Molina Enríquez, and José Vasconcelos who suggested that the lack of ethnic integration was at the root of many of Mexico's problems. They advocated a type of ethnic unity—arguably homogeneity—to integrate the divided Mexico. By encouraging individual groups to lose their distinctive characteristics and become *mestizo*, different groups could become part of the Mexican nation. In promoting *mestizaje* as the basis of being Mexican, the *mestizo* construction aimed to diminish the role of foreigners and the indigenous, thereby limiting ethnocultural plurality and allowing for a hegemonic discourse. Despite the intellectuals' attempts to construct a monolithic Mexico, the Mexican populace, including diverse immigrants, developed into a pluralistic society that has allowed many ways of being Mexican.

Consider an episode of a popular Mexican *telenovela* that showed a heroine whispering to her friends as they left a Middle Eastern merchant's apartment, "The Turk is cheap."[4] The Middle Eastern merchant sports a comically bushy mustache with the ends twisted up and has a large, hooked nose. This character is not particularly important to the story line; yet, he appears in the soap opera with his oversized nose and cartoonish mustache trying to swindle Mexican women, a stereotypical Middle Eastern presence in Mexican popular culture.

The story of Middle Eastern immigrants arriving at the end of the nineteenth century and becoming peddlers and merchants in the twentieth century illuminates a neglected aspect of Mexican history. As the Mexican nation evolved from the Porfiriato to the regime of Lázaro Cárdenas, the treatment of Middle Eastern immigrants fluctuated. While immigrants encountered a mixed reception in Mexico, events in the Levant caused many Middle Easterners to settle permanently in Mexico. After World War I, the Ottoman Empire lost its power in the Levant, and the French took over. In 1943 and 1946, Lebanon and Syria, respectively, were declared independent states.

Against this backdrop of political change, Middle Eastern immigrants found an environment in which their network enabled them to settle in Mexico or continue migration to the United States and in many cases to make a profit. Their settlement entailed acculturating in multiple ways, depending on their economic and social positions. Some identify themselves as Mexicans, as does my *tío-abuelo,* while others such as Carlos Slim Helú identify with being Lebanese Mexican, and still others identify with being Arab.

The diversity of this immigrant population offers new ways to conceptualize the Mexican nation as tolerating ethnic difference. It suggests that Mexicanness is anything but monolithic. The influx of Lebanese, Syrians, "Arabs" (again, whether Saudi Arabians or other immigrants who self-identified as "Arabs"), Egyptians, Iraqis, Persians, Jordanians, Palestinians, and Arab Jews suggests an alternative to the notion that only the Lebanese came to Mexico and that Lebanese Mexicans quickly positioned themselves to dominate Mexico. Rather, the data have shown that Middle Eastern immigrants were from all parts of the Middle East and of various religious orientations and that all encountered challenges in joining the Mexican nation.

The multicultural aspects of Mexicanness have roots in the Mexican foreign tradition, which dates back to the Spanish Conquest and continues to the present. The foreign citizen paradigm allows some outsiders to maintain multiple identities in Mexico while becoming citizens. The process of joining the Mexican nation has also enabled wealthy Middle Eastern Mexicans to position themselves politically and economically in Mexican society. Those Middle Eastern Mexicans who did not attain great economic fortunes were not able to participate in the Lebanese historical construction. Rather, these lower- and middle-class Middle Eastern Mexicans became absorbed into the *mestizo* discourse and saw themselves primarily as Mexicans.

How the Mexican national discourse has evolved reflects the changes in Mexican identities and the instability of the categories of legal and political personhood, nationality, and ethnicity generally. The categories of *turco, árabe, sirio-libanés,* and *libanés* reflect the dynamics of Middle Eastern politics, the historical imagination, and the changing Mexican discourse of what is Mexican and who can belong to the nation. Middle Eastern immigration to Mexico in the late nineteenth and early twentieth centuries sheds light on how one immigrant group played a pivotal role in revolutionary Mexico. The immigrants' early roles as merchants later enabled some of them to become economic and political leaders in present-day Mexico.

Turco sojourners left the Middle East because of political instability, increased competition in the Levant economy, and religious tensions. At that time, Porfirian development initiatives drew some immigrants to Mexico, and others sought easier entrance into the United States through Mexico. The analysis of immigrant registration cards and immigrant histories reveals that the majority of immigrants came from Lebanon and Syria and settled throughout Mexico. Middle Eastern immigrant networks that gave them money and information greatly facilitated their migration experiences. The early sojourners' network also provided an infrastructure that enabled Middle Easterners to continue with commercial activities during the chaos of the Mexican Revolution. Middle Eastern immigrants often provided food and arms to Villa and Zapata by using their ability to cross into the United States to obtain goods. While the rest of the country was fighting, these and other Middle Eastern immigrants and their descendants were able to amass large profits. At the same time, the immigrants faced great risks from anti-foreign sentiments and revolutionary violence.

After the violent decade of the Revolution, Middle Eastern immigrants continued migrating, with nearly 50 percent of the study sample (1878–1951) coming to Mexico in the 1920s. Mexican citizens became increasingly uncomfortable with the immigrants' presence and commercial practices. As Mexicans voiced their opposition to the Middle Eastern immigrants, wealthy Middle Eastern families became more unified, consolidating their economic enterprises with more kinship ties.

Economic hardship led to more anti-foreign policies during the Depression. This can be attributed both to the larger numbers of immigrants who had arrived in the 1920s and to a Mexican citizenry demanding help from the federal government in times of crisis. Complaints against Middle Easterners came in the form of letters from citizens, chambers of commerce, and state governments. While Middle Eastern immigration decreased in the 1930s, Mexico was a nation searching for a way to handle its immigrant populations in the midst of economic, social, and political change. For although Mexican citizens excluded Middle Easterners from the mainstream, Mexicans thus helped establish Middle Easterners as "foreigners," which in turn became a point of differentiation for elite Lebanese Mexicans.

In the Laguna region, immigrants fulfilled specific needs of the northern Mexican economy. Immigrant testimonies showed the tensions between *laguneros* and immigrants as well as the Middle Easterners' continuous economic positioning for themselves. Although the Laguna's economic demands during and after the Revolution drove many immigrants to risk their lives in an effort to succeed financially, Mexican historiography has given little attention to their mercantile activities. Instead, regional documents combined with immigrant narratives downplay anti-Arab attitudes expressed to federal authorities and portray the Middle Eastern community as overcoming Mexican economic difficulties.

Speaking more broadly, Middle Eastern immigrants have positioned themselves between Mexican society and their own ethnic groups within the Middle Eastern community. Their identities have been largely rooted in their economic roles of realizing profits, especially during conflict. While profiting, Middle Eastern immigrants sought to define themselves in relation to events in the Middle East and in Mexico. In response to Mexican nation building, the immigrants aimed to unite themselves and perpetuate their foreignness. The construction of the Lebanese community created a hegemonic voice for those of Middle Eastern descent with money in Mexico. Middle Eastern immigrants and their descendants with few economic resources have been absorbed into the *mestizo* Mexican construction, thus contributing to a history that tends to ignore the diversity of the immigrants and their contradictory reception in Mexico.

The examination of Middle Eastern immigrant registration, immigrant testimony, and government letters challenges the Lebanese Mexican historical construction and the notion of a monolithic *mestizo* nation. Middle Easterners have simultaneously acculturated into Mexican culture, adding to the diversity of *mestizaje,* and become foreign citizens. Their presence therefore implicates a Mexican multiculturalism. This multiculturalism appears in the ways in which Middle Eastern immigrants have successfully positioned their ambivalent role in Mexican society by exploiting conflictual moments and building on the Mexican tradition of immigrant entrepreneurship. It is perhaps best captured in a 1936 editorial in the Palestinian-Lebanese magazine *Palmira* that quoted a Mexican immigration official as saying:

> It is among those peoples (referring to Syrians, Lebanese, etc.) whom we can find the sons who are proud to be Mexicans. Not with that Mexicanism of our drunkards nor that shouted by our agitators. We know full well that the citizens coming from prosperous, rich and glorious countries come to us as if they were doing us a favor with their presence. On the other hand, the others, those who come from lowly countries, come here with the desire to honorably deserve to be taken as Mexicans.[5]

This study has revealed a Mexican multiculturalism by examining how Middle Eastern immigrants and their descendants have become Mexican citizens and how they have created their own Lebaneseness. If scholars

Figure 7.1. Statue of Emigrant, Beirut

begin to include Middle Eastern immigrants and other ethnic groups in explorations of Mexican history, new questions arise as to what it means to
be Mexican. If Mexicans can be seen as ethnically and culturally diverse,
then scholars may also need to reexamine who are the Mexican immigrants
coming to the United States. These questions challenge current understand-
ings of Mexican migration and integration into North American society.
Are immigrants from Mexico "Mexican," or are they, for example, Lebanese Mexican, Chinese Mexican, or Zapotec Mexican? What significance

do these categories command? Given the fluidity of the U.S.-Mexican border, how does one identify these individuals and their contributions from such diverse backgrounds? How do scholars begin to meaningfully differentiate between Mexicans and Mexican Americans in the United States? Such questions, derived from the historical experiences of Middle Eastern and other immigrants to Mexico, underscore the complexity of twentieth-century constructions of the Mexican nation and *mexicanidad*.

Postscript

As I mentioned in the introduction, I traveled to Lebanon and Syria in June 2004. Upon arrival, I learned that the Lebanese community in Mexico had donated a statue to the Lebanese government in October 2003. This statue of a nineteenth-century immigrant towers over bustling traffic on Avenue Charles Helou in Beirut (East Beirut, as it was referred to during the Lebanese civil war). His eyes look out toward the port, the Mediterranean Sea, the Atlantic Ocean, and beyond. The emigrant appears Middle Eastern in dress, yet he is a gift from Mexico. As I looked at the statue, I reflected on how far Middle Eastern women and men had traveled to improve their lives, finding both success and failure and often feeling very far from their "Allah." The Centro Libanés proudly displays the immigrant statue on its Website, and the Mexican government has issued a postage stamp bearing a similar image to commemorate "125 Years of Lebanese Presence in Mexico." They show how close Middle Eastern immigrants have come to Mexico.

APPENDIX: TABLES

Table 1. Middle Eastern Immigrants and Resident Foreign Nationals in Mexico, by Source of Documentation

	Mexican Census		Mexican Immigrant Registration Cards[c]	
Year	Birthplace[a] N	Nationality[b] N	Years	N
1895	470	457	1878-1899	166
1900	768	647	1900-1909	2,111
1910	4,518	4,508	1910-1919	919
1921	10,516	5,973	1920-1929	3,657
1930	9,879	15,139	1930-1939	585
1940	Not available	4,984	1940-1951	598
1950	6,753	4,167		

[a] Delia Salazar Anaya, *La población extranjera en México (1895-1990): Un recuento con base en los Censos Generales de Población* (Mexico City: Instituto Nacional de Antropología e Historia [INAH], 1996), 105-106. The data used to construct this column are based on the Mexican census takers' questions on place of birth. I used Saudi Arabia, Lebanon, Syria, Palestine, Turkey, Iran, Egypt, and Morocco to calculate this column.
[b] Ibid., 297-298. I used Arab, Lebanese, Palestinian, Iranian, Syrian, and Turkish nationalities to calculate this column.
[c] Author's calculations from the National Registry of Foreigners, Departamento de Migración (DM), 1926-1951, Archivo General de la Nación (AGN), Mexico City. The archive dates from 1926 to 1951, the years the Mexican government required immigrant registration, and includes information on immigrants who entered Mexico before 1926 as well.

Table 2. Middle Eastern Immigrants and Resident Foreign Nationals in Mexico, by Nationality and Sex

Nationality	1878–1909 N	1878–1909 %	1910–1919 N	1910–1919 %	1920–1929 N	1920–1929 %	1930–1939 N	1930–1939 %	1940–1951 N	1940–1951 %
Lebanese										
Male	953		303		1,009		218		195	
Female	650		187		576		117		140	
Subtotal	1,613	70.84	490	53.32	1,585	43.34	335	57.26	335	56.02
Syro-Lebanese										
Male	180		69		311		32		3	
Female	93		33		99		17		2	
Subtotal	273	11.99	102	11.10	410	11.21	49	8.38	5	0.84
Syrian										
Male	137		107		632		75		121	
Female	48		69		315		53		77	
Subtotal	185	8.12	176	19.15	947	25.90	128	21.88	198	33.11
Arab										
Male	111		81		345		29		13	
Female	53		54		284		17		11	
Subtotal	164	7.20	135	14.69	629	17.20	46	7.86	24	4.01
Egyptian										
Male	3		3		18		0		7	
Female	1		4		8		7		10	
Subtotal	4	0.18	7	0.76	26	0.71	7	1.20	17	2.84
Palestinian										
Male	1									
Female	2									
Subtotal	3	0.13								
Iraqi										
Male	2		1		10		5		6	
Female	0		0		3		4		1	
Subtotal	2	0.08	1	0.11	13	0.36	9	1.54	7	1.17
Turkish										
Male	2									
Female	0									
Subtotal	2	0.08								
Armenian										
Male					4					
Female					2					
Subtotal					6	0.16				

Table 2. Continued

Nationality	1878–1909 N	%	1910–1919 N	%	1920–1929 N	%	1930–1939 N	%	1940–1951 N	%
Transjordanian										
Male							1			
Female							0			
Subtotal							1	0.17		
Ottoman										
Male					1					
Female					0					
Subtotal					1	0.03				
Persian										
Male					2					
Female					0					
Subtotal					2	0.05				
British										
Male									3	
Female									1	
Subtotal									4	0.67
North American										
Male									3	
Female									0	
Subtotal									3	0.50
By Marriage (Female)										
Lebanese	13				4		3			
Syro-Lebanese	2				1					
Syrian	3		1		2					
Other					1		1			
Total	18	0.79	1	0.11	9	0.25	4	0.68		
Not available	13	0.57	7	0.76	29	0.79	6	1.03	5	0.84
Total	2,277	99.98	919	100.00	3,657	100.0	585	100.00	598	100.00

Source: Author's calculations from National Registry of Foreigners, DM (1926–1951), AGN.

Table 3. Lebanese-Born Immigrants and Resident Foreign Nationals in Mexico, by City/Town of Birth

City/Town	1878–1909 N	1878–1909 %	1910–1919 N	1910–1919 %	1920–1929 N	1920–1929 %	1930–1939 N	1930–1939 %	1940–1951 N	1940–1951 %
Beirut	156	12.8	78	13.4	248	12.40	39	10.60	39	11.10
Bikfaya (Bakafra)	67	5.5								
Tripoli	61	5.0	22	3.8	126	6.30	15	4.07	12	3.41
Monte Lebanon	58	4.8	23	3.9	89	4.40	8	2.17		
Tannourine	42	3.5							6	1.70
Kartaba	24	2.0	13	2.2						
Zgharta	22	1.8	23	3.9	64	3.20	13	3.53	15	4.26
Jounieh	21	1.7								
Nabatiyeh	19	1.6			28	1.40				
Saida	19	1.6					6	1.60		
Jezzine			12	2.0			8	2.17	13	3.69
Jounieh			12	2.0						
Deir el Qammar			12	2.0	25	1.25				
Beiteddine			11	1.9						
Bacassin			11	1.9						
Beit Mellat					27	1.35	16	4.35		
Douma					26	1.30			7	1.99
Kartaba					26	1.30			6	1.70
Batroun					24	1.20	10	2.72	11	3.13
Saida					23	1.15				
Salima					23	1.15				
Braachit					22	1.10				
Sarba					21	1.05				
Meniara							11	2.99		
Shouaifat									8	2.27
Bhamdoun									6	1.70
Ghazir									6	1.70
City/town with fewer than x emigrants	727	59.7	367	63.0	1,189	59.40	242	65.80	223	63.35
	x = 17		x = 10		x = 20		x = 5		x = 5	
Total	1,216	100.0	584	100.0	2,002	100.00	368	100.00	352	100.00

Source: Author's calculations from National Registry of Foreigners, DM (1926–1951), AGN.

Table 4. Syrian-Born Immigrants and Resident Foreign Nationals in Mexico, by City/Town of Birth

City/Town	1878–1909		1910–1919		1920–1929		1930–1939		1940–1951	
	N	%	N	%	N	%	N	%	N	%
Damascus	42	22.7	42	22.7	299	25.0	28	19.6	37	19.1
Aleppo	18	9.7	18	9.7	432	35.0	54	37.8	97	50.0
Homs	16	8.6	16	8.6	73	6.0	9	6.3	14	7.2
Lattakia	7	3.8	7	3.8	13	1.0				
Hama	6	3.2	6	3.2						
Safita					10	1.0				
City/town with fewer than x emigrants	96	52.0	96	52.0	395	32.0	52	36.3	46	23.7
	x = 5		x = 5		x = 9		x = 2		x = 2	
Total	185	100.0	185	100.0	1,222	100.0	143	100.0	194	100.0

Source: Author's calculations from National Registry of Foreigners, DM (1926–1951), AGN.

Table 5. Middle Eastern Immigrants and Resident Foreign Nationals in Mexico, by Country of Birth

Country of Birth	1878–1909 N	1878–1909 %	1910–1919 N	1910–1919 %	1920–1929 N	1920–1929 %	1930–1939 N	1930–1939 %	1940–1951 N	1940–1951 %
Lebanon	1,216	53.40	584	63.55	2,002	54.74	368	62.91	352	58.86
Syria	185	8.12	237	25.78	1,222	33.42	143	24.44	194	32.44
Arabia	12	0.53	8	0.87	57	1.56	3	0.51	3	0.50
Egypt	6	0.26	12	1.31	31	0.85	9	1.54	9	1.50
Iraq	3	0.13	7	0.87	56	1.53	10	1.71	9	1.50
Palestine	2	0.09	1	0.11	7	0.19			1	0.17
Turkey	2	0.09	4	0.44	38	1.04	8	1.37	4	0.67
Transjordan (Jordan)	1	0.04			23	0.63	3	0.51	2	0.34
Iran					4	0.11	1	0.17		
Armenia					2	0.05				
North and South American Countries	15	0.66	20	2.18	39	1.07	8	1.37		
European Countries	5	0.22	1	0.11	3	0.08	3	0.51	11	1.84
Not available	71	3.12	40	4.35	157	4.29	11	1.88	4	0.67
Born in Mexico	759	33.33	5	0.54	16	0.44	18	3.08	7	1.17
Total	2,277	99.99	919	100.00	3,657	100.00	585	100.00	598	100.00

Source: Author's calculations from National Registry of Foreigners, DM (1926–1951), AGN.

Table 6. Middle Eastern Immigrants and Resident Foreign Nationals in Mexico, by Religion and Sex

Religion	1878–1909 N	1878–1909 %	1910–1919 N	1910–1919 %	1920–1929 N	1920–1929 %	1930–1939 N	1930–1939 %	1940–1951 N	1940–1951 %
Catholic										
Male	1,145		372		1,215		162		161	
Female	810		254		725		101		111	
Subtotal	1,955	85.86	626	68.12	1,940	53.05	263	44.96	272	45.48
Jewish										
Male	51		101		557		52		109	
Female	24		70		403		61		73	
Subtotal	75	3.30	171	18.61	960	26.25	113	19.32	182	30.43

Table 6. Continued

Religion	1878–1909 N	%	1910–1919 N	%	1920–1929 N	%	1930–1939 N	%	1940–1951 N	%
Orthodox										
Male	53		32		148		58		22	
Female	18		18		89		21		18	
Subtotal	71	3.12	50	5.44	237	6.48	79	13.50	40	6.70
Maronite										
Male							27		14	
Female							14		15	
Subtotal							41	7.01	29	4.85
Muslim										
Male	47		25		191		21		16	
Female	4		2		23		3		7	
Subtotal	51	2.24	27	2.94	214	5.85	24	4.10	23	3.85
None										
Male	34		13		41		4		4	
Female	5		2		4		1		1	
Subtotal	39	1.71	15	1.63	45	1.23	5	0.85	5	0.84
Free Thinker										
Male	20		7							
Female	0		0							
Subtotal	20	0.88	7	0.76						
Druze										
Male	15		9		81		24		10	
Female	0		0		8		7		4	
Subtotal	15	0.66	9	0.98	88	2.41	31	5.30	14	2.34
Romanist										
Male					29					
Female					18					
Subtotal					47	1.29				
Other	38	1.66	8	0.87	98	2.68	26	4.44	21	3.51
Not available	13	0.57	6	0.65	28	0.76	3	0.51	12	2.00
Total	2,277	100.00	919	100.00	3,657	100.00	585	99.99	598	100.00

Source: Author's calculations from National Registry of Foreigners, DM (1926–1951), AGN.

Table 7. Middle Eastern Immigrants and Resident Foreign Nationals in Mexico, by State of Residence in Mexico

State	1878–1909 N	1878–1909 %	1910–1919 N	1910–1919 %	1920–1929 N	1920–1929 %	1930–1939 N	1930–1939 %	1940–1951 N	1940–1951 %
Aguascalientes	16	0.70	7	0.76	24	0.66	1	0.17	0	0
Baja California	11	0.48	2	0.22	12	0.33	5	0.86	1	0.17
Campeche	40	1.76	17	1.85	19	0.52	1	0.17	1	0.17
Chiapas	28	1.23	19	2.07	44	1.20	2	0.34	1	0.17
Chihuahua	132	5.80	36	3.92	128	3.50	19	3.25	4	0.67
Coahuila	107	4.70	16	1.74	163	4.45	16	2.74	2	0.33
Colima	5	0.22	0	0	7	0.19	1	0.17	0	0
Distrito Federal	494	21.70	348	37.86	1,792	49.00	291	49.74	108	18.06
Durango	113	4.96	20	2.18	78	2.13	6	1.03	0	0
Guanajuato	11	0.48	7	0.76	20	0.55	2	0.34	0	0
Guerrero	30	1.31	10	1.09	22	0.60	3	0.51	0	0
Hidalgo	50	2.20	22	2.39	45	1.23	4	0.68	0	0
Jalisco	26	1.14	6	0.65	46	1.26	4	0.68	6	1.00
Mexico	43	1.89	12	1.31	47	1.29	7	1.20	0	0
Michoacán	58	2.55	14	1.52	25	0.68	2	0.34	0	0
Morelos	36	1.58	7	0.76	11	0.30	0	0	0	0
Nayarit	25	1.09	3	0.33	18	0.49	3	0.51	0	0
Nuevo León	72	3.16	25	2.72	89	2.43	18	3.08	6	1.00
Oaxaca	40	1.76	27	2.94	79	2.16	10	1.71	0	0
Puebla	230	10.10	54	5.88	146	3.99	24	4.10	1	0.17
Querétaro	21	0.92	3	0.33	17	0.46	0	0	0	0
Quintana Roo			1	0.11	1	0.03	0	0	0	0
San Luis Potosí	67	2.94	16	1.74	88	2.40	7	1.20	0	0
Sinaloa	14	0.60	8	0.87	47	1.29	4	0.68	0	0
Sonora	8	0.35	1	0.11	12	0.33	3	0.51	0	0
Tabasco	9	0.40	6	0.65	7	0.19	0	0	0	0
Tamaulipas	58	2.54	43	4.68	137	3.75	7	1.20	3	0.50
Tlaxcala	12	0.53	4	0.44	11	0.30	0	0	0	0
Veracruz	347	15.24	117	12.72	298	8.15	26	4.44	11	1.84
Yucatán	111	4.87	59	6.42	101	2.76	16	2.74	4	0.67
Zacatecas	50	2.20	7	0.76	31	0.85	1	0.17	0	0
Not available	14	0.60	2	0.22	92	2.52	102	17.43	450	75.25
Total	2,277	100.00	919	100.00	3,657	99.99	585	99.99	598	100.00

Source: Author's calculations from National Registry of Foreigners, DM (1926–1951), AGN.

Table 8. Middle Eastern Immigrants and Resident Foreign Nationals in Mexico, by Occupation and Sex

Occupation	1878–1909 N	%	1910–1919 N	%	1920–1929 N	%	1930–1939 N	%	1940–1951 N	%
In Commerce										
Merchants										
Male	853		428		1,698		217		241	
Female	69		43		64		2		8	
Subtotal	922	40.49	471	51.25	1,762	48.18	219	37.43	249	41.64
Peddlers										
Male	29		17		107		11		3	
Female	3		0		3		0		0	
Subtotal	32	1.40	17	1.85	110	3.01	11	1.88	3	0.50
Clothing Merchants										
Male	31		15		65		18		2	
Female	6		0		2		0		0	
Subtotal	37	1.62	15	1.63	67	1.83	18	3.08	2	0.33
Property Merchants										
Male	45		13		44		8		9	
Female	7		1		3		3		0	
Subtotal	52	2.28	14	1.52	47	1.29	11	1.88	9	1.51
Employees in Commerce										
Male	23		4		21		4			
Female	4		0		2		0			
Subtotal	27	1.19	4	0.44	23	0.63	4	0.68		
Other Commerce										
Male					15					
Female					0					
Subtotal					15	0.41				
Subtotal in										
Commerce	1,070	46.99	521	56.69	2,024	55.35	263	44.95	263	43.98
Homemakers										
Male	16		7		21		2		5	
Female	718		300		1,160		202		220	
Subtotal	734	32.24	307	33.40	1,181	32.29	204	34.87	225	37.63
Employees in Unspecified Sectors										
Male	77		12		77		6		5	
Female	9		0		18		0		2	
Subtotal	86	3.78	12	1.31	95	2.60	6	1.02	7	1.17

Table 8. Continued

	1878–1909		1910–1919		1920–1929		1930–1939		1940–1951	
Occupation	N	%	N	%	N	%	N	%	N	%
Employees in Specified Sectors[a]										
Male	10		4		7					
Female	0		0		0					
Subtotal	10	0.44	4	0.44	7	0.19				
Farmers										
Male	57		16		50		11		5	
Female	1		0		0		0		1	
Subtotal	58	2.55	16	1.74	50	1.37	11	1.88	6	1.00
None										
Male	21		2		17		8		2	
Female	19		0		6		1		1	
Subtotal	40	1.76	2	0.22	23	1.64	9	1.54	3	0.50
Students										
Male	67		1		46		44		18	
Female	25		0		14		7		9	
Subtotal	92	4.04	1	0.11	60	0.63	51	8.73	27	4.52
Landlords										
Male					16					
Female					1					
Subtotal					17	0.46				
Industrialists										
Male					16				14	
Female					0				0	
Subtotal					16	0.44			14	2.34
Other	181	7.95	52	5.65	166	4.54	41	7.01	49	8.19
Not available	6	0.26	4	0.44	18	0.49			4	0.67
Total	2,277	100.00	919	100.00	3,657	100.00	585	100.00	598	100.00

Source: Author's calculations from National Registry of Foreigners, DM (1926–1951), AGN.
[a] Specified sectors include office work, industry, municipal service, accounting, jewelry, and lingerie.

Table 9. Middle Eastern Immigrants and Resident Foreign Nationals in Mexico, by Marital Status and Sex

Marital Status	1878–1909		1910–1919		1920–1929		1930–1939		1940–1951	
	N	%	N	%	N	%	N	%	N	%
Married										
Male	727		351		1,101		162		200	
Female	494		241		869		123		131	
Subtotal	1,221	53.62	592	64.42	1,970	53.87	285	48.72	331	55.35
Single										
Male	584		185		1,215		192		137	
Female	267		57		264		57		51	
Subtotal	851	37.37	242	26.32	1,479	40.44	249	42.56	188	31.44
Widowed										
Male	73		30		33		6		11	
Female	116		49		161		39		58	
Subtotal	189	8.30	79	8.60	194	5.30	45	7.70	69	11.54
Divorced										
Male	13		3		4		1		4	
Female	2		1		7		2		4	
Subtotal	15	0.66	4	0.44	11	0.30	3	0.51	8	1.34
Not available	1	0.04	2	0.22	3	0.08	3	0.51	2	0.33
Total	2,277	99.99	919	100.00	3,657	99.99	585	100.00	598	100.00

Source: Author's calculations from National Registry of Foreigners, DM (1926–1951), AGN.

Table 10. Middle Eastern Immigrants and Resident Foreign Nationals in Mexico, by Sex

Years	Male N	Male %	Female N	Female %	Total N	Total %
1878–1909	1,397	61.4	880	38.6	2,277	100.0
1910–1919	571	62.0	348	38.0	919	100.0
1920–1929	2,354	64.4	1,303	35.6	3,657	100.0
1930–1939	364	62.2	221	37.8	585	100.0
1940–1951	353	59.0	245	41.0	598	100.0

Source: Author's calculations from National Registry of Foreigners, DM (1926–1951), AGN.

Table 11. Middle Eastern Immigrants and Resident Foreign Nationals in Mexico, by Place of Entry

Place of Entry	1878–1909		1910–1919		1920–1929		1930–1939		1940–1951	
	N	%	N	%	N	%	N	%	N	%
Veracruz, Veracruz	1,330	58.41	766	83.35	3,118	85.26	381	65.13	16	2.68
Progreso, Yucatán	101	4.44	39	4.24	68	1.86	26	4.44		
Tampico, Tamaulipas	37	1.62	39	4.24	308	8.42	14	2.39		
Ciudad Juárez, Chihuahua			26	2.83	17	0.46	17	2.91	19	3.18
Nuevo Laredo, Tamaulipas			25	2.72	28	0.77	40	6.84	47	7.86
Mariscal, Chiapas					16	0.44				
Distrito Federal							25	4.27	283	47.32
Mérida, Yucatán									14	2.34
Other places of entry in Mexico by fewer than x immigrants	30	1.32	17	1.85	40	1.09	32	5.47	90	15.05
	x = 10		x = 7		x = 11		x = 10		x = 10	
Consulate in France					28	0.77				
Consulate in Beirut					18	0.49	36	6.15	58	9.70
Consulate in Jerusalem									41	6.86
Consulate in Havana, Cuba									13	2.17
Not available	20	0.88	4	0.44	16	0.44	12	2.05	17	2.84
Born in Mexico	759	33.33	3	0.33	0	0	2	0.34		
Total	2,277	100.00	919	100.00	3,657	100.00	585	99.99	598	100.00

Source: Author's calculations from National Registry of Foreigners, DM (1926–1951), AGN.

Table 12. Middle Eastern Immigrants in Mexico, Endogamy and Exogamy, 1948

Marriage Pattern	N	%
Endogamy	9,546	86.98
Exogamy	1,114	10.15
Unknown	314	2.86
Total	10,974	99.90

Source: Louis J. Maloof, "A Sociological Study of Arabic-Speaking People in Mexico" (Ph.D. dissertation, University of Florida, January 1959), Table 24, pp. 254–255. Maloof based his calculations on Directorio libanés: Censo general de las colonias—libanesa—palestina—siria: Residentes en la República, compiled and published by Julián Nasr and Salim Abud (Mexico City, 1948).

Table 13. Lebanese Immigrants in Mexico, Endogamy and Exogamy, 1948

Marriage Pattern	N	%
Endogamy	3,005	72.6
Exogamy	1,136	27.4
Total	4,141	100.0

Source: Carmen Mercedes Páez Oropeza, Los libaneses en México: Asimilación de un grupo étnico (Mexico City: Instituto Nacional de Antropología e Historia, 1984), Table 17, p. 124; Oropeza calculations based on Directorio libanés, Nasr and Abud, 1948.

Table 14. Middle Easterners Living in Mexico at the End of 1948, by Nationality and Sex

	Period of Arrival in Mexico							
Nationality	1880–1889	1890–1899	1900–1909	1910–1919	1920–1929	1930–1939	1940–1948	Total
Lebanese								
Male	20	61	751	432	1,274	76	33	2,647
Female	24	64	495	378	802	38	24	1,825
Subtotals	44	125	1,246	810	2,076	114	57	4,472
Syrian								
Male	2	0	46	57	188	7	4	304
Female	1	0	37	40	102	4	3	187
Subtotals	3	0	83	97	290	11	7	491
Palestinian								
Male	0	3	86	39	122	5	8	263
Female	0	2	71	27	92	4	5	201
Subtotals	0	5	157	66	214	9	13	464
Iraqi								
Male	0	0	6	7	24	0	1	38
Female	0	0	1	5	14	0	1	21
Subtotals	0	0	7	12	38	0	2	59
Jordanian								
Male	0	0	0	0	12	1	0	13
Female	0	0	0	0	4	0	0	4
Subtotals	0	0	0	0	16	1	0	17
Egyptian								
Male	0	0	2	1	1	2	0	6
Female	0	0	0	0	0	0	0	0
Subtotals	0	0	2	1	1	2	0	6
TOTAL	47	130	1,495	986	2,635	137	79	5,509

Source: Maloof, "Sociological Study," Table 1, p. 147; Maloof calculations based on *Directorio libanés,* compiled by Nasr and Abud, 1948.

Notes

Introduction

1. Caroline R. Nagel and Lynn A. Staeheli, "Citizenship, Identity, and Transnational Migration: Arab Immigrants to the United States," *Space and Polity* 8, no. 1 (April 2004), 4–5.

2. "Hidden transcript" refers to the discourse that takes place "offstage," beyond direct observation by power holders. "The hidden transcript is thus derivative in the sense that it consists of those offstage speeches, gestures, and practices that confirm, contradict, or inflect what appears in the public transcript." James Scott, *Domination and the Arts of Resistance: Hidden Transcripts* (New Haven, CT: Yale University Press, 1990), 4–5 and n8: "this is not to assert that subordinates have nothing more to talk among themselves."

3. For rich ethnographic work on the Lebanese community in Mexico see Teresa Cuevas Seba and Miguel Mañana Plasencio, *Los libaneses de Yucatán* (Mérida, Mexico: Impresiones Profesionales, 1990); María Beatriz de Lourdes Cáceres Menéndez and María Patricia Fortuny Loret de Mola, " 'Gebel-Libnan' (Montaña Blanca): La migración libanesa a Yucatán" (undergraduate thesis, Universidad de Yucatán, March 1977); and Diana Urow Schifter, "La inmigración a México durante el porfiriato: Un estudio de caso: Torreón, Coahuila" (undergraduate thesis, Universidad Iberoamericana, Mexico City, 1994).

4. Zidane Zéraoui, "Los árabes en México: El perfil de la migración, 1997," in *Destino México: Un estudio de las migraciones asiáticas a México, siglos XIX a XX,* edited by María Elena Ota Mishima (Mexico City: Colegio de México, 1997).

5. These immigration officials included Alejandro M. Bravo, Andrés Landa y Piña, Angel Escudero, Captain Salvador Amezcua F., Carlos A. Gómez, Carlos Guzmán, E. Soto Ruíz, Edmundo Butrón, Enrique Flores Magón, Enrique Ortíz, Francisco de P. Jiménez, Francisco A. de Icaza, Jorge Ferrestis, José Gallo Real, José Trinidad Ramos, Vicente E. Matus, Lorenzo Gallo, M. Torner, Manuel Gamio, Manuel Ramírez Arriaga, María Elena Gómez, and Pedro Molina E. There were others, but these individuals processed the majority of the immigration cards. Carlos Guzmán in particular, handled nearly 32 percent (1,848) of all the immigrant

cards, and José Trinidad Ramos handled 19 percent (1,071). Andrés Landa y Piña and José Gallo Real each processed 248 immigrants. Enrique Ortíz, who handled most of the later immigration, registered 4 percent (237 cases).

6. For a detailed discussion of Arabic-to-Spanish name changes see Jacques Najm Sacre, *Directorio por familias de los descendientes libaneses de México y Centroamérica* (Mexico City: Centro de Difusión Cultural de la Misión de México, 1981), 487–491.

7. With this concern in mind, in March 2005 I visited with Dr. Martha Díaz de Kuri, a Centro Libanés board member and author of various books on the Lebanese community in Mexico. She indicated that some community newsletters had been lost or destroyed.

Chapter 1

1. Jonathan Kandell, "Yo Quiero Todo Bell," *Wired*, January 2001, 136. For a detailed description of Carlos Slim Helú see José M. Martínez, *Carlos Slim. Retrato inédito* (Mexico City: Océano, 2002), and Patricia Jacobs Barquet, *Diccionario enciclopédico de mexicanos de origen libanés y de otros pueblos del Levante* (Mexico City: Solar, 2000), 368–369. It should be noted that sources used to describe Slim Helú are sometimes subsidized by his companies and his affiliates; therefore information from business presses and community-generated sources needs to be more closely examined. Alexandra Kirkman, "The Global Elite: The World's Best Telecom Companies," *Forbes,* April 10, 2002.

2. Tim Weiner, "Mexico City Vendors Survived Cortéz, but Now . . . ," *New York Times,* October 10, 2002.

3. *Forbes* says, "Just call him Midas," reinforcing the notion that everything Slim Helú touches becomes a lucrative business. *Forbes.com,* "The World's Billionaires: Carlos Slim Helu," March 10, 2005, at http://www.forbes.com/static/bill2005/LIRWYDJ.html?passListId=10&passYear=2005&passListType=Person&uniqueId=WYDJ&datatype=Person. Also see Geri Smith, "Slim's New World," *Business Week,* March 6, 2000, 162.

4. Kandell, "Yo Quiero Todo Bell," 132.

5. Nancy P. Appelbaum, "Post-Revisionist Scholarship on Race," *Latin American Research Review* 40, no. 3 (October 2005): 206–217. Ileana Rodríguez, editor, *The Latin American Subaltern Studies Reader* (Durham, NC: Duke University Press, 2001). Gilbert M. Joseph and Daniel Nugent, editors, *Everyday Forms of State Formation: Revolution and the Negotiation of Rule in Modern Mexico* (Durham, NC: Duke University Press, 1994).

6. Armenians do not typically consider themselves Arabs. Indeed, some Middle Eastern immigrants feigned an Armenian identity, believing that Armenians were more desirable than Arabs in the eyes of Mexican immigration officials.

7. I thank Carlos Martínez Assad for bringing this point to my attention at the seminar Xenofobia y Xenofilia en la Historia de México, Siglos XIX y XX, Homenaje a Moisés González Navarro, by the Dirección de Estudios Históricos, Instituto Nacional de Antropología e Historia (INAH), Mexico City, November 5, 2001.

8. Roberto Marín-Guzmán and Zidane Zéraoui, *Arab Immigration in Mexico*

in the Nineteenth and Twentieth Centuries: Assimilation and Arab Heritage (Austin/ Monterrey: Augustine Press/Instituto Tecnológico de Monterrey, 2003).

9. Ignacio Klich and Jeffrey Lesser, "Introduction: '*Turco*' Immigrants in Latin America," *Americas* 53, no. 1 (July 1996): 5.

10. National Registry of Foreigners, Migration (1926–1951), Archivo General de la Nación (AGN), Mexico City (hereafter cited as National Registry of Foreigners, 1926–1951).

11. According to Asher Kaufman, "The Phoenicians actually called themselves Canaanites and their land Canaan, at least until the 1st century AD as documented in the New Testament where it is written that Jesus reached the borders of Tyre and Sidon and cured there a Canaanite woman. (New Testament, Matthew 15:21–28; Mark 7:24–30). The term *Cna'ani* in biblical Hebrew implies a merchant, which suggests that, as with the word *phoinix*, the name of the country may have derived from the most popular profession of the ancient Lebanese—commerce." Asher Kaufman, *Reviving Phoenicia: In Search of Identity in Lebanon* (London: I. B. Tauris, 2004), 2n5.

12. Kaufman, *Reviving Phoenicia*, 78. Also see the pioneering work of Kamal Salibi, *A House of Many Mansions: The History of Lebanon Reconsidered* (Berkeley: University of California Press, 1988), 167–181.

13. Kaufman, *Reviving Phoenicia*, 79; also see 103n101.

14. Ricardo Flores Magón, an early opponent of the Díaz regime, foresaw this tendency in 1914. Moisés González Navarro, *Historia moderna de México: El porfiriato. La vida social* (Mexico City: Editorial Hermes, 1957), 160.

15. Nancy Leys Stepan, *"The Hour of Eugenics": Race, Gender, and Nation in Latin America* (Ithaca, NY: Cornell University Press, 1991).

16. Roger Bartra, *The Cage of Melancholy: Identity and Metamorphosis in the Mexican Character*, translated by Christopher J. Hall (New Brunswick, NJ: Rutgers University Press, 1992).

17. During the Porfiriato, Germans invested heavily in Mexico's public debt. British investors relied on El Aguila Oil Company, which by 1910 controlled 58 percent of Mexico's oil production. This company became vitally important to the British Empire as it moved away from coal to oil as a primary fuel source. Friedrich Katz, *The Secret War in Mexico: Europe, the United States, and the Mexican Revolution* (Chicago: University of Chicago Press, 1981), 24–25. Also see Sandra Kuntz Ficker, *Empresa extranjera y mercado interno: El Ferrocarril Central Mexicano (1880–1907)*, (Mexico City: El Colegio de México, 1995); Flavia Derossi, *El empresario mexicano* (Mexico City: Universidad Nacional Autónoma de México [UNAM], 1977); Stephen H. Haber, *Industry and Underdevelopment: The Industrialization of Mexico, 1890–1940* (Stanford, CA: Stanford University Press, 1989).

18. Serge Gruzinski notes that "rape, concubines, and, more rarely, marriages generated a new category of population—mestizos—of ambiguous status. It was not clear whether mestizos should be integrated into the Spanish world or the indigenous community." Serge Gruzinski, *The Mestizo Mind: The Intellectual Dynamics of Colonialization and Globalization*, translated by Deke Dusinberre (New York: Routledge, 2002), 42. José Vasconcelos, *The Cosmic Race: La raza cósmica, misión de la raza iberoamericana*, translated and annotated by Didier T. Jaén (Baltimore: Johns Hopkins University Press, 1925/1979).

19. Susanna Rostas notes: "*Indigenismo,* as an official policy, aimed to encourage those indigenous activities and attitudes that would best engender a sense of Mexican nationalism. It targeted for eradication certain practices, such as language and others related to other core aspects of indigenous culture (such as medicine and agricultural techniques), in the interests of turning Mexico's indigenous people into mestizos and establishing Mexico as a nation" (60–61). Rostas argues that *mexicanidad* is an "invented tradition" (56). Susanna Rostas, "Performing 'Mexicanidad'; Popular 'Indigenismo' in Mexico City," in *Encuentros Antropológicos: Power, Identity and Mobility in Mexican Society,* edited by Valentina Napolitano and Xochitl Leyva Solano (London: University of London, Institute of Latin American Studies, 1998).

D. A. Brading describes one of the founding Creole patriots, Servando de Mier, as having "succeeded brilliantly in endowing the Mexican nation with a patriotic pedigree in which Moctezuma and Cuauhtémoc figured as the predecessors of Hidalgo and Morelos, united in their stand against the cruel tyranny of Spain." D. A. Brading, *The First America: The Spanish Monarchy, Creole Patriots, and the Liberal State, 1492–1867* (Cambridge, England: Cambridge University Press, 1991), 602. Creole identity is a strange hybrid of legitimized exploitation of the indigenous peoples and a history paradoxically "borrowed" from them. Mexican Creole identity was perhaps more extreme than its Latin American counterparts because Mexican Creoles saw themselves as the center of the New World, as Mexico was by far the most valuable of Spain's American possessions. Benedict Anderson, *Imagined Communities: Reflections on the Origin and Spread of Nationalism* (London: Verso, 1991), 62.

20. Vasconcelos, *Cosmic Race,* 17.

21. Justo Sierra, *The Political Evolution of the Mexican People,* translated by Charles Ramsdell (Austin: University of Texas Press, 1969), 368.

22. Andrés Molina Enríquez, *Los grandes problemas nacionales* (Mexico City: Colección Problemas de México, Ediciones Era, 1909/1978), 393. Moisés González Navarro writes, "Andrés Molina Enríquez described the mestizo as the strongest, largest, and most patriotic element in the country since it possessed common origin as well as unity of religion, physical characteristics, language, values, and aspirations." González Navarro, "*Mestizaje* in Mexico During the National Period," in *Race and Class in Latin America,* edited by Magnus Mörner (New York: Columbia University Press, 1970), 149.

23. Alan Knight, "Racism, Revolution, and Indigenismo, Mexico, 1910–1940," in *The Idea of Race in Latin America, 1870–1940,* edited by Richard Graham (Austin: University of Texas Press, 1990), 85.

24. Greg Grandin argues that Guatemalan nationalism is very different from Mexican nationalism. Grandin, *The Blood of Guatemala: A History of Race and Nation* (Durham, NC: Duke University Press, 2000), 82. Grandin contends that "by promoting racial assimilation while at the same time permitting no middle ground for cultural mestizaje, Ladinos [non-Indian political elites] developed a nationalism that deployed culture and class to affirm racial identities" (230). For an interesting analysis of the "myth of mestizaje" in Nicaragua see Jeffrey L. Gould, *To Die in This Way: Nicaraguan Indians and the Myth of Mestizaje, 1880–1965* (Durham,

NC: Duke University Press, 1998), 10, 13. Also see Jeffrey Gould, "Gender, Politics, and the Triumph of Mestizaje in Early 20th Century Nicaragua," *Journal of Latin American Anthropology* 2, no. 1 (1996): 23, and in the same issue Charles R. Hale, "*Mestizaje,* Hybridity, and the Cultural Politics of Difference in Post-Revolutionary Central America," 49.

25. Arthur Schmidt, "Mexicans, Migrants, and Indigenous Peoples: The Work of Manuel Gamio in the United States, 1925–1927," in *Strange Pilgrimages: Exile, Travel, and National Identity in Latin America, 1800–1990s,* edited by Ingrid E. Fey and Karen Racine (Wilmington, DE: Scholarly Resources, 2000), 174.

26. Ibid.

27. D. A. Brading, "Manuel Gamio and Official Indigenismo in Mexico," *Bulletin of Latin American Research* 7, no. 1 (1988), 88.

28. Gruzinski, *Mestizo Mind,* 19. For more on *mestizaje* see Luz María Martínez Montiel, *La gota de oro: Migración y pluralismo étnico en América Latina* (Veracruz, Mexico: Instituto Veracruzano de Cultura, 1988), 12–13. Néstor García Canclini writes, "I prefer this last term [hybridization] because it includes diverse intercultural mixtures—not only the racial ones to which *mestizaje* tends to be limited—and because it permits the inclusion of the modern forms of hybridization better than does 'syncretism,' a term that almost always refers to religious fusions or traditional symbolic movements." Néstor García Canclini, *Hybrid Cultures: Strategies for Entering and Leaving Modernity,* translated by Christopher L. Chiappari and Silvia L. López (Minneapolis: University of Minnesota Press, 1995), 11n1.

29. Marilyn Grace Miller, *Rise and Fall of the Comic Race: The Cult of Mestizaje in Latin America* (Austin: University of Texas Press, 2004), 6. Knight, "Racism, Revolution, and Indigenismo," 85.

30. Miller, *Rise and Fall of the Comic Race,* 28.

31. Agustín Basave Benítez, *México mestizo: Análisis del nacionalismo mexicano en torno a la mestizofilia de Andrés Molina Enríquez* (Mexico City: Fondo de Cultura Económica, 1992), 14.

32. Henry C. Schmidt, *The Roots of Lo Mexicano: Self and Society in Mexican Thought, 1900–1934* (College Station: Texas A&M University Press, 1978).

33. Bartra, *Cage of Melancholy,* 2–3.

34. In Brazil, "members of a growing immigrant elite . . . engaged actively in a public discourse about what it meant to be Brazilian," while Mexicans have remained attached to constructions of the *mestizo.* Jeffrey Lesser, *Negotiating National Identity: Immigrants, Minorities, and the Struggle for Ethnicity in Brazil* (Durham, NC: Duke University Press, 1999), 2.

35. Bartra, *Cage of Melancholy,* 2.

36. For a more detailed discussion of the myth of the Mexican Revolution see Thomas Benjamin, *La Revolución: Mexico's Great Revolution as Memory Myth and History* (Austin: University of Texas Press, 2000). For more information on revolutionary leaders see Friedrich Katz, *The Life and Times of Pancho Villa.* (Stanford, CA: Stanford University Press, 1998); Alan Knight, *The Mexican Revolution* (Lincoln: University of Nebraska Press, 1986); Samuel Brunk, *¡Emiliano Zapata!: Revolution and Betrayal in Mexico* (Albuquerque: University of New Mexico, 1995); and John Womack Jr., *Zapata and the Mexican Revolution* (New York: Random House,

Vintage Books, 1968). Also see Ilene V. O'Malley, *The Myth of the Revolution: Hero Cults and the Institutionalization of the Mexican State, 1920–1940* (New York: Greenwood Press, 1986).

37. Rodolfo Stavenhagen and Tania Carrasco, "La diversidad étnica y cultural," in *El Patrimonio Nacional de México,* coordinated by Enrique Florescano (Mexico City: Consejo Nacional Para la Cultura y Las Artes and Fondo de Cultura Económica, 1997), 259.

38. Alexandra Minna Stern, "From Mestizophilia to Biotypology: Racialization and Science in Mexico, 1920–1960," in *Race and Nation in Modern Latin America,* edited by Nancy P. Appelbaum, Anne S. Macpherson, and Karin Alejandra Rosemblatt (Chapel Hill: University of North Carolina Press, 2003), 121–122.

39. Paulette Kershenovich delineates groups and subgroups among Mexican Jews. "There are three ethnic groups within this community: the *Ashkenazim,* the *Sepharadim* and the *Mizrahim* (originating mainly in Syria and called Arab by Mexican Jews). The *Mizrahim* are divided into the *Halebis* (also called *Maguen David*) from Aleppo, and the *Shamis* (also called *Monte Sinai*) from Damascus . . . 39.5 percent [of the Jewish Mexican community is] Ashkenazi, 47.4 percent Sephardic and Arabic sectors combined, 13.1 percent unknown or indifferent to their origins." Paulette Kershenovich, "Jewish Women in Mexico," in *Jewish Women 2000: Conference Papers from the Hadassah Research Institute on Jewish Women International Scholarly Exchanges 1997–1998,* edited by Helen Epstein (Boston: Brandeis University, 1999), 98n13. A 1989 publication on Jews from Aleppo, Syria, indicates that between 1907 and 1930, only 540 Sephardic Jews migrated to Mexico. This same study suggested that 8,914 Jews from Eastern Europe migrated to Mexico between 1921 and 1929; Liz Hamui de Halabe, coordinator, *Los judíos de Alepo en México* (Mexico City: Maguén David, 1989), 101nn47–48. Corinne Azen Krause, "The Jews in Mexico: A History with Special Emphasis on the Period from 1850 to 1930" (Ph.D. diss., University of Pittsburgh, 1970), 65.

40. Jürgen Buchenau argues that "Mexico has proven a 'salad bowl' rather than a 'melting pot,' as most immigrant families sought to retain their native language and customs." He suggests that "trade conquistadors," the upper and middle classes from France, Germany, Great Britain, and Spain, dominated much of the nineteenth-century mining, money-lending, and wholesale trade. Buchenau, "Small Numbers, Great Impact: Mexico and Its Immigrants, 1821–1973," *Journal of American Ethnic History* 20, no. 3 (Spring 2001): 23, 27.

41. For excellent studies on Japanese, Korean, Chinese, Arab, Palestinian, Philippine, and Indian immigrant groups in Mexico see *Destino México,* edited by Ota Mishima.

42. William H. Beezley, *Judas at the Jockey Club and Other Episodes of Porfirian Mexico* (Lincoln: University of Nebraska Press, 1987), 67.

43. Charles F. Nunn, *Foreign Immigrants in Early Bourbon Mexico, 1700–1760* (Cambridge, England: Cambridge University Press, 1979), 12.

44. Ibid., 31.

45. D. A. Brading, *Miners and Merchants in Bourbon Mexico 1763–1810* (Cambridge, England: Cambridge University Press, 1971), 95, 105.

46. Bonnie Honig, *Democracy and the Foreigner* (Princeton, NJ: Princeton University Press, 2001), 12, 80n15.

47. Luz María Martínez Montiel and Araceli Reynoso Medina, "Inmigración europea y asiática, siglos XIX y XX," in *Simbiosis de culturas: Los inmigrantes y su cultura en México,* edited by Guillermo Bonfil Batalla (Mexico City: Fondo de Cultura Económica, 1993), 273.

48. Jürgen Buchenau suggests that foreigners "enjoyed considerable power and wealth precisely due to their status as outsiders." This power enabled them to enjoy their cultural niches and form enclaves or "colonies." Buchenau, "Small Numbers, Great Impact," 29, 34.

49. Identity in this context implies the shared and interactive process for the actor and his/her relationship with the environment. "The process of identity construction, adaptation and maintenance always has two aspects: the internal complexity of an actor (the plurality of orientations which characterizes him), and the actor's relationship with the environment (other actors, opportunities and constraints)." Alberto Melucci, "Getting Involved: Identity and Mobilization in Social Movements," in *International Social Movement Research: From Structure to Action— Comparing Social Movements Research Across Cultures,* volume 1, edited by Hansperter Kriesi, Sidney Tarrow, and Bert Klandermans (London: JAI Press, 1988), 342. Also see Arturo Escobar, "Culture, Economics, and Politics in Latin American Social Movements Theory and Research," in *The Making of Social Movements in Latin America: Identity, Strategy, and Democracy,* edited by Arturo Escobar and Sonia E. Alvarez (Boulder, CO: Westview Press, 1992), 72.

50. Peter Sahlins, *Unnaturally French: Foreign Citizens in the Old Regime and After* (Ithaca, NY: Cornell University Press, 2004).

51. Ibid., 9.

52. Ibid., 66.

53. Florencia Mallon, in *Peasant and Nation,* argues that during the late nineteenth century in the Sierra de Puebla and in Morelos, peasants developed their own sense of nation and loyalty to the *patria.* Mallon, *Peasant and Nation: The Making of Postcolonial Mexico and Peru* (Berkeley: University of California Press, 1995). Luis González, in *San José de Gracia,* illustrates how some villages in the state of Michoacán were relatively unaffected by the Mexican Revolution, yet they become heavily involved in the Cristero Revolt. This case study shows how meanings of nation and loyalty to the *patria* clearly varied by region and time period in Mexico. Luis González, *San José de Gracia: Mexican Village in Transition,* translated by John Upton (Austin: University of Texas Press, 1974).

54. In studying Arabs in Argentina, Gladys Jozami notes that home locality and religion often determined the immigrants' identity. For instance, she describes how an immigrant would label himself or herself: "I am an Orthodox of Farbo, I am a Muslim of Yabrut [Yabroud], and I am a Protestant from Hama." Jozami, "Identidad religiosa e integración cultural en cristianos sirios y libaneses en Argentina, 1890–1990," *Estudios Migratorios Latinoamericanos* 9 (April 1994): 97–98.

55. *Llevamos una doble vida, cuando estoy en la casa soy libanesa y en la calle yucateca.* Quoted in Cuevas Seba and Mañana Plasencio, *Los libaneses de Yucatán,* 117.

56. As Liliana R. Goldin describes, "processes of displacement, exile, and settlement occur at psychological, cultural, and social levels and these can operate at 'home' as well as 'abroad.'" Goldin, "Transnational Identities: The Search

for Analytical Tools," in *Identities on the Move: Transnational Processes in North America and the Caribbean Basin,* edited by Liliana R. Goldin (Albany, NY: Institute for Mesoamerican Studies, State University of New York, 1999), 2. Also see Nina Glick Schiller, Linda Basch, and Cristian Blanc-Szanton, "Transnationalism: A New Analytic Framework for Understanding Migrations," in *Towards a Transnational Perspective on Migration: Race, Class, Ethnicity, and Nationalism Reconsidered* (New York: New York Academy of Science, 1992), 1–2.

57. See Prasenjit Duara, "Historicizing National Identity, or Who Imagines What and When," in *Becoming National: A Reader,* edited by Geoff Eley and Ronald Grigor Suny (New York: Oxford University Press, 1996), 151–177.

58. Ibid., 162.

59. Jorge Nacif Mina best captures the sense of dual identity by noting that the immigrants must respect, love, and defend both countries equally. Jorge Nacif Mina, *Crónicas de un inmigrante libanés en México* (Mexico City: Jorge Nacif Mina and Instituto Cultural Mexicano Libanés, 1995), 95. Antonio Mouhanna, "La comunidad árabe en la ciudad de México: La comunidad libanesa," in *BaBel, Ciudad de México* 4, Medio Oriente (June 1999): 23, Mexico City. Cáceres Menéndez and Fortuny Loret de Mola, " 'Gebel-Libnan' (Montaña Blanca)," 98.

60. Interview by author with Omar in Mexico City, April 27, 1999.

61. Donna Gabaccia, in discussing Sicilians in New York City, notes that "the conservatism of the immigrant was not necessarily Sicilian in origin; more likely it was a product of the migration experience." Donna R. Gabaccia, *From Sicily to Elizabeth Street: Housing and Social Change Among Italian Immigrants, 1880–1930* (Albany: State University of New York Press, 1984), 116.

Chapter 2

1. Jorge Amado, *Gabriela, Clove and Cinnamon,* translated by James L. Taylor and William Grossman (New York: Avon Books, 1962), 35–36.

2. Klich and Lesser, "Introduction: '*Turco*' Immigrants," 5.

3. Charles Gibson, *The Aztecs Under Spanish Rule: A History of the Indians of the Valley of Mexico, 1519–1810* (Stanford, CA: Stanford University Press, 1964), 4.

4. Ibid., 24. Frances F. Berdan, *The Aztecs of Central Mexico: An Imperial Society* (Orlando, FL: Harcourt Brace Jovanovich, 1982), 111.

5. Brading, *Miners and Merchants in Bourbon Mexico,* 95, 105. Louisa Schell Hoberman, *Mexico's Merchant Elite, 1590–1660: Silver, State, and Society* (Durham, NC: Duke University Press, 1991), 2–3. Hoberman notes that Latin American merchants have been seen as parasitic and for some reason have been hardly mentioned in social history. Another issue rarely addressed is what specifically these merchants sold and produced. In the twentieth century, the foreign merchants provided their own goods and services, imports, and Mexican-produced goods.

6. Harold Dana Sims, *The Expulsion of Mexico's Spaniards 1821–1836* (Pittsburgh, PA: University of Pittsburgh Press, 1990), 16–17.

7. See Ida Altman, *Transatlantic Ties in the Spanish Empire: Brihuega, Spain, and Puebla, Mexico, 1560–1620* (Stanford, CA: Stanford University Press, 2000).

8. Magnus Mörner with Harold Sims, *Adventurers and Proletarians: The*

Story of Migrants in Latin America (Pittsburgh, PA: University of Pittsburgh Press; UNESCO, 1985), 6–9.

9. For an interesting account by this Chaldean priest from Baghdad see Elias al-Mûsili, *An Arab's Journey to Colonial Spanish America: The Travels of Elias al-Mûsili in the Seventeenth Century*, translated and edited by Caesar E. Farah (Syracuse, NY: Syracuse University Press, 2003), 78–85.

10. Colin M. MacLachlan and Jaime E. Rodríguez O., *The Forging of the Cosmic Race: A Reinterpretation of Colonial Mexico* (Berkeley: University of California Press, 1990), 214, 218, 222.

11. Brading, *Miners and Merchants in Bourbon Mexico*, 249. His Chapter 7, "A Census," provides an excellent description of the number of Europeans versus Creoles participating in the Guanajuato workforce. Charles Nunn notes that "foreigners did represent a small number of the total population of New Spain, but they comprised some 3 percent of the European born." Nunn, *Foreign Immigrants in Early Bourbon Mexico*, 2.

12. Luz María Martínez Montiel, coordinator, *Presencia Africana en México* (Mexico City: Dirección General de Publicaciones del Consejo Nacional para la Cultura y las Artes, 1994). Also see Luz María Martínez Montiel, "La cultura africana: Tercera raíz," in *Simbiosis de culturas: los inmigrantes y su cultura en México*, edited by Guillermo Bonfil Batilla (Mexico City: Fondo de Cultura Económica, 1993), 111–180.

13. Regions that have been marked off as black and Indian (such as southern Mexico) have been "labeled backward in relation to more modern, whiter regions . . . Regions identified as black or Indian . . . have not been considered fully part of the nation." Nancy P. Appelbaum, Anne S. Macpherson, and Karin Alejandra Rosemblatt, "Introduction: Racial Nations," *Race and Nation in Modern Latin America*, edited by Appelbaum, Macpherson, and Rosemblatt, 10n34.

14. See Patrick J. Carroll, *Blacks in Colonial Veracruz: Race, Ethnicity, and Regional Development* (Austin: University of Texas Press, 2001). Ben Vinson III, *Bearing Arms for His Majesty: The Free-Colored Militia in Colonial Mexico* (Stanford, CA: Stanford University Press, 2001). Gonzalo Aguirre Beltrán, *La población negra de México: Estudio etnohistórico* (Mexico City: Fondo de Cultura Económica, 1972).

15. Michael Kenny, Virginia García, Carmen Icazuriaga, Clara Elena Suárez, and Gloria Artís, *Inmigrantes y refugiados españoles en México (siglo XX)* (Mexico City: Ediciones de la Casa Chata, 1979), 30.

16. Sims, *Expulsion of Mexico's Spaniards*, 18.

17. Delia Salazar Anaya, *La población extranjera en México (1895-1990): Un recuento con base en los censos generales de población* (Mexico City: INAH, 1996), 103.

18. For a more detailed discussion of French financial interests during and after French occupation see Steven C. Topik, "When Mexico Had the Blues: A Transatlantic Tale of Bonds, Bankers, and Nationalists, 1862–1910," *American Historical Review* 105, no. 3 (June 2000): 714–738.

19. Delia Salazar Anaya, "Extraños en la ciudad. Un acercamiento a la inmigración internacional a la ciudad de México, en los censos de 1890, 1895, 1900 y 1910," in *Imágenes de los inmigrantes en la ciudad de México, 1753-1910*, coordinated by Delia Salazar Anaya (Mexico City: INAH and Plaza y Valdés, 2002), 239. Buche-

nau, "Small Numbers, Great Impact," 27. Colin M. MacLachlan and William H. Beezley, *El Gran Pueblo: A History of Greater Mexico* (Englewood Cliffs, NJ: Prentice Hall, 1994), 39.

20. Brian Hamnett, *Juárez* (New York: Longman, 1994), 111.

21. W. H. Ellis, who worked with the Agricultural, Industrial, and Colonization Company of Tlahualilo, along with Robert A. ("Peg-Leg") Williams claimed that they would take more than 100,000 blacks from the American South to Mexico. Later Ellis said that only 10,000 were expected in the first year. William Cohen, *At Freedom's Edge: Black Mobility and the Southern Quest for Racial Control, 1861-1915* (Baton Rouge: Louisiana State University Press, 1991), 261n38. Margaret Maud McKellar's account of life on a northern Mexican ranch describes a black settlement in Coahuila at the end of the nineteenth century. "When the Negroes learned that we would buy all they brought, they brought them over in quantities, each egg carefully tied in the shucks of corn." Margaret Maud McKellar, *Life on a Mexican Ranche*, edited by Dolores L. Latorre (Bethlehem, PA: Lehigh University Press, 1994), 54.

22. Jerry Garcia, "Japanese Immigration and Community Development in México, 1897-1940" (Ph.D. diss., Washington State University, 1999), Appendix 4, 225.

23. Chinese Exclusion Act of May 6, 1882, 22 United States Statutes-at-Large 58 (1882).

24. Evelyn Hu-DeHart. "Immigrants to a Developing Society: The Chinese in Northern Mexico, 1875-1932," *Journal of Arizona History* 21, no. 3 (August 1980), 277.

25. Moisés González Navarro, *Los extranjeros en México y los mexicanos en el extranjero, 1821-1970* (Mexico City: Colegio de Mexico, 1994), 2:100.

26. In the case of Mexico see Martha Díaz de Kuri and Lourdes Macluf, *De Líbano a México: Crónica de un pueblo emigrante* (Mexico City: Gráfica, Creatividad y Diseño, 1995); Nacif Mina, *Crónicas de un inmigrante libanés*.

27. Jorge Amado, *Gabriela*, 34-35.

28. Ignacio Klich and Jeffrey Lesser, editors, *Arab and Jewish Immigrants in Latin America: Images and Realities* (London: Frank Cass, 1998); also see their "Introduction: 'Turco' Immigrants." Albert Hourani and Nadim Shehadi, editors, *The Lebanese in the World: A Century of Emigration* (London: Centre for Lebanese Studies and I. B. Taurus, 1992).

29. Luz María Martínez Montiel, "Lebanese Immigration to Mexico," in *Asiatic Migrations in Latin America*, edited by Luz María Martínez Montiel, 147-161 (Mexico City: 30th International Congress of Human Sciences in Asia and North Africa [1976], Colegio de Mexico, 1981); Carmen Páez Oropeza, *Los libaneses en México: Asimilación de un grupo étnico* (Mexico City: INAH, Colección Científica, 1984); Rebeca Inclán Rubio, "Inmigración libanesa en la Ciudad de Puebla, 1890-1930: Proceso de aculturación" (undergraduate thesis, Universidad Nacional Autónoma de México [UNAM], Mexico City, 1978); Angelina Alonso Palacios, *Los libaneses y la industria textil en Puebla* (Mexico City: Centro de Investigaciones y Estudios Superiores en Antropología Social [CIESAS] and Cuadernos de la Casa Chata, 1983); Zidane Zéraoui, "Los árabes en México: El perfil de la migración," in *Destino México*, edited by Ota Mishima, 257-293; Doris Musalem

Rahal, "La migración palestina a México, 1893-1949," in *Destino México*, edited by Ota Mishima, 305-364; Roberto Marín-Guzmán, "Los inmigrantes árabes en México en los siglos XIX y XX: un estudio de historia social," in *El mundo árabe y América Latina*, coordinated by Raymundo Kabchi (Madrid: UNESCO, 1997).

30. Salazar Anaya, *La población extranjera en México*, 5.

31. Centro Libanés Website, www.centrolibanes.org. Also see Sam Dagher, "Nation's Lebanese Distant from Arab Conflicts but Hold Close Ties to Those in Power," *News Mexico*, October 25, 2001, 4. Dagher reports that about 400,000 people of Lebanese Christian descent reside in Mexico.

32. Albert Hourani, introduction to *Lebanese in the World*, edited by Hourani and Shehadi, 7.

33. Luz María Martínez Montiel, "The Lebanese Community in Mexico: Its Meaning, Importance, and the History of Its Communities," in *Lebanese in the World*, edited by Hourani and Shehadi, 381.

34. Ibid., 382.

35. William Meyers notes that in the Laguna's small towns, one or two stores provided the necessities to part-time agricultural and mining workers. These small towns became holding centers for marginal laborers waiting for work. Arab peddlers therefore provided an important service to Mexican elite in need of labor. William Meyers, *Forge of Progress, Crucible of Revolt: Origins of the Mexican Revolution in La Comarca Lagunera, 1880-1911* (Albuquerque: University of New Mexico Press, 1994), 83-86.

36. Sarah Elizabeth John argues that many Syrians "slipped through America's 'back door'" at the beginning of the twentieth century when they were turned away from U.S. ports of entry. "'Trade Will Lead a Man Far': Syrian Immigration to the El Paso Area, 1900-1935" (master's thesis, University of Texas at El Paso, December 1982), 24-25.

37. Alan M. Kraut, *Silent Travelers: Germs, Genes, and the "Immigrant Menace"* (New York: BasicBooks, 1994), 51, 55. Immigration Act of March 3, 1891, 26. United States Statutes-at-Large 1084 (1891).

38. Kraut, *Silent Travelers*, 51. Also see Gerald L. Neuman, *Strangers to the Constitution: Immigrants, Borders, and Fundamental Law* (Princeton, NJ: Princeton University Press, 1996), 31-34.

39. The disease tends to affect more women who are in close contact with children and are therefore three times more likely to suffer from trachoma blindness than men. International Trachoma Initiative, at http://www.trachoma.org/trachoma.php. Also see U.S. National Library of Health and National Institutes of Health MedlinePlus article at http://www.nlm.nih.gov/medlineplus/ency/article/001486.htm.

40. "In a study of trachoma diagnosis at all immigration stations from 1908 to 1910 in the United States, the PHS [Public Health Service] officer Victor Safford concluded that Chinese, Japanese, Syrian, and Asian Indian immigrants were more likely to be certified for trachoma than the most 'susceptible' southern and eastern European 'races.'" Nayan Shah, *Contagious Divides: Epidemics and Race in San Francisco's Chinatown* (Berkeley: University of California Press, 2001), 188.

41. Maurice Fishberg, Immigrant Inspector, to Hon. Frank P. Sargent, *Commissioner-General of Immigration, Washington, D.C. Annual Report of the Commis-*

sioner-General of Immigration to the Secretary of Commerce and Labor for the Fiscal Year Ended June 30, 1905 (Washington, DC: Government Printing Office, 1905), 54. This document is located at the U.S. Citizenship and Immigration Services Historical Reference Library in Washington, D.C., and was brought to my attention by historian Marion Smith in 2003.

42. A. Seraphic to Commissioner-General of Immigration, Department of Commerce and Labor, Immigration Service, January 8, 1907, Seraphic Report, Document No. 51,423-11, Record Group (RG) 85, INS, National Archives, Washington, DC (NA), hereafter cited as Seraphic Report.

43. Ibid., 12.

44. Grace Delgado, "In the Age of Exclusion: Race, Region and Chinese Identity in the Making of the Arizona-Sonora Borderlands, 1863–1943" (Ph.D. diss., University of California, Los Angeles, 2000), 210–211n70.

45. Commissioner-General F.P. Sargent of Department of Commerce and Labor, Bureau of Immigration and Naturalization, Washington, D.C. to T.F. Schmucker, Inspector in Charge, El Paso, Texas, February 11, 1907, Document No. 51,423-1, RG 85, INS, NA.

46. Commissioner-General F.P. Sargent of Department of Commerce and Labor, Bureau of Immigration and Naturalization, Washington, D.C. to Luther C. Steward, Inspector in Charge, San Antonio, Texas, February 11, 1907, Document No. 51,423-1, RG 85, INS, NA.

47. Seraphic Report, 2.

48. Ibid., 3.

49. Ibid., 3.

50. Ibid., 4.

51. Statement of Fares Nasser of St. Louis, Missouri. August 27, 1906, Document No. 51,423-11, RG 85, INS, NA, 1, 2, 4.

52. *Mexican Herald,* July 8, 1906, Document No. 50,275–5, RG 85, INS, NA.

53. Ibid.

54. *San Antonio Express,* December 2, 1906, Document No. 51,423-4, RG 85, INS, NA.

55. Seraphic Report, 14.

56. Ibid, 14.

57. Ibid., 15.

58. Ibid., 20.

59. Sink claimed that interpreter Salim Mattar was taking bribes from Syrian immigrants. He also mentioned another Syrian smuggler named Alexander Lemon. See Dr. E. D. Sink testimony on December 31, 1906, El Paso Texas, Document No. 51,423-11A, RG 85, INS, NA.

60. Seraphic Report, 17, 18, 24.

61. Commissioner-General of Immigration, Office of the Commissioner, Philadelphia, PA, Department of Commerce and Labor, Washington, D.C., May 16, 1907, File No. 1407, Document No. 51,615/10, RG 85, INS, NA, 6.

62. See Sworn Statement of S. M. Mattar, El Paso, Texas, January 1, 1906, Document No. 51,423-11A, RG 85, INS, NA. Mattar defended himself and tried to implicate Dr. Sinks.

63. Inspector in Charge, El Paso, Texas to Commissioner-General of Immigra-

tion, Department of Commerce and Labor, Washington, D.C. December 21, 1906, Document No. 51,423-11A, RG 85, INS, NA, 2.

64. Office of Inspector in Charge, El Paso, Texas to Commissioner General of Immigration, Department of Commerce and Labor, Immigration Service, February 21, 1907, Document No. 51,423-11-A, RG 85, E9, INS, NA.

65. Chief Bureau of Investigation, Department of Justice, Washington, D.C. to Anthony Caminetti, Commissioner-General of Immigration, Department of Interior, December 7, 1915, Document No. 51,423-2, RG 85, INS, NA.

66. Seraphic Report, 24.

67. Office of Inspector in Charge, El Paso, Texas to Commissioner-General of Immigration, Department of Commerce and Labor, Immigration Service, March 23, 1907, Document No. 51,423-11-A, RG 85, E9, INS, NA.

68. Braun Report, New York, June 10, 1907, Document No. 51,403/22, RG 85, INS, NA, 2.

69. Delgado, "Age of Exclusion," 283n106–107.

70. Memorandum as to Efforts Made to Perfect an Agreement with the Railways of Mexico Concerning of Aliens, February 3, 1903, Document No. 51,463, RG 85, INS, NA.

71. D. E. Thompson to Ignacio Mariscal, Embassy of Mexico, June 7, 1906. Document No. 51, 463/A, RG 85, INS, NA. Expediente (Exp.) 14-28-79, 1906–1907, Siglo XX, Secretaría de Relaciones Exteriores (SRE).

72. Exp. 14-28-79, May 25, 1906, Siglo XX, SRE.

73. Ibid.

74. On June 7, 1906, Thompson wrote Mariscal again highlighting contagious diseases and how the Canadian government was helping in the cause to curb Syrian immigration. He wrote that "the Mexican government has always shown much alacrity in cooperating with the United States with respect to the suppression of common evils . . . I would be sincerely pleased to learn of their adoption, or of any other measures which Your Excellency's government may have the goodness to enact regarding the matter." Exp. 14-28-79, June 30, 1906, Siglo XX, SRE.

75. Exp. 14-28-79, July 3, 1906, Siglo XX, SRE.

76. Thompson acknowledged the proposed measures to stem Syrian immigration in a letter to Mariscal dated August 27, 1906. Through Thompson, however, the United States continued asserting pressure on Mexico regarding its immigration policy. Thompson complained in the letter of how a Syrian with trachoma, John Shahadie Jacob, "secured unlawful entry into the United States from Mexico." He indicated that another Syrian accompanied Mr. Shahadie, but the other Syrian's whereabouts were unknown. Thompson closed the letter stating, "Should these remedial measures meet with the views of Your Excellency's government, I would be sincerely glad to learn of their adoption." Exp. 14-28-79, August 26, 1906, Siglo XX, SRE.

77. Memorandum as to Efforts Made to Perfect an Agreement with the Railways of Mexico Concerning of Aliens, February 3, 1903, Document No. 51,463, RG 85, INS, NA, 3.

78. Exp. 14-28-79, January 3, 1907, Siglo XX, SRE.

79. Surgeon-General of the Public Health and Marine Hospital Service of the United States, April 13, 1907, Exp. 14-28-79, 1906–1907, Siglo XX, SRE.

80. George H. Winters, American Vice Consul U.S. State Department, "Review of Mexican Department of Migration Report Entitled: 'The Migration Service in Mexico', and Discussing Mexican Migration To and From the United States," Document No. 812.5511.87, M274, October 25, 1929, U.S. State Department Records, RG 85, U.S. National Archives, College Park, MD (NACP).

81. Moisés González Navarro, *Población y sociedad en México (1900–1970)* (Mexico City: UNAM, 1974), 2:37.

82. Francisco J. Ituarte to Licenciado Don Francisco Alfaro, Caja 31, Exp. 303, Folios 24, December 14, 1908, Archivo Histórico, Don Rafael Chousal, Secretaría Particular, Archivo Histórico, UNAM, Mexico City, 8.

83. Maurice Fishberg, *Annual Report*, 55.

84. Ibid.

85. Ibid., 50. In a 1906 report in Havre, France, the on-site surgeon reported that "the medical examination work at this station, so far as I can see, compares very favourably with other European Stations. The Compagne [steamship company] evidently prefer[s] to reject passengers at Havre rather than take the risk of the trouble and expense involved in rejections at New York—Mindful probably also of the fact that the hardship in the case as it affects the poor emigrant will be increased in proportion to the distance he finds himself from home when misfortune befalls him." To Commissioner-General, U.S. Immigration Service, Washington from Havre, France, August 11, 1906, Document No. 51,841–129, p. 3, RG 85, INS, NA.

86. Immigrant Inspector Marcus Braun, Mexico City, Bureau of Immigration and Naturalization, Department of Commerce and Labor, May 7, 1907, Document No. 51,564, RG 85, INS, NA.

87. "Negotiating with Mexicans," February 12, 1908, Document No. 51,463–B, p.5, RG 85, INS, NA.

88. Stephen Castles and Mark J. Miller, *The Age of Migration: International Population Movements in the Modern World* (New York: Guilford Press, 1993), 62–63.

Chapter 3

1. Examination of Mahmoud, Soulaiman. El Paso, Texas, June 20, 1907, Document No. 51,634-180, RG 85, INS, NA, 3.

2. *Mexican Herald*, Mexico City, August 17, 1907, Document No. 51,463-B, RG 85, INS, NA.

3. Carlos Marichal argues that "the pattern of loan cycles was not circumstantial, but rather the result of the interaction between the economic cycles of the more-advanced capitalist nations and the processes of economic change in Latin America." Carlos Marichal, *A Century of Debt Crises in Latin America: From Independence to the Great Depression, 1820–1930* (Princeton, NJ: Princeton University Press, 1989), 5.

4. Haber, *Industry and Underdevelopment*, 22.

5. Edward Beatty, *Institutions and Investment: The Political Basis of Industrialization in Mexico Before 1911* (Stanford, CA: Stanford University Press, 2001), 196.

6. Mauricio Tenorio-Trillo says, "Universal scientific politics proved to be a selective ideological discourse that depended on both the circumstances of each specific country and the interests of its national elite." Tenorio-Trillo, *Mexico at the World's Fairs: Crafting a Modern Nation* (Berkeley: University of California Press, 1996), 23.

7. Rodney D. Anderson, *Outcasts in Their Own Land: Mexican Industrial Workers, 1906–1911* (DeKalb: Northern Illinois University Press, 1976), 34n38.

8. Francois-Xavier Guerra, *México: Del antiguo régimen a la Revolución*, 2 volumes (Mexico City: Fondo de Cultura Económica, 1988). Beatty suggests that Díaz "effectively micro-managed politics throughout the country to maintain order and authority, and limited office holding to a narrow and beholden elite." Beatty, *Institutions and Investment*, 20–21. Also see Tenorio-Trillo, *Mexico at the World's Fairs*, 19, 35, 176.

9. Anderson, *Outcasts in Their Own Land*, 18.

10. Ibid.

11. Gladys Jozami, in writing about Arabs in Argentina, notes that there is a pattern of Arab immigrants in search of markets for their wares settling along railroad routes. Jozami, "Aspectos demográficos y comportamiento espacial de los inmigrantes árabes en el noroeste argentino," *Estudios Migratorios Latinoamericanos* (hereafter cited as EML) 2, no. 5 (April 1987): 78.

12. Leila Tarazi Fawaz, *Merchants and Migrants in Nineteenth-Century Beirut* (Cambridge, MA: Harvard University Press, 2000), 66–67. Roger Owen, *The Middle East and the World Economy, 1800–1914* (London: I. B. Tauris, 1993), 154.

13. Albert Hourani, *A History of the Arab Peoples* (New York: Warner Books, 1991), 286–287.

14. Charles Issawi, "The Transformation of the Economic Position of the *Millets* in the Nineteenth Century," in *Christians and Jews in the Ottoman Empire: The Functioning of a Plural Society*, edited by Benjamin Braude and Bernard Lewis, volume 1, *The Central Lands* (New York: Holmes and Meier, 1982), 262.

15. Sarah Gualtieri, "From Internal to International Migration: Migratory Movements in Late-Ottoman Syria," paper presented at Middle Eastern Migrations to Latin America conference, University of Chicago, May 31, 2003, 17–18.

16. Charles Issawi, "The Historical Background of Lebanese Emigration: 1800–1914," in *Lebanese in the World*, edited by Hourani and Shehadi, 25.

17. Ibid., 25–27.

18. Najib E. Saliba, *Emigration from Syria and the Syrian-Lebanese Community of Worcester, MA* (Ligonier, PA: Antakya Press, 1992), 6.

19. Michael W. Suleiman, "Introduction: The Middle Eastern Immigrant Experience," in *Arabs in America: Building a New Future*, edited by Michael W. Suleiman (Philadelphia: Temple University Press, 1999), 2n9. Also see Akram Fouad Khater, "'House' to 'Goddess of the House': Gender, Class, and Silk in 19th-Century Mount Lebanon," *International Journal of Middle East Studies* 28, no. 3 (1996): 325–348.

20. Douglas Massey, "Social Structure, Household Strategies, and the Cumulative Causation of Migration," *Population Index* 56, no. 1 (1990): 3–26.

21. Robert Brenton Betts, *Christians in the Arab East: A Political Study* (Atlanta, GA: John Knox Press, 1978), 25.

22. For an interesting discussion on sectarian identities see Akram Fouad Khater, *Inventing Home: Emigration, Gender, and the Middle Class in Lebanon, 1870–1920* (Berkeley: University of California Press, 2001), 181n2. Ussama Makdisi, *The Culture of Sectarianism: Community, History, and Violence in Nineteenth-Century Ottoman Lebanon* (Berkeley: University of California Press, 2000). Leila Tarazi Fawaz, *An Occasion for War: Civil Conflict in Lebanon and Damascus in 1860* (Berkeley: University of California Press, 1994).

23. Elizabeth Picard notes that the European diplomatic missions in Beirut played roles in the intrigues and manipulations in the Middle East, and each great power identified local clientele. "France, which stole the first place with Catholics away from Italy, bet on the Maronites. Austria did the same, but with less ambitious economic designs and smaller means. Russia had openly offered its protection to the Orthodox ever since 1744. To Great Britain, long anxious to save the great Muslim unit of the Ottoman Empire from being dismantled and tempted to intrigue with the Maronites, remained the Druze community, through which it pursued its rivalry with France." Elizabeth Picard, *Lebanon, A Shattered Country: Myths and Realities of the Wars in Lebanon,* translated by Franklin Philip (New York: Holmes and Meier, 1996), 20. Also see Alixa Naff, *Becoming American: The Early Arab Immigrant Experience* (Carbondale: Southern Illinois University Press, 1985), 28.

24. Suleiman, introduction to *Arabs in America,* 3.

25. Ibid.

26. Saliba, *Emigration from Syria,* 1; Naff, *Becoming American,* 28.

27. Naff, *Becoming American,* 29. Also see Owen, *The Middle East and the World Economy,* 163.

28. Samir Khalaf, "Communal Conflict in Nineteenth-Century Lebanon," in *Christians and Jews in the Ottoman Empire: The Functioning of a Plural Society,* edited by Braude and Lewis, volume 2, *The Arabic-Speaking Lands,* 1982, 120.

29. Ignacio Klich, "*Criollos* and Arabic Speakers in Argentina: An Uneasy *Pas de Deux,* 1888–1914," in *Lebanese in the World,* edited by Hourani and Shehadi, 1982, 247n4.

30. Naff, *Becoming American,* 84.

31. Interview with Hugo by author, February 19, 1999, in Torreón.

32. Engin Deniz Akarli, "Ottoman Attitudes Towards Lebanese Emigration, 1885–1910," in *Lebanese in the World,* edited by Hourani and Shehadi, 1992, 125.

33. Kemal H. Karpat, "The Ottoman Emigration to America, 1860–1914," *International Journal of Middle Eastern Studies* 17 (May 1985): 182.

34. Ibid.

35. According to Juan Abusaid's immigrant registration card, he was born in Sasud, Lebanon. However, I could not locate a city with that spelling.

36. Interview with Mae by author, February 8, 1999, in Torreón.

37. Charles Issawi, *An Economic History of the Middle East and North Africa, 1800–1914* (New York: Columbia University Press, 1982), 86.

38. Saliba, *Emigration from Syria,* 17n46.

39. Hearing of Abdallah Abraham, El Paso, Texas, October 27, 1906, Seraphic Report, Document No. 51,423, RG 85, INS, NA.

40. Karpat, "Ottoman Emigration," Appendix X, Beirut travel agency advertisement 1896, 205.

41. Samir Khalaf, "The Background and Causes of Lebanese/Syrian Immigration to the United States Before World War I," in *Crossing the Waters: Arabic-Speaking Immigrants to the United States Before 1940*, edited by Eric Hooglund (Washington, DC: Smithsonian Institution Press, 1987), 31.

42. Naff, *Becoming American*, 81.

43. Ibid., 92.

44. Case No. 51,615/106, Hearing of Abraham Assad, May 15, 1907, RG 85, INS, NA.

45. Elmaz Abinader, *Children of the Roojme: A Family's Journey from Lebanon* (Madison: University of Wisconsin Press, 1997), 190.

46. A Presbyterian Seventy-Second Annual Report, 1907, 431–432. Also see Clark Knowlton, "The Social and Spatial Mobility of the Syrian and Lebanese Community in São Paulo, Brazil," in *Lebanese in the World*, edited by Hourani and Shehadi, 1992, 288n11.

47. Patricia Nabti, "Emigration from a Lebanese Village: A Case Study of Bishmizzine," in *Lebanese in the World*, edited by Hourani and Shehadi, 1992, 137.

48. Fabre Steamship Company, New York to U.S. Commission of Immigration, Ellis Island, NY, June 5, 1907, Document No. 51,615/107, RG 85, INS, NA.

49. David Nicholls, "They Came from the Middle East," *Jamaica Journal* (March 1970): 51.

50. Alixa Naff notes that "none . . . developed a Syrian port colony comparable to that of Marseilles." Naff, *Becoming American*, 92.

51. Interview with Hugo by author, February 19, 1999, in Torreón.

52. Cuevas Seba and Mañana Plasencio, *Los libaneses de Yucatán*, 27.

53. Exp. III-297-12, 1934, Siglo XX, SRE, Mexico City.

54. Fernando Mota Martínez, *Más forjadores de México* (Mexico City: Panorama Editorial, 1995), 51–54.

55. Interview with Ahmed by author, April 26, 1999, in Mexico City.

56. Díaz de Kuri and Macluf, *De Líbano a México*, 52, 63, 67. However, according to a 1929 government publication, El Arca de Noé located at Independence Avenue 60 and 62 in Veracruz was owned by Salomón Nasta and Company. Comité Oficial del Libro de Oro de la Revolución Mexicana, editor, *Libro de oro de la Revolución Mexicana: Forjando los nuevos moldes de la nacionalidad* (Mexico City, 1929).

57. Interview with Badía Yapur, January 1988, in Cuevas Seba and Mañana Plasencio, *Los libaneses de Yucatán*, 28.

58. For a comprehensive discussion of the evolution on racial thinking see Moisés González Navarro, "Las ideas raciales de los científicos, 1890–1910," *Historia Mexicana* 37, no. 4 (1988): 565–583.

59. For a further discussion on how Arabs are classified by race see Helen Hatab Samhan, "Not Quite White: Race Classification and the Middle Eastern-American Experience," in *Arabs in America*, edited by Michael W. Suleiman, 209–226. Also see Nancy Faires Conklin and Nora Faires, " 'Colored' and Catholic: The Lebanese in Birmingham, Alabama," in *Crossing the Waters*, edited by Hooglund, 1987, 69–84. For the comparative case of Argentina see Theresa Alfaro-Velcamp, "The Historiography of Arab Immigration to Argentina: The Intersection Between the Imaginary and Real Country," in *Arab and Jewish Immigrants*, edited by Klich

and Lesser, 1998, 231–232. Also see Stepan, *Hour of Eugenics*, 105, 110, 120, 140, 142, 146–153.

60. Klich and Lesser, "Introduction: '*Turco*' Immigrants," 6.

61. González Navarro, *Historia moderna de México*, 159.

62. Jo Carolyn Gibbs Sekaly notes that early Syrian-Lebanese immigrants in Texas often went into the black districts of Beaumont, Texas, to peddle. The Middle Eastern immigrants in Mexico followed a similar trajectory of targeting marginalized communities. Sekaly, "The Syrian-Lebanese Immigration into Southeast Texas and Their Progeny" (master's thesis, Lamar University, Beaumont, Texas, December 1987), 117. In their study of immigrants in Alabama, Conklin and Faires note: "Like their Italian, Jewish, and Greek counterparts, the Lebanese traded with both blacks and whites." Conklin and Faires, " 'Colored' and Catholic," 73.

63. González Navarro, *Los extranjeros en México*, 3:137.

64. Cáceres Menéndez and Loret de Mola, " 'Gebel-Libnan,' " 78. This anecdote is repeated throughout the Yucatán. Cuevas Seba and Mañana Plasencio, *Los libaneses de Yucatán*, 66.

65. Jeffrey Rubin, *Decentering the Regime: Ethnicity, Radicalism, and Democracy in Juchitán, Mexico* (Durham, NC: Duke University Press, 1997), 1, 65. On petty capitalists in Oaxaca see Leigh Binford, "Peasants and Petty Capitalists in Southern Oaxacan Sugar Cane Production and Processing, 1930–1980," *Journal of Latin American Studies* 24: 33–55 (Feb. 1992); also see Scott Cook and Leigh Binford, *Obliging Need: Rural Petty Industry in Mexican Capitalism* (Austin: University of Texas Press, 1990).

66. I thank INAH anthropologist Leticia Reina for generously sharing her findings on Middle Easterners in Oaxaca.

67. Anya Peterson Royce, *Ethnic Identity: Strategies of Diversity* (Bloomington: Indiana University Press, 1982), 111.

68. Ibid., 121–122. For a more in-depth discussion of Zapotec women and the marketplace see Beverly Newbold Chiñas, *The Isthmus Zapotecs: A Matrifocal Culture of Mexico* (Fort Worth, TX: Harcourt Brace Jovanovich College, 1992); Beverly Newbold Chiñas, *La Zandunga: Of Fieldwork and Friendship in Southern Mexico* (Prospect Heights, IL: Waveland Press, 1993); and Lynn Stephen, *Zapotec Women* (Austin: University of Texas Press, 1991).

69. Royce, *Ethnic Identity*, 122.

70. Rebeca Inclán Rubio, "Así hicieron la América. Características generales de la inmigración libanesa en México," paper presented at the Seminario de los Inmigrantes en la Historia de México, Dirección de Estudios Históricos, INAH, November 24, 1982, 60.

71. R. Bayly Winder, "The Lebanese in West Africa," *Comparative Studies in Society and History* 4, no. 3 (1962): 310.

72. Carlos Montfort Rubín, *La cultura del algodón: Torreón de la Laguna* (Torreón, Coahuila, Mexico: Editorial del Norte Mexicano, 1997), 244.

73. Díaz de Kuri and Macluf, *De Líbano a México*, 75.

74. Special Board of Inquiry in the Matter of Milet and Heikel Zakarya, Laredo, Texas, March 25, 1905, Document No. 47,340, RG 85, INS, NA.

75. La Historia de Yamil, Exp. 059, 1922–1942, Archivo Histórico Papeles de Familias, Universidad Iberoamericana, Laguna (AHPF), 16–22.

76. Monica Boyd, "Family and Personal Networks in International Migration: Recent Developments and New Agendas," *International Migration Review* 23, no. 3 (1989), 654.

77. Interview with Hassan Zain Chamut by Urow Schifter, "La inmigración a México durante el porfiriato," 59.

78. Sekaly, "Syrian-Lebanese Immigration into Southeast Texas," 99.

79. Interview with Zacchia Ayoub, February 19, 1982, by John, " 'Trade Will Lead a Man Far,' " 46n6.

80. Sarah E. John, "Arabic-Speaking Immigration to the El Paso Area, 1900–1935," in *Crossing the Waters*, edited by Hooglund, 1987, 107n18.

81. Evelyn Hu-DeHart, "From Immigrant Minority to Racial Minority: The Chinese of Mexico, 1876–1930," paper presented at the 10th Conference of Mexican and North-American Historians, Dallas, Texas, November 1999, 18.

82. Gerardo Rénique, "Race, Region, and Nation: Sonora's Anti-Chinese Racism and Mexico's Postrevolutionary Nationalism, 1920s-1930s," in *Race and Nation in Modern Latin America*, edited by Appelbaum, Macpherson, and Rosemblatt.

83. Meyers, *Forge of Progress*, 121-122. William Meyers, "Second Division of the North: Formation and Fragmentation of the Laguna's Popular Movement, 1910-1911," in *Riot, Rebellion, and Revolution: Rural Social Conflict in Mexico*, edited by Friedrich Katz (Princeton, NJ: Princeton University Press, 1988), 459.

84. In her interviews with Middle Eastern immigrants in southeastern Texas, Jo Carolyn Gibbs Sekaly has found that some immigrants obtained food items from the black community, whose members often were sharecroppers. Sekaly, "Syrian-Lebanese Immigration into Southeast Texas," 104.

85. Francisco Marcos to Commissioner of Immigration, NY, October 28, 1910. Document No. 53,084-373, RG 85, INS, NA.

86. Mexican Consul General C. Romero to A.T. Sherman, Acting Commissioner of Immigration, Ellis Island, New York Harbor, NY, October 31, 1910. Document No. 53,084-373, RG 85, INS, NA.

87. *Diario Oficial, Órgano del Gobierno de los Estados Mexicanos*, 28 de mayo de 1886, capítulo III, artículos 12, 13, 27, 28, 29.

88. Susan Sanderson, Phil Sadel, and Harold Sims, "East Asians and Arabs in Mexico: A Study of Nationalized Citizens (1886–1941)," in *Asiatic Migrations in Latin America*, edited by Luz María Martínez Montiel, 175.

89. Ley Extranjería y Naturalización, Artículo 2, Exp. IV IV-338-1, May 28, 1886, Siglo XIX, SRE.

90. Sanderson, Sadel, and Sims, "East Asians and Arabs in Mexico," 173.

91. "Capítulo 1, Artículo 4 — La mexicana que se case con extranjero no pierde su nacionalidad por el hecho del matrimonio." Ley de Nacionalidad y Naturalización, *Diario Oficial*, January 20, 1934.

92. Ley Extranjería y Naturalización, Articulo IV, Exp. IV-338-1, May 28, 1886, Siglo XIX, SRE. Also see Pablo Yankelevich, "Nación y extranjería en el México revolucionario," *Cuicuilco Nueva Época* 11, no. 31 (May–August 2004): 116.

93. See Katherine Elaine Bliss, *Compromised Positions: Prostitution, Public Health, and Gender Politics in Revolutionary Mexico* (University Park: Pennsylvania State University Press, 2001).

94. These were the decrees of December 1894 and February 1915, in conjunction with the October 1902 decree in Uruguay. Ignacio Klich, "Introduction to the Sources for History of the Middle Easterners in Latin America," *Temas de Africa y Asia* 2 (1993): 209.

95. Ibid.

96. Romana Falcón, "Logros y límites de la centralización porfirista: Coahuila vista desde arriba," in *El dominio de las minorías república restaurada y porfiriato*, compiled by Anne Staples, Gustavo Verduzco Igartúa, Carmen Blázquez Domínguez, and Romana Falcón (Mexico City: Colegio de Mexico, 1989), 132.

97. Cuevas Seba and Mañana Plasencio, *Los libaneses de Yucatán*, 42.

98. I should note that more than one hundred immigrants indicated *Arabia* as their place of birth.

99. Sergio Camposortega Cruz, "Análisis demográfico de las corrientes migratorias a México desde finales del siglo XIX," in *Destino México*, edited by Ota Mishima, 41.

100. Mónica Almeida, "Phoenicians of the Pacific: Lebanese and Other Middle Easterners in Ecuador," *Americas* 53 (July 1996): 92n15. Also see Gladys Jozami, "El retorno de los 'turcos' en la Argentina de los 90," paper presented at the international seminar Discriminación y Racismo en América Latina, University of Buenos Aires, November 23-24, 1994.

101. Cuevas Seba and Mañana Plasencio, *Los libaneses de Yucatán*, 34, 38. Also see Guadalupe Zarate Miguel, *México en la diaspora judía* (Mexico City: INAH, 1986), 71.

102. Cuevas Seba and Mañana Plasencio, *Los libaneses de Yucatán*, 38.

103. Karpat, "Ottoman Emigration," 182.

104. Documents located at the Lebanese Emigration Research Center, Notre Dame University, Beirut, Lebanon (LERC). All documents from LERC were translated by Hayat Abu-Saleh from Arabic to English.

105. Priest Daoud Ass'ad, July 1893, Mexico City, LERC.

106. Priest Daoud Ass'ad, 1894?, LERC.

107. Abdo Yousef Maron, January 12, 1892, Mexico City, LERC.

108. Priest Daoud Ass'ad to Father Yousef Dryian, Mexico City, Mexico, April 2, 1896, LERC.

109. Priest Daoud Ass'ad, Mexico City, Mexico, September 16, 1894, LERC.

110. Ibid.

111. Ibid.

112. Díaz de Kuri and Macluf, *De Líbano a México*, 68-69.

113. Martínez Montiel, *La gota de oro*, 79.

114. Seraphic Report, February 2, 1907, Document No. 51,423-1, RG 85, INS, NA.

115. Marcus Braun Report, New York, June 10, 1907, Document No. 51,403/22, RG 85, INS, NA, 4.

116. Ibid., 5.

Chapter 4

1. B. Traven, "Scenes from a Lumber Camp," in *The Rebellion of the Hanged*, translated by Esperanza López Mateos and Josef Wieder (Farrar, Straus and Giroux, 1952/1980), and reprinted in *The Mexican Reader: History, Culture, Politics*, edited by Gilbert Joseph and Timothy Henderson (Durham, NC: Duke University Press, 2002), 280-281.

2. Thomas Benjamin astutely notes that "this talking and writing [by Mexicans] was also part of an older, larger, and greater project of *forjando patria*, forging a nation, inventing a country, imagining a community across time and space called Mexico. *La Revolución* became part of a master narrative." Thomas Benjamin, *La Revolución: Mexico's Great Revolution as Memory, Myth, and History* (Austin: University of Texas Press, 2000), 14, 20-21.

3. Although this chapter shows that Middle Eastern immigrants often crossed the U.S.-Mexican border to enter the United States, Middle Eastern immigrants often used other ports of entry, such as Havana, Cuba. In 1911, six "Turkish Hebrews" were deported from New York after originally trying to migrate to Cuba. Department of Commerce and Labor, Bureau of Immigration and Naturalization. October 9, 1911. Document No. 53,370-260, RG 85, INS, NA.

4. See Mark Wasserman's introduction to *Provinces of the Revolution: Essays on Regional Mexican History, 1910-1929*, edited by Thomas Benjamin and Mark Wasserman (Albuquerque: University of New Mexico, 1990), 1-14. Also see Nora Hamilton, *The Limits of State Autonomy: Post-Revolutionary Mexico* (Princeton, NJ: Princeton University Press, 1982).

5. John Tutino, "Revolutionary Confrontation, 1913-1918: Regional Factions, Class Conflicts, and the New National State," in *Provinces of the Revolution*, edited by Benjamin and Wasserman, 1990, 41.

6. See Linda B. Hall, *Álvaro Obregón: Power and Revolution in Mexico, 1911-1920* (College Station: Texas A&M University Press, 1981).

7. Brunk, *¡Emiliano Zapata!*, 31-32, n16.

8. A 1998 amendment recognizes Mexican nationality as transmitted by birth but limits nationality to the first generation born abroad.

9. Yankelevich, "Nación y extranjería."

10. Hall, *Álvaro Obregón*, 224.

11. Arnaldo Córdova, *La Revolución en crisis: La aventura del maximato* (Mexico City: Cal y Arena, 1995), 38-39.

12. Benjamin, *La Revolución*, 80. Nora Hamilton states that "there is another element underlying Cárdenas' action during the Maximato which also explained certain of his subsequent actions in the presidency: his concern for the stability of the new institutions of the state." Hamilton, *Limits of State Autonomy*, 119.

13. John Womack, "The Mexican Economy During the Revolution, 1910-1920: Historiography and Analysis," *Marxist Perspectives* (Winter 1978): 83, 300n32. Also see Allen Wells and Gilbert M. Joseph, *Summer of Discontent, Seasons of Upheaval: Elite Politics and Rural Insurgency in Yucatán, 1876-1915* (Stanford, CA: Stanford University Press, 1996).

14. Ibid.

15. Board of Special Inquiry in the Matter of Cecilia Attal, 30, October 18, 1913. Document No. 53,598-165, RG 85, INS, NA.

16. Ibid.

17. Statement made by Heleney Attal, Office of Supervising Inspector, El Paso, Texas, October 29, 1913. Document No. 53,598-165, RG 85, INS, NA.

18. Board of Special Inquiry in the Matter of Cecilia Attal, 30, November 3, 1913. Document No. 53,598-165, RG 85, INS, NA.

19. Office of Supervising Inspector, El Paso, Texas to Commissioner-General of Immigration, Washington, D.C., December 10, 1913. Document No. 53,598-165, RG 85, INS, NA.

20. Board of Special Inquiry, El Paso Texas, November 16, 1914. Document No. 53,598-165, RG 85, INS, NA, 8.

21. Oscar L. Bower, Attorney for Alien, to the Secretary of Labor, Washington, D.C. in the Matter of Cecilia Attal, November 21, 1914, El Paso, Texas. Document No. 53,598-165, RG 85, INS, NA, 8.

22. Supervising Inspector F.W. Berkshire, El Paso, Texas to Commissioner-General of Immigration, U.S. Department of Labor, Immigration Service, Washington, D.C., October 29, 1915. Document No. 53,598-165, RG 85, INS, NA.

23. Board of Special Inquiry held at Laredo, Texas, December 23, 1913. Document No. 53,598-186. RG 85, INS, NA.

24. Ibid., 3.

25. Ibid.

26. Walter S. Reynolds, Attorney at Law, New Castle, PA to Commissioner of Immigration, October 27, 1913. Document No. 53,598-162, RG 85, INS, NA.

27. Report of Execution of Department Decision, Department of Commerce and Labor, Immigration Service, El Paso, Texas, November 12, 1913. Document No. 53,598-162, RG 85, INS, NA.

28. Board of Special Inquiry in the Matter of Tokokichi Saito, November 14, 1913. Document No. 53,598-173, RG 85, INS, NA, 3–4.

29. Ibid., 4.

30. Board of Special Inquiry in the Matter of Shinkichi Kitagawa, El Paso, Texas, June 20, 1912. Document No. 53,387-42, RG 85, INS, NA.

31. Interview with Mae by author, February 8, 1999, in Torreón.

32. Martínez Montiel, "Lebanese Immigration to Mexico," 158.

33. Samuel Brunk, in discussing Zapatistas in Jojutla, notes that "money . . . when there was any, generally came from hacendados and wealthy merchants and officials, who were forced to cooperate or suffer the consequences in terms of scorched cane-fields and sugar mills and looted shops and homes. By March 1912, this policy of intimidation was quite so successful that the principal citizens of Jojutla caused a scandal in the Mexico City press with a meeting to decide how best to pay Zapata to leave them alone." Brunk *¡Emiliano Zapata!*, 73n42.

34. Rebeca Inclán Rubio, "Inmigración libanesa en la Ciudad de Puebla," 118–119. Also see Jacobs Barquet, *Diccionario enciclopédico*, 133.

35. Their interview with Said Assam Rabay was among more than 150 that Martha Díaz de Kuri and Lourdes Macluf conducted with Lebanese descendants; *De Líbano a México*, 66.

36. González Navarro, *Los extranjeros en México*, 2:49.

37. I calculated this number by examining Mexican census data and the foreign-born in 1910. The category of "Arabia Saudita" shows 1,546 immigrants. See Salazar Anaya, *La población extranjera en México*, 105.

38. Díaz de Kuri and Macluf, *De Líbano a México*, 89.

39. Ibid., 88.

40. Meyers, *Forge of Progress*, 33n37.

41. Hu-DeHart, "Immigrants to a Developing Society," 209. William Meyers notes that "in the next few hours, the rampaging mob indiscriminately murdered over three hundred defenseless Chinese and five Japanese, 'owing to the similarity of features.' " Meyers, *Forge of Progress*, 239.

42. Knight, "Racism, Revolution, and Indigenismo," 96–97. Pierre van den Berghe, *Race and Racism: A Comparative Perspective* (New York: Wiley, 1967), 29–30.

43. Katz, *Life and Times of Pancho Villa*, 626. Katz does not elaborate any further on the anti-Arab sentiments in Chihuahua during the Revolution.

44. Evelyn Hu-DeHart describes an incident in which the wives of mine workers gathered at the Ronquillo district in Cananea, Sonora, "making speeches attacking all foreigners. The group grew into an angry mob of almost 500 men and women who marched to a Chinese laundry, ransacked it inside and out, and beat up three Chinese workers trapped on the premises. . . . Finally, thirty mounted soldiers managed to disperse the Mexicans." Hu-DeHart, "Immigrants to a Developing Society," 285. For a detailed discussion of women rioting in the colonial period see William Taylor, *Drinking, Homicide, and Rebellion in Colonial Mexican Villages* (Stanford, CA: Stanford University Press, 1979).

45. Nicolás Abusamra, Victoria Martínez de Peña, and Hassan Zain Chamut, "Como llegaron los libaneses," *Puente: Revista de Historia y Cultura de La Laguna* 1, no. 4 (May–June 1991): 50.

46. José Chamut helped protect the Chinese during the Revolution, in particular the Juan Wu family. The Chinese were considered below Middle Easterners. Chamut also protected six Jewish families. Interview with Lucero by the author, February 10, 1999, in Torreón.

47. Nazas is approximately 150 miles (two to three hours' drive) from Torreón and has a population of less than 3,000. Interview with Elena, librarian in Paso Nacional, Durango, by the author, February 6, 1999, in Paso Nacional, Durango.

48. According to immigrant registration cards, three other Muslim Lebanese went to Nazas: Jacinto (Hassan) Farjat arrived in 1924; Abraham Alejandro Mussa arrived in 1924; and Narciso Chab Ramadan arrived in 1922.

49. Theodore Hamm, American Consul, to Secretary of State, Durango, Mexico, January 14, 1913. Document No. 812.00/5930, M274, U.S. State Department Records, RG 59, U.S. National Archives, College Park, MD (hereafter NACP).

50. Domingo Kuri was perhaps the best-known Middle Easterner for using his diplomatic skills to help incoming immigrants as well as saving many Arabs' lives during the Revolution. Jacobs Barquet, *Diccionario enciclopédico*, 133.

51. Interview with Mae by author, February 8, 1999, in Torreón.

52. Interview with Leonardo by author, February 21, 1999, in Torreón.

53. Bartley F. Yost, American Consul to Juan Abusaid, March 18, 1924, Abusaid Private Family Collection, Torreón, Coahuila.

54. Glick Schiller, Basch, and Blanc-Szanton, "Transnationalism: A New Analytic Framework," 1–2.

55. Interviews with Alonzo and Rodrigo by author, February 22, 1999, in San Pedro de las Colonias.

56. Interview with Mae by author, February 8, 1999, in Torreón. During a conversation with Friedrich Katz in March 23, 1999, he was not able to confirm this rumor nor the role of Middle Easterners helping *villistas* mentioned in his *Life and Times of Pancho Villa*.

57. Díaz de Kuri and Macluf, *De Líbano a México*, 94.

58. John, "Arabic-Speaking Immigration to the El Paso Area," 105–117. Also see Charles H. Harris and Louis R. Sadler, "The 'Underside' of the Mexican Revolution: El Paso, 1912," *Americas* 39, no. 1 (July 1982): 69–83; and Gilbert Malooly, "The Syrian People in El Paso" (paper submitted for history course 390-11, University of Texas at San Antonio, Texas Cultural Institute, May 22, 1953), 30.

59. Friedrich Katz describes Pancho Villa and his men looting stores in Chihuahua. Katz, *Life and Times of Pancho Villa*, 626. It should be noted that Article 27 of the 1917 Constitution declared that all property rights were subordinate to the needs of society. The article also attempted to eliminate ownership of property by aliens. At the same time, the Secretaría de Gobernación in 1917 prohibited enemies of the Mexican government, meaning those who collaborated with Victoriano Huerta. *Gazeta de Saltillo:* Organo Informativo del Archivo Municipal de Saltillo, August 24, 1917, Año VII, No. 18, Archivo Municipal de Saltillo.

60. "Breves Apuntes Biográficos de Nicolás Abusamra Hadad," Exp. 047, 1890–1943, AHPF, 3.

61. "Breves Apuntes Biográficos de Nicolás Abusamra Hadad," Exp. 047, 1890–1943, AHPF, 3.

62. Ibid.

63. Enrique Castro Farías, *Aporte libanés al progreso de América* (Mexico City, Editorial Impacto, 1965), 114.

64. Salomón Bujdud Chain from Nabatiyeh, Lebanon, first went to New York City in 1910 and then emigrated to Mexico.

65. "La letra es la mitad de la mirada," Celia Jalife de Iriate, Exp. 118, 1910–1991, AHPF.

66. *La Opinión*, November 27, 1917, 4. Celia Jalife de Iriate, Exp. 118, 1910–1991, AHPF.

67. Ibid.

68. Adib Khalife to Ahmad Khalife (Carlos Jalife), Beirut, September 4, 1919. Celia Jalife de Iriate, Exp. 118, 1910–1991, AHPF.

69. "Suleiman Baddour founded *al-bayyaan* [bold in original text] (The Declaration) in New York in 1910." Mohammad Sawaie, "Language Loyalty and Language Shift Among Early (1890's–1930's) Arabic-Speaking Immigrants in the United States of America," *Journal of the Humanities* 20, no. 5 (1985): 325.

70. Abdallah Omar Saleh to Ahmad Mustafa Khalife (Carlos Jalife) April 2, 1919. Celia Jalife de Iriate, Exp. 118, 1910–1991, AHPF.

71. John, "Arabic-Speaking Immigration to the El Paso Area," 106n8.

72. Ibid., 105–117. Also see Malooly, "Syrian People in El Paso," 30.

73. Assistant Secretary of Labor to Frederic C. Howe, Commissioner of Immi-

gration, Ellis Island, N.Y.H., May 14, 1917. Document No. 54,254-78, RG 85, INS, NA.

74. Assistant Secretary Memorandum, "In re 56 Chinese and Japanese entered without inspection recently from Mexico at Calexico or vicinity." September 20, 1917. Document No. 54,321-105, RG 85, INS, NA. For more in-depth accounts of the Chinese in the borderlands see Delgado, "In the Age of Exclusion," and Robert Chao Romero, "The Dragon in Big Lusong: Chinese Immigration and Settlement in Mexico, 1882–1940" (Ph.D. diss., University of California, Los Angeles, 2003).

75. James Patrick McGuire, *The Lebanese Texans and The Syrian Texans* (San Antonio: Institute of Texan Cultures, University of Texas, 1974), 4. *Su vida en expansión* (Mexico City: no publisher, no date), Saltillo Municipal Archive, 32.

76. Carlos Macías Richard, *Vida y temperamento: Plutarco Elías Calles, 1877–1920* (Mexico City: Instituto Sonorese de Cultura, Fideicomiso Archivos Plutarco Elías Calles y Fernando Torreblanca, and Fondo de Cultura Económica, 1995), 65, 129.

77. Macías Richard, *Vida y temperamento*, 130n43.

78. Ibid., 129.

79. The James Garfield papers and the Chandler Anderson papers in the Manuscript Division of the U.S. Library of Congress illustrate the complicated dealings American business interests faced with the revolutionary factions. Also see Katz, *Secret War in Mexico.*

80. Lay, *War, Revolution, and the Ku Klux Klan, 63.*

81. Alexandra Minna Stern. "Buildings, Boundaries, and Blood: Medicalization and Nation-Building on the U.S.-Mexico Border, 1910-1930," *Hispanic American Historical Review* 79, no. 1 (February 1999): 41.

82. Ibid., 49.

83. Department of State to Department of Labor, the Immigration and Naturalization Service, May 28, 1921. Microfilm 2032, Slide No. 0261, RG 85, National Archives at Laguna Niguel, California (NALN).

84. Immigration Act of August 3, 1882 (U.S. 22 Statutes-at-Large 214), and Immigration Act of February 20, 1907 (U.S. 34 Statutes-at-Large 898).

85. Acting Secretary, Department of Labor and Commerce, to Hon. John N. Garner, House of Representatives, Washington, D.C., May 23, 1918. Document No. 54,261-12, RG 85, INS, NA.

86. Willis A. Myers, American Vice Consul in Charge, Veracruz, Mexico, to Secretary of State, June 21, 1921. 1921-1931, Microfilm M2032, File 811.1, RG 85, NALN.

87. See case of Gabriel Jorge Matook, age fifteen, March 11, 1911. Document No. 53,147-6, RG 85, INS, NA. Also see case of Sarey Hanna El Baba, age fifteen, August 26, 1911. Document No. 53,303-13, RG 85, INS, NA.

88. Supervising Inspector F.W. Berkshire, El Paso, Texas, to Commissioner-General of Immigration, Department of Commerce and Labor, Immigration Service, Washington, D.C., August 19, 1911. Document No. 53,303-13, RG 85, INS, NA.

89. Board of Special Inquiry in the Matter of Sarey Hanna El Baba, August 11, 1911. Document No. 53,303-13, RG 85, INS, NA.

90. Board of Special Inquiry in the Matter of Khalil Shaaban, Laredo, Texas, April 24, 1912. Document No. 53,387-41, RG 85, INS, NA, 2.

91. Matter of the Appeal of Khalil Shaaban, Laredo, Texas, April 24, 1912. Document No. 53,387-41, RG 85, INS, NA.

92. Board of Special Inquiry in the Matter of Mohammed Ramadan, Laredo, Texas, April 24, 1912. Document No. 53,387-41, RG 85, INS, NA.

93. Commissioner-General, Memorandum for the Acting Secretary, U.S. Department of Labor, Bureau of Immigration, Washington, September 19, 1913. Document No. 53,598/121-130, RG 85, INS, NA.

94. Board of Special Inquiry in the Matter of Youssef Daher, Laredo, Texas, September 10, 1913. Document No. 53,598/121-130, RG 85, INS, NA, 2.

95. Immigrant Inspector A.D. Faulkner to Inspector in Charge, Immigration Service, Cleveland, Ohio, September 12, 1913. Document No. 53,598/121-130, RG 85, INS, NA.

96. Board of Special Inquiry in the Matter of Moustafa Khaleel, Laredo, Texas, August 18, 1913. Document No. 53,598/156, RG 85, INS, NA, 2.

97. Immigration Office, Chicago, August 11, 1913. Document No. 53,598-156, RG 85, INS, NA, 2.

98. Memorandum for the Acting Secretary, U.S. Department of Labor, Bureau of Immigration, Washington, November 1, 1913. Document No. 53,598-156, RG 85, INS, NA.

99. Act. Supervising Inspector, El Paso, Texas to Commissioner-General of Immigration, Washington, D.C., U.S. Department of Labor, Immigration Service, October 24, 1913. Document No. 53,598-159, RG 85, INS, NA.

100. Ibid., 2.

101. Exp. 11-14-273, 1915, Siglo XX, SRE, Mexico City.

102. Exp. 11-14-273, May 24, 1915, Siglo XX, SRE.

103. Exp. 16-25-87, March 25, 1918, Siglo XX, SRE. The document also states: "While the shipment in question is to be permitted to go forward, this action is in no way derogatory to the right of the United States to withhold the re-exportation of merchandise destined for firms in neutral territory who names appear on the Enemy Trading List, irrespective of the point at which the shipment began."

104. Saliba, *Emigration from Syria,* 3.

105. On the eve of World War I, Mount Lebanon had 159 inhabitants per square kilometer, compared to 34 in the *vilayet* of Beirut, 25 in Jerusalem, and 13 in Damascus. Issawi, "Historical Background of Lebanese Emigration," 23.

106. Ibid., 27. George Orfalea challenges Alixa Naff because she "barely mentions the Druze-Maronite massacres and is strangely silent about what to many Syrian immigrants is *the* most traumatic collective experience (whether firsthand or through relatives)—the starvation in World War I." George Orfalea, *Before the Flames: A Quest for the History of Middle Eastern Arab Americans* (Austin: University of Texas Press, 1988), 52.

107. Abinader, *Children of the Roojme,* 150–151.

108. Ibid., 145.

109. Elizabeth Thompson, *Colonial Citizens: Republican Rights, Paternal Privilege, and Gender in Syria and Lebanon* (New York: Columbia University, 1995).

110. Hashen Alazar and Rashid Khalifa, Merida, Mexico, to Ayub Al-'Alami of Mar Elias, October 1919, LERC.

111. Priest Yousef Zghieb, Parroquia, Mexico to Father Butrus of Mar Elias, January 15, 1924, LERC.

112. Anton Halayl, Chief of Tanauring Association, Mexico, July 1919, LERC.

113. Lois J. Roberts, *The Lebanese in Ecuador: A History of Emerging Leadership* (Boulder, CO: Westview Press, 2000), 19.

114. Ibid.

115. Saliba, *Emigration from Syria*, 11n27.

116. Khater, *Inventing Home*, 62.

117. Naff, *Becoming American*, 82.

118. Khater, *Inventing Home*, 10.

119. Interview with Salma by author, February 11, 1999 in Torreón, Coahuila.

120. Mohamed M. Khalife to Ahmed Khalife (Carlos Jalife), Beirut, February 13, 1926. Celia Jalife de Iriate, Exp. 118, 1910-1991, AHPF.

121. Ibrahim Khalife to Ahmed M. Khalife (Carlos Jalife), Beirut, April 11, 1928. Celia Jalife de Iriate, Exp. 118, 1910-1991, AHPF.

122. Khadiya Khalife and signed by Ibrahim Khalife, Ridah Khalife, Muhammad Khalife, and Adib Khalife to Ahmed Khalife (Carlos Jalife), April 27, 1934. Celia Jalife de Iriate, Exp. 118, 1910-1991, AHPF.

123. Salvador Jalife to Cecila García (his wife), Damas, Lebanon, June 7, 1955. Celia Jalife de Iriate, Exp. 118, 1910-1991, AHPF.

124. Álvaro, Diego, and Hugo had visited Lebanon. Interviews by author, February 1999 in Torreón.

125. Evelyn Hu-DeHart notes that "the Chinese colony in Sonora reached a high point in 1919, indicating heavy Chinese immigration to Mexico during the turbulent revolutionary years (1910-1917)." Hu-DeHart, "From Immigrant Minority to . Racial Minority," 2.

126. Alonso Palacios, *Los libaneses y la industria textil*, 111-112.

127. A letter to President Cárdenas in 1938 indicates that the foreigners with organizations in Ciudad Juárez were guilty of hurting Mexican merchants. Exp. 546.2/48, January 10, 1938, Lázaro Cárdenas Files, AGN.

128. John W. Dye, American Consul to Secretary of State, Ciudad Juárez, Mexico, November 21, 1927. Document No. 812.5611/14, RG 59, NACP.

129. The Immigration and Naturalization Service, May 5, 1921. Document No. 55,079/290, Microfilm 2032, Slide No. 0271, RG 85, NALN.

130. The Immigration and Naturalization Service, March 31, 1921, Microfilm 2032, Slide No. 0291, RG 85, NALN.

131. Acting Assistant Surgeon Irving McNeil to Assistant Surgeon J.W. Tappan, El Paso, Texas. This report came in response to concern over standardization of medical inspections. In April 1925 Surgeon J. C. Perry of the U.S. Public Health Service reported on the status of Arizona's Border Immigration Stations in Ajo, San Fernando, Tucson, Nogales, Naco, and Douglas. The Immigration and Naturalization Service, Medical Exams, December 22, 1923. Document No. 52,903-29, RG 85, INS, NA, 1.

132. Medical Exams, December 13, 1923. Document No. 52,903-29, RG 85, INS, NA, 1-2.

133. The Immigration and Naturalization Service, April 21, 1921. Document

No. 55,079/290, Microfilm 2032, Slide No. 0274, RG 85, NALN. In particular, three aliens of "Jewish race" had entered the United States from Mexico unlawfully. May 2, 1921. Microfilm 2032, Slide No. 0277-0279, RG 85, NALN.

134. Shawn Lay writes that "in 1923, for example, out of 80,793 Mexicans legally emigrated to the United States, more than 40,000 were processed through El Paso. These immigrants were supplemented by thousands of illegal aliens who did not bother with the technicalities of documentation." Lay, *War, Revolution and the Ku Klux Klan*, 56n33.

135. The Immigration and Naturalization Service, May 5, 1921. Document No. 55,079/290, Microfilm 2032, Slide No. 0284-0285, RG 85, NALN.

136. Secretary James J. Davis Memorandum for the Bureau of Immigration, November 17, 1923. Document No. 52,903-29, RG 85, INS, NA.

137. The Immigration and Naturalization Service, July 29, 1922. Microfilm 2032, Slide No. 0015, RG 85, NALN.

138. American Consulate General, Berlin, December 3, 1921, Robert Mayhofer in Koemisberg, Germany, Microfilm 2032, Slide No. 0212, RG 85, NALN.

139. The Immigration and Naturalization Service, American Consulate, Veracruz. June 17, 1921, Microfilm 2032, Slide No. 0258, RG 85, NALN.

140. American Consulate, Antwerp, Belgium, May 13, 1922. Microfilm 2032, Slide No. 0131-0138, RG 85, NALN.

141. John Wood, Veracruz, Mexico, to Secretary of State, October 11, 1922. Document No. 812.55.63, M274, Roll 204, U.S. State Department Records, RG 59, NACP.

142. In September 1924 an incident was recorded with two Arabs accusing one another of defamation and injury. Najib N. Bitar of Tepic, Nayarit, accused Julio Abunader of *delito de injurias,* for which Abunader was sentenced to prison in December 1924. Whether Abunader served his sentence is not known, only that two Syrians went to court over a dispute and one lost. Exp. 9-19-137, September 6, 1924, December 10, 1924, Siglo XX, SRE.

143. José Helú helped found La Liga Literaria in the 1930s and wrote editorials in the various Lebanese community newsletters. For a more detailed discussion of José Helú see Díaz de Kuri and Macluf, *De Líbano a México,* 83, 210.

144. Exp. 9-18-316, January 9, 1922, Siglo XX, SRE.

145. Álvaro Obregón to Naoum A. Mokarzell, c/o José C. Helú, Exp. 802-L-19, September 25, 1922, Álvaro Obregón Files, AGN.

146. *El Universal* (Mexico City), September 23, 1923. I would like to thank Sarah Buck for bringing this article to my attention.

147. Ibid. The article reads: *Árabes casi siempre que se dedican a vender ropa en abonos* (Arabs almost always dedicate themselves to selling clothes on installments).

148. For a critical discussion about Calles see Córdova, *La Revolución en crisis.* For a more autobiographical account of Calles see Macías Richard, *Vida y temperamento.*

149. In reading over several cases, I encountered letters to Mexican presidents that discussed how certain Arabs had aligned with the *delahuertistas.* I found a specific case, for example, in Exp. 2.362.2(26)28, December 5, 1927, Dirección General de Gobierno (DGG), AGN.

150. For the list of illnesses see Moisés González Navarro, *Población y sociedad*

en México, 2:42. Martínez Montiel and Reynoso Medina, "Inmigración europea y asiática," 265.

151. Exp. 18-19-236, June 25, 1926, Siglo XX, SRE.

152. Liz Hamui-Halabe, "Re-creating Community: Christians from Lebanon and Jews from Syria in Mexico, 1900–1938," in *Arab and Jewish Immigrants in Latin America*, edited by Klich and Lesser, 129n10.

153. Marín Guzmán, "Los inmigrantes árabes en México," 130.

154. *Diario Oficial*, July 15, 1927, volume 43, no. 13.

155. Daniela Gleizer Salzman, "La política mexicana frente a la recepción de refugiados judíos (1934–1942)," in *México, país refugio: La experiencia de los exilios en el siglo XX*, coordinated by Pablo Yankelevich (Mexico City: INAH and Plaza y Valdés, 2002), 120.

156. "It is not believed that the importance of the cause prompting this restriction, as set forth in the decree, has been exaggerated, particularly since a large number of the immigrants subject to the restrictive measure are known to come to this country in the belief that their entry into the United States may be effected more easily than from their native countries." Alexander W. Weddell, American Consul General, Mexico City, to Secretary of State, July 20, 1927, 1910–1929. Document No. 812.55, RG 59, NACP.

157. Exp. 2.3622 (5-1)-29, July 22, 1926, DGG, AGN.

158. Exp. 2.362.(10) 2, January 9, 1928, DGG, AGN.

159. How Alejandro Athié became a *hacendado* is not addressed in the records. However, it is quite possible that during the Revolution, someone owed him some favors and repaid him with these *haciendas*.

160. Exp. 2.362.(10) 2, January 9, 1928, DGG, AGN.

161. For an insightful fictional depiction of post-revolutionary tensions over land seizures see Carlos Fuentes' 1962 novel, *The Death of Artemio Cruz*, translated by Alfred Mac Adam (New York: Noonday Press, 1991).

162. Exp. 2.363.2 (29) 91, November 22, 1927, DGG, AGN.

163. Exp. 2.362.2(26)28, December 5, 1927, DGG, AGN.

164. It was not clear if the father of the baby was Señor Aguilar or someone else. In her testimony in 1930 she does not mention an abortion. However, in other documents, a doctor testifies that she had the abortion at eight months due to an infected placenta. Exp. 2363.3 (26)8, January 1, 1928, DGG, AGN.

165. Exp. 2.362.2 (26) 28, December 5, 1927, DGG, AGN.

166. Exp. 2.362.2 (26) 28, April 21, 1928, DGG, AGN.

167. Exp. 2.362.2 (26) 28, June 16, 1930, DGG, AGN.

168. Pablo Yankelevich, "Extranjeros indeseables en México (1911–1940). Una aproximación cuantitativa a la aplicación del artículo 33 constitucional," *Historia México* 53, no. 3 (January–March 2004): 706, 734.

169. This is a simplified version of a rather complex political struggle. For more in-depth discussion see Córdova, *La Revolución en crisis*, 89–144.

170. Ibid.

171. Exp. 2.363.2 (6) 9, DGG, AGN.

172. Exp. 2.362.2(50) 18, October 27, 1928, DGG, AGN.

173. Exp. 2.362.2(50) 18, January 12, 1928, DGG, AGN.

174. "Accord prohibiting the immigration of foreigners to enter the country to

engage in manual labor for wages." *Diario Oficial,* April 27, 1929, first section. Hamui-Halabe, "Re-creating Community," 142n11.

175. Instituto Nacional de Migración, *Compilación histórica de la legislación migratoria en México 1821–2002* (Mexico City, 2002), 151.

176. Exp. IV-136-18, October 21, 1929, Siglo XX, SRE.

177. Ibid.

178. Ibid.

179. As many in the Middle Eastern community relied on France and its protectorate status, the United States appealed to the British government, as Protectorate of Palestine, for assistance with immigrants as well. In 1924 the Bureau of Immigration wrote the British Embassy asking that Justin Kirreh (or Kirrel), a native of Palestine, be deported for polygamy. Bureau of Immigration, Department of Labor, Washington, D.C., British Embassy, Washington, D.C. to W.W. Sibray, October 11, 1924. Case File No. 1906-1932, Document No. 55,079-142, RG 85, INS, NA.

180. In 1921 the first quota law was passed in the United States, limiting immigration of each nationality to 3 percent of the number of foreign-born persons of that nationality living in the United States in the 1910 Census. In 1924 the National Origins Act was enacted in the United States to limit immigration of each nationality to 2 percent of the number of persons of that nationality as determined in the 1890 Census and set a minimum of 100 persons for each country. And in 1929 the National Quota Law of 1924 was announced, setting the annual quotas of 1924 for each country apportioned according to each nationality's percentage in the 1920 Census. Charles Keely, "Immigration in the Interwar Period," in *Immigration and U.S. Foreign Policy,* edited by Robert Tucker, Charles Keely, and Linda Wrigley (Boulder, CO: Westview Press, 1990), 44–50.

181. During the 1920s, twenty-three recorded Ottoman, Palestinian, and Syrian immigrants went to Saltillo. *Gazeta Saltillo:* Organo Informativo del Archivo Municipal de Saltillo, 1920, Año VII, No. 20, Archivo Municipal de Saltillo.

Chapter 5

1. This process of Arabs becoming store owners also occurred in Argentina. Gabriela Olivera notes that in La Rioja, a northwestern province in Argentina, "commercial houses comprised various shops and stores, generally in the hands of one family, often of Arab immigrant origin." She notes that "85 percent of the total owners of such businesses were 'Arab' (Syrians and Lebanese) immigrants or sons of immigrants." Gabriela Olivera, "Forestry in the *Llanos* of La Rioja (1900–1960)," in *Region and Nation: Politics, Economy, and Society in Twentieth-Century Argentina,* edited by James P. Brennan and Ofelia Pianetto (New York: St. Martin's Press, 2000), 137, n20.

2. Jonathan Brown and Alan Knight, *The Mexican Petroleum Industry in the Twentieth Century* (Austin: University of Texas Press, 1992), and Lorenzo Meyer, *Mexico and the United States in the Oil Controversy, 1917–1942* (Austin: University of Texas Press, 1972).

3. Francisco E. Balderrama and Raymond Rodríguez, *Decade of Betrayal:*

Mexican Repatriation in the 1930s (Albuquerque: University of New Mexico Press, 1995), 121.

4. Western Union Cable from MacCormack to Washington D.C., December 19, 1933. Document No. 55,817-902-A, RG 85, INS, NA.

5. Chamber of Commerce of the United States of America, Washington, D.C. to D.W. MacCormack, Commissioner General, Bureau of Immigration, Department of Labor, July 25, 1933. Document No. 55,817-902-A, RG 85, INS, NA, 2.

6. William P. Blocker, American Consul, Ciudad Juárez to R. Henry Norweb, Esquire, Chargé d' Affaires ad interim, American Embassy, México, D.F., June 23, 1934. Document No. 55,817-902-A, RG 85, INS, NA.

7. "24-Hour Ports Recommended at Conference," *El Paso Herald Post,* January 31, 1934.

8. "Telegramas Falsificados," *El Universal: El Gran Diario de México,* Mexico City, September 13, 1940. "Falsificación de pasaportes en relaciones," *Excelsior: El Periódico de la Vida Nacional,* Mexico City, September 13, 1940.

9. He married into Porfirian elite. Díaz de Kuri and Macluf, *De Líbano a México,* 82, 84.

10. Exp. IV-397-19, December 30, 1930, Siglo XX, SRE, Mexico City, 1.

11. Ibid., 2.

12. Ibid. Despite these strong feelings, six months later Almanza submitted a report on Amado E. Afif to be naturalized as a Mexican citizen. Exp. IV-195-51, June 23, 1931, Siglo XX, SRE.

13. Stepan, *"Hour of Eugenics",* 142.

14. The United States implemented a similar policy with the Alien Registration Act of 1940.

15. Secretaría Oficial de Gobierno to C. Presidente Municipal, Torreón, Coahuila, March 28, 1932, Oficios 1932, Torreón Municipal Archive.

16. Oficios 1937, Torreón Municipal Archivo, Torreón, Coahuila.

17. For instance, Isidro Attie Dayan was not at the address that he indicated, so they left a message with his wife. León N. Martínez, Inspección Gral. De Policía, Torreón, Coahuila to C. Presidente Municipal, Torreón, Coahuila, March 8, 1934, Oficios 1934, Torreón Municipal Archive.

18. The Secretary of the Interior wrote in 1934 that Torreón should only be registering definitive immigrants, not tourists. Lic. José Magro Soto of Secretaría Oficial de Gobierno to C. Presidente Municipal, Torreón, Coahuila, April 28, 1934, Oficios 1934, Torreón Municipal Archive.

19. Exp. 546.2/13, December 28, 1934, Lázaro Cárdenas Files, AGN.

20. Interview with Mae by author, February 21, 1999, in Torreón. Ruth Elizabeth Arboleyda Castro, "La crisis del ejido en la Comarca Lagunera. Tres casos," in *Boletín del Proyecto Archivo Agrarios,* no. 9 (January–April 2000), 6. Also see Iván Restrep and Salomón Eckstein, *La agricultura colectiva en México: La experiencia de la Laguna* (Mexico City: Siglo Veintiuno, 1975), 23–44.

21. Exp. 546.2/75, May 21, 1936, Lázaro Cárdenas Files, AGN.

22. Exp. 546.2/80, July 22, 1936, Lázaro Cárdenas Files, AGN.

23. A. García Toledo to Gobernador de Saltillo, Coahuila, Exp. 2/367(3)25440, June 4, 1937, Lázaro Cárdenas Files, AGN.

24. Lay, *War, Revolution, and the Ku Klux Klan,* 57, 155.

25. R. Medina Guzmán to Alejandro Chaib, José Name and Owszei Sladownik, Nueva Rosita, Coahuila, Exp. 2/367(3)25440, June 4, 1937, Lázaro Cárdenas Files, AGN.

26. Summary of directive, *Diario Oficial*. Secretaría Oficial de Gobierno to C. President Municipal, Torreón, Coahuila, July 29, 1937, Oficios 1937, Torreón Municipal Archive.

27. Cámara Nacional de Comercio de Industria de Torreón to C. President Municipal, Torreón, Coahuila, July 19, 1937, Torreón, Coahuila. Oficios 1937, Torreón Municipal Archive.

28. Ota Mishima, preface to *Destino México*, 13n10.

29. President Municipal, Torreón, Coahuila to Secretaría del Ejecutivo del Estado, Saltillo, Coahuila, December 14, 1938, Oficios 1938, Torreón Municipal Archive.

30. Exp. 546.2/48, August 26, 1937, Lázaro Cárdenas Files, AGN.

31. Ibid.

32. Manuel Sánchez Cuen of the Secretaría de la Economía Nacional to President Cárdenas. Exp. 546-2/48, April 16, 1938, Lázaro Cárdenas Files, AGN.

33. Exp. 2.360(3)35883, December 30, 1938, Lázaro Cárdenas Files, AGN.

34. Lic. Armando Flores, Secretaría de Relaciones Exteriores to President Municipal, Torreón, Coahuila, June 20, 1939, Oficios 1939, Torreón Municipal Archive.

35. Neuman, *Strangers to the Constitution*, 19–43.

36. Ernesto Hidalgo of Secretaría de Relaciones Exteriores to President Municipal, Torreón, Coahuila, December 15, 1939. Oficios 1939, Torreón Municipal Archive.

37. It should be noted that Juan Abusaid's son was a Torreón municipal president sometime in the 1960s or 1970s.

38. Exp. II-474-18, February 5, 1931, Buenos Aires, Siglo XX, SRE, 4.

39. Exp. 2.360 (29)-59, February 24, 1931, Pascual Ortíz Rubio Files, AGN.

40. Ibid.

41. Exp. 2.360 (29)-59, March 24, 1931, Pascual Ortíz Rubio Files, AGN.

42. Exp. 2.360 (29)-59, June 12, 1931, Pascual Ortíz Rubio Files, AGN.

43. Ota Mishima, *Destino México*, 12–13.

44. E.W. Easton, American Vice Consul, Mazatlán, Sinaloa, Mexico to Secretary of State, January 16, 1932. Document No. 812.111/335, M1370, RG 59, U.S. State Department Records, NACP.

45. Henry T. Unverzagt, American Vice Consul, San Luis Potosí to Secretary of State, January 7, 1932. Document No. 812.43, RG 59, NACP. The vice-consul summarized the organization's aims.

46. Exp. 181/11, December 12, 1933, Abelardo Rodríguez Files, AGN.

47. Exp. 181/11, October 25, 1933, Abelardo Rodríguez Files, AGN, 2. This twelve-page constitution outlined the group's concern about secret mafias, and one of the solutions was to boycott foreign stores and products.

48. Exp. 181/11, November 23, 1933, Abelardo Rodríguez Files, AGN.

49. In January 1934 Antonio G. Díaz, the Secretary of Conflict of the Committee for Race, asked for a restriction on Jewish immigration. Exp. 181/11, January 5, 1934, Abelardo Rodríguez Files, AGN.

50. Martínez Montiel and Reynoso Medina, "Inmigración europea y asiática," 270n50.

51. Exp. 241-R-B-28, July 12, 1927, Plutarco Elías Calles Files, AGN.

52. Exp. 21-26-51, November 17, 1927, Siglo XX, SRE.

53. Ibid.

54. Exp. III-297-12, 1934, Siglo XX, SRE. The document continues: "Aliens Excluded: Contract laborers, also aliens who, because of old age, deformity, physical defect, etc. may be incapable of work, illiterates, drug fiends, anarchists, also natives and/or subjects of Syria, Lebanon, Palestine, Arabia and Turkey are excluded from admission to Mexico."

55. Julián Slim to President Abelardo Rodríguez, Exp. 519.5/81, June 8, 1934, President Abelardo Rodríguez Files, AGN.

56. Lic. José Magro Soto to Julián Slim, Exp. 2.362.2.(6)23, June 13, 1934, President Abelardo Rodríguez Files, AGN.

57. Paulo Tacla to President Abelardo Rodríguez, Exp. 210.33, April 2, 1934, Abelardo Rodríguez Files, AGN.

58. According to Jeffrey Lesser, this letter came four months after the Brazilian Ministry of Labor allowed Assyrians, under certain conditions, to migrate to Brazil: "from January to April 1934, the story [of Assyrian emigration] was constantly in the news, . . . *Correio da Manhã* and *Diário Carioca,* the two papers most ardently opposed to Assyrian entry, frequently ran more than one article on the same day." Lesser, *Negotiating National Identity,* 69n136.

59. Nora Hamilton describes how Cárdenas constructed state power through his personal style and use of the party. "The most dramatic method used by Cárdenas to centralize his control was his personal style of government—the attempt to make himself immediately accessible to the people and to directly intervene in important programs and reforms." In addition, "the Cárdenas government in effect had given legitimacy to the state as representative of the revolution." Hamilton, *Limits of State Autonomy,* 134, 162.

60. See Luis Medina Peña, *Hacia el nuevo estado: México, 1920-1924* (Mexico City: Fondo de Cultura Económica, 1994), on how post-revolutionary leaders constructed the Mexican state.

61. *El Hombre Libre,* January 12, 1934, quoted in Laura Pérez Rosales, "Anticardenismo and Anti-Semitism in Mexico, 1934–1940," translated by Alejandro Pescador, in *The Jewish Diaspora in Latin American: New Studies on History and Literature,* edited by David Sheinin and Lois Baer Barr (New York: Garland, 1996), 189.

62. *Omega,* February 2, 1934, quoted in Pérez Rosales, "Anticardenismo and Anti-Semitism," 191.

63. Exp. 545.2/56, October 1935, Lázaro Cárdenas Files, AGN, 2.

64. Ibid., 7.

65. Exp. 546.2/48, December 14, 1935, Lázaro Cárdenas Files, AGN.

66. Exp. 546.2/48, April 3, 1936, July 14, 1936, Lázaro Cárdenas Files, AGN.

67. Exp. 546.2/48, July 27, 1936, Lázaro Cárdenas Files, AGN.

68. Instituto Nacional de Migración, *Compilación histórica,* 181. Mónica Palma Mora, " 'Una inmigración bienvenida'. Los ejecutivos de empresas extranjeras en

México durante la segunda mitad del siglo XX," in *Los inmigrantes en el mundo de los negocios siglos XIX y XX,* coordinated by Rosa María Meyer and Delia Salazar Anaya (Mexico City: CONACULTA and INAH, 2003), 237.

69. González Navarro, *Los extranjeros en México,* 41–42.

70. "To save Mexico for Mexicans and to save Mexicans for Mexico is, in synthesis, the Mexican Revolution," stated Moisés Saenz in 1926. Thomas Benjamin, "Rebuilding the Nation," in *The Oxford History of Mexico,* edited by Michael C. Meyer and William H. Beezley (New York: Oxford University Press, 2000), 478.

71. Exp. 546.2/48, September 2, 1937, Lázaro Cárdenas Files, AGN.

72. Exp. 546.2/48, September 6, 1937, Lázaro Cárdenas Files, AGN.

73. Exp. 546.2/97, April 2, 1937, Lázaro Cárdenas Files, AGN.

74. Ibid.

75. Exp. 546.2/48, December 6, 1937, Lázaro Cárdenas Files, AGN.

76. Ibid., 2.

77. Evelyn Hu-DeHart, in describing the Chinese, notes that "while working as cooks or domestics, in their restaurants and laundries, these disease-ridden Chinese spread contagious diseases to their unsuspecting, innocent Mexican clients." Hu-DeHart, "From Immigrant Minority to Racial Minority," 21. Also see Howard Markel and Alexandra Minna Stern, "The Foreignness of Germs: The Persistent Association of Immigrants and Disease in American Society," *Milbank Quarterly* 80, no. 4 (2002): 766.

78. Exp. 546.2/48, June 24, 1938, Lázaro Cárdenas Files, AGN.

79. Exp. 546.2/48, November 29, 1940, Lázaro Cárdenas Files, AGN.

80. In May 1936, through Decrees 1813 and 1823 the Guatemalan government prohibited the establishment of commercial activities of those of Turkish, Syrian, Lebanese, Arab, Palestinian, Armenian, Egyptian, Persian, or Afghan descent. Klich, "Introduction to the Sources," 210. Also see Lelio Mármora, "La fundamentación de las políticas migratorias internacionales en América Latina," *Estudios Migratorios Latinoamericanos* (December 1988), 380–381.

81. El Salvador also singled out its Turkish, Palestinian, Arab, Syrian and Lebanese immigrants by forbidding them from translating into Spanish or Hispanicizing their names in September 1930, through Decree 65. Klich, "Introduction to the Sources," 209.

82. Nicaragua, through it immigration legislation in 1930, banned the entry of Turks, Arabs, Syrians, and Armenians and those of black and gypsy races.

83. The Honduran government in March 1934 restricted the entry of Arabs, Turks, Lebanese, Syrians, Armenians, and Palestinians unless they could devote themselves solely to agriculture. Klich, "Introduction to the Sources," 210. Darío Euraque notes that "according the 1929 legislation, immigrant *Arabes, Turcos, Sirios, Armenios, Negros,* and 'Coolies' were required to deposit 2,500 dollars when entering the country. Local relatives from these 'races' could secure temporary permits for immigrant kinship of the same races. The Immigration Law of 1934 restated many elements of the 1929 legislation." Darío A. Euraque, "The Arab-Jewish Economic Presence in San Pedro Sula, the Industrial Capital of Honduras: Formative Years, 1880s–1930s," in *Arab and Jewish Immigrants in Latin America,* edited by Klich and Lesser, 105.

84. In February 1937, by Decree 397 Colombia imposed more difficult require-

ments for Egyptians, Greeks, Moroccans, Palestinians, Syrians, and Turks to enter the country.

85. Article 121 limited the influx by nationality to 2 percent of the number of those who had arrived in the previous fifty years from the same country. Jeffrey Lesser, *Welcoming the Undesirables: Brazil and the Jewish Question* (Berkeley: University of California Press, 1995), 66, 67n120. Brazilian constitution of July 16, 1934, art. 121, par. 6.

86. Lesser, *Welcoming the Undesirables*, 92.

87. Medina Peña, *Hacia el nuevo estado*.

88. Kenny et al., *Inmigrantes y refugiados españoles*, 33. Clara E. Lida, *Inmigración y exilio: Reflexiones sobre el caso español* (Mexico City: Colegio de México and Siglo Ventiuno, 1979).

89. Mörner with Sims, *Adventurers and Proletarians*, 93.

90. González Navarro, *Población y sociedad en México*, 2:51.

91. "The idea of the extended family was important to early Syrian immigrants, especially in economic terms. . . . Family members knew that if they all worked together, concentrating wholeheartedly on developing their economic base, they would have a better chance to survive economically and become successful." John, "Arabic-Speaking Immigration to the El Paso Area," 106.

92. For a detailed discussion of Mexico during World War II see Rafael Loyola, coordinator, *Entre la guerra y estabilidad política El México de los 40* (Mexico: Grijalbo and CONACULTA, 1986).

93. Exp. 550/104, November 22, 1943, Manuel Ávila Camacho files, AGN.

94. Exp. 550/104, October 3, 1944, Manuel Ávila Camacho files, AGN.

95. Angélica Reyna Bernal, "El pensamiento y la política poblacionista en el México de la primera mitad del siglo XX," in *El poblamiento de México: Una visión histórica demográfica*, volume 4: *México en el siglo XX.* (Mexico City, Secretaría de Gobernación, n.d.), 70.

96. Instituto Nacional de Migración, *Compilación histórica*, 215–219. Marín-Guzmán and Zéraoui, *Arab Immigration in Mexico*, 53.

97. Meyer and Salazar Anaya, introduction to *Los inmigrantes en el mundo de los negocios*, 12.

98. Klich, "Introduction to the Sources," 210.

99. Document No. 56,146–140, Acc. 58A 734, INS, RG 85, NA.

100. Historical accounts are not clear about what happened in the 1930s and 1940s to Domingo Kuri, who had aided so many of the early Middle Eastern immigrants arriving in Veracruz.

101. Jo Carolyn Gibbs Sekaly describes how Syrians in southeastern Texas sought out fellow countrymen when migrating and settling. "Once one of their 'neighbors' was established there it was an automatic occurrence for others from the same town to migrate to the same area. It was important for them to know someone who could set them up with some kind of business, whether it was a brother, uncle, cousin, friend or friend of a friend." Sekaly, "Syrian-Lebanese Immigration into Southeast Texas," 62–63.

102. Alonso, *Los libaneses y la industria textil*, 137, 140–141. A character in Ángeles Mastretta's novel *Arráncame la vida* (New York: Vintage Español, 1986) is an Arab named Julián Amed, who owns the La Victoria store in Puebla (77).

103. Alonso, *Los libaneses y la industria textil,* 143–144.

104. Mónica Almeida, in discussing Middle Easterners in Ecuador, notes a similar pattern: "Nowadays a number of financial institutions, hotels, media companies and industries are controlled by Ecuadorans of Arab origin. But the Middle Easterners still remain active as well in importing fabrics, appliances, toys, perfume and other goods." Almeida, "Phoenicians of the Pacific," 101.

105. Cáceres Menéndez and Loret de Mola, " 'Gebel-Libnan' (Montaña Blanca)," 66–67.

106. Luz María Martínez Montiel argues that the Lebanese and Jewish immigrants formed ethnic minorities in Mexico because of the way Mexican society marginalized and rejected them both socially and economically. Martínez Montiel, *La gota de oro,* 4, 9.

Chapter 6

1. Cáceres Menéndez and Loret de Mola, " 'Gebel-Libnan' (Montaña Blanca)," 27.

2. For a strong case on how Arabs have assimilated into Mexican society see Marín-Guzmán and Zéraoui, *Arab Immigration in Mexico.*

3. "Breves Apuntes Biográficos de Nicolás Abusamra Hadad," Exp. 047, 1890–1943, AHPF, 3.

4. Interviews in Cáceres Menéndez and Loret de Mola, " 'Gebel-Libnan' (Montaña Blanca)," 66–67.

5. Martínez Montiel and Reynoso Medina, "Inmigración europea y asiática," 273.

6. Foreign elitism dates back to the Spanish Empire. Octavio Paz calls it "imperialism," whereby "imperialism has not allowed us to achieve 'historical normality,' and the ruling classes of Mexico have no other mission than to collaborate, as administrators or associates, with a foreign power." Octavio Paz, *The Labyrinth of Solitude,* translated by Lysander Kemp, Yara Milos, and Rachel Phillips Belash (New York: Grove Weidenfeld, 1985), 146.

7. Samuel L. Baily, *Immigrants in the Lands of Promise: Italians in Buenos Aires and New York City, 1870–1914* (Ithaca, NY: Cornell University Press, 1999), 13, see nn11–12.

8. "Networks brought into being by immigration serve to create and perpetuate inequality. Lest anyone think that solidarity and mutual aid have nothing but gratifying results, we should recognize two things: 1) members of immigrant groups often exploited one another as they would not have dared to exploit the native-born, and 2) every inclusion also constitutes an exclusion." Charles Tilly, "Transplanted Networks," in *Immigration Reconsidered: History, Sociology, and Politics,* edited by Virginia Yans-McLaughlin (New York: Oxford University Press, 1990), 92.

9. "La Historia de Yamil," Exp. 059, 1922–1942, AHPF, 16–22.

10. Dib Morrillo, *Memorias y biografía* (Actopán, Hidalgo: N.p., September 3, 1957), 55. At Colegio de México library, Mexico City.

11. Throughout Latin America, Middle Easterners are often referred to as *abo-*

neros for their system of selling merchandise in installments, or *abonos*. "Se trataba de los famosos buhoneros que vendían prácticamente todo tipo de mercancía en abonos, por lo que se les conocía también como 'aboneros.'" Urow Schifter, "La inmigración a México durante el porfiriato," 59. Also see Alonso Palacios, *Los libaneses y la industria textil*, 107.

12. Carlos Martínez Assad, *En el verano, la tierra: Un viaje de amor y misterio; un diálogo encantado entre México y Líbano* (Mexico City: Editorial Planeta de México, 1994), 39.

13. Cáceres Menéndez and Loret de Mola, "'Gebel-Libnan' (Montaña Blanca)," 83.

14. Buyers also get free Internet access. Geri Smith, "Mexico's Richest Man is Betting Big on U.S. Computer Retailing: Slim's New World," *Business Week*, March 6, 2000, 167.

15. Alonso Palacios, *Los libaneses y la industria textil*, 111–112.

16. Cáceres Menéndez and Loret de Mola, "'Gebel-Libnan' (Montaña Blanca)," 87.

17. Interview with Álvaro by author, February 12, 1999, in Torreón.

18. Jacobs Barquet, *Diccionario enciclopédico*, 133.

19. The Abusaids were rumored to be one of the wealthiest families in Torreón; however, as Arab tradition dictates, Juan Abusaid's eldest son inherited his wealth, and the younger Abusaid apparently lost most of the family fortune.

20. Luis Alfonso Ramírez Carrillo, *Secretos de familia: Libaneses y élites empresariales en Yucatán* (Mexico City: CONACULTA, 1994), 187.

21. Díaz de Kuri and Macluf, *De Líbano a México*, 185.

22. Alonso Palacios, *Los libaneses y la industria textil*, 116.

23. Ibid., 137, 140–141.

24. Interviews in Cáceres Menéndez and Loret de Mola, "'Gebel-Libnan' (Montaña Blanca)," 86.

25. This construction continued into the 1990s. The Centro Libanés in 1997 published *Líbano, crisol de culturas*, whose authors indicate that it is important to give a historic vision of a people little known but with a history going back 6,000 years. The emphasis on this extensive history of trading and their Phoenician roots is echoed throughout Lebanese literature; Exp. 216, 1997, AHPF. Also see Kaufman, *Reviving Phoenicia*, and Kamal Salibi, *A House of Many Mansions: The History of Lebanon Reconsidered* (Berkeley: University of California Press, 1988).

26. Anderson, *Imagined Communities*, 6.

27. This notion of mutual constructions occurring simultaneously and intersecting is drawn from José Limón's discussion of culture in both Greater Mexico and the American South. José E. Limón, *American Encounters: Greater Mexico, the United States, and the Erotics of Culture* (Boston: Beacon Press, 1998), 19.

28. Lesser, *Negotiating National Identity*, 51. Boyd, "Family and Personal Networks," 654.

29. In studying Arab immigrants in Argentina, Lilia Bertoni and Gladys Jozami provide comprehensive analyses of how the immigrants established their social networks. Lilia Bertoni, "De Turquía a Buenos Aires. Una colectividad nueva a fines del siglo XIX," 87; Jozami, "Identidad religiosa e integración cultural," 108.

30. Walter P. Zenner, "Arabic-Speaking Immigrants in North America as

Middleman Minorities," *Ethnic and Racial Studies* 5, no. 4 (October 1982): 457–458.

31. The category of *comerciante* may have glossed over some other, illegal occupations such as smuggling.

32. These percentages are derived from my sample of 8,240 immigrant registration cards. In examining the variable of occupation, only 8,196 immigrant responses were available.

33. Cáceres Menéndez and Loret de Mola, "'Gebel-Libnan' (Montaña Blanca)," 85.

34. Jacobs Barquet, *Diccionario enciclopédico,* 129–130.

35. For a further discussion see Theresa Alfaro-Velcamp, "La recepción ambivalente: Los inmigrantes del Medio Oriente en la Laguna en México durante el siglo veinte," *Xenofobia y xenofilia en la historia de México, siglos XIX y XX. Homenaje a Moisés González Navarro,* edited by Delia Salazar Anaya (Mexico City: Dirección de Estudios Históricos del INAH, forthcoming).

36. Louis J. Maloof, who interviewed Salim Abud in Central America in 1950 and several times in Mexico City in 1957, noted that Abud "was persistent in upholding the contention that the census had a 70 percent coverage." Abud, a Lebanese Melkite, was editor of *Al-Gurbal.* His rival, Alfonso N. Aued, a Maronite and editor of *Emir,* confirmed Abud's claims. Louis J. Maloof, "Sociological Study of Arabic-Speaking People in Mexico" (Ph.D. diss., University of Florida, January 1959), 42n3.

37. In Ecuador, Mónica Almeida notes, "for a long time the Arabs themselves only allowed endogamic marriages which can be viewed as a way of refusing to assimilate into Ecuadorian society but also served to strengthen their network of ethnic solidarity." Almeida, "Phoenicians of the Pacific," 104.

38. See Marín-Guzmán and Zéraoui, *Arab Immigration in Mexico,* 107.

39. Interviews with Professor Juan Estafan by Louis J. Maloof, Mexico City, June 9–11, 1957, in Maloof, "Sociological Study"; also see 321n4.

40. Cáceres Menéndez and Loret de Mola, "'Gebel-Libnan' (Montaña Blanca)," 49.

41. In discussing Middle Eastern Ecuadorans, Mónica Almeida observes that "one sees a certain persistence of traditional Arab marriage customs, under which a man marries a first cousin on his father's side or at least keeps the family patrimony within the line of descendancy." Almeida, "Phoenicians of the Pacific," 104.

42. Khater, *Inventing Home,* 141.

43. "It [the Directory] omitted Arabic-speaking Jews, even those in Mexico who immigrated mainly from Syria and Lebanon, and Mexico's little known Moriscos or Moros." Maloof, "Sociological Study," 40.

44. "The Arabic census dealt not merely with the family as it is popularly known in the United States . . . but with the patriarchal-structured family. This means in general that the census compilers were thinking characteristically as Arabs; . . . in terms of the large patriarchal family with its ironclad organization and Arab East folkway of recognizing the general household head of the greater family." Ibid., 48.

45. Virginia Yans-McLaughlin, in discussing Italian immigrant women in Buffalo, New York, notes how women negotiated their roles within patriarchy: "Cul-

ture, then, acted as an interface between family and economy, dictating which options were acceptable and which were not." What makes Yans-McLaughlin's analysis relevant to Middle Eastern immigrant women is that both groups of immigrant women were constantly negotiating between their homeland culture and their adopted countries' culture. Virginia Yans-McLaughlin, *Family and Community: Italian Immigrants in Buffalo, 1880–1930* (Ithaca, NY: Cornell University Press, 1977), 53. Also see Martínez Montiel and Reynoso Medina, "Inmigración europea y asiática," 311–312.

46. Evelyn Shakir argues that Arab women who migrated to the United States were active agents in the immigration process. Women came alone to support their families back in Lebanon. Evelyn Shakir, *Bint Arabs: Arab and Arab American Women in the United States.* (Westport, CT: Praeger, 1997), 28, 42. Elizabeth Ewen notes that among Jewish immigrants, "peddling was also a way of avoiding the discipline of factory labor. Many Orthodox Jewish men became peddlers because it allowed time for study and was a way to avoid breaking the Sabbath taboo on work. But many were women. For some it was a part of a family economy: the 1906 Mayor Pushcart Commission found that many men had 'other occupations regularly and let their wives and children attend to the pushcarts.' " Elizabeth Ewen, *Immigrant Women in the Land of Dollars: Life and Culture on the Lower East Side, 1890–1925* (New York: Monthly Review Press, 1985), 168n11.

47. "Diasporic" describes those living outside their natal or imagined natal territories who acknowledge that the old country has a claim to their loyalty and emotions. Robin Cohen, *Global Diasporas,* (Seattle: University of Washington Press, 1997), ix. I have chosen to use the term *diasporic elements* because the Middle Eastern immigrants in Mexico do not fit a clear *diaspora*.

48. William Safran notes that those in a diaspora "retain a collective memory, vision or myth about their original homeland—its physical location, history, and achievements." William Safran, "Diasporas in Modern Societies: Myth of Homeland and Return," *Diaspora* (spring 1991): 83.

49. "How long does it take for a diaspora consciousness to develop, and what are the necessary and sufficient conditions for its survival? Does such consciousness weaken with the passage of decades or centuries, as the relationship with the real homeland is lost, or conversely, does the homeland focus become more deeply embedded in the collective consciousness of a minority as concrete experience is replaced by myth? What factors or conditions—for example, language, religion, relative deprivation, and political disabilities—are necessary or sufficient for the maintenance of a homeland myth?" Ibid., 95.

50. Adina Cimet, *Ashkenazi Jews in Mexico: Ideologies in the Structuring of a Community* (New York: State University of New York Press, 1997).

51. Álvaro Obregón to Naoum A. Mokarzell, c/o José C. Helú, Exp. 802-L-19, September 25, 1922, Álvaro Obregón Files, AGN, Mexico City.

52. This observation is based on a photograph found in the Abusamra family papers with Miguel Abed described as "presidente del Comite Central Pro aliados y Pro Francia Libre." Nicolás Abusamra was listed as one of those in the photograph. Breves Apuntes Biográficos de Nicolás Abusamra Hadad," Exp. 047, 1890–1943, AHPF.

53. Díaz de Kuri and Macluf, *De Líbano a México*, 130.

54. Ministère des affaires étrangères, Série E Levant, Paris, France. I would like to thank Sarah Gualtieri for bringing this document to my attention.

55. Juan Rohana was second voice, Nicolás Jaik was third voice, and Ramon Iza was fourth voice. Other members included: Antonio Farhak, Aldo Chible, Elías Jaik, Pedro Jaik, Jorge Chible, Nahadar Najul, Hasib Ahuad, Elías March, Antonio Chible, Miguel Koran, Baltasar Bassol, Asad Helú, and Abraham Milán.

56. "Breves Apuntes Biográficos de Nicolás Abusamra Hadad," Exp. 047, 1890–1943, AHPF.

57. Naff, *Becoming American*, 16.

58. This dominant voice becomes a hegemonic discourse. Michel Foucault argues that discourses are a form of power: "What makes power hold, what makes it accepted, is simply the fact that it doesn't only weigh on us as a force that says no, but that it traverses and produces things, it induces pleasure, forms knowledge, produces discourse." Michel Foucault, "Truth and Power," in *The Foucault Reader*, edited by Paul Rabinow (New York, Pantheon Books, 1984), 61.

59. Print media have played an often critical role in unifying national identity. "Yet it is obvious that while today almost all modern self-conceived nations—and also nation-states—have 'national print-languages', many of them have these languages in common, and in others only a tiny fraction of the population 'uses' the national language in conversation or on paper." Anderson, *Imagined Communities*, 46.

60. In March 1983 *Al Gurbal* indicated that the magazine began in 1922.

61. Castro Farías, *Aporte libanés*, 103.

62. Jacobs Barquet, *Diccionario enciclopédico*, 324.

63. Nemesio García Naranjo, "El orgullo de la raza," in *Líbano* i, no. 2 (September 1937), Mexico City, edited by Nasre M. Ganem.

64. Valentina Abdo, "¡Que vibra ante los hermosos testimonios que nos brinda la Naturaleza humana!" Femininas, *Líbano* i, no. 5 (December 1937), Mexico City, edited by Nasre M. Ganem.

65. *Emir* issues in its first year, 1937.

66. Anne Rubenstein, "How *Las futbolistas* Became Mexican: Historical Memory and the Revolutionary Woman's Body," paper presented at Washington Area Symposium on Modern Latin America, Washington, DC, September 2000, 22.

67. Rubenstein suggests that by 1940 "the image of the New Woman was sometimes derided as a picture of the stereotypical *marimacho*, film and other media had helped popularize the look of the New Woman among working-class Mexicans." Ibid., 23n57.

68. *Emir*, September 1937, 20–21.

69. Steve Stern argues that colonial women in Mexico were encouraged to conform and avoid deviant behavior. Ironically, he finds that the deviant women faced less violence than the "family-attached" women. Steve Stern, *The Secret History of Gender: Women, Men, and Power in Late Colonial Mexico* (Chapel Hill: University of North Carolina Press, 1995). Stern, Ana María Alonso, and Mary Kay Vaughan suggest that a patriarchal bargain is often struck where women are relegated to the spiritual and moral sphere of the community (as mothers, teachers, and caregivers). Ana María Alonso, *Thread of Blood: Colonialism, Revolution, and Gender on Mexico's Northern Frontier* (Tucson: University of Arizona Press, 1995); Mary Kay

Vaughan, *Cultural Politics in Revolution: Teachers, Peasants, and Schools in Mexico, 1930–1940* (Tucson: University of Arizona Press, 1997). However, Matthew Gutmann, Lynn Stephen, and Pierrette Hondagneu-Sotelo illustrate that this patriarchal structure has been challenged by transitions to capitalism. Matthew C. Gutmann, *The Meanings of Macho: Being a Man in Mexico City* (Berkeley: University of California Press, 1996); Lynn Stephen, *Zapotec Women;* Pierrette Hondagneu-Sotelo, *Gendered Transitions: Mexican Experiences of Immigration* (Berkeley: University of California Press, 1994).

70. María Dib, Dita Noemí, Emilia y Rosita Wabí, and Lili Rosado were the founders; interviews in January 1988 in Mérida, Yucatán, in Cuevas Seba and Mañana Plasencio, *Los libaneses de Yucatán*, 108.

71. *Emir*, November 25, 1943, 14.

72. Josefina Estrada, *Joaquín Pardavé: El señor del espectáculo*, volume 2 (Mexico: Editorial Clío, Libros y Videos, 1996), 35–36. Joaquín Pardavé (1900–1955) acted in seven films in 1942 and four films in 1945. Paulo Antonio Paranaguá, *Mexican Cinema*, translated by Ana M. López (London: British Film Institute, IMCINE, and CONACULTA, 1995), 292.

73. Emilio García Riera, *Historia Documental del Cine Mexicano 2, 1938–1942* (Jalisco: Universidad de Guadalajara and CONACULTA, 1993), 264.

74. For a more in-depth discussion of Mexican cinema in the 1940s see Seth Fein, "Myths of Cultural Imperialism and Nationalism in Golden Age Mexican Cinema," in *Fragments of a Golden Age: The Politics of Culture in Mexico Since 1940*, edited by Gilbert Joseph, Anne Rubenstein, and Eric Zolov (Durham, NC: Duke University Press, 2001), 159–198; and Joanne Hershfield, "Race and Ethnicity in the Classical Cinema," in *Mexico's Cinema: A Century of Film and Filmmakers*, edited by Joanne Hershfield and David R. Maciel (Wilmington, DE: Scholarly Resources, 1999), 81–100.

75. Carl Mora says that "among the 'star' fixtures of the cinema, was 'the mother of Mexico,' Sara García." Carl J. Mora, *Mexican Cinema: Reflections of a Society, 1896–1980* (Berkeley: University of California Press, 1982), 57. Also see Carl J. Mora, "Feminine Images in Mexican Cinema: The Family Melodrama; Sara García, 'The Mother of México'; and the Prostitute," *Studies in Latin American Popular Culture* 4 (1985): 228–235.

76. Paranaguá, *Mexican Cinema*, 4.

77. While many second- and third-generation Arabs pursued careers in medicine, law, and engineering, a few went into producing and directing movies. Miguel Zacarías and his brother Mario Zacarías produced many films. Miguel Zacarías made such films as *Rosario, El peñon de las ánimas* and many more. Díaz de Kuri and Macluf, *De Líbano a México*, 213–216.

78. Lesser comments that in the context of Brazil, immigrants "sought to interpret class status as a marker of Brazilian identity, allowing ethnicity to be maintained even as its importance was dismissed." Lesser, *Negotiating National Identity*, 4.

79. Páez Oropeza, *Los libaneses en México*, 207–208.

80. See Winder, "The Lebanese in West Africa," 324.

81. Marín-Guzmán, "Los inmigrantes árabes en México," 145. Also see Centro Libanés Website, http://www.centrolibanes.org.

82. Alonso Palacios, *Los libaneses y la industria textil*, 156.
83. Interview by author with Omar, April 27, 1999, in Mexico City.
84. Martha Díaz de Kurí, e-mail to author, January 18, 2005.
85. Díaz de Kuri and Macluf, *De Líbano a México*, 179.
86. Páez Oropeza, *Los libaneses en México*, 166.
87. Ibid., 200.
88. See http://www.jomali.org.
89. Alfonso Ramírez Carrillo contends that the Lebanese identity matters only as a secondary cultural characteristic for middle-class Mexicans, whereas the elite accentuate their Lebanese identity. Ramírez Carrillo, *Secretos de familia*, 198.
90. David Nicholls, *Haiti in Caribbean Context: Ethnicity, Economy and Revolt* (New York: St. Martin's Press, 1985), 161.
91. Gabriela Legaspi Velázquez, "Medio siglo de relaciones diplomáticas México-El Líbano" (undergraduate thesis, Universidad Iberoamericana, Mexico City, 1990), 60.
92. When I asked about Muslims in the Centro Libanés, I was told there were very few, if any. See Alfaro-Velcamp, "Mexican Muslims in the Twentieth Century."
93. National Registry of Foreigners, DM (1926–1951), AGN, Mexico City.
94. Marín-Guzmán and Zéraoui, *Arab Immigration in Mexico*, 90, Table 18.
95. For a more detailed examination of Mexican Muslims see Alfaro-Velcamp, "Mexican Muslims in the Twentieth Century."
96. Alfonso Ramírez Carrillo goes as far as to say that the Lebanese community was a sociohistorical product of Mexico rather than a group rooted in a shared history. Ramírez Carrillo, *Secretos de familia*, 190–191.
97. Alfonso Negib Aued, *Historia del Líbano* (Mexico City: Ediciones Emir, 1945).
98. José Vasconcelos, prologue to William Nimeh's *Historia del Líbano* (Mexico City: Impresora Mena, 1945).
99. Jacobs Barquet, *Diccionario enciclopédico*, 335–336.
100. Ibid., 163.
101. Ibid., 400–401. Marín-Guzmán and Zéraoui state that Villanueva Hallal was an ambassador in Algeria; *Arab Immigration in Mexico*, 163.
102. Jacobs Barquet, in *Diccionario enciclopédico*, describes the following on the respective pages noted in parentheses: In 1952 Juan del Socorro Sabines Gutiérrez, a son of Middle Eastern immigrants, was supposedly the first Middle Easterner to enter politics as a *diputado federal* (congressman); he became governor of Chiapas from 1979 to 1982 (345). Jorge Salomón Azar García was governor of Campeche from 1991 to 1998 (76). José Antonio González Curi, of Lebanese ancestry, was elected governor of Campeche in 1997. Prior to this position, González Curi was a *diputado federal* from 1991 to 1994 (177–178). In southern Mexico, Miguel Borge Martín, of Lebanese origins, was governor of Quintana Roo from 1987 to 1992 (94). In the state of Morelos, Jorge Morales Barud, whose family was from Tanurín, Lebanon, became governor in 1998 (285). José Murat Casab, whose family was from Iraq, was a *diputado federal* for the PRI from 1973 to 1976, 1979 to 1982, and 1988 to 1991; and in 1998, he was elected governor of Oaxaca (288). Jesús Murillo Karam, of Lebanese ancestry, was also a federal *diputado* from 1979 to 1982 and 1985 to 1988, governor of Hidalgo from 1993 to 1998, and in 1998 was named under-

secretary of Public Security and Social Security (subsecretario de Seguridad Pública y Previsión Social de la Secretaría de Gobernación) (288). In 2000 Murrillo Karam became *secretario general adjunto* of the PRI. The late Salvador José Neme Castillo, also of Lebanese ancestry, was governor of Tabasco from 1989 to 1992 and died in 1996 (306).

103. For an excellent discussion of political and economic elite in Yucatán see Ramírez Carrillo, *Secretos de familia.*

104. Jacobs Barquet, *Diccionario enciclopédico,* 331-332.

105. Ibid., 119. According to Marín-Guzmán and Zéraoui, Chuayffet Chemor was President of the Municipality of Toluca (1982), Secretary of Education, Culture and Social Welfare of the State of Mexico (1983-1987), Secretary of the Government of the State of Mexico (1987), and General Director of the Federal Electoral Institute (1991-1992). Marín-Guzmán and Zéraoui state that "his political career suddenly ended in 1998, due to the tragic events of the massacre of Acteal, Chiapas"; *Arab Immigration in Mexico,* 105.

106. For a comprehensive list of Middle Eastern descendants in political positions see Marín-Guzmán and Zéraoui, *Arab Immigration in Mexico,* 161-168, and for their discussion see 105-107.

107. Alfonso Dau, the "scion of a wealthy Lebanese textile family in Guadalajara," invested $3 million in the newspaper *Siglo 21* in 1991. The paper did well until editor Jorge Zepeda Patterson and Dau had a falling out in 1997. For more details see Julia Preston and Samuel Dillon, *Opening Mexico: The Making of a Democracy* (New York: Farrar, Straus and Giroux, 2004), 427-439.

108. *Forbes.com,* "The World's Billionaires: #3 Carlos Slim Helu," at http://www.forbes.com/lists/2006/10/WYDJ.html.

109. *Latin Business Chronicle,* "The Billionaires: Latin America's Wealthiest Individuals, According to Forbes," November 9, 2004, online at http://www.latinbusinesschronicle.com/topics/billionaires04.htm. Also see Kirkman, "Global Elite."

110. Kandell, "Yo Quiero Todo Bell," 128.

111. Ibid., 130.

112. Ramírez Carrillo, *Secretos de familia,* 195.

113. When U.S. Senator Carl Levin asked Amy Elliott, a Citibank employee, about Raúl Salinas de Gortari, she indicated that Telmex, among other Mexican companies, made monthly deposits of roughly $60,000 into Raúl's accounts. Martínez, *Carlos Slim. Retrato inédito,* 184.

114. *Latin Business Chronicle,* "Billionaires."

115. During a research trip to Lebanon in June 2004 when I asked several Lebanese to describe themsleves, they responded that they were "Phoenicians."

116. Picard, *Lebanon, A Shattered Country,* 19.

117. Meir Zamir, "From Hegemony to Marginalism: The Maronites of Lebanon," in *Minorities and the State in the Arab World,* edited by Ofra Bengio and Gabriel Ben-Dor (Boulder, CO: Lynne Rienner, 1999), 111-112.

118. Ibid.

119. Inclán Rubio, "Inmigración libanesa en México: Un caso de diversidad cultural," *Historias 33* (October 1994-March 1995), 62.

120. Zamir, "From Hegemony to Marginalism," 126.

121. Interview by author with Omar, April 27, 1999, in Mexico City.

122. Alonso Palacios, *Los libaneses y la industria textil,* 149n59. *Emir,* September–October, 1945.

Conclusion

1. González Navarro, *Los extranjeros en México,* 3:314.

2. This is based on the notion that citizenship derives from the father—*juis sanguinis* (citizenship derived from blood and can apply to mothers or fathers or parents, generally).

3. Sahlins, *Unnaturally French,* 126n61.

4. *El privilegio de amar* aired on Mexico City broadcaster TV Azteca from September 1998 to February 26, 1999.

5. Jorge Ferretis summarized an August 1936 editorial from *Palmira* of Monterrey, Nuevo León. Edward I. Nathan, American Consul General, to Secretary of State, Monterrey, Mexico, 812.5590B/1, M1370, Roll 116, September 3, 1936, 1930–1939, U.S. State Department Records, RG 59, NACP.

Selected Bibliography

Abbreviations

AGN	Archivo General de la Nación, Mexico City
DGG	Dirección General de Gobierno
DM	Departamento de Migración
AHPF	Archivo Histórico Papeles de Familias, Universidad Iberoamericana, Laguna, Torreón, Coahuila
CIESAS	Centro de Investigaciones y Estudios Superiores en Antropología Social
CONACULTA	Consejo Nacional para la Cultura y las Artes
IMCINE	Instituto Mexicano de Cinematografía
INAH	Instituto Nacional de Antropología y Historia
INS	U.S. Immigration and Naturalization Service, now U.S. Citizenship and Immigration Services
LERC	Lebanese Emigration Research Center, Notre Dame University, Beirut, Lebanon
NA	National Archives, Washington, DC
NACP	National Archives, College Park, MD
NALN	National Archives, Laguna Niguel, CA
SRE	Secretaría de Relaciones Exteriores, Mexico City
UNAM	Universidad Nacional Autónoma de México
UNESCO	United Nations Educational, Social, and Cultural Organization

Primary Sources

Archives

In France

Ministère des Affaires Étrangères, Série E Levant, Paris

In Lebanon

Fondation Arabe pour l'Image (FAI), Studio Yazbeck Collection, Beirut
Lebanese Emigration Research Center (LERC), Notre Dame University, Beirut

In Mexico

Archivo Agrario, Mexico City
Archivo General de la Nación (AGN), Mexico City
 Departamento de Migración (DM), Registro de Extranjeros, 1926–1951
 Dirección General de Gobierno (DGG)
 Presidential Files
 Álvaro Obregón
 Plutarco Elías Calles
 Emilio Portes Gil
 Pascual Ortíz Rubio
 Abelardo L. Rodríguez
 Lázaro Cárdenas del Río
 Manuel Ávila Camacho
 Miguel Alemán Valdés
Archivo Histórico, Don Rafael Chousal, Secretaría Particular, Universidad Nacional, Mexico City
Archivo Municipal de Saltillo, Coahuila
Gazeta de Saltillo, Organo Informativo del Archivo Municipal de Saltillo, 1861–1863, Año VI, No. 8
Archivo Plutarco Elías Calles, Mexico City
Archivo de Relaciones Exteriores, Secretaría de Relaciones Exteriores (SRE), Mexico City
Archivo de Testimonios Familiares y Documentos Históricos, Proyectos de Investigación del Archivo Histórico, Universidad Iberoamericana, Laguna, Torreón, Coahuila
Diario Oficial, Mexico City
Instituto Municipal de Documentación, Torreón, Coahuila

In the United States

Citizenship and Immigration Services Historical Reference Library, formerly U.S. Immigration and Naturalization Service Library, Washington, DC.
Immigration from Mexico, Hearings Before the Committee on Immigration and Naturalization, House of Representatives, 71st Congress, 2nd session on H.R. 12382, May 15, 1930, Washington, DC.
International, Foreign, and Comparative Law Collection, Columbia Law Library, New York, New York.
Library of Congress, Manuscript Division, Chandler Anderson and James Garfield Papers, Washington, DC.
National Archives, College Park, MD (NACP), Record Group (RG) 59, State Department Records, and RG 84, Consular Reports from Torreón, Mexico

National Archives, Laguna Niguel, CA (NALN), RG 85, Immigration and Natural-
ization Service Records (INS), and RG 21, Records of U.S. District Courts, Dis-
trict of Arizona
National Archives, Washington, DC (NA), RG 85, INS
Stanford University Library, Special Collections and University Archives, Mexican
Movie Stills Collection, Stanford, CA
University of Texas, Benson Latin American Collection, Austin, Sánchez Navarro
Family Papers, Coahuila, 1658–1895, and Lázaro de la Garza Papers, 1905–1939
University of Texas at El Paso, Institute of Oral History, C. L. Sonnichsen Special
Collections Department

Private Family Collections

Abusaid Family Collection, Torreón, Coahuila, Mexico
Saab-Nasr Family Collection, Beirut, Lebanon

Interviews

In Mexico City

Ahmed, April 26, 1999
Centro Libanés, January 26, 1999
Miguel, January 25, 1999, and April 24, 1999
Omar, April 27, 1999
Pablo, January 25, 1999

In Paso Nacional, Durango

Elena, librarian, February 6, 1999

In San Pedro de las Colonias, Coahuila

Alonzo, February 22, 1999
Rodrigo, February 22, 1999

In Torreón, Coahuila

Álvaro, February 12, 1999
Beto, February 9, 1999
Cruz, February 10, 1999
Diego, February 15, 1999
Emilio, February 21, 1999
Francisco, February 10, 1999
Hugo, February 19, 1999
Javier, February 9, 1999
Leonardo, February 21, 1999

Lucero, February 10, 1999
Mae, February 8, 1999
Pilar, February 9, 1999
Salma, February 11, 1999

Secondary Sources

Abdo, Valentina. "¡Que vibra ante los hermosos testimonios que nos brinda la Naturaleza humana!" Femininas, *Líbano* 1, no. 5 (December 1937), Mexico City, edited by Nasre M. Ganem.
Abinader, Elmaz. *Children of the Roojme: A Family's Journey from Lebanon.* Madison: University of Wisconsin Press, 1997.
Aboites Aguilar, Luis. *Norte Precario: Poblamiento y Colonización en México (1760–1940).* Mexico City: Colegio de México, 1995.
Abraham, Sameer Y., and Nabeel Abraham. *Arabs in the New World: Studies on Arab-American Communities.* Detroit, MI: Center for Urban Studies, Wayne State University, 1983.
Abu-Laban, Baha, and Michael Suleiman. *Arab Americans: Continuity and Change.* Belmont, MA: Association of Arab-American University Graduates, 1989.
Abusamra, Nicolás, Victoria Martínez de Peña, and Hassan Zain Chamut. "Como llegaron los libaneses." *Puente: Revista de Historia y Cultura de La Laguna* 1, no. 4 (May–June 1991): 43–50.
Adler Hellman, Judith. "The Role of Ideology in Peasant Politics: Peasant Mobilization and Demobilization in the Laguna Region." *Journal of Interamerican Studies and World Politics* 25, no. 1 (February 1993): 3–29.
Aguilar Camín, Héctor. *La frontera nómada: Sonora y la Revolución Mexicana.* Mexico City: Siglo Veintiuno, 1985.
Aguirre Beltrán, Gonzalo. *El proceso de aculturación y el cambio socio-cultural en México.* Mexico City: Universidad Ibero-Americana Editorial Comunidad, Instituto de Ciencias Sociales, 1970.
———. *La población negra de México: Estudio etnohistórico.* Mexico City: Fondo de Cultura Económica, 1972.
Akarli, Engin Deniz. *The Long Peace: Ottoman Lebanon, 1861–1920.* Berkeley: University of California Press, 1993.
———. "Ottoman Attitudes Towards Lebanese Emigration, 1885–1910." In *Lebanese in the World: A Century of Emigration,* edited by Albert Hourani and Nadim Shehadi. London: Centre for Lebanese Studies and I. B. Tauris, 1992.
Alfaro-Velcamp, Theresa. "The Historiography of Arab Immigration to Argentina: The Intersection Between the Imaginary and Real Country." In *Arabs and Jewish Immigrants in Latin America: Images and Realities,* edited by Ignacio Klich and Jeffrey Lesser. London: Frank Cass, 1998.
———. "Immigrant Positioning in Twentieth-Century Mexico: Middle Easterners, Foreign Citizens, and Multiculturalism." *Hispanic American Historical Review* 86, no. 1 (February 2006): 61–91.
———. "Mexican Muslims in the Twentieth Century: Challenging Stereotypes and

Negotiating Space." In *Muslims in the West: Sojourners to Citizens,* edited by Yvonne Yazbeck Haddad. New York: Oxford University Press, 2002.

————. "La recepción ambivalente: Los inmigrantes del Medio Oriente en la Laguna en México durante el siglo veinte." In *Xenofobia y xenofilia en la historia de México, siglos XIX y XX. Homenaje a Moisés González Navarro,* edited by Delia Salazar Anaya. Mexico City: Dirección de Estudios Históricos del INAH, forthcoming.

Allswang, John M. *A House for All Peoples: Ethnic Politics in Chicago, 1890-1936.* Lexington: University Press of Kentucky, 1971.

Almeida, Mónica, "Phoenicians of the Pacific: Lebanese and Other Middle Easterners in Ecuador." *Americas* 53 (July 1996): 87–112.

al-Mûsili, Elias. *An Arab's Journey to Colonial Spanish America: The Travels of Elias al-Musili in the Seventeenth Century.* Translated and edited by Caesar E. Farah. Syracuse, NY: Syracuse University Press, 2003.

Alonso, Ana María. *Thread of Blood: Colonialism, Revolution, and Gender on Mexico's Northern Frontier.* Tucson: University of Arizona Press, 1995.

Alonso Palacios, Angelina. *Las aventuras del paisano Yusef.* Mexico City: Instituto de Investigaciones Dr. José María Luis Mora, 1993.

————. *Los libaneses y la industria textil en Puebla.* Mexico City: CIESAS and Cuadernos de la Casa Chata, 1983.

Altman, Ida. *Transatlantic Ties in the Spanish Empire: Brihuega, Spain, and Puebla, Mexico, 1560-1620.* Stanford, CA: Stanford University Press, 2000.

Amado, Jorge. *Gabriela, Clove and Cinnamon.* Translated by James L. Taylor and William Grossman. New York: Avon Books, 1962.

Anderson, Benedict. *Imagined Communities: Reflections on the Origin and Spread of Nationalism.* London: Verso, 1991.

Anderson, Rodney. *Outcasts in Their Own Land: Mexican Industrial Workers, 1906-1911.* DeKalb: North Illinois University Press, 1976.

Anguiano, Arturo. *El estado y la política obrera del cardenismo.* Mexico City: Colección Problemas de México, Ediciones Era, 1975.

Antonius, Soraya. *Architecture in Lebanon.* Beirut: Khayats, 1965.

Appelbaum, Nancy P. "Post-Revisionist Scholarship on Race." *Latin American Research Review* 40, no. 3 (October 2005): 206–217.

Appelbaum, Nancy P., Anne S. Macpherson, and Karin Alejandra Rosemblatt, editors. *Race and Nation in Modern Latin America.* Chapel Hill: University of North Carolina Press, 2003.

Arboleyda Castro, Ruth Elizabeth. "La crisis del ejido en la Comarca Lagunera. Tres casos." *Boletín del Proyecto Archivo Agrarios,* no. 9 (January–April 2000), 5–12.

Arrom, Silvia Marina. *The Women of Mexico City, 1790-1857.* Stanford, CA: Stanford University Press, 1985.

Aswad, Barbara C. *Arabic Speaking Communities in American Cities.* New York: Center for Migration Studies of New York and Association of Arab-American University Graduates, 1974.

Avni, Haim. "Cárdenas, México y los refugiados: 1938-1940." *Estudios Interdisciplinarios de América Latina y el Caribe* 3, no. 1 (1992): 5–22.

―――. "Mexico—Immigration and Refuge." Latin American Program Working Papers 177. Washington, DC: Woodrow Wilson International Center for Scholars, 1989.

Ayalon, Ami. "The Arab Discovery of America in the Nineteenth Century." *Middle Eastern Studies* 20, no. 4 (1984): 5–17.

Baily, Samuel L. *Immigrants in the Lands of Promise: Italians in Buenos Aires and New York City, 1870–1914.* Ithaca, NY: Cornell University Press, 1999.

Balderrama, Francisco E., and Raymond Rodríguez. *Decade of Betrayal: Mexican Repatriation in the 1930s.* Albuquerque: University of New Mexico Press, 1995.

Balibar, Etienne, and Immanuel Wallerstein. *Race, Nation, Class: Ambiguous Identities.* London: Verso, 1991.

Barak, Oren. "Intra-Communal and Inter-Communal Dimensions of Conflict and Peace in Lebanon." *International Journal of Middle East Studies* 34 (2002): 619–644.

Barakat, Halim. *The Arab World: Society, Culture, and State.* Berkeley: University of California Press, 1993.

Bartra, Roger. *Blood, Ink, and Culture: Miseries and Splendors of the Post-Mexican Condition.* Translated by Mark Alan Healey. Durham, NC: Duke University Press, 2002.

―――. *The Cage of Melancholy: Identity and Metamorphosis in the Mexican Character.* Translated by Christopher J. Hall. New Brunswick, NJ: Rutgers University Press, 1992.

Basave Benítez, Agustín. *México mestizo: Análisis del nacionalismo mexicano en torno a la mestizofilia de Andrés Molina Enríquez.* Mexico City: Fondo de Cultura Económica, 1992.

Beatty, Edward. *Institutions and Investment: The Political Basis of Industrialization in Mexico Before 1911.* Stanford, CA: Stanford University Press, 2001.

Becker, Marjorie. *Setting the Virgin on Fire: Lázaro Cárdenas, Michoacán Peasants, and the Redemption of the Mexican Revolution.* Berkeley: University of California Press, 1995.

Beezley, William H. *Judas at the Jockey Club and Other Episodes of Porfirian Mexico.* Lincoln: University of Nebraska Press, 1987.

Béjar, Raúl, and Héctor Rosales, coordinators. *La identidad nacional mexicana como problema político y cultural. Los desafíos de la pluralidad.* Cuernavaca, Morelos, Mexico: UNAM, 2002.

Benjamin, Thomas. "Rebuilding the Nation." In *The Oxford History of Mexico,* edited by Michael C. Meyer and William H. Beezley. New York: Oxford University Press, 2000.

―――. *La Revolución: Mexico's Great Revolution as Memory, Myth, and History.* Austin: University of Texas Press, 2000.

Benjamin, Thomas, and Mark Wasserman, editors. *Provinces of the Revolution: Essays on Regional Mexican History, 1910–1929.* Albuquerque: University of New Mexico, 1990.

Berdan, Frances F. *The Aztecs of Central Mexico: An Imperial Society.* Orlando, FL: Harcourt Brace Jovanovich, 1982.

Bertoni, Lilia. "De Turquía a Buenos Aires. Una colectividad nueva a fines del siglo XIX." *Estudios Migratorios Latinoamericanos* 9 (April 1994).

Bessie, Susan K. *Restructuring Patriarchy: The Modernization of Gender Inequality in Brazil, 1914–1940.* Chapel Hill: University of North Carolina Press, 1996.

Betts, Robert Brenton. *Christians in the Arab East: A Political Study.* Atlanta, GA: John Knox Press, 1978.

———. *The Druze.* New Haven, CT: Yale University Press, 1988.

Binford, Leigh. "Peasants and Petty Capitalists in Southern Oaxacan Sugar Cane Production and Processing, 1930–1980." *Journal of Latin American Studies* 24 (Feb. 1992): 33–55.

Blancarte, Roberto, compiler. *Cultura e identidad nacional.* Mexico City: CONACULTA and Fondo de Cultura Económica, 1994.

Bliss, Katherine Elaine. *Compromised Positions: Prostitution, Public Health, and Gender Politics in Revolutionary Mexico.* University Park: Pennsylvania State University Press, 2001.

Bodnar, John. *The Transplanted: A History of Immigrants in Urban America.* Bloomington: Indiana University Press, 1985.

Bonfil Batalla, Guillermo. *México Profundo: Reclaiming a Civilization.* Translated by Philip A. Dennis. Austin: University of Texas Press, 1996.

———. *Pensar nuestra cultura.* Mexico City: Alianza Editorial Estudios, 1991.

———. *Simbiosis de culturas: Los inmigrantes y su cultura en México.* Mexico City: Fondo de Cultura Económica, 1993.

Boyd, Monica. "Family and Personal Networks in International Migration: Recent Developments and New Agendas." *International Migration Review* 23, no. 3 (1989): 638–670.

Brading, D. A. *Caudillo and Peasant in the Mexican Revolution.* Cambridge, England: Cambridge University Press, 1980.

———. *The First America: The Spanish Monarchy, Creole Patriots, and the Liberal State, 1492–1867.* Cambridge, England: Cambridge University Press, 1991.

———. "Manuel Gamio and Official Indigenismo in Mexico," *Bulletin of Latin American Research* 7, no. 1 (1988): 75–89.

———. *Mexican Nationalism.* Cambridge, England: Cambridge University Press, 1985.

———. *Miners and Merchants in Bourbon Mexico, 1763–1810.* Cambridge, England: Cambridge University Press, 1971.

Braude, Benjamin, and Bernard Lewis. *Christians and Jews in the Ottoman Empire: The Functioning of a Plural Society.* 2 volumes. New York: Holmes and Meier, 1982.

Brennan, James P., and Ofelia Pianetto, editors. *Region and Nation: Politics, Economics, and Society in Twentieth-Century Argentina.* New York: St. Martin's Press, 2000.

Brown, Jonathan, and Alan Knight. *The Mexican Petroleum Industry in the Twentieth Century.* Austin: University of Texas Press, 1992.

Brunk, Samuel. *¡Emiliano Zapata!: Revolution and Betrayal in Mexico.* Albuquerque: University of New Mexico Press, 1995.

Buchenau, Jürgen. "Small Numbers, Great Impact: Mexico and Its Immigrants, 1821–1973." *Journal of American Ethnic History* 20, no. 3 (spring 2001): 23–49.

Burdiel de las Heras, María Cruz. *La emigración libanesa en Costa Rica.* Madrid: Cant Arabia, 1991.

Cáceres Menéndez, María Beatriz de Lourdes, and María Patricia Fortuny Loret de Mola. " 'Gebel-Libnan' (Montaña Blanca): La migración libanesa a Yucatán." Undergraduate thesis, Universidad de Yucatán, March 1977.

Camposortega Cruz, Sergio. "Análisis demográfico de las corrientes migratorias a México desde finales del siglo XIX." In *Destino México: Un estudio de las migraciones asiaticas a México, siglos XIX y XX*, edited by María Elena Ota Mishima. Mexico City: Colegio de México, 1997.

Cardoso, Ciro, compiler. *México en el siglo XIX 1821-1910: historia económica y de la estructura social*. Mexico City: Nueva Imagen, 1988.

Carr, Barry. "The Mexican Community Party and Agrarian Mobilization in the Laguna 1920-1940: A Worker-Peasant Alliance?" *Hispanic American Historical Review* 67, no. 3 (1987): 371-404.

Carroll, Patrick J. *Blacks in Colonial Veracruz: Race, Ethnicity, and Regional Development*. Austin: University of Texas Press, 2001.

Castles, Stephen, and Mark J. Miller. *The Age of Migration: International Population Movements in the Modern World*. New York: Guilford Press, 1993.

Castro Farías, Enrique. *Aporte libanés al progreso de América*. Mexico City: Unión Libanesa Mundial, 1965.

———. *Libro de oro de los pueblos de habla árabe*. Santiago, Chile: N.p., 1949.

Cerutti, Mario, and Juan Ignacio Barragán. "Empresarios y empresas en México (1840-1930). Jabonera de La Laguna: un recuento historiográfico a partir de su archivo," *América Latin en la Historia Económica. Boletín de Fuentes*, no. 4, (July–December 1995): 77-87.

Chance, John K. *Race and Class in Colonial Oaxaca*. Stanford, CA: Stanford University Press, 1978.

Chiñas, Beverly Newbold. *The Isthmus Zapotecs: A Matrifocal Culture of Mexico*. Fort Worth, TX: Harcourt Brace Jovanovich College, 1992.

———. *La Zandunga: Of Fieldwork and Friendship in Southern Mexico*. Prospect Heights, IL: Waveland Press, 1993.

Cimet, Adina. *Ashkenazi Jews in Mexico: Ideologies in the Structuring of a Community*. New York: State University of New York Press, 1997.

Civantos, Christine Elsa. "Between Argentines and Arabs: The Writing of National and Immigrant Identities." Ph.D. diss., University of California at Berkeley, 1999.

Cleveland, William L. *A History of the Modern Middle East*. 2d edition. Boulder, CO: Westview Press, 2000.

Coatsworth, John H. *Growth Against Development: The Economic Impact of Railroads in Porfirian Mexico*. DeKalb: Northern Illinois University Press, 1981.

Cobban, Helena. *The Making of Modern Lebanon*. Boulder, CO: Westview Press, 1985.

Cockroft, James. *Intellectual Precursors of the Mexican Revolution, 1900-1913*. Austin: University of Texas Press, 1968.

Cohen, Robin. *Global Diasporas*. Seattle: University of Washington Press, 1997.

Cohen, William. *At Freedom's Edge: Black Mobility and the Southern Quest for Racial Control, 1861-1915*. Baton Rouge: Louisiana State University Press, 1991.

Comaroff, John L., and Jean Comaroff. *Ethnography and the Historical Imagination*. Boulder, CO: Westview Press, 1992.

————. *Of Revelation and Revolution: The Dialectics of Modernity on a South African Frontier*, volume 2. Chicago: University of Chicago Press, 1997.

Comité Oficial del Libro de Oro de la Revolución Mexicana, editor. *Libro de oro de la Revolución Mexicana: Forjando los nuevos moldes de la nacionalidad*. Mexico City, 1929.

Conklin, Nancy Faires, and Nora Faires. " 'Colored' and Catholic: The Lebanese in Birmingham, Alabama." In *Crossing the Waters: Arabic-Speaking Immigrants to the United States Before 1940*, edited by Eric Hooglund. Washington, DC: Smithsonian Institution Press, 1987.

Cook, Scott, and Leigh Binford. *Obliging Need: Rural Petty Industry in Mexican Capitalism*. Austin: University of Texas Press, 1990.

Cope, Douglas R. *The Limits of Racial Domination: Plebian Society in Colonial Mexico City 1660-1720*. Madison: University of Wisconsin Press, 1994.

Córdova, Arnaldo. *La Revolución en crisis: La aventura del maximato*. Mexico City: Cal y Arena, 1995.

Corona Páez, Sergio Antonio. *San Juan Bautista de los González: Cultura material, producción y consumo en una hacienda saltillense del siglo XVII*. Torreón, Mexico: Plantel Laguna, 1997.

Cosío Villegas, Daniel. *Historia moderna de México: El porfiriato, la vida económica*. Buenos Aires: Editorial Hermes, 1965.

Cott, Kennett. "Mexican Diplomacy and the Chinese Issue, 1876-1910." *Hispanic American Historical Review* 67, no. 1 (February 1987): 63-84.

Cuevas Seba, Teresa, and Miguel Mañana Plasencio. *Los libaneses de Yucatán*. Mérida, Mexico: Impresiones Profesionales, 1990.

Dagher, Sam. "Nation's Lebanese Distant from Arab Conflicts but Hold Close Ties to Those in Power." *News Mexico*, October 25, 2001.

Jacques, Leo M. Dambourges. "The Chinese Massacre in Torreón (Coahuila) in 1911." *Arizona and the West* 16 (1974): 234-247.

Daniels, Roger. *Coming to America: A History of Immigration and Ethnicity in American Life*. Bloomington: Indiana University Press, 1985.

Deeds, Susan. "Rural Work in Nueva Vizcaya: Forms of Labor Coercion on the Periphery." *Hispanic American Historical Review* 69, no. 3 (1989): 425-449.

De Ferrari, Gabriella. *Gringa Latina: A Woman of Two Worlds*. Boston: Houghton Mifflin, 1995.

Deger, Robert John Jr. "Porfirian Foreign Policy and Mexican Nationalism: A Study of Cooperation and Conflict in Mexican-American Relations, 1884-1904." Ph.D. diss., Indiana University, 1979.

de la Vega Alfaro, Eduardo. "The Decline of the Golden Age and the Making of the Crisis." In *Mexico's Cinema: A Century of Film and Filmmakers*, edited by Joanne Hershfield and David R. Maciel. Wilmington, DE: Scholarly Resources, 1999.

————. "Origins, Development, and Crisis of the Sound Cinema (1929-1964)." In *Mexican Cinema*, edited by Paulo Antonio Paranaguá and translated by Ana M. López. London: British Film Institute, IMCINE, and CONACULTA, 1995.

Delgado, Grace. "In the Age of Exclusion: Race, Region, and Chinese Identity in the Making of the Arizona-Sonora Borderlands, 1863-1943." Ph.D. diss., University of California at Los Angeles, 2000.

DellaPergola, Sergio. *World Jewry Beyond 2000: The Demographic Prospects*. Occasional Papers 2, Third Frank Green Lecture. Oxford Centre for Hebrew and Jewish Studies. Swindon, England: Acorn Press, 1999.

Dermenghem, Émile. *Vida de Mahoma*. Translated by Raymundo Mayoral. Barcelona: Talles Gráficos Agustín Nuñez, 1942.

Derossi, Flavia. *El empresario mexicano*. Mexico City: UNAM, 1977.

Díaz de Kuri, Martha, and Lourdes Macluf. *De Líbano a México: Crónica de un pueblo emigrante*. Mexico City: Gráfica, Creatividad y Diseño, 1995.

Díaz Sánchez, Ramón. *Líbano: Una historia de hombres y de pueblos. Los libaneses en América y en Venezuela*. Caracas: N.p., 1965.

Divine, Robert A. *American Immigration Policy, 1924-1952*. New Haven, CT: Yale University Press, 1957.

Duara, Prasenjit. *Culture, Power, and the State: Rural North China 1900-1942*. Stanford, CT: Stanford University Press, 1988.

———. "Historicizing National Identity, or Who Imagines What and When." In *Becoming National: A Reader*, edited by Geoff Eley and Ronald Grigor Suny. New York: Oxford University Press, 1996.

———. *Rescuing History from the Nation: Questioning Narratives of Modern China*. Chicago: University of Chicago Press, 1995.

Duben, Alan, and Cem Behar. *Istanbul Households: Marriage, Family, and Fertility, 1880-1940*. Cambridge, England: Cambridge University Press, 1991.

Echánove Trujillo, Carlos. *Manual del Extranjero*. Mexico City: Editorial Porrúa, 1976.

Eley, Geoff, and Ronald Grigor Suny, editors. *Becoming National. A Reader*. New York: Oxford University Press, 1996.

Elkin, Judith Laikin. *The Jews of Latin America*. Revised edition. New York: Holmes and Meier, 1998.

Emir. Mexico City, 1937-1972.

Escalante Gonzalbo, Fernando. *Ciudadanos imaginarios*. Mexico City: Colegio de México, 1992.

Escobar, Arturo. "Culture, Economics, and Politics in Latin American Social Movements Theory and Research." In *The Making of Social Movements in Latin America: Identity, Strategy, and Democracy*, edited by Arturo Escobar and Sonia E. Alvarez. Boulder, CO: Westview Press, 1992.

Estrada, Josefina. *Joaquín Pardavé: El señor del espectáculo*, volume 2. Mexico City: Editorial Clío, Libros y Videos, 1996.

Euraque, Darío A. "The Arab-Jewish Economic Presence in San Pedro Sula, the Industrial Capital of Honduras: Formative Years, 1880s-1930s." In *Arab and Jewish Immigrants in Latin America*, edited by Klich and Lesser, 1998.

———. "Formación nacional, mestizaje, y la inmigración árabe palestina a Honduras, 1880-1930." *Estudios Migratorios Latinoamericanos* 9, no. 26 (April 1994): 47-66.

Ewen, Elizabeth. *Immigrant Women in the Land of Dollars: Life and Culture on the Lower East Side, 1890-1925*. New York: Monthly Review Press, 1985.

Falcón, Romana. "Logros y límites de la centralización porfirista: Coahuila vista desde arriba." In *El dominio de las minorías república restaurada y porfiriato*, compiled by Anne Staples, Gustavo Verduzco, Carmen Blázquez Domínguez, and Romana Falcón. Mexico City: Colegio de Mexico, 1989.

————. *Las rasgaduras de la descolonización: Españoles y mexicanos a mediados del siglo XIX.* Mexico City: Colegio de México, 1996.

————. *Revolución y caciquismo San Luis Potosí, 1910-1938.* Mexico City: Colegio de Mexico, 1984.

Fawaz, Leila Tarazi. "The City and the Mountain: Beirut's Political Radius in the Nineteenth Century as Revealed in the Crisis of 1860." *International Journal of Middle East Studies* 16 (1984): 489-495.

————. *Merchants and Migrants in Nineteenth-Century Beirut.* Cambridge: Harvard University Press, 2000.

————. *An Occasion for War: Civil Conflict in Lebanon and Damascus in 1860.* Berkeley: University of California Press, 1994.

Fein, Seth. "Myths of Cultural Imperialism and Nationalism in Golden Age Mexican Cinema." In *Fragments of a Golden Age: The Politics of Culture in Mexico Since 1940,* edited by Gilbert Joseph, Anne Rubenstein, and Eric Zolov. Durham, NC: Duke University Press, 2001.

Fernandes, Florestan. *The Negro in Brazilian Society.* New York: Columbia University Press, 1969.

Fey, Ingrid Elizabeth. "First Tango in Paris: Latin Americans in Turn-of-the-Century France, 1880-1920." Ph.D. diss., University of California at Los Angeles, 1996.

Firro, Kais. "Silk and Agrarian Changes in Lebanon, 1860-1914," *International Journal of Middle East Studies* 22, no. 2 (May 1990): 151-169.

Florescano, Enrique. *Etnia, estado y nación.* Mexico City: Taurus, 2001.

————, coordinator. *El patrimonio nacional de México.* Mexico City: CONACULTA and Fondo de Cultura Económica, 1997.

Forbes.com. "The World's Billionaires: Carlos Slim Helu." March 10, 2005. At http://www.forbes.com/static/bill2005/LIRWYDJ.html?passListId=10&pass Year=2005&passListType=Person&uniqueId=WYDJ&datatype=Person.

————. "The World's Billionaires: #3 Carlos Slim Helu." March 9, 2006. At http://www.forbes.com/lists/2006/10/WYDJ.html.

Foucault, Michel. "Truth and Power." In *The Foucault Reader,* edited by Paul Rabinow. New York, Pantheon Books, 1984.

French, William. "Imagining and the Cultural History of Nineteenth Century Mexico." *Hispanic American Historical Review* 79, no. 2 (May 1999).

————. "Progreso Forzado: Workers and the Inculcation of the Capitalist Work Ethic in the Parral Mining District." In *Rituals of Rule, Rituals of Resistance,* edited by William H. Beezley, Cheryl English Martin, and William E. French. Wilmington, DE: Scholarly Resources, 1994.

Freyre, Gilberto. *The Masters and the Slaves.* Translated by Samuel Putnam. New York: Knopf, 1956.

Frye, David. *Indians into Mexicans: History and Identity in a Mexican Town.* Austin: University of Texas Press, 1996.

Fuller, Graham E., and Rend Rahim Francke. *The Arab Shi'a: The Forgotten Muslims.* New York: St. Martin's Press, 1999.

Gabaccia, Donna R. *From the Other Side: Women, Gender, and Immigrant Life in the U.S., 1820-1990.* Bloomington: Indiana University Press, 1994.

————. *From Sicily to Elizabeth Street: Housing and Social Change Among Italian Immigrants, 1880-1930.* Albany: State University of New York Press, 1984.

Gamio, Manuel. *Forjando patria.* Mexico: Editorial Porrúa, 1982.

————. *The Mexican Immigrant.* New York: Arno Press and New York Times, 1969.

Garcia, Jerry. "Japanese Immigration and Community Development in Mexico, 1897-1940." Ph.D. diss., Washington State University, 1999.

García Canclini, Néstor. *Hybrid Cultures: Strategies for Entering and Leaving Modernity.* Translated by Christopher L. Chiappari and Silvia L. López. Minneapolis: University of Minnesota Press, 1995.

García Naranjo, Nemesio. "El orgullo de la raza." *Líbano* 1, no. 2 (September 1937), edited by Nasre M. Ganem. Mexico City.

García Riera, Emilio. *Historia Documental del Cine Mexicano 2, 1938-1942.* Jalisco, Mexico: Universidad de Guadalajara and CONACULTA, 1993.

Garza Villarreal, Gustavo. *El proceso de industrialización en la ciudad de México (1821-1970).* Mexico City: Colegio de México, 1985.

Geertz, Clifford. *The Interpretation of Cultures.* New York: Basic Books, 1973.

————. *Peddlers and Princes: Social Change and Economic Modernization in Two Indonesian Towns.* Chicago: University of Chicago Press, 1963.

Gibson, Charles. *The Aztecs Under Spanish Rule: A History of the Indians of the Valley of Mexico, 1519-1810.* Stanford, CA: Stanford University Press, 1964.

Gilsenan, Michael. *Lords of the Lebanese Marches: Violence and Narrative in an Arab Society.* Berkeley: University of California Press, 1996.

Glade, W. "The Levantines in Latin America." *American Economic Review* 73, no. 2. (May 1983): 118-122.

Gleizer Salzman, Daniela. "La política mexicana frente a la recepción de refugiados judíos (1934-1942)." In *México, país refugio: La experiencia de los exilios en el siglo XX,* coordinated by Pablo Yankelevich. Mexico City: INAH and Plaza y Valdés, 2002.

Glick Schiller, Nina, Linda Basch, and Cristian Blanc-Szanton. "Transnationalism: A New Analytic Framework for Understanding Migration." In *Towards a Transnational Perspective on Migration: Race, Class, Ethnicity, and Nationalism Reconsidered.* New York: New York Academy of Science, 1992.

Gojman de Backal, Alicia. *Camisas, escudos y desfiles militares: Los dorados y el antisemitismo en México (1934-1940).* Mexico City: Fondo de Cultura Económica, 2000.

————. *Generaciones judías en México. La Kehilá Ashkenazí (1922-1992).* Mexico City: Comunidad Ashkenazí de México, 1993.

————. "Minorías, estado y movimientos nacionalistas de la clase media en México. La Liga Antichina y Antijudía." In *Judaica latinoamericana.* Amilat, Jerusalem: Editorial Universitaria Magnes, 1988.

Goldin, Liliana. "Transnational Identities: The Search for Analytical Tools." In *Identities on the Move: Transnational Processes in North America and the Caribbean Basin,* edited by Liliana R. Goldin. Albany, NY: Institute for Mesoamerican Studies, State University of New York, 1999.

Gómez Izquierdo, José Jorge. *El movimiento antichino en México (1871-1934):*

Problemas del racismo y del nacionalismo durante la Revolución Mexicana. Mexico City: INAH, 1991.

González, Luis. *San José de Gracia: A Mexican Village in Transition.* Translated by John Upton. Austin: University of Texas Press, 1972.

González, Nancie L. *Dollar, Dove, and Eagle: One Hundred Years of Palestinian Migration to Honduras.* Ann Arbor: University of Michigan, 1992.

González Montes, Soledad, and Julia Tuñón, compilers. *Familias y mujeres en México.* Mexico City: Colegio de México: 1997.

González Navarro, Moisés. *Los extranjeros en México y los mexicanos en el extranjero 1821–1970.* 3 volumes. Mexico City: Colegio de México, 1994.

———. *Historia moderna de México: El porfiriato. La vida social.* Mexico City: Editorial Hermes, 1957.

———. "Las ideas raciales de los científicos, 1890–1910." *Historia Mexicana* 37, no. 4 (July–June 1987–1988): 565–581.

———. "*Mestizaje* in Mexico in the Nineteenth Century." In *Race and Class in Latin America,* edited by Magnus Mörner. New York: Columbia University Press, 1970.

———. *Población y sociedad en México (1900–1970).* 2 volumes. Mexico City: UNAM, 1974.

Gordon, Milton. *Assimilation in American Life: The Role of Race, Religion, and National Origins.* New York: Oxford University Press, 1964.

Gould, Jeffery L. "Gender, Politics, and the Triumph of Mestizaje in early 20th Century Nicaragua." *Journal of Latin American Anthropology* 2, no. 1 (1996): 4–33.

———. *To Die in This Way: Nicaraguan Indians and the Myth of Mestizaje, 1880–1965.* Durham, NC: Duke University Press, 1998.

Grandin, Greg. *The Blood of Guatemala: A History of Race and Nation.* Durham, NC: Duke University Press, 2000.

Gruzinski, Serge. *The Mestizo Mind: The Intellectual Dynamics of Colonization and Globalization.* Translated by Deke Dusinberre. New York: Routledge, 2002.

Gualtieri, Sarah. "From Internal to International Migration: Migratory Movements in Late-Ottoman Syria." Paper presented at Middle Eastern Migrations to Latin America Conference, University of Chicago, May 31, 2003.

———. "Making the Mahjar Home: The Construction of Syrian Ethnicity in the United States, 1870–1930." Ph.D. diss., University of Chicago, 2000.

Guerra, Eduardo. *Historia de la Laguna.* Torreón, Mexico: Editorial del Norte Mexicano, 1996.

———. *Historia de Torreón.* Torreón, Mexico: Editorial del Norte Mexicano, 1996.

Guerra, Francois-Xavier. *México: Del antiguo régimen a la Revolución.* 2 volumes. Mexico City: Fondo de Cultura Económica, 1988.

Guillermoprieto, Alma. *The Heart That Bleeds: Latin America Now.* New York: Vintage Books, 1994.

Gutmann, Matthew C. *The Meanings of Macho: Being a Man in Mexico City.* Berkeley: University of California Press, 1996.

Haber, Stephen, editor. *How Latin America Fell Behind: Essays on the Economic Histories of Brazil and Mexico, 1800–1914.* Stanford, CA: Stanford University Press, 1997.

————. *Industry and Underdevelopment: The Industrialization of Mexico, 1890–1940*. Stanford, CA: Stanford University Press, 1989.

Haddad, Yvonne. "Make Room for the Muslims." In *Religious Diversity/American Religious History*, edited by Walter Conser and Sumner Twiss. Athens: University of Georgia Press, 1997.

Hagopian, Elaine C., and Ann Paden, editors. *The Arab-Americans: Studies in Assimilation*. Wilmette, IL: Medina University Press International, 1969.

Haim, Sylvia G. *Arab Nationalism: An Anthology*. Berkeley: University of California Press, 1962.

Hale, Charles R. "*Mestizaje*, Hybridity, and the Cultural Politics of Difference in Post-Revolutionary Central America." *Journal of Latin American Anthropology* 2, no. 1 (1996): 34–61.

————. *Mexican Liberalism in the Age of Mora, 1821–1853*. New Haven, CT: Yale University Press, 1968.

Hall, Linda B. *Álvaro Obregón: Power and Revolution in Mexico, 1911–1920*. College Station: Texas A&M University Press, 1981.

Hamilton, Nora. *The Limits of State Autonomy: Post-Revolutionary Mexico*. Princeton, NJ: Princeton University Press, 1982.

Hamnett, Brian. *Juárez*. New York: Longman, 1994.

Hamui de Halabe, Liz, coordinator. *Los judíos de Alepo en Mexico*. Mexico City: Maguén David, 1989.

————. "Re-creating Community: Christians from Lebanon and Jews from Syria in Mexico, 1900–1938." In *Arab and Jewish Immigrants in Latin America*, edited by Klich and Lesser, 1998.

Handlin, Oscar. *Immigration as a Factor in American History*. Englewood Cliffs, NJ: Prentice-Hall, 1959.

————. *The Uprooted*. Boston: Brown Little, 1973.

Harik, Iliya. *Politics and Change in a Traditional Society: Lebanon, 1711–1845*. Princeton, NJ: Princeton University Press, 1968.

Harris, Charles H., and Louis R. Sadler. "The 'Underside' of the Mexican Revolution: El Paso, 1912." *Americas* 39, no. 1 (July 1982): 69–83.

Hart, John Mason. *Empire and Revolution: The Americans in Mexico Since the Civil War*. Berkeley: University of California Press, 2002.

————. *Revolutionary Mexico: The Coming and Process of the Mexican Revolution*. Berkeley: University of California Press, 1997.

Herberg, Will. *Protestant-Catholic-Jew: An Essay in American Religious Sociology*. Garden City, NY: Anchor Books, 1960.

Hershfield, Joanne. "Race and Ethnicity in the Classical Cinema." In *Mexico's Cinema: A Century of Film and Filmmakers*, edited by Joanne Hershfield and David R. Maciel. Wilmington, DE: Scholarly Resources, 1999.

Higham, John. *Strangers in the Land: Patterns of American Nativism, 1860–1925*. New Brunswick, NJ: Rutgers University Press, 1955.

Hitti, Philip K. *The Arabs: A Short History*. Washington, DC: Gateway Editions, Regnery, 1970.

————. *The History of the Arabs*. 2d Edition. London: MacMillan, 1940.

Hoberman, Louisa Schell. *Mexico's Merchant Elite, 1590–1660: Silver, State, and Society*. Durham, NC: Duke University Press, 1991.

Hobsbawm, Eric. *The Age of Empire 1875–1914*. New York: Vintage Books, 1987.
———. *Nations and Nationalism Since 1780: Programme, Myth, Reality*. Cambridge, England: Cambridge University Press, 1995.
Hobsbawm, Eric, and Terence Ranger, editors. *The Invention of Tradition*. Cambridge, England: Cambridge University Press, 1992.
Hondagneu-Sotelo, Pierrette. *Gendered Transition in Mexico: Mexican Experiences of Immigration*. Berkeley: University of California Press, 1994.
Honig, Bonnie. *Democracy and the Foreigner*. Princeton, NJ: Princeton University Press, 2001.
Hooglund, Eric J., editor. *Crossing the Waters: Arabic-Speaking Immigrants to the United States Before 1940*. Washington, DC: Smithsonian Institution Press, 1987.
Hourani, Albert. *A History of the Arab Peoples*. New York: Warner Books, 1991.
———. Introduction to *Lebanese in the World*, edited by Hourani and Shehadi, 1992.
———. *Syria and Lebanon: A Political Essay*. New York: Oxford University Press, 1954.
Hourani, Albert, and Nadim Shehadi, editors. *The Lebanese in the World: A Century of Emigration*. London: Centre for Lebanese Studies and I. B. Tauris, 1992.
Hu-DeHart, Evelyn, editor. *Across the Pacific: Asian Americans and Globalization*. Philadelphia: Temple University Press, 1999.
———. "Los chinos de Sonora, 1875 a 1930: La formación de una pequeña burguesía regional." Paper presented at the colloquium Los Inmigrantes en el Mundo de los Negocios, Dirección de Estudios Históricos, INAH, Mexico City, October 25–27, 2000.
———. "From Immigrant Minority to Racial Minority: The Chinese of Mexico, 1876–1930," Paper presented at the Tenth Conference of Mexican and North-American Historians, Dallas, Texas, November 1999.
———. "Immigrants to a Developing Society: The Chinese in Northern Mexico, 1875–1932." *Journal of Arizona History* 21, no. 3 (August 1980): 274–312.
———. *Yaqui Resistance and Survival: The Struggle for Land and Autonomy, 1821–1900*. Madison: University of Wisconsin Press, 1984.
Hudson, Michael. *The Precarious Republic: Political Modernization in Lebanon*. New York: Random House, 1968.
Humphrey, Michael. "The Lebanese War and Lebanese Immigrant Communities: A Comparative Study of Lebanese in Australia and Uruguay." *Ethnic and Racial Studies* 9, no. 4 (October 1986): 445–460.
Hutchinson, Edward Prince. *Legislative History of American Immigration Policy, 1789–1965*. Philadelphia: University of Pennsylvania Press, 1981.
Inclán, Rebeca, Antonio Mouhanna, Doris Musalem, and Ulises Casab. "Medio Oriente en la ciudad de México." *BaBel Ciudad de México* 4, Medio Oriente (June 1999). Mexico City.
Inclán Rubio, Rebeca. "Así hicieron la América. Características generales de la inmigración libanesa en México." Paper presented at the Seminario de los Inmigrantes en la Historia de México, Dirección de Estudios Históricos, INAH, November 24, 1982.
———. "Inmigración libanesa en la ciudad de Puebla, 1890–1930: Proceso de aculturación." Undergraduate thesis, UNAM, 1978.

———. "Inmigración libanesa en México: Un caso de diversidad cultural." *Historias 33* (October 1994–March 1995): 61–68.

Instituto Nacional de Migración. *Compilación histórica de la legislación migratoria en México 1821–2002.* Mexico City, 2002.

Issawi, Charles. *The Economic History of the Middle East and North Africa, 1800–1914.* New York: Columbia University, 1982.

———. "The Historical Background of Lebanese Emigration: 1800–1914." In *Lebanese in the World,* edited by Hourani and Shehadi, 1992.

———. "The Transformation of the Economic Position of the *Millets* in the Nineteenth Century." In *Christians and Jews in the Ottoman Empire,* edited by Braude and Lewis. Volume 1, *The Central Lands.*

Jacobs Barquet, Patricia. *Diccionario enciclopédico de mexicanos de origen libanés y de otros pueblos del Levante.* Mexico City: Solar, 2000.

Jacobson, Mathew Frye. *Whiteness of a Different Color: European Immigrants and the Alchemy of Race.* Cambridge, MA: Harvard University Press, 1998.

Jamieson, Tulitas. *Tulitas of Torreón: Reminiscences of Life in Mexico.* As told to Evelyn Payne. El Paso: Texas Western Press, 1969.

Jankowski, James, and Israel Gershoni, editors. *Rethinking Nationalism in the Arab Middle East.* New York: Columbia University Press, 1997.

John, Sarah Elizabeth. "Arabic-Speaking Immigration to the El Paso Area, 1900–1935." In *Crossing the Waters,* edited by Hooglund.

———. " 'Trade Will Lead a Man Far': Syrian Immigration to the El Paso Area, 1900–1935." Master's thesis, University of Texas at El Paso, December 1982.

Joseph, Gilbert M., and Timothy J. Henderson, editors. *The Mexico Reader: History, Culture, Politics.* Durham, NC: Duke University Press, 2002.

———. *Revolution from Without: Yucatán, Mexico, and the United States, 1880–1924.* Durham, NC: Duke University Press, 1995.

Joseph, Gilbert M., and Daniel Nugent, editors. *Everyday Forms of State Formation: Revolution and the Negotiation of Rule in Modern Mexico.* Durham, NC: Duke University Press, 1994.

Jozami, Gladys. "Aspectos demográficos y comportamiento espacial de los inmigrantes árabes en el noroeste argentino." *Estudios Migratorios Latinoamericanos* 2, no. 5 (April 1987): 57–90.

———. "Identidad religiosa e integración cultural en cristianos sirios y libaneses en Argentina, 1890–1990." *Estudios Migratorios Latinoamericanos* 9, no. 26 (April 1994): 95–114.

———. "El retorno de los 'turcos' en la Argentina de los 90." Paper presented at the international seminar Discriminación y Racismo en América Latina, University of Buenos Aires, November 23–24, 1994.

Jung, Courtney. *Then I was Black: South African Political Identities in Transition.* New Haven, CT: Yale University Press, 2000.

Kandell, Jonathan. "Yo Quiero Todo Bell." *Wired,* January 2001, 126–183.

Kandiyoti, Deniz. "Islam and Patriarchy: A Comparative Perspective." In *Women in Middle Eastern History: Shifting Boundaries in Sex and Gender,* edited by Nikke R. Keddie and Beth Baron. New Haven, CT: Yale University Press, 1991.

Karpat, Kemal H. *An Inquiry into the Social Foundations of Nationalism in the Otto-*

man State: From Social Estates to Classes, From Millets to Nations. Research Monograph No. 39. Princeton, NJ: Princeton University Press, 1973.

———. "*Millets* and Nationality: The Roots of the Incongruity of Nation and State in the Post-Ottoman Era." In *Christians and Jews in the Ottoman Empire,* edited by Braude and Lewis. Volume 1, *The Central Lands.*

———. "The Ottoman Emigration to the Americas, 1860–1914." *International Journal of Middle Eastern Studies* (May 1985): 175–209.

Katz, Friedrich. *The Life and Times of Pancho Villa.* Stanford, CA: Stanford University Press, 1998.

———, editor. *Riot, Rebellion, and Revolution: Rural Social Conflict in Mexico.* Princeton, NJ: Princeton University Press, 1988.

———. *The Secret War in Mexico: Europe, the United States, and the Mexican Revolution.* Chicago: University of Chicago Press, 1981.

Kaufman, Aby, and Yoram Shapira. "Jews and Arabs in Latin America." *Patterns of Prejudice* 10, no. 1 (January–February 1976): 15–26.

Kaufman, Asher. "Phoenicianism: The Formation of an Identity in Lebanon in 1920." *Middle Eastern Studies* 37, no. 1 (2001).

———. *Reviving Phoenicia: In Search of Identity in Lebanon.* London: I. B. Tauris, 2004.

Kayal, Philip M., and Joseph M. Kayal. *The Syrian-Lebanese in America: A Study in Religion and Assimilation.* Boston: Twayne, 1975.

Kayali, Hasan. *Arabs and Young Turks: Ottomanism, Arabism, and Islamism in the Ottoman Empire, 1908–1918.* Berkeley: University of California Press, 1997.

Keely, Charles B. *American Immigration: The Continuing Tradition.* New York: Co-ordinating Committee for Ellis Island, 1989.

———. "Immigration in the Interwar Period." In *Immigration and U.S. Foreign Policy,* edited by Robert Tucker, Charles Keely, and Linda Wrigley. Boulder, CO: Westview Press, 1990.

Kenny, Michael, Virginia García, Carmen Icazuriaga, Clara Elena Suárez, and Gloria Artís. *Inmigrantes y refugiados españoles en México (siglo XX).* Mexico City: Ediciones de la Casa Chata, 1979.

Keremitsis, Dawn. "Latin American Women Workers in Transition: Sexual Division of the Labor Force in Mexico and Colombia in the Textile Industry." *Americas* 11 (April 1984).

Kerr, Malcolm. *Lebanon in the Last Years of Feudalism, 1840–1860: A Contemporary Account by Antun Dahir al-ʿAqiqi and Other Documents.* Edited and translated version of Antun Dahir al-ʿAqiqi, *Thawra wa fitna fi Lubnan: Safha majhula min tarikh al-jabal min 1841 ila 1873.* Beirut: American University of Beirut, 1959.

Kershenovich, Paulette. "Jewish Women in Mexico." In *Jewish Women 2000: Conference Papers from the Hadassah Research Institute on Jewish Women International Scholarly Exchanges 1997–1998,* edited by Helen Epstein. Boston: Brandeis University, 1999.

Kessner, Thomas. *The Golden Door: Italian and Jewish Immigrant Mobility in New York City, 1880–1915.* New York: Columbia University Press, 1975.

Kettani, M. Ali. *Muslim Minorities in the World Today.* London: Mansell, 1986.

Khalaf, Samir. "The Background and Causes of Lebanese/Syrian Immigration to the United States Before World War I." In *Crossing the Waters*, edited by Hooglund, 1987.

———. *Civil and Uncivil Violence in Lebanon: A History of Internationalization of Communal Conflict*. New York: Columbia University Press, 2002.

———. "Communal Conflict in Nineteenth-Century Lebanon." In *Christians and Jews in the Ottoman Empire: The Functioning of a Plural Society*, edited by Braude and Lewis. Volume 2, *The Arabic-Speaking Lands*. New York: Holmes and Meier, 1982.

Khashan, Hilal. *Arabs at the Crossroads: Political Identity and Nationalism*. Gainesville: University Press of Florida, 2000.

Khater, Akram Fouad. " 'House' to 'Goddess of the House': Gender, Class, and Silk in 19th-Century Mount Lebanon." *International Journal of Middle Eastern Studies* 28 (1996): 325–348.

———. *Inventing Home: Emigration, Gender, and the Middle Class in Lebanon, 1870–1920*. Berkeley: University of California Press, 2001.

Khater, Akram F., and Antoine F. Khater. "Assaf: A Peasant of Mount Lebanon." In *Struggle and Survival in the Modern Middle East,* edited by Edmund Burke III. Berkeley: University of California Press, 1993.

Khoury, P. Salomón. *La iglesia melquita*. Mexico City: Curia del Arzobispado de México, 1969.

Kirkman, Alexandra. "The Global Elite: The World's Best Telecom Companies." *Forbes,* April 10, 2002.

Klich, Ignacio. "*Criollos* and Arabic Speakers in Argentina: An Uneasy *Pas de Deux, 1888–1914*." In *Lebanese in the World*, edited by Hourani and Shehadi, 1992.

———. "Introduction to the Sources for the History of the Middle Easterners in Latin America." *Temas de Africa y Asia* 2 (1993): 205–233.

Klich, Ignacio, and Jeffrey Lesser, editors. *Arab and Jewish Immigrants in Latin America: Images and Realities*, edited by Ignacio Klich and Jeffrey Lesser. London: Frank Cass, 1998.

———. "Introduction: '*Turco*' Immigrants in Latin America." *Americas* 53, no. 1 (July 1996).

Knight, Alan. *The Mexican Revolution*. 2 volumes. Lincoln: University of Nebraska Press, 1986.

———. "Popular Culture and the Revolutionary State in Mexico, 1910–1940." *Hispanic American Historical Review* 74, no. 3 (August 1994): 393–444.

———. "Racism, Revolution, and Indigenismo, Mexico, 1910–1940." In *The Idea of Race in Latin America, 1870–1940*, edited by Richard Graham. Austin: University of Texas Press, 1990.

Knowlton, Clark. "The Social and Spatial Mobility of the Syrian and Lebanese Community in São Paulo, Brazil." In *Lebanese in the World*, edited by Hourani and Shehadi, 1992.

———. "Spatial and Social Mobility of Syrians and Lebanese in the City of São Paulo, Brazil." Ph.D. diss., Vanderbilt University, 1955.

Kourí, Emilio. "Interpreting the Expropriation of Indian Pueblo Lands in Porfirian Mexico: The Unexamined Legacies of Andrés Molina Enríquez." *Hispanic American Historical Review* 82, no. 1 (2002): 69–117.

Krause, Corinne Azen. "The Jews in Mexico: A History with Special Emphasis on the Period from 1857 to 1930." Ph.D. diss., University of Pittsburgh, 1970.

Kraut, Alan M. *Silent Travelers: Germs, Genes, and the "Immigrant Menance."* New York: BasicBooks, 1994.

Kuntz Ficker, Sandra. *Empresa extranjera y mercado interno: El Ferrocarril Central Mexicano, 1880-1907.* Mexico City: Colegio de México, 1995.

Kusmer, Kenneth. "The Next Agenda in American Ethnic History." *Reviews in American History* 20 (1992): 580–584.

La Botz, Dan. "Roberto Haberman and the Origins of Modern Mexico's Jewish Community." *American Jewish Archives* 43, no. 1 (spring/summer 1991): 7–21.

Langston, William Stanley. "Coahuila: Centralization Against State Autonomy." In *Other Mexicos: Essays on Regional Mexican History, 1876-1911,* edited by Thomas Benjamin and William McNellie. Albuquerque: University of New Mexico Press, 1984.

Latin Business Chronicle. "The Billionaires: Latin America's Wealthiest Individuals, According to Forbes," November 9, 2004. At http://www.latinbusiness chronicle.com/topics/billionaires04.htm.

Lay, Shawn. *War, Revolution, and the Ku Klux Klan: A Study of Intolerance in a Border City.* El Paso: Texas Western Press, 1985.

Legaspi Velázquez, Gabriela. "Medio siglo de relaciones diplomáticas México-El Líbano." Undergraduate thesis, Universidad Iberoamericana, Mexico City, 1990.

Lesser, Jeffrey. *Negotiating National Identity: Immigrants, Minorities, and the Struggle for Ethnicity in Brazil.* Durham, NC: Duke University Press, 1999.

———. *Welcoming the Undesirables: Brazil and the Jewish Question.* Berkeley: University of California Press, 1995.

Lewis, Oscar. *Pedro Martínez: A Mexican Peasant and His Family.* New York: Vintage Books, 1964.

Líbano, Revista Mensual (Mexico City) 1 (1937), nos. 1, 2, 5, 6.

Lida, Clara E. *Inmigración y exilio: Reflexiones sobre el caso español.* Mexico City: Colegio de México and Siglo Veintiuno, 1997.

Liebman, Seymour B. *A Guide to Jewish References in the Mexican Colonial Era, 1521-1821.* Philadelphia: University of Pennsylvania Press, 1964.

Light, Ivan, and Parminder Bhachu, editors. *Immigration and Entrepreneurship: Culture, Capital, and Ethnic Networks.* New Brunswick, NJ: Transaction Publishers, 1993.

Limón, José E. *American Encounters: Greater Mexico, the United States, and the Erotics of Culture.* Boston: Beacon Press, 1998.

López, Kathleen. "The Chinese in *Cubanidad:* Historical and Contemporary Perspectives on Chinese Cuban Ethnic Identity." Paper presented at Graduate Student Speaker Series, Center for the Study of Ethnicity and Race, Columbia University, February 19, 2003.

Loyd, Jane-Dale. "*Rancheros* and Rebellion: The Case of Northwestern Chihuahua, 1905-1909." In *Rural Revolt in Mexico: U.S. Intervention and the Domain of Subaltern Politics,* edited by Daniel Nugent. Durham, NC: Duke University Press, 1998.

Loyola, Rafael, coordinator. *Entre la guerra y la estabilidad política: El México de los 40.* Mexico City: Grijalbo and CONACULTA, 1986.

Macías, Anna. *Against All Odds: The Feminist Movement in Mexico to 1940.* Westport, CT: Greenwood Press, 1982.

Macías Richard, Carlos. *Vida y temperamento: Plutarco Elías Calles, 1877–1920.* Mexico City: Instituto Sonorense de Cultura, Gobierno del Estado de Sonora, Fideicomiso Archivo Plutarco Elías Calles y Fernando Torreblanca, and Fondo de Cultura Económica, 1995.

MacLachlan, Colin M., and William H. Beezley. *El Gran Pueblo: A History of Greater Mexico.* Englewood Cliffs, NJ: Prentice Hall, 1994.

MacLachlan, Colin M., and Jaime E. Rodríguez O. *The Forging of the Cosmic Race: A Reinterpretation of Colonial Mexico.* Berkeley: University of California Press, 1990.

Macluf, Lourdes, and Martha Díaz de Kuri. *De Líbano a México: La vida alrededor de la mesa.* Mexico City: Impresos Castellanos, 2002.

Makdisi, Ussama. *The Culture of Sectarianism: Community, History, and Violence in Nineteenth-Century Ottoman Lebanon.* Berkeley: University of California Press, 2000.

Malet, Alberto. *Historia del Oriente: Egipto, Caldea, Palestina, Fenicia, Persia.* Paris: Libreria Hachette, 1922.

Mallon, Florencia. *Peasant and Nation: The Making of Postcolonial Mexico and Peru.* Berkeley: University of California Press, 1995.

Maloof, Louis J. "Sociological Study of Arabic-Speaking People in Mexico." Ph.D. diss., University of Florida, January 1959.

Malooly, Gilbert. "The Syrian People in El Paso." Paper submitted for history course 390-11, University of Texas at San Antonio, Texas Cultural Institute, May 22, 1953.

Marichal, Carlos. *A Century of Debt Crises in Latin America: From Independence to the Great Depression, 1820–1930.* Princeton, NJ: Princeton University Press, 1989.

Marín-Guzmán, Roberto. "Las causas de la emigración libanesa durante el siglo XIX y principios del XX. Un estudio de historia económica y social." *Estudios de Asia y Africa* 31, no. 3 (September–December 1996): 557–606.

———. *A Century of Palestinian Immigration into Central America: A Study of Their Economic and Cultural Contributions.* San José, Costa Rica: Editorial de la Universidad de Costa Rica, 2000.

———. "Los inmigrantes árabes en México en los siglos XIX y XX: Un estudio de historia social." In *El mundo árabe y América Latina,* coordinated by Raymundo Kabchi. Madrid: UNESCO, 1997.

Marín-Guzmán, Roberto, and Zidane Zéraoui. *Arab Immigration in Mexico in the Nineteenth and Twentieth Centuries: Assimilation and Arab Heritage.* Austin/Monterrey: Augustine Press/Instituto Tecnológico de Monterrey, 2003.

Markel, Howard, and Alexandra Minna Stern. "The Foreignness of Germs: The Persistent Association of Immigrants and Disease in American Society." *Milbank Quarterly* 80, no. 4 (2002): 757–788.

Mármora, Lelio. "La fundamentación de las políticas migratorias internacionales en América Latina." *Estudios Migratorios Latinoamericanos* (December 1988).

Marroni de Velázquez, María Da Gloria. *Los orígenes de la sociedad industrial en Coahuila, 1840-1940.* Saltillo, Mexico: Archivo Municipal de Saltillo, 1992.

Martinez, John. *Mexican Emigration to the U.S. 1910-1930.* Berkeley: University of California, 1971.

Martínez, José. *Carlos Slim: Retrato inédito.* Mexico City: Océano, 2002.

Martínez Assad, Carlos. "La aculturación de los libaneses en México." In *BaBel, Ciudad de México* 4, Medio Oriente (June 1999). Mexico City.

———. *Memoria de Líbano.* Mexico City: Océano, 2003.

———. *En el verano, la tierra: Un viaje de amor y misterio, un diálogo encantado entre México y Líbano.* Mexico City: Planeta, 1994.

Martínez Guzmán, Gabino, and Juan Ángel Chávez Ramírez. *Durango: Un volcán en erupción.* Durango, Mexico: Gobierno del Estado de Durango, Secretaría de Educación, Cultura y Deporte, and Fondo de Cultura Económica, 1998.

Martínez Montiel, Luz María, editor. *Asiatic Migrations in Latin America.* 30th International Congress of Human Sciences in Asia and North Africa (1976). Mexico City: Colegio de México, 1981.

———. "La cultura africana: Tercera raíz." In *Simbiosis de culturas: Los inmigrantes y su cultura en México,* edited by Guillermo Bonfil Batilla. Mexico City: Fondo de Cultura Económica, 1993.

———. *La gota de oro: Migración y pluralismo étnico en América Latina.* Veracruz, Mexico: Instituto Veracruzano de Cultura, 1988.

———. "The Lebanese Community in Mexico: Its Meaning, Importance and the History of Its Communities." In *Lebanese in the World,* edited by Hourani and Shehadi, 1992.

———. "Lebanese Immigration to Mexico." In *Asiatic Migrations in Latin America,* edited by Luz María Martínez Montiel, 1981.

———. "Nuestra tercera raíz. La presencia africana en los pueblos de América." *Temas de África y Asia* 2 (1993): 135-145.

———, coordinator. *Presencia Africana en México.* Mexico City: CONACULTA, 1994.

Martínez Montiel, Luz María, and Araceli Reynoso Medina. "Inmigración europea y asiática, siglos XIX y XX." In *Simbiosis de culturas: Los inmigrantes y su cultura en México,* edited by Guillermo Bonfil Batalla. Mexico City: Fondo de Cultura Económica, 1993.

Martínez Peláez, Severo. *La patria del criollo: Ensayo de interpretación de la realidad colonial guatemalteca.* San José, Costa Rica: Editorial Universitaria Centroaméricana, 1973.

Massey, Douglas. "Social Structure, Household Strategies, and the Cumulative Causation of Migration." *Population Index* 56, no. 1 (1990): 3-26.

Massey, Douglas, Rafael Alarcón, Jorge Durand, and Humberto González. *Return to Aztlan. The Social Process of International Migration from Western Mexico.* Berkeley: University of California Press, 1987.

Masters, Bruce. *Christians and Jews in the Ottoman Arab World: The Roots of Sectarianism.* Cambridge, England: Cambridge University Press, 2001.

Masterson, Daniel M., with Sayaka Funada-Classen. *The Japanese in Latin America.* Urbana: University of Illinois Press, 2004.

Mastretta, Ángeles. *Arráncame la vida.* New York: Vintage Español, 1986.

McCarus, Ernest. *The Development of Arab-American Identity*. Ann Arbor: University of Michigan Press, 1994.

McGuire, James Patrick. *The Lebanese Texans and The Syrian Texans*. San Antonio: Institute of Texan Cultures, University of Texas, 1974.

McKellar, Margaret Maud. *Life on a Mexican Ranche*, edited by Dolores L. Latorre. Bethlehem, PA: Lehigh University Press, 1994.

McLaurin, R. D., editor. *The Political Role of Minority Groups in the Middle East*. New York: Praeger, 1979.

Medina Peña, Luis. *Hacia el nuevo estado: México, 1920-1994*. Mexico City: Fondo de Cultura Económica, 1994.

Mehdi, Beverlee Turner. *The Arabs in America 1492-1977*. Dobbs Ferry, NY: Oceana Publications, 1978.

Melucci, Alberto. "Getting Involved: Identity and Mobilization in Social Movements." In *International Social Movement Research: From Structure to Action — Comparing Social Movements Research Across Cultures*, volume 1, edited by Hansperter Kriesi, Sidney Tarrow, and Bert Klandermans. London: JAI Press, 1988.

Meyer, Jean. *The Cristero Rebellion: The Mexican People Between Church and State*. Translated by Richard Southern. New York: Oxford University Press, 1978.

Meyer, Lorenzo. *Mexico and the United States in the Oil Controversy, 1917-1942*. Austin: University of Texas Press, 1972.

Meyer, Rosa María, and Delia Salazar Anaya, coordinators. *Los inmigrantes en el mundo de los negocios siglos XIX y XX*. Mexico City: CONACULTA and INAH, 2003.

Meyers, William K. *Forge of Progress, Crucible of Revolt: The Origins of the Mexican Revolution in La Comarca Lagunera, 1880-1911*. Albuquerque: University of New Mexico Press, 1994.

———. "Second Division of the North: Formation and Fragmentation of the Laguna's Popular Movement, 1910-1911." In *Riot, Rebellion, and Revolution: Rural Social Conflict in Mexico*, edited by Friedrich Katz. Princeton, NJ: Princeton University Press, 1988.

Miller, Marilyn Grace. *Rise and Fall of the Cosmic Race: The Cult of Mestizaje in Latin America*. Austin: University of Texas Press, 2004.

Molina Enríquez, Andrés. *Los grandes problemas nacionales*. 1909. Reprint, Mexico City: Colección Problemas de México, Ediciones Era, 1978.

Montejo Baquiero, Francisco D. "La colonia sirio-libanesa en Mérida." In *Enciclopedia yucatanense*, volume 12, edited by Carlos Echánove Trujillo. Mérida, Mexico: Gobierno del Estado de Yucatán, 1981.

Montfort Rubín, Carlos. *La cultura del algodón: Torreón de la Laguna*. Torreón, Mexico: Editorial del Norte Mexicano, 1997.

Moosa, Matti. *The Maronites in History*. New York: Syracuse University Press, 1986.

Mora, Carl J. "Feminine Images in Mexican Cinema: The Family Melodrama; Sara García, 'The Mother of México'; and the Prostitute." *Studies in Latin American Popular Culture* 4 (1985): 228-235.

———. *Mexican Cinema: Reflections of a Society, 1896-1980*. Berkeley: University of California Press, 1982.

Mörner, Magnus, editor. *Race and Class in Latin America.* New York: Columbia University Press, 1970.

Mörner, Magnus, with Harold Sims. *Adventurers and Proletarians: The Story of Migrants in Latin America.* Pittsburgh, PA: University of Pittsburgh Press; UNESCO, 1985.

Morrillo, Dib. *Memorias y biografía.* Actopán, Hidalgo: N.p., September 3, 1957. At Colegio de México library, Mexico City.

Morris, Katherine, editor. *Odyssey of Exile: Jewish Women Flee the Nazis for Brazil.* Detroit, MI: Wayne State University Press, 1996.

Moser, Diane. "Hometown and Family Ties: The Marriage Registers of the Lebanese-Syrian Orthodox Churches of Montreal, 1905–1950." Master's thesis, McGill University, Montreal, Canada, March 1990.

Mota Martínez, Fernando. *Más forjadores de México.* Mexico City: Panorama Editorial, 1995.

Mouhanna, Antonio. "La comunidad árabe en la ciudad de México: La comunidad libanesa." In *BaBel, Ciudad de México* 4, Medio Oriente (June 1999). Mexico City.

Moya, José. *Cousins and Strangers: Spanish Immigrants in Buenos Aires, 1850–1930.* Berkeley: University of California Press, 1998.

Musalem Rahal, Doris. "La migración palestina a México, 1893–1949." In *Destino México,* edited by Ota Mishima, 1997.

Nabti, Patricia. "Emigration from a Lebanese Village: A Case Study of Bishmizzine." In *Lebanese in the World,* edited by Hourani and Shehadi, 1992.

———. "International Emigration from a Lebanese Village: Bishmizzinis on Six Continents." Ph.D. diss., University of California at Berkeley, 1989.

Nacif Mina, Jorge. *Crónicas de un inmigrante libanés en México.* Mexico City: Edición de Jorge Nacif Mina and Instituto Cultural Mexicano Libanés, 1995.

Nader, Laura. "Chapter 11: Moving On—Comprehending Anthropologies of Law." In *Practicing Ethnography in Law: New Dialogues, Enduring Methods,* edited by June Starr and Mark Goodale. New York: Palgrave, MacMillan, 2002.

———. "Communication Between Village and City in the Modern Middle East." *Human Organization* 24, no. 1 (spring 1965): 18–24.

Naff, Alixa. *Becoming American: The Early Arab Immigrant Experience.* Carbondale: Southern Illinois Press, 1985.

Nagel, Caroline R., and Lynn A. Staeheli. "Citizenship, Identity, and Transnational Migration: Arab Immigrants to the United States." *Space and Polity* 8, no. 1 (April 2004): 3–23.

Najm Sacre, Jacques. *Directorio por familias de los descendientes libaneses de México y Centroamérica.* Mexico City: Centro de Difusión Cultural de la Misión de México, 1981.

———. *Historia y memoría del Primer Congreso Mundial Maronita.* Mexico City: Centro de Difusión Cultural de la Misión de México, 1979.

Nasr, Julián, and Salim Abud. *Directorio libanés: Censo general de las colonias libanesa-palestina-siria residentes en la República Mexicana.* Mexico City: Privately published, 1948.

Negib Aued, Alfonso. *Historia del Líbano.* Mexico City: Ediciones Emir, 1945.

Nelli, Humbert. *Italians in Chicago, 1880-1930: A Study in Ethnic Mobility*. New York: Oxford University Press, 1970.

Neuman, Gerald L. *Strangers to the Constitution: Immigrants, Borders, and Fundamental Law*. Princeton, NJ: Princeton University Press, 1996.

Niblo, Stephen R. *Mexico in the 1940s: Modernity, Politics, and Corruption*. Wilmington, DE: Scholarly Resources, 1999.

Nicholls, David. *Haiti in Caribbean Context: Ethnicity, Economy and Revolt*. New York: St. Martin's Press, 1985.

———. "The Syrians of Jamaica." *Jamaican Historical Review* 15 (1986): 50-62.

———. "They Came from the Middle East." *Jamaica Journal* (March 1970).

Nimeh, William. *Historia del Líbano*. Mexico City: Impresora Mena, 1945.

Nisan, Mordechai. *Minorities in the Middle East: A History of Struggle and Self-Expression*. Jefferson, NC: McFarland, 1991.

Nunn, Charles F. *Foreign Immigrants in Early Bourbon Mexico, 1700-1760*. Cambridge, England: Cambridge University Press, 1979.

Offutt, Leslie. *Saltillo, 1770-1810: Town and Region in the Mexican North*. Tucson: University of Arizona Press, 2001.

Olivera, Gabriela. "Forestry in the *Llanos* of La Rioja (1900-1960). In *Region and Nation: Politics, Economy, and Society in Twentieth-Century Argentina*, edited by James P. Brennan and Ofelia Pianetto. New York: St. Martin's Press, 2000.

O'Malley, Ilene V. *The Myth of the Revolution: Hero Cults and the Institutionalization of the Mexican State, 1920-1940*. New York: Greenwood Press, 1986.

Omi, Michael, and Howard Winant. *Racial Formation in the United States: From the 1960s to the 1990s*. 2d Edition. New York: Routledge, 1994.

Orfalea, Gregory. *Before the Flames: A Quest for the History of Arab Americans*. Austin: University of Texas Press, 1988.

Ota Mishima, María Elena, editor. *Destino México: Un estudio de las migraciones asiaticas a México, siglos XIX y XX*. Mexico City: Colegio de México, 1997.

———. *Siete migraciones japonesas en México 1890-1978*. Mexico City: Colegio de México, 1982.

Owen, Roger. *The Middle East in the World Economy, 1800-1914*. London: I. B. Tauris, 1993.

Páez Oropeza, Carmen Mercedes. *Los libaneses en México: Asimilación de un grupo étnico*. Mexico City: INAH, Colección Científica, 1984.

Palma, Mónica Mora. " 'Una inmigración bienvenida'. Los ejecutivos de empresas extranjeras en México durante la segunda mitad del siglo XX." In *Los inmigrantes en el mundo de los negocios siglos XIX y XX*, coordinated by Rosa María Meyer and Delia Salazar Anaya, 2003.

Paranaguá, Paulo Antonio. *Mexican Cinema*. Translated by Ana M. López. London: British Film Institute, IMCINE, and CONACULTA, 1995.

Paz, Octavio. *The Labryrinth of Solitude*. Translated by Lysander Kemp, Yara Milos, and Rachel Phillips Belash. New York: Grove Weidenfeld, 1985.

Pérez Rosales, Laura. "Anticardenismo and Anti-Semitism in Mexico, 1934-1940." Translated by Alejandro Pescador, in *The Jewish Diaspora in Latin American: New Studies on History and Literature*, edited by David Sheinin and Lois Baer Barr. New York: Garland, 1996.

Picard, Elizabeth. *Lebanon, A Shattered Country: Myths and Realities of the Wars in Lebanon.* Translated by Franklin Philip. New York: Holmes and Meier, 1996.

Pilcher, Jeff. *¡Que Vivan los Tamales! Food and the Making of Mexican Identity.* Albuquerque: University of New Mexico Press, 1998.

Piore, Michael J. *Birds of Passage: Migrant Labor in Industrial Societies.* Cambridge, England: Cambridge University Press, 1979.

Plana, Manuel. *El reino del algodón en México: La estructura agraria de La Laguna (1855–1910).* Torreón and Monterrey, Mexico: Universidad Autónoma de Nuevo León, Universidad Iberoamericana, Laguna, and Centro de Estudios Sociales y Humanísticos de Saltillo, 1996.

Plummer, Brenda Gayle. "Race, Nationality, and Trade in the Caribbean: The Syrians in Haiti, 1903–1934." *International History Review* (October 1981).

Preston, Julia, and Samuel Dillon. *Opening Mexico: The Making of a Democracy.* New York: Farrar, Straus and Giroux, 2004.

Prothro, Edwin Terry, and Lutfy Najib Diab. *Changing Family Patterns in the Arab East.* Beirut: American University of Beirut, 1974.

Ragette, Friedrich. *Architecture in Lebanon: The Lebanese House During the 18th and 19th Centuries.* Beirut: American University of Beirut, 1974.

Ramírez Carrillo, Luis Alfonso. "De buhoneros a empresarios la inmigración libanesa en el sureste de México." *Historia Mexicana* 43, no. 3 (January–March 1994): 451–486.

———. *Secretos de familia: Libaneses y élites empresariales en Yucatán.* Mexico City: CONACULTA, 1994.

Ramos, Samuel. *Profile of Man and Culture in Mexico.* Translated by Peter G. Earle. Austin: University of Texas Press, 1969.

Rashkin, Elissa J. *Women Filmmakers in Mexico: The Country of Which We Dream.* Austin: University of Texas Press, 2001.

Reimers, David M. *Still the Golden Door: The Third World Comes to America.* New York: Columbia University Press, 1992.

Reis, João José. *Slave Rebellion in Brazil: African Muslim Uprising in Bahia, 1835.* Translated by Arthur Brakel. Baltimore, MD: Johns Hopkins University Press, 1993.

Reisler, Mark. *By the Sweat of Their Brow: Mexican Immigrant Labor in the United States, 1900–1940.* Westport, CT: Greenwood Press, 1976.

Rénique, Gerardo. "Race, Region, and Nation: Sonora's Anti-Chinese Racism, and Mexico's Postrevolutionary Nationalism, 1920s–1930s." In *Race and Nation in Modern Latin America,* edited by Appelbaum, Macpherson, and Rosemblatt, 2003.

Restrep, Iván, and Salomón Eckstein. *La agricultura colectiva en México: La experiencia de la Laguna.* Mexico City: Siglo Veintiuno, 1975.

Reyna Bernal, Angélica. "El pensamiento y la política poblacionista en el México de la primera mitad del siglo XX." In *El poblamiento de México: Una visión histórica demográfica,* volume 4, *México en el siglo XX.* Mexico City, Secretaría de Gobernación, no date.

Richmond, Douglas W. "Mexican Immigration and Border Strategy During the Revolution, 1910–1920." *New Mexico Historical Review* 57, no. 3 (1982): 269–288.

Roberts, Lois J. *The Lebanese in Ecuador: A History of Emerging Leadership*. Boulder, CO: Westview Press, 2000.

Rodinson, Maxime. *The Arabs*. Translated by Arthur Goldhammer. Chicago: University of Chicago Press, 1981.

Rodríguez, Ileana, editor. *The Latin American Subaltern Studies Reader*. Durham, NC: Duke University Press, 2001.

Rodríquez, Martha. *La guerra entre bárbaros y civilizados: El exterminio del nómada en Coahuila, 1840–1880*. Saltillo, Mexico: Centro de Estudios Sociales y Humanísticos, 1998.

Romero, Robert Chao. "The Dragon in Big Lusong: Chinese Immigration and Settlement in Mexico, 1882–1940." Ph.D. diss., University of California at Los Angeles, 2003.

Rostas, Susanna. "Performing 'Mexicanidad': Popular 'Indigenismo' in Mexico City." In *Encuentros Antropológicos: Power, Identity, and Mobility in Mexican Society*, edited by Valentina Napolitano and Xochitl Leyva Solano. London: Institute of Latin American Studies, University of London, 1998.

Royce, Anya Peterson. *Ethnic Identity: Strategies of Diversity*. Bloomington: Indiana University Press, 1982.

Rubenstein, Anne. "How *Las futbolistas* Became Mexican: Historical Memory and the Revolutionary Woman's Body." Paper presented at Washington Area Symposium on Modern Latin America, Washington, DC, September 2000.

Rubin, Jeffrey W. *Decentering the Regime: Ethnicity, Radicalism, and Democracy in Juchitán, Mexico*. Durham, NC: Duke University Press, 1997.

Ruíz, Vicky L. *Cannery Women Cannery Lives: Mexican Women, Unionization, and the California Food Processing Industry, 1930–1950*. Albuquerque: University of New Mexico Press, 1987.

———. " 'Star Struck': Acculturation, Adolescence, and the Mexican American Woman, 1920–1950." In *Between Two Worlds: Mexican Immigrants in the United States*, edited by David G. Gutiérrez. Wilmington, DE: Scholarly Resources, 1996.

Safran, William. "Diasporas in Modern Societies: Myth of Homeland and Return." *Diaspora* (Spring 1991): 83–99.

Sahlins, Peter. *Unnaturally French: Foreign Citizens in the Old Regime and After*. Ithaca, NY: Cornell University Press, 2004.

Said, Edward W. *Culture and Imperialism*. New York: Vintage Books, 1994.

———. *Orientalism*. New York: Vintage Books, 1979.

Salazar Anaya, Delia. "Extraños en la ciudad. Un acercamiento a la inmigración internacional a la ciudad de México, en los censos de 1890, 1895, 1900 y 1910." In *Imágenes de los inmigrantes en la ciudad de México, 1753–1910*, coordinated by Delia Salazar Anaya. Mexico City: INAH and Plaza y Valdés, 2002.

———. *La población extranjera en México (1895–1990): Un recuento con base en los Censos Generales de Población*. Mexico City: INAH, 1996.

Saleh, Marta, and Susan Budeguer. *El aporte de los sirios y libaneses a Tucumán*. Tucumán, Argentina: Editorial América Latina, 1979.

Saliba, Najib. *Emigration from Syria and the Syrian Lebanese Community of Worcester, MA*. Ligonier, PA: Antakya Press, 1992.

Salibi, Kamal. *Crossroads to Civil War: Lebanon 1958–1976.* Delmar, NY: Caravan Books, 1976.

———. *A House of Many Mansions: The History of Lebanon Reconsidered.* Berkeley: University of California Press, 1988.

Samhan, Helen Hatab. "Not Quite White: Race Classification and the Middle Eastern-American Experience." *Arabs in America: Building a New Future,* edited by Michael W. Suleiman. Philadelphia: Temple University Press, 1999.

Sánchez, George J. *Becoming Mexican American: Ethnicity, Culture, and Identity in Chicano Los Angeles, 1900–1945.* New York: Oxford University Press, 1993.

Sanderson, Susan, Phil Sadel, and Harold Sims. "East Asians and Arabs in Mexico: A Study of Nationalized Citizens (1886–1941)." In *Asiatic Migrations in Latin America,* edited by Luz María Martínez Montiel, 1981.

Saragoza, Alex M. *The Monterrey Elite and the Mexican State, 1880–1940.* Austin: University of Texas Press, 1988.

Sariego, Juan Luis. *Enclaves y minerales en el norte de México: Historia social de los mineros de Cananea y Nueva Rosita 1900–1970.* Mexico City: CIESAS and Ediciones de la Casa Chata, 1988.

Sawaie, Mohammad. "Language Loyalty and Language Shift Among Early (1890's–1930's) Arabic-Speaking Immigrants in the United States of America." *Journal for the Humanities* 20, no. 5 (1985): 324–336.

Schmidt, Arthur. "Mexicans, Migrants, and Indigenous Peoples: The Work of Manuel Gamio in the United States, 1925–1927." In *Strange Pilgrimages: Exile, Travel, and National Identity in Latin America, 1800–1990s,* edited by Ingrid E. Fey and Karen Racine. Wilmington, DE: Scholarly Resources, 2000.

Schmidt, Henry C. *The Roots of Lo Mexicano: Self and Society in Mexican Thought, 1900–1934.* College Station: Texas A&M University Press, 1978.

Scott, James. *Domination and the Arts of Resistance: Hidden Transcripts.* New Haven, CT: University of Yale Press, 1990.

Sekaly, Jo Carolyn Gibbs. "The Syrian-Lebanese Immigration into Southeast Texas and Their Progeny." Master's thesis, Lamar University, Beaumont, Texas, December 1987.

Shah, Nayan. *Contagious Divides: Epidemics and Race in San Francisco's Chinatown.* Berkeley: University of California Press, 2001.

Shakir, Evelyn. *Bint Arabs: Arab and Arab American Women in the United States.* Westport, CT: Praeger, 1997.

Shulewitz, Malka Hillel, editor. *The Forgotten Millions: The Modern Jewish Exodus from Arab Lands.* London: Cassell, 1999.

Shulgovski, Anatoli. *México en la encrucijada de su historia.* Mexico City: Ediciones de Cultura Popular, 1968.

Sierra, Justo. *The Political Evolution of the Mexican People.* Translated by Charles Ramsdell. Austin: University of Texas Press, 1969.

Sims, Harold Dana. *The Expulsion of Mexico's Spaniards 1821–1836.* Pittsburgh, PA: University of Pittsburgh Press, 1990.

Smith, Geri. "Mexico's Richest Man is Betting Big on U.S. Computer Retailing: Slim's New World." *Business Week,* March 6, 2000.

———. "A Secretive Tycoon Gets Investor-Friendly," *Business Week,* May 18, 1998.

———. "Slim's New World." *Business Week,* March 6, 2000.

Solberg, Carl. *Immigration and Nationalism: Argentina and Chile, 1890–1914*. Austin: University of Texas Press, 1970.

Spitzer, Leo. *Lives in Between: Assimilation and Marginality in Austria, Brazil, and West Africa, 1780–1945*. Cambridge, England: Cambridge University Press, 1989.

Staples, Anne, Gustavo Verduzco Igartúa, Carmen Blázquez Domínguez, and Romana Falcón, compilers. *El dominio de las minorías república restaurada y porfiriato*. Mexico City: Colegio de México, 1989.

Stavenhagen, Rodolfo, and Tania Carrasco. "La diversidad étnica y cultural." In *El patrimonio nacional de México*, coordinated by Enrique Florescano. Mexico City: CONACULTA and Fondo de Cultura Económica, 1997.

Stepan, Nancy Leys. *"The Hour of Eugenics": Race, Gender, and Nation in Latin America*. Ithaca, NY: Cornell University Press, 1991.

Stephen, Lynn. *Zapotec Women*. Austin: University of Texas Press, 1991.

Stern, Alexandra Minna. "Buildings, Boundaries, and Blood: Medicalization and Nation Building on the U.S.-Mexico Border, 1910–1930." *Hispanic American Historical Review* 79, no. 1 (February 1999): 41–81.

———. "From Mestizophilia to Biotypology: Racialization and Science in Mexico, 1920–1960." In *Race and Nation in Modern Latin America*, edited by Appelbaum, Macpherson, and Rosemblatt, 2003.

Stern, Steve J. *The Secret History of Gender: Women, Men, and Power in Late Colonial Mexico*. Chapel Hill, NC: University of North Carolina Press, 1995.

Stolarik, M. Mark, and Murray Friedman. *Making It in America: The Role of Ethnicity in Business Enterprise, Education, and Work Choices*. Lewisburg, PA: Bucknell University Press, 1986.

Su vida en expansión. Mexico City: N.p., n.d. At Saltillo Municipal Archive.

Suleiman. Michael W., editor. *Arabs in America: Building a New Future*. Philadelphia: Temple University Press, 1999.

Talhami, Ghada Hashem. *Syria and the Palestinians: The Clash of Nationalisms*. Gainesville: University Press of Florida, 2001.

Tannous, Afif. "Acculturation of an Arab-Syrian Community in the Deep South." *American Sociological Review* 8, no. 3 (1943): 264–271.

Taylor, William B. *Drinking, Homicide, and Rebellion in Colonial Mexican Villages*. Stanford, CA: Stanford University Press, 1979.

———. *Magistrates of the Sacred*. Stanford, CA: Stanford University Press, 1996.

Taylor Hansen, Lawrence Douglas. "La Gran Aventura en México: El papel de los voluntarios extranjeros en los ejércitos revolucionarios mexicanos, 1910 a 1915." Undergraduate thesis, Centro de Estudios Históricos, Colegio de México, Mexico City, 1990.

Tenorio-Trillo, Mauricio. *Mexico at the World's Fairs: Crafting a Modern Nation*. Berkeley: University of California Press, 1996.

Terrazas, Silvestre. *El verdadero Pancho Villa*. Mexico: Colección Problemas de México, Ediciones Era, 1985.

Thompson, Elizabeth. *Colonial Citizens: Republican Rights, Paternal Privilege, and Gender in Syria and Lebanon*. New York: Columbia University, 1995.

Tilly, Charles. "Transplanted Networks." In *Immigration Reconsidered: History, Sociology, and Politics*, edited by Virginia Yans-McLaughlin. New York: Oxford University Press, 1990.

Topik, Steven C. "When Mexico Had the Blues: A Transatlantic Tale of Bonds, Bankers, and Nationalists, 1862–1910." *American Historical Review* 105, no. 3 (June 2000): 714–738.

Traven, B. "Scenes from a Lumber Camp." In *The Rebellion of the Hanged*, translated by Esperanza López Mateos and Josef Wieder; Farrar, Straus and Giroux, 1952/1980. Reprinted in *The Mexican Reader: History, Culture, Politics*, edited by Gilbert Joseph and Timothy Henderson. Durham, NC: Duke University Press, 2002.

Tuñón, Julia. "Españoles y libaneses en pantalla. La imagen fílmica mexicana de los años cuarenta." N.p., n.d.

Tutino, John. *From Insurrection to Revolution in Mexico*. Princeton, NJ: Princeton University Press, 1986.

———. "The Revolution in Mexican Independence: Insurgency and the Renegotiation of Property, Production, and Patriarchy in the Bajío, 1800–1855." *Hispanic American Historical Review* 78, no. 3 (August 1998): 367–418.

———. "Revolutionary Confrontation, 1913–1918: Regional Factions, Class Conflicts, and the New National State." In *Provinces of the Revolution*, edited by Benjamin and Wasserman, 1990.

Urow Schifter, Diana. "La inmigración a México durante el porfiriato. Un estudio de caso: Torreón, Coahuila." Undergraduate thesis, Universidad Iberoamericana, Mexico City, 1994.

U.S. National Library of Health and National Institutes of Health. "Trachoma." *MedlinePlus Encyclopedia*. At http://www.nlm.nih.gov/medlineplus/ency/article/001486.htm.

van den Berghe, Pierre. *Race and Racism: A Comparative Perspective*. New York: Wiley, 1967.

Van Leeuwen, Richard. *Notables and Clergy in Mount Lebanon: The Khazin Sheiks and the Maronite Church (1726–1840)*. Leiden, Netherlands: E. J. Brill, 1994.

Van Young, Eric. "The New Cultural History Comes to Old Mexico." *Hispanic American Historical Review* 79, no. 2 (May 1999): 211–247.

———. *The Other Rebellion: Popular Violence, Ideology, and the Mexican Struggle for Independence, 1810–1821*. Stanford, CA: Stanford University Press, 2001.

Vanderwood, Paul. *The Power of God Against the Guns of Government*. Stanford, CA: Stanford University Press, 1998.

Vargas-Lobsinger, María. *La hacienda de "La Concha": Una empresa algodonera de la Laguna, 1883–1917*. Mexico City: UNAM, 1984.

Vasconcelos, José. *The Cosmic Race: La raza cósmica, misión de la raza iberoamericana*. 1925. Translated by Didier T. Jaen. Reprint, Baltimore, MD: John Hopkins University Press, 1979.

———. Prologue to *Historia del Líbano*, by William Nimeh. Mexico City: Impresora Mena, 1945.

Vaughan, Mary Kay. *Cultural Politics in Revolution: Teachers, Peasants, and Schools in Mexico, 1930–1940*. Tucson: University of Arizona Press, 1997.

Villarello Vélez, Ildefonso. *Historia de la Revolución Mexicana en Coahuila*. Mexico City: Biblioteca del Instituto Nacional de Estudios Históricos de la Revolución Mexicana, 1970.

Vinson, Ben III. *Bearing Arms for His Majesty: The Free-Colored Militia in Colonial Mexico.* Stanford, CA: Stanford University Press, 2001.

Vizcaíno, Fernando. "Los cambios recientes del nacionalismo mexicano." *La identidad nacional mexicana como problema político y cultural. Los desafíos de la pluralidad,* coordinated by Raúl Béjar and Héctor Rosales. Cuernavaca, Morelos, Mexico: UNAM, 2002.

Von Mentz, Brigida, Verena Radkau, Beatriz Scharrer, and Guillermo Turner. *Los pioneros del imperialismo alemán en México.* Mexico City: Ediciones de la Casa Chata, 1982.

Walker, David. "Homegrown Revolution: The Hacienda Santa Catalina del Alamo y Anexas and Agrarian Protest in Eastern Durango, Mexico, 1897-1913." *Hispanic American Historical Review* 72, no. 2 (1992): 239-273.

Wasserman, Mark. *Capitalists, Caciques, and Revolution: The Native Elite and Foreign Enterprise in Chihuahua, Mexico, 1854-1911.* Chapel Hill, NC: University of North Carolina Press, 1984.

———. Introduction to *Provinces of the Revolution: Essays on Regional Mexican History, 1910-1929,* edited by Benjamin and Wasserman, 1990.

———. *Persistent Oligarchs: Elites and Politics in Chihuahua, Mexico, 1910-1940.* Durham, NC: Duke University Press, 1993.

Weber, Devra. "Historical Perspectives on Mexican Transnationalism: With Notes from Angumacutiro." *Social Justice* 26, no. 3 (Fall 1999): 39-58.

Weiner, Tim. "Mexico City Vendors Survived Cortéz, but Now . . .". *New York Times,* October 10, 2002.

Wells, Allen. *Yucatán's Gilded Age: Haciendas, Henequen, and International Harvester, 1860-1915.* Albuquerque: University of New Mexico Press, 1985.

Wells, Allen, and Gilbert M. Joseph. *Summer of Discontent, Seasons of Upheaval: Elite Politics and Rural Insurgency in Yucatán, 1876-1915.* Stanford, CA: Stanford University Press, 1996.

Wilkie, Mary Elizabeth. "The Lebanese in Montevideo, Uruguay—A Study of an Entrepreneurial Ethnic Minority." Ph.D. diss., University of Wisconsin, 1973.

Winder, R. Bayly. "The Lebanese in West Africa." *Comparative Studies in Society and History* 4, no. 3 (April 1962): 297-336.

Womack, John. "The Mexican Economy During the Revolution, 1910-1920: Historiography and Analysis." *Marxist Perspectives* 1 (Winter 1978): 80-123.

———. *Zapata and the Mexican Revolution.* New York: Random House, Vintage Books, 1968.

Worthy, James C. *Shaping an American Institution: Robert E. Wood and Sears, Roebuck.* Urbana: University of Illinois Press, 1984.

Yankelevich, Pablo. "Extranjeros indeseables en México (1911-1940). Una aproximación cuantitativa a la aplicación del artículo 33 constitucional." *Historia México* 53, no. 3 (2004): 693-744.

———, coordinator. *México, país refugio: La experiencia de los exilios en el siglo XX.* Mexico City: INAH and Plaza y Valdés, 2002.

———. "Nación y extranjería en el México revolucionario." *Cuicuilco Nueva Época* 11, no. 31 (May-August 2004): 105-133.

Yans-McLaughlin, Virginia. *Family and Community: Italian Immigrants in Buffalo. 1880-1930.* Ithaca, NY: Cornell University Press, 1977.

——, editor. *Immigration Reconsidered: History, Sociology, and Politics.* New York: Oxford University Press, 1990.

Younis, Adele. "Growth of Arabic Speaking Settlements." In *The Arab-Americans: Studies in Assimilation,* edited by Hagopian and Paden, 1969.

Zamir, Meir. "From Hegemony to Marginalism: The Maronites of Lebanon." In *Minorities and the State in the Arab World,* edited by Ofra Bengio and Gabriel Ben-Dor. Boulder, CO: Lynne Rienner, 1999.

Zarate Miguel, Guadalupe. *México en la diáspora judía.* Mexico City: INAH, 1986.

Zenner, Walter P. "Arabic-Speaking Immigrants in North America as Middleman Minorities." *Ethnic and Racial Studies* 5, no. 4 (October 1982): 457–477.

Zéraoui, Zidane. "Los árabes en México: El perfil de la migración." In *Destino México,* edited by Ota Mishima, 1997.

Zilli Manica, José Benigno. *Italianos en México: Documentos para la historia de los colonos italianos en México.* Xalapa, Mexico: Ediciones San José, 1981.

Zogby, John. *Arab America Today: A Demographic Profile of Arab Americans.* Washington, DC: Arab American Institute, 1990.

Index

Uruguay, 61
U.S. Commerce and Labor Department, 43, 84
U.S. Immigration and Naturalization Service (INS), 8, 39, 58, 77, 85, 95–97
U.S. Immigration Bureau, 84
U.S. Labor Department, 75, 83–85, 96, 111
U.S. Public Health Service (PHS), 32, 84, 96, 191n.40
U.S. State Department, 39, 41, 42–43, 84–85, 88, 103

Van den Berghe, Pierre, 78
Vargas, Getúlio, 123
Vasconcelos, José, 16–17, 150, 159
Veracruz: Middle Eastern immigrants in, 67, 100, 127, 130, 153; peddlers and merchants in, 116; as port of entry for immigrants, 94, 99, 127, 130; textile mills in, 47
Verdugo, Inés, 106
Villa, Francisco (Pancho), 19, 72, 79–81, 136, 161, 204n.56, 204n.59
Villanueva Hallal, Ricardo, 151–152

Wallerstein, Gregorio, 145–147
Warren, Albert, 74
wealth of Middle Eastern immigrants, 104, 131, 133, 134–138, 141–142, 153–154
Wehbe, Julián, 78
West Africa, 57, 148
Wilson, Woodrow, 72, 143
Winder, R. Bayly, 57
Womack, John, 73–74, 77
women: citizenship of Mexican women married to foreigners, 60–61; and commercial activities, 68, 131, 139, 141–142; and foreigners, 122; as immigrants, 87–88, 219n.46; and New Woman image, 144, 220n.67; newspaper sections on women's issues, 144; occupa-

tions of, 68, 173–174; roles of, in families, 141–142, 144; social clubs for, 144; statistics on female immigrants, 98, 125, 129, 166–167, 170–171, 173–175, 179; stereotypes of Middle Eastern women, 105; and trachoma, 191n.39; Zapotec women in Oaxaca, 56–57
World War I, 29, 88, 89–92, 206n.106
World War II, 125, 128–131, 137, 142, 148
World War II refugees, 129–131

xenophobia, 20, 21, 23, 71, 78–79, 134, 136, 151. *See also* anti-Arab sentiment

Yabur, Badía, 55
Yamo, Brom, 83–84
Yankelevich, Pablo, 105
Yans-McLaughlin, Virginia, 218–219n.45
Yucatán: discrimination against Middle Eastern immigrants in, 134; hometowns of Middle Eastern immigrants in, 62; immigrant registration records in, 64; Maya language in, 56; merchants in, 117, 137; Middle Eastern immigrants in, 56, 67, 94, 127, 134; property ownership in, 136–137

Zacarías, Mario, 221n.77
Zacarías, Miguel, 221n.77
Zakarya, Zelim, 57–58
Zamir, Meir, 155
Zapata, Emiliano, 19, 71, 72, 78, 161, 202n.33
Zapatistas, 72, 78, 202n.33
Zarzar, Jacobo, 115
Zenner, Walter, 138–139
Zepeda Patterson, Jorge, 223n.107
Zéraoui, Zidane, 6, 13–14, 150, 153, 223n.105
Zghieb, Yosef, 65